In this innovative textbook Alessandro Duranti introduces linguistic anthropology as an interdisciplinary field which studies language as a cultural resource and speaking as a cultural practice. He shows that it relies on ethnography as an essential element of linguistic analyses, and that it draws its intellectual inspiration from interactionally oriented perspectives on human activity and understanding. Unlike other current accounts of the subject, it emphasizes that communicative practices are constitutive of the culture of everyday life and that language is a powerful tool rather than a simple mirror of pre-established social realities. An entire chapter is devoted to the notion of culture, and there are invaluable methodological chapters on ethnography and transcription. The theories and methods of linguistic anthropology are introduced through a discussion of linguistic diversity, grammar in use, the role of speaking in social interaction, the organization and meaning of conversational structures, and the notion of participation as a unit of analysis.

Original in its treatment and yet eminently clear and readable, *Linguistic Anthropology* will appeal to upper-level undergraduate and graduate students.

CAMBRIDGE TEXTBOOKS IN LINGUISTICS

General Editors: S. R. ANDERSON, J. BRESNAN, B. COMRIE,
W. DRESSLER, C. EWEN, R. HUDDLESTON, R. LASS, D. LIGHTFOOT,
J. LYONS, P. H. MATTHEWS, R. POSNER, S. ROMAINE, N. V. SMITH,
N. VINCENT

LINGUISTIC ANTHROPOLOGY

In this series

LINGUISTIC ANTHROPOLOGY

ALESSANDRO DURANTI

PROFESSOR OF ANTHROPOLOGY,
UNIVERSITY OF CALIFORNIA AT LOS ANGELES

CAMBRIDGE
UNIVERSITY PRESS

PUBLISHED BY THE PRESS SYNDICATE OF THE UNIVERSITY OF CAMBRIDGE
The Pitt Building, Trumpington Street, Cambridge CB2 1RP, United Kingdom

CAMBRIDGE UNIVERSITY PRESS
The Edinburgh Building, Cambridge CB2 2RU, United Kingdom
40 West 20th Street, New York, NY 10011–4211, USA
10 Stamford Road, Oakleigh, Melbourne 3166, Australia

© Cambridge University Press 1997

First published 1997

Printed in the United Kingdom at the University Press, Cambridge

Typeset in Times Ten

A catalogue record for this book is available from the British Library

Library of Congress cataloguing in publication data

Duranti, Alessandro.
Linguistic anthropology / Alessandro Duranti.
    p.   cm. – (Cambridge textbooks in linguistics)
Includes bibliographical references and indexes.
ISBN 0 521 44536 1 (hardback) ISBN 0 521 44993 6 (paperback)
1. Anthropological linguistics.   I. Title. II. Series.
P35.D87   1997
306.44'089–dc21   96–44608   CIP

ISBN 0 521 44536 1 hardback
IBSN 0 521 44993 6 paperback

CP

To my students

CONTENTS

Contents

Contents

PREFACE

Linguistic anthropology has undergone a considerable transformation in the last few decades. In this book I present some of the main features of this transformation. Rather than striving for a comprehensive treatise of what linguistic anthropology has been up to now, I have been very selective and often avoided topics that could have reinforced what I see as a frequent stereotype of linguistic anthropologists, namely, descriptive, non-theoretically oriented, technicians who know about phonemic analysis, historical linguistics, and "exotic" languages and can teach these subjects to anthropology students who may be wary of taking courses in linguistics departments. Rather than a comprehensive "everything-you-always-wanted-to-know-about-language-but-were-afraid-to-ask" for cultural anthropologists and other social scientists, this volume is conceived as a statement about contemporary research on language and culture from a particular point of view. This view is my own but it also echoes the work of a number of productive researchers in departments of anthropology, linguistics, applied linguistics, sociology, folklore, performance studies, philosophy, ethnomusicology, and communication. Whether or not they see themselves as doing linguistic anthropology, the researchers from whose work I extensively drew are all concerned with the study of language as a cultural resource and with speaking as a cultural practice, rely on ethnography as an essential element of their analyses and find intellectual inspiration from a variety of philosophical sources in the social sciences and the humanities. What unites them is the emphasis on communicative practices as constitutive of the culture of everyday life and a view of language as a powerful tool rather than a mirror of social realities established elsewhere.

The focus on the history, logic, and ethics of research found in this book is unusual in linguistics but common among anthropologists, who have long been concerned with the politics of representation and the effects of their work on the communities they study.

Like any other writer of introductory books, for every chapter, section, or paragraph I had to choose among dozens of possible ways of presenting a concept, making connections with other fields, or finding appropriate examples from the literature or my own research experience. Simplicity of exposition and recognition of historical sources were often in conflict and I am aware of the fact that I have not given adequate space to many important authors and topics. In particular, I said very little about three areas that are traditionally associated with linguistic anthropology, namely, language change, areal linguistics, and pidgins and creoles. These and related topics are however dealt with in other volumes in this series such as Hudson's *Sociolinguistics* and Bynon's *Historical Linguistics*. I have also said relatively little about such classic pragmatic notions as conversational implicatures and presuppositions; these themes receive adequate attention in Levinson's *Pragmatics* and Brown and Yule's *Discourse Analysis*, also in this series. Finally, I hardly touched the burgeoning literature on language socialization and did not include the impressive body of work currently devoted to literacy and education. I hope that future volumes in the series will develop these important areas to the readers' satisfaction.

There is another way in which this volume complements the other volumes in the series, namely, in the attention given to culture and the methods for its study. I have dedicated an entire chapter to current theories of culture. I have also written two methods chapters: one on ethnography and the other on transcribing live discourse. Finally, I have discussed several paradigms – structuralist analysis, speech act theory, conversation analysis – from the point of view of their contribution to an anthropological theory of language.

The book is aimed at upper-division undergraduate courses and introductory graduate seminars on linguistic anthropology or (as they are often called) "language *and* (or *in*) culture" courses. Instructors who like challenges should be able to experiment with at least some of the chapters for lower division classes that deal with culture and communication. I have for instance used the chapters on theories of cultures and ethnography with some success with freshmen. I also believe that instructors can easily remedy whatever thematic, methodological, and theoretical lacunae they will detect in the book by integrating its chapters with additional articles or monographs in linguistic anthropology. Finally, all chapters are written to stand on their own. Hence, students and researchers interested in selected issues or paradigms should be able to read selectively without feeling lost.

When I was an undergraduate student at the University of Rome, one day I discovered a small library on the third floor of the Faculty of Letters and Philosophy. It was filled with books and journals about languages, many of which had names I had never heard before. As I became acquainted with the people who frequented that library – instructors, students, and visiting scholars from other parts of Italy or from other countries –, I also developed a sense of

curiosity for the knowledge contained in those rich descriptions of linguistic phenomena. My later experiences – as a graduate student, fieldworker, university
researcher, and teacher – have not altered that earlier curiosity for linguistic
forms and their description. In the meantime, I have also developed something
new: a commitment to understanding language as the voice, tool, and foundation
for any human experience. It is this commitment that I have tried to articulate in
this book.

ACKNOWLEDGMENTS

Over the last twenty-five years I have ventured into a number of fields and paradigms, searching for a way of studying languages that would preserve the richness of linguistic communication as we live it and know it in everyday encounters. This book is my first attempt to put many of these strands together in a systematic way. Many teachers and colleagues have guided me in this unending quest, suggesting models of communication, cognition, and interaction that are increasingly sensitive to the fluid, co-constructed, constitutive force of language as a system of tools among other tools, stock of knowledge among other stocks of knowledge, semiotic resources among other resources, physical sounds or marks on paper among other physical objects in our lifeworld. At the University of Rome, in the early 1970s, I was fortunate to be around a group of young and innovative scholars who were shaping new ways of making connections between language, cognition and culture. Among them, it was Giorgio Raimondo Cardona who first introduced me to linguistic anthropology and encouraged me to work on my first article, on Korean speech levels. My graduate years in the Department of Linguistics at the University of Southern California coincided with what I regard as the golden age of that department and perhaps of linguistics in the US, when linguistics students and teachers with the most diverse backgrounds and interests easily conversed with each other and believed that no one paradigm could alone provide all the answers or should be used as a measure for the success of everyone's accomplishments. My two postdoctoral experiences, at the Australian National University, in the Department of Anthropology of the Research School of Pacific Studies in 1980–81, and at the Laboratory of Comparative Human Cognition at the University of California at San Diego in 1983–84, opened up several new intellectual horizons, including an interest in new technologies for research and education, Vygotskian psychology, and Bakhtinian linguistics. During the 1980s, I held positions at the University of Rome, in the newly formed department of Studi Glottoantropologici, at the University of California, San Diego (Department of Communication) and at Pitzer College, where I taught courses on linguistics, computers as tools, and film theory and production. These appointments and the people I interacted with kept me intellectually engaged and hopeful during difficult years, when I wasn't sure I would be able to stay in academia. My appointment in linguistic anthropology at the University of California, Los Angeles, in 1988 provided an ideal working environment that has recently culminated with the establishment of an interdisciplinary center for the study of language, interaction, and culture. It is quite obvious to me that this book is partly coauthored by the voices and ideas of the many scholars I interacted with in these and other institutions over more than two decades. Among them, I owe the most to one person: my wife Elinor Ochs, the most creative linguistic anthropologist I have ever met. From our fieldwork experience in Western Samoa to the postdoctoral fellowship at ANU and all the way to the more recent years together at UCLA, Elinor has shown me again and again how to transform primitive intuitions and precarious associations into stories that can be shared with an audience. I hope this book will be one of those stories.

A number of people generously gave me feedback on earlier drafts. Elizabeth Keating worked as my editor for my first draft, providing many crucial insights on content and format; Rowanne Henry, Jennifer Schlegel, and Diana Wilson gave me useful comments on several chapters; Jennifer Reynolds and Melissa Lefko Foutz helped me locate references. Special thanks go to Asif Agha and Lisa Capps for many detailed suggestions and positive reinforcement on my second draft. Finally, I owe a great deal to four colleagues who acted as reviewers for Cambridge University Press: Jane Hill (who carefully read and gave feedback on two drafts), Paul Garrett, Susanne Romaine, and Bambi Schieffelin. Their comments and questions made the text more readable and hopefully more useful. Any remaining shortcomings are, of course, my own responsibility.

The idea of this book came out of a conversation at the Congo Cafe in Santa Monica with my editor Judith Ayling in the Spring of 1992. She didn't know then how much work – including countless messages over electronic mail – this would cost her. I am very thankful to Judith for her encouragement and her wise decisions at different stages of this project.

The less obvious and yet most important help in writing this book came from my family. The warm and stimulating environment Elinor and I routinely enjoy in our house owes a great deal to our son Marco's affection, generosity, and unique thirst for learning. My parents' emotional and material support in running our household during the winter, when they come to stay with us in California, is invaluable. Between Christmas and Easter, I can afford to sit writing at the computer or reading an article only because I know that my mother is preparing a delicious dinner and my father is fixing the latest problem with the roof in some very original and inexpensive way.

This book is dedicated to the people that have made this effort meaningful, my students. In large undergraduate courses just as much as in small graduate seminars, I often perceive the overwhelming passion and determination with which many students implicitly ask for a lesson about language that could go beyond the rigid canons of academia and reach into the meaning of life. Needless to say, very rarely do I feel able to even come close to delivering such a precious message, but their confidence that I might do it one day is a reward for my efforts to communicate across generational and cultural boundaries. This book is a modest but sincere acknowledgment of their trust and an invitation to continue our conversations.

1
The scope of linguistic anthropology

This book starts from the assumption that linguistic anthropology is a distinct discipline that deserves to be studied for its past accomplishments as much as for the vision of the future presented in the work of a relatively small but active group of interdisciplinary researchers. Their contributions on the nature of language as a social tool and speaking as a cultural practice have established a domain of inquiry that makes new sense of past and current traditions in the humanities and the social sciences and invites everyone to rethink the relationship between language and culture.

To say that linguistic anthropology is an interdisciplinary field means that it draws a great deal from other, independently established disciplines and in particular from the two from which its name is formed: linguistics and anthropology. In this chapter, I will introduce some aspects of this intellectual heritage – other aspects will be discussed in more depth later in the book. I will also begin to show how, over the last few decades, the field of linguistic anthropology has developed an intellectual identity of its own. It is the primary goal of this book to describe this identity and to explain how it can enhance our understanding of language not only as a mode of thinking but, above all, as a cultural practice, that is, as a form of action that both presupposes and at the same time brings about ways of being in the world. It is only in the context of such a view of language that linguistic anthropology can creatively continue to influence the fields from which it draws while making its own unique contribution to our understanding of what it means to be human.

1.1 Definitions

Since the term **linguistic anthropology** (and its variant **anthropological linguistics**)[1] is currently understood in a variety of ways, it is important to clarify the way

---

[1] The two terms "linguistic anthropology" and "anthropological linguistics" have been used in the past more or less interchangeably and any attempt to trace back semantic or

in which it will be used in this book. Engaging in this task at the beginning puts me in a somewhat difficult position given that the entire book is dedicated to the definition of the field and therefore I could never hope to do justice to its many aspects and subfields in a few introductory remarks. At the same time, it is important to recognize the need to give a first, however sketchy, idea of the type of enterprise pursued by the discipline described in this book. I will thus start with a brief definition of the field of linguistic anthropology and will then proceed to expand and clarify its apparent simplicity in the rest of this chapter. I should mention at this point that much of what I will discuss in this book has also been called **ethnolinguistics**, a term that enjoyed only a limited popularity in the US in the late 1940s and early 1950s (Olmsted 1950; Garvin and Riesenberg 1952), but has been quite common in European scholarship,[2] perhaps following the general preference, up to recently, in Continental Europe for "ethnology" and its cognates over "anthropology."[3] As will become clear in the rest of this chapter, my choice of "linguistic anthropology" over both "anthropological linguistics" and "ethnolinguistics" is part of a conscious attempt at consolidating and redefining the study of language and culture as one of the major subfields of anthropology. This view of the field was clearly stated by Hymes (1963: 277), when he defined it as *"the study of speech and language within the context of anthropology."*

Simply stated, in this book linguistic anthropology will be presented as *the study of language as a cultural resource and speaking as a cultural practice*. As an

---

practical distinctions risks rewriting history. Hymes tried to stabilize the use of the term linguistic anthropology in a number of essays in the early 1960s (Hymes 1963, 1964c). But even Hymes, as scrupulous an historian as he is, can be found alternating between the two. In *Language in Culture and Society*, he uses "linguistic anthropology" when defining the field in the introduction (Hymes 1964a: xxiii) – see also note 6 below – and both "linguistic anthropology" and "anthropological linguists" when discussing Boas's influence: "Boas and other shapers of linguistic anthropology in America ..." and, in the next paragraph, "Boas et al. (1916) defines a style that characterizes the field work of both Boas and a generation or more of American anthropological linguists" (p. 23).

2 Cardona (1973, reprinted in 1990: 13–44) mentions several cognates of the English *ethnolinguistics* in other European languages, such as the Russian *ètnolingvistika*, the French *ethnolinguistique*, the German *Ethnolinguistik*, the Spanish *etnolingüística*, and the Portuguese *etnolinguística*. Cardona himself eventually followed this European trend by abandoning *linguistica antropologica* in favor of *etnolinguistica* in his introduction to the field (Cardona 1976).

3 Malinowski also used the term *ethnolinguistic* in his early writings, where he made explicit "an urgent need for an ethnolinguistic theory, a theory for the guidance of linguistic research to be done among natives and in connection with ethnographic study" (1920: 69) (quoted in Hymes 1964c: 4).

inherently interdisciplinary field, it relies on and expands existing methods in other disciplines, linguistics and anthropology in particular, with the general goal of providing an understanding of the multifarious aspects of language as a set of cultural practices, that is, as a system of communication that allows for interpsychological (between individuals) and intrapsychological (in the same individual) representations of the social order and helps people use such representations for constitutive social acts. Inspired by the work of a number of leading anthropologists in the first half of this century who made language a central theoretical concern and an indispensable tool of cultural anthropology, linguistic anthropologists work at producing ethnographically grounded accounts of linguistic structures as used by real people in real time and real space. This means that linguistic anthropologists see the subjects of their study, that is, **speakers**, first and above all as **social actors**, that is, members of particular, interestingly complex, communities, each organized in a variety of social institutions and through a network of intersecting but not necessarily overlapping sets of expectations, beliefs, and moral values about the world.

Contrary to earlier definitions of the field and some commonsense understanding of the term by non-practitioners, linguistic anthropology in this book is not synonymous with just *any* study of language done by anthropologists. Nor is it equivalent to the collection of "exotic" texts studied by anthropologists – texts, that is, usually produced by members of technologically less advanced, non-literate societies.[4] The act of providing a written account of some aspects of the grammar of a language spoken by a people without writing – in the Brazilian jungle or in the Kalahari desert – does not qualify someone as a linguistic anthropologist. It is rather specific goals and methods that distinguish a linguistic anthropology project from a linguistic study or survey, on the one hand, and from an ethnographic account on the other.

What distinguishes linguistic anthropologists from other students of language is not only the interest in language use – a perspective that is shared by other researchers, dialectologists and sociolinguists in particular (Hudson 1980) –, but their focus on language as a set of symbolic resources that enter the constitution of social fabric and the individual representation of actual or possible worlds. Such a focus allows linguistic anthropologists to address in innovative ways some of the issues and topics that are at the core of anthropological research such as the politics of representation, the constitution of authority, the legitimation of

---

4 My position here is in sharp contrast with Hoijer's (1961: 110) definition of anthropological linguistics as "... an area of research which is devoted in the main to studies, synchronic and diachronic, of the languages of the people who have no writing."

power, the cultural basis of racism and ethnic conflict, the process of socialization, the cultural construction of the person (or self), the politics of emotion, the relationship between ritual performance and forms of social control, domain-specific knowledge and cognition, artistic performance and the politics of aesthetic consumption, cultural contact and social change.

Linguistic anthropology is often presented as one of the four traditional branches of anthropology (the others being archaeological, biological or physical, and sociocultural anthropology[5]). However, being an anthropologist and working on language are two conditions that do not necessarily qualify someone as a linguistic anthropologist. It is in fact quite possible to be an anthropologist and produce a grammatical description of a language that has little or nothing to offer to linguistic anthropological theory and methods. Linguistic anthropology must be viewed as part of the wider field of anthropology not because it is a kind of linguistics practiced in anthropology departments, but because it examines language through the lenses of anthropological concerns. These concerns include the transmission and reproduction of culture, the relationship between cultural systems and different forms of social organization, and the role of the material conditions of existence in a people's understanding of the world. This view of linguistic anthropology, however, does not mean that its research questions must always be shaped by the other subfields in anthropology. On the contrary, the very existence of an independent field of linguistic anthropology is justified only to the extent to which it can set its own agenda, which is informed by anthropological issues but needs not be led exclusively by such issues.[6] In particular, as I will discuss below, not all views of culture within sociocultural anthropology are equally conducive to the dynamic and complex notion of language presently assumed by most linguistic anthropologists. Many cultural anthropologists continue to see language primarily as a system of classification and representation and when linguistic forms are used in ethnographies, they tend to be used as labels for some independently established meanings. Linguistic anthropologists, on the other hand, have been stressing a view of language as a set of practices, which play an essential role in mediating the ideational and material aspects of

---

[5] For the purpose of this discussion I am conflating the distinction that is at times made between social anthropology – which is concerned with the reproduction of particular social systems – and cultural anthropology – which is the study of the more cognitively oriented notions of culture proposed by Boas and his students.

[6] I am here reformulating an earlier definition given by Hymes (1964a: xxiii): "In one sense, [linguistic anthropology] is a characteristic activity, the activity of those whose questions about language are shaped by anthropology ... Its scope may include problems that fall outside the active concern of linguistics, and *always it uniquely includes the problem of integration with the rest of anthropology.*"

human existence and, hence, in bringing about particular ways of being-in-the-world. It is such a dynamic view of language that gives linguistic anthropology its unique place in the humanities and the social sciences.

1.2 The study of linguistic practices

As a domain of inquiry, linguistic anthropology starts from the theoretical assumption that words matter and from the empirical finding that linguistic signs as representations of the world and connections to the world are never neutral; they are constantly used for the construction of cultural affinities and cultural differentiations. The great success of structuralism in linguistics, anthropology, and other social sciences can be partly explained by the fact that so much of interpretation is a process of comparison and hence entails differentiation. What linguistic anthropologists add to this fundamental intuition is that differences do not just live in the symbolic codes that represent them. Differences are not just due to the substitution of a sound with another (/pit/ vs. /bit/) or of a word with another (*a big fan of yours* vs. *a big dog of yours*). Differences also live through concrete acts of speaking, the mixing of words with actions, and the substitution of words *for* action. It is from structuralists that we learned to pay attention to what is not said, to the alternative questions and the alternative answers, to the often dispreferred and yet possible and hence meaningful silence (Basso 1972; Bauman 1983). When we think about what is said in contrast with what is not said, we set up a background against which to evaluate the said (Tyler 1978). But how wide and how deep should we search? How many levels of analysis are sufficient? This is not just a question about the number of utterances, speakers, and languages that should be studied. It is about the function of ethnography, its merits and limits. It is about the range of phenomena that we take as relevant to what language is and does. Such a range is infinitely wide but *de facto* constrained by human action and human understanding. We can't think about the whole world at once and much of the work done by linguistic anthropologists is about the ways in which the words said on a given occasion give participants first and researchers later a point of view, a way of thinking about the world and the nature of human existence. As pointed out by the great philosophers of the past, humans are the only creatures who think about themselves thinking. Such an awareness is closely connected with symbolic representation and hence with the language faculty. But language is more than a reflective tool whereby we try to make sense of our thoughts and actions. Through language use we also enter an interactional space that has been partly already shaped for us, a world in which some distinctions seem to matter more than others, a world where every choice we make is partly contingent on what happened before and contributes to the definition of what will happen next.

Consider greetings, for example. In many societies, greetings take the form of questions about a person's health, e.g. the English "how are you?" In other societies, greetings include questions about the participants' whereabouts, e.g. the pan-Polynesian "where are you going?" discussed by Firth (1972). There are many questions we can ask and hypotheses we can entertain in studying such phenomena. Are these questions formulaic? And, if so, why does the way in which one answers matter? Does the content of such routine exchanges reveal something about the users, their ancestors, humanity at large? Why do people greet at all? How do they know *when* to greet or *who* to greet? Do the similarities and differences in greetings across language varieties, speech communities, and types of encounters within the same community reveal anything interesting *about* the speakers or *to* the speakers?

Although linguistic anthropology is also defined by its ethnographic methods (see chapter 4), such methods are by no means unique; there are other disciplines concerned with the empirical investigation of human behavior that follow similar, although not necessarily identical procedures. Linguistic anthropologists also attach a great deal of importance to writing practices, that is, the ways in which both speech and other symbolic activities are documented and made accessible first for analysis and later for argumentation through a variety of transcription conventions and new technologies (see chapter 5). But, again, there are other disciplines that can claim expertise in such procedures. Although they can help establish a creative tension between theory and practice, methods can never exhaust or define a discipline's uniqueness.

What is unique about linguistic anthropology lies somewhere else, namely, in its interest in speakers as social actors, in language as both a resource for and a product of social interaction, in speech communities as simultaneously real and imaginary entities whose boundaries are constantly being reshaped and negotiated through myriad acts of speaking. Linguistic anthropology is partly built upon the work of structuralist linguists, but provides a different perspective on the object of their study, language, and ultimately shapes a new object. Such a new object includes the "language instinct" discussed by formal grammarians who underscore the biological foundations of the language faculty (Pinker 1994), but it also manifests a different set of concerns and hence a different research agenda.

As discussed in the following chapters, grammarians typically deal with language as an abstract system of rules for the combination of distinct but meaningless elements (phonemes) into meaningful units (morphemes), which, in turn, are combined into higher-level units (words, phrases, sentences). The implied theoretical separation found in structuralist linguistics between language as an abstract system and language as a concrete one restricts the range of phenomena relevant to the theory.[7] This kind of idealization has meant considerable progress in the understanding of formal properties of languages. Its ultimate goal, however, is not the understanding of the role and place of linguistic forms and contents (grammar included) in people's individual and collective lives, but the universal properties of the human mind entailed by the formal properties of the linguistic systems inferred from the study of intuitions. In such a perspective, speakers only count as representatives of an *abstract* human species. What one particular speaker or one particular dialect can or cannot do compared to others is interesting only in so far as it reveals something about the human brain and our innate capacity to have a language at all. It is the faculty of speaking more than speaking itself that is the object of study of much of contemporary formal linguistics. It is hence a very abstract and removed *homo sapiens* that is being studied by most formal grammarians, not the kids in a Philadelphia neighborhood or the Akan orators of Ghana. For linguistic anthropology, instead, the object and goal of study is, to borrow Toni Morrison's (1994) inspiring metaphor, *language as the measure of our lives*. This is one of the reasons for which linguistic anthropologists tend to focus on linguistic performance and situated discourse. Rather than exclusively concentrating on what makes us cognitively equal, linguistic anthropologists also focus on how language allows for and creates differentiations – between groups, individuals, identities.

Language is the most flexible and most powerful intellectual tool developed by humans. One of its many functions is the ability to reflect upon the world, including itself. Language can be used to talk about language (see chapter 3). More generally, as argued by Michael Silverstein (1976b, 1981, 1993), the possibility of cultural descriptions and hence the fate of cultural anthropology depend on the extent to which a given language allows its speakers to articulate what is being done by words in everyday life. As Boas, Malinowski, and the other founders of modern anthropology knew from the start, it is language that provides the interpretations of the events that the ethnographer observes. In fact, without language there are no reported events. Much before interpretive anthropologists proposed to think of culture as a text, it was mostly texts that ethnographers went home with, that is, notebooks full of descriptions, stories, list of names and objects, a few drawings, and some awkward attempts at translation. What really count are the stories ethnographers heard and the descriptions they collected of people, relationships, places, and events. This aspect of their work makes it even more compelling for all ethnographers to become expert discourse analysts.

But a culture is not just contained in the stories that one hears its members

---

[7] I am here thinking of the well-known distinction originally made by Saussure (1959) and later reframed by Chomsky first in terms of competence and performance (Chomsky 1965) and then as I-language and E-language (Chomsky 1986).

recount. It is also in the encounters that make the tellings possible, in the types of organization that allow people to participate or be left out, be competent or incompetent, give orders or execute them, ask questions or answer them. As discussed in the next chapters, to be an ethnographer of language means to have the instruments to first hear and then listen carefully to what people are saying when they get together. It means to learn to understand what the participants in the interactions we study are up to, what counts as meaningful *for them,* what they are paying attention to, and for what purposes. Tape recorders and video cameras are a great help, of course, but we also need sophisticated analytical instruments. The discussion of *units of analysis* in this book has been guided by the idea that analysis means to divide the continuous flow of experience that characterizes one's perception of the world into manageable chunks that can be isolated and scrutinized, in some none too *ad hoc,* hopefully reproducible ways. An anthropological approach to the problem of establishing units of analysis implies a concern for whether the segmentation we as analysts propose is consistent with what the participants themselves believe. Unfortunately (or fortunately, depending on the point of view), we cannot just ask people whether it makes sense for us to analyze what they do in terms of the notions developed by language analysts. Such concepts as morphemes, sentences, language games, adjacency pairs, participant frameworks usually make little sense outside of a particular research paradigm. The issue then is how to find analytical concepts that are consistent with the participants' perspective without turning every informant into an anthropologist with our own analytical preferences.

Linguistic anthropologists' quest for the relevant dimensions of human understanding, for the criteria of relevance has entailed an attention to the details of face-to-face encounters that has been seen by some social theorists as implying a separation between the interactions studied and the societal forces operating outside such interactions. Thus, Pierre Bourdieu (1990; Bourdieu and Wacquant 1992) argues that certain analyses done by conversation analysts and linguistic anthropologists fall into what he calls the "occasionalist fallacy" of believing that each encounter is created on the spot. Instead, Bourdieu argues, the world of any encounter is predefined by broader racial, gender, and class relations (Bourdieu and Wacquant 1992: 144f).

But no linguistic anthropologist would argue against the potential relevance of "broader relations," and in fact much of the discipline's empirical work is dedicated to establishing ways to connect the micro-level phenomena analyzable through recordings and transcripts with the often invisible background of people's relations as mediated by particular histories, including institutional ones. The fact that such connections are hard to make at times – and there is certainly room for improvement in this area – is not always a sign of theoretical weakness or political naiveté. What might appear as a theoretical gap to sociocultural anthropologists is in fact due to the unwillingness to embrace theories and categories born out of questionable empirical work. Too often the just assumption that "[e]very linguistic exchange contains the *potentiality* of an act of power" (Bourdieu and Wacquant 1992: 145) means that analysts can ignore the details of how such acts of power are actually produced. Too often we are presented with phenomena that seem to be out of a script based on the political wisdom of the moment. This wisdom includes the attention to what we do as analysts. If one of the basic ethnographic questions is "Who does this matter for?", we must be prepared to say that in some cases something matters for us, that *we* are the context, as contemporary critical anthropologists have taught us (Clifford and Marcus 1986). But such a recognition – and the reflexivity that it implies – cannot be the totality of our epistemological quest. Other times we must decenter, suspend judgment, and hence learn to "remove ourselves," to be able to hear the speakers' utterances in a way that is hopefully closer to – although by no means identical with – the way in which *they* heard them. Knowledge of the participants' social class, family background, or gender gives us only a portion – albeit a potentially important one – of the story that is being constructed. As pointed out by Susan Gal (1989), the recent work on women's language rightly rejects any essentialist idealization of a "woman's voice" and its implicit notion of a women's separate culture and puts forward the hypothesis of "more ambiguous, often contradictory linguistic practices, differing among women of different classes and ethnic groups and ranging from accommodation to opposition, subversion, rejection or reconstruction of reigning cultural definitions" (Gal 1989: 4). If we want to talk about gender, speech, and power, Gal argues, the first thing we need to do is to find out what counts as power and powerful speech crossculturally. We must be prepared for the possibility that power means different things within different cultures. For the linguistic anthropologist, a differentiated notion of power means that we are likely to find linguistic practices distributed differently across gender, class, and ethnic boundaries. But such distribution cannot be determined once and for all exclusively on the basis of a language-independent assumption of dominance or hegemony.

Linguistic anthropologists start from the assumption that there are dimensions of speaking that can only be captured by studying what people actually *do* with language, by matching words, silences, and gestures with the context in which those signs are produced. A consequence of this programmatic position has been the discovery of many ways in which speaking is a social act and as such is subject to the constraints of social action. It has also allowed us to see how speaking *produces* social action, has consequences for our ways of being in the world, and ultimately for humanity.

1.3   Linguistic anthropology and other disciplines in the humanities and social sciences

In the last twenty years, the field of linguistic anthropology has grown to include or draw from a vast array of other fields including folklore and performance studies (Bauman 1975; 1977; 1986; Bauman and Briggs 1990; 1992; Briggs 1988; Hymes 1981), literacy and education (Cook-Gumperz 1986; Heath 1983; Schieffelin and Gilmore 1986; Scollon and Scollon 1981; Scribner and Cole 1981), cognitive sociology (Cicourel 1973), interactional sociology (Goffman 1961, 1963, 1972, 1974, 1981), social cognition (Hutchins 1995; Lave 1988; Lave and Wenger 1991; Rogoff 1990; Rogoff and Lave 1984), and child language acquisition (Ochs and Schieffelin 1984; 1995; Schieffelin and Ochs 1986). Some linguistic anthropologists have also been influenced by an active group of culturally minded psychologists (Michael Cole and James Wertsch in particular) who brought into American scholarship the work of the Soviet sociohistorical school of psychology headed by Lev Vygotsky and his associates and helped revive the interest of cognitive and social scientists in the theoretical contributions of other Russian scholars, in particular, in the writings of the literary critic Mikhail Bakhtin and his circle (Bakhtin 1968, 1973, 1981a; Clark and Holquist 1984; Cole and Griffin 1986; Vološinov 1973; Wertsch 1985a; 1985b; 1991). As we shall see in later chapters, some of the concepts introduced by these scholars such as activity, reported speech, voice, and heteroglossia, have an important role in contemporary models of language use.

Ethnomethodology, as the study of the methods used by social actors in interpreting their everyday life (Garfinkel 1972), also offered several important and innovative ideas for those researchers interested in applying traditional ethnographic methods to the study of everyday speaking. From this phenomenologically inspired approach, linguistic anthropologists can learn or see confirmed several recurrent intuitions about the constitution of culture and society in communicative encounters. First, they can easily relate to the ethnomethodological principle that social structure is not an independent variable, which exists outside of social practices, whether in the form of social categories like "status" and "role" (Cicourel 1972) or in assumptions about what constitutes someone's gender (Garfinkel 1967). Social structure is an emergent product of interactions, in which social actors produce culture by applying native (typically implicit) methods of understanding and communicating what they are and what they care about. In other words, members of society work at making their actions (words included) accountable, i.e. rational and meaningful for all practical purposes.

Second, if knowledge is implicit, it follows that we cannot just go and ask people what they think (that often just gives us more data to analyze – and if we kept using interviews we would produce an infinite regress). Rather, we must look at how participants carry out their daily interactions and solve everyday problems such as getting along with others, making or maintaining friends, getting directions, giving orders, filling out forms, looking for jobs, paying traffic tickets. In engaging in these everyday activities, members first of all must often make available to others their own understanding of what is going on. Given that so much of mutual monitoring of what is going on in any given interaction is done through speech – as well as through other semiotic resources (e.g. gestures and postures, artifacts and documents of various sorts), language use has become an important area of study for ethnomethodologically oriented sociologists. Among them, conversation analysts have introduced ideas and methods that have been influential on many linguistic anthropologists interested in the sequential organization of everyday talk (see chapter 8).

Linguistic anthropologists have also benefited from the work of contemporary social theorists who pay particular attention to the constitution of society and culture in everyday life. This is particularly true of Bourdieu's (1977, 1990) practice theory, Anthony Giddens's (1979, 1984) structuration theory, and Michel Foucault's historical study of technologies of knowledge as technologies of power (e.g. 1973, 1979, 1980a, 1988).

Bourdieu has been particularly influential in the critique of culture as a rational system made up of beliefs or hierarchically organized rules. He has stressed the importance of socialization and the priority of our lived experience over our rationalization and thematization of distinct social categories and norms. This perspective, which attempts to integrate the Heideggerian theme of the primacy of our being-in-the-world with traditional social science methods,[8] provides a model of symbolic domination based on unconscious dispositions inculcated through participation in routine interactions rather than through cognitive processes ascribed to a rational subject.

In Giddens's view, social agents and social structures represent a temporally and spatially organized reproductive process whereby society provides resources for organizing the social life of its members while members' use of such resources in turn reproduces them. The idea of the structual properties of social systems as both medium and outcome of the practices they recursively organize – Giddens's principle of the "duality of structure" – is consistent with the perspective of linguistic anthropologists who view talk not simply as a medium for the representation of a language-independent reality but also as a ubiquitous resource for reproducing social reality, and hence existing relations of power and dependence.

---

[8] As pointed out by Dreyfus (1991: 205), Heidegger and Bourdieu share the view that "much of human behavior could and does take place as ongoing skillful coping without the need for mental states (i.e. beliefs, desires, intentions, etc.)..."

Giddens's work on *regionalization*, defined as the "zoning of time-space in relation to routinized social practices" (Giddens 1984: 119) is particularly relevant to that of those linguistic anthropologists who are engaged in the analysis of how talk and material resources, including the built environment and other existing artifacts, are used by speakers in their daily interactions and communicative practices (see section 9.6). Synthesizing earlier work by Teun Hägerstrand and others, Giddens brought attention to how a living space like a house is a *locale*, a place that becomes "a 'station' for a large cluster of interactions in the course of a typical day. Houses in contemporary societies are regionalized into floors, halls and rooms. But the various rooms of the house are zoned differently in time as well as space" (1984: 119).

Space is the pervasive field of study and metaphor of social thought used by Foucault in his discussion of the relation between knowledge and power. For Foucault the nineteenth century was obsessed with history and hence with time and the twentieth century will be known as the epoch of space (Foucault 1980b; Soja 1989). To understand how knowledge is never neutral and always a form of power, Foucault suggests that we think of it in terms of spatial concepts such as "region, domain, implantation, displacement, transposition" (1980b: 69). Once we start doing this, we are faced with the political or militaristic connotations of such terms and we may then soon realize that such connotations are not accidental. They correspond to frames of reference that inform how we understand and use language within particular institutions.

Foucault uses the term "discourse" as something much wider than a text or a sequence of speech acts. Discourse, for Foucault, is a particular way of organizing knowledge through speech but also through other semiotic resources and practices (e.g. the way of conceptualizing and institutionalizing hygiene in eighteenth-century France) – this use explains why Foucault speaks of discourses (in the plural). This widening of the meaning of the term "discourse" has important consequences for anyone interested in the relationship between language and context, given that it draws attention to the fact that particular uses of language, particular speech acts (see chapter 7), turn sequences (see chapter 8), and participant frameworks (see chapter 9) are connected to particular spatio-temporal arrangements such that speakers have access to one another in limited spatial configurations and for limited periods of time. Finally, this emphasis on discourses as technologies of knowledge makes us aware of the role of language in institutional efforts (in schools, hospitals, prisons) to organize and hence control the private lives of members of society, including their conceptualizations of self, ethnic identity, and gender relations.

1.3.1   Linguistic anthropology and sociolinguistics

Among the disciplines in the social sciences and humanities that study communication, sociolinguistics is the closest to linguistic anthropology. In fact, looking back at the history of the two disciplines, it is sometimes difficult to tell them apart. Although many sociolinguists favor quantitative methods and tend to work in urban environments whereas most linguistic anthropologists favor qualitative methods and tend to work in small scale societies, the overall goals of their research agendas appear very similar to outsiders – especially as more and more anthropologists turn their attention to urban contexts. Some of the differences between the two disciplines have to do with their history. Linguistic anthropology was one of the four subfields of anthropology when the discipline was officially defined by Boas and his colleagues at the beginning of the twentieth century (see section 3.1). Sociolinguistics came out of urban dialectology in the late 1950s and early 1960s. The closeness between the two disciplines was partly enhanced in the 1960s and 1970s by several efforts to merge them, including Dell Hymes's attempt to define an interdisciplinary field centered around *language use*. This is evident in the introduction to Gumperz and Hymes's (1964) collection, where Hymes worked hard at constituting the field of the **ethnography of communication** by creating links with almost everything one could think of at the time as even marginally relevant to the study of the interface between language and culture or language and society. When we examine the articles and authors included in the 1964 collection, we find the following fields represented: sociological linguistics (Bernstein), folklore (Arewa & Dundes), interactional sociolinguistics (Ervin-Tripp), comparative sociolinguistics (Ferguson), cognitive anthropology and ethnoscience (Frake), historical linguistics (Malkiel), quantitative sociolinguistics (Labov), and interactional (micro)sociology (Goffman). In the later collection (Gumperz and Hymes 1972), we find some of the same contributors with several additions, most notably, non-verbal (or kinesic) communication, represented by Birdwhistell, and the ethnomethodological school, represented by Garfinkel, Sacks, and Schegloff.

Gumperz and Hymes helped shape intellectual connections and collaborations that continue to be an important part of linguistic anthropology as an interdisciplinary field, but they did not succeed in the ecumenical effort to create a unified field in which all of the authors and schools mentioned above could recognize themselves. This becomes evident when we examine the main foci of theoretical interest in contemporary sociolinguistics and linguistic anthropology.

Sociolinguists have continued to work on language choice and language change, while trying to engage in a dialogue with formal grammarians, with whom they share an interest in how to represent linguistic competence, while disagreeing on

13

the criteria by which to evaluate such competence and its boundaries. Sociolinguists also continue to be concerned with the definition of the speech community as a reference point for investigating the limits of individual variation in language use. For these intellectual pursuits, the study of phenomena like pidgins and creole languages or language planning have proved to be rich testing grounds.[9] Other areas of study, such as speech register, language and gender, speech acts, and discourse, have been more often shared with linguistic anthropologists and have thus provided opportunities for crossfertilization between the two disciplines. In addition to the importance of the concept of culture (see chapter 2), which alone makes linguistic anthropological methods and theoretical goals quite distinct from sociolinguistic research, there are a number of theoretical concerns that have developed as more uniquely associated with the work of linguistic anthropologists. I will turn to three of these concerns in the next sections.

1.4   Theoretical concerns in contemporary linguistic anthropology

There are three major theoretical areas that have been developed within linguistic anthropology in the last few decades. Each of these areas is devoted to the understanding of one of the following analytical notions: (i) performance, (ii) indexicality, and (iii) participation. As it will be made clear in the following discussion, the three notions are interconnected.

1.4.1   *Performance*

The concept of performance draws from a number of sources and can thus be interpreted in a number of ways. One use of the term originates in the theoretical work of Noam Chomsky and the distinction he made in *Aspects of the Theory of Syntax* (1965) between **competence** and **performance**. This distinction was in part inspired by de Saussure's contrast between *langue* and *parole* (Saussure 1959), with the first being the system as a whole, independent of particular uses by particular speakers, and the second the language of a particular user of the system. In this context, competence describes the capacity for language, that is, the knowledge – mostly unconscious – that a native speaker has of the principles that allow for the interpretation and use of a particular language. Performance, instead, is the actual use of a language and is not only seen by Chomsky as based upon competence but also following principles such as attention, perception, and memory which do not need to be invoked for the notion of competence as the abstract knowledge speakers have independent of their use of

---

[9] See Hymes (1971), Jourdan (1991), Mülhäusler (1986), Romaine (1986, 1994: ch. 6), Thomason and Kaufman (1988). For a survey of the structure of pidgin and creole languages, see Holm (1988, 1989).

language.[10] Competence in this case is the knowledge of a language that an ideal speaker has.[11] Performance instead is the implementation of that knowledge in acts of speaking.

This notion of performance is different from the one used by the philosopher J. L. Austin (1962) in his category of *performative verbs*, which make explicit the type of action a particular utterance is trying to achieve (see chapter 7). In the utterance *I order you to leave the room* said by a person who has the authority to issue such a command to another who is in a position to execute the command, the verb *order* is not describing what the speaker believes to be true about an independently existing reality. It is instead an attempt to affect reality, by making it conform to the speaker's wants and expectations. This is an example of the ways in which words *do* things. For Austin, it turned out, all utterances do something, even those that seem to simply describe a state of affairs (the sky is blue). They do the job of informing.

There is no question that linguistic anthropologists are interested in what speakers *do* with language. In this sense, their work can be seen as falling either within Chomsky's notion of performance as "use of the linguistic system" or within Austin's notion of performance as the "doing of things with words." However, either one of these understandings of linguistic anthropologists' interest in performance would leave out a third and equally important sense of the term, which comes from folklore studies, poetics, and, more generally, the arts (Bauman 1992b; Bauman and Briggs 1992; Palmer and Jankowiak 1996). Performance in this sense refers to a domain of human action where special attention is given to the ways in which communicative acts are executed. This special attention to the form of the message is what Roman Jakobson (1960) called the "poetic function" of speech (see section 9.2). Performance is "something creative, realized, achieved" (Hymes 1981: 81). It is a dimension of human life that is most typically emphasized in music, theater, and other public displays of artistic abilities and creativity. It is for instance found in verbal debates, story tellings, singing, and other speech activities in which what speakers say is evaluated according to aesthetic canons, that is, for the beauty of

---

[10] In Chomsky's more recent writings, the distinction between competence and performance is revived through the distinction between what he calls "internal language" (I-language) and "external language" (E-language) (Chomsky 1986) (see section 3.5.1).

[11] Chomsky's notion of competence was criticized by Dell Hymes (1972b) who introduced the alternative notion of **communicative competence**. This is the knowledge that a speaker needs to have in order to function as a member of a social group. Although Hymes's notion tries to solve some of the problems inherent in Chomsky's notion, it subscribes to the same epistemological assumptions. Some of these assumptions have been questioned by more recent theoretical perspectives such as practice theory and distributed cognition (see chapter 2).

their phrasing or delivery, or according to the effect it has on an audience, namely, for their ability to "move" the audience (Briggs 1988). But this notion of performance can also describe what is often found in the most ordinary of encounters, when social actors exhibit a particular attention to and skills in the delivery of a message. To subscribe to and focus on this other notion of performance is more than the recognition of the fact that in speaking there is always an aesthetic dimension, understood as an attention to the form of what is being said. It also means to stress the fact that speaking itself always implies an exposure to the judgment, reaction, and collaboration of an audience, which interprets, assesses, approves, sanctions, expands upon or minimizes what is being said (Duranti and Brenneis 1986). In this other meaning of performance, in addition to the dimension of accountability, there is also a dimension of risk or challenge (Bauman 1977). Even the most competent speaker can say the wrong word at the wrong time just like the best of actors can miscalculate a pause or an opera singer can fail to control the pitch of his voice. This dramatic dimension of verbal performance is recognized in a number of approaches in the social sciences, including Goffman's use of dramaturgic metaphors like *actor, stage, foreground/background, frame,* and Bourdieu's (1977) criticism of objectivist paradigms in anthropology that, in trying to spell out the "logic" of human action, miss the importance of the "unknown" – with its tension and uncertainty – during the different phases of an exchange (see section 2.1.5).

Performance in this sense is an ever-present dimension of language use because it is an ever-present dimension of language evaluation and there is no use without evaluation. We are constantly being evaluated by our listeners and by ourselves as our own listerners.

Finally, the notion of performance implies a notion of creativity (Palmer and Jankowiak 1996) and improvisation (Sawyer 1996). This is found across all kinds of speech activities and speech events, from the most ritualized and formal to the most ordinary and casual. In the NorthYemeni tradition studied by Steven Caton, the poet's skill in actual performance is not just to recite memorized verses, but to "situate the performance in its concrete setting by little details of reference and address" (Caton 1990: 106). This means that the poet must know how to connect traditional verses to the here-and-now. This is true in general of verbal performance. One of the attributes of a great orator in Samoan society is to know what to include and what to leave out of a speech while connecting well-known metaphors and proverbs to the occasion on which the speech is delivered, including the names and titles of the people present.

To be a fluent speaker of a language means to be able to enter any conversation in ways that are seen as appropriate and not disruptive. Such conversational skills, which we usually take for granted (until we find someone

16

who does not have them or ignore their social implications) are not too different from the ways in which a skilled jazz musician can enter someone else's composition, by embellishing it, playing around with its main motiv, emphasizing some elements of the melody over others, quoting other renditions of the same piece by other musicians, and trying out different harmonic connections – all of this done without losing track of what everyone else in the band is doing (Berliner 1994).

1.4.2 Indexicality

Philosophers have long recognized that there are different kinds of signs. Immanuel Kant, in his *Anthropology from a pragmatic point of view* ([1798] 1974), distinguished between **arbitrary** and **natural** signs. Letters representing linguistic sounds would be an example of arbitrary sounds. There is no necessary relationship between the shape of a particular letter and the quality of the sound or sounds it stands for, as shown by the fact that the same sound can be represented by different letters in the same alphabets or by different symbols in different orthographic traditions (e.g. Latin vs. cyrillic). A letter represents a sound and can evoke that sound in a reader because a convention has been established and accepted by a community. On the other hand, the smoke alerting us that there is fire is a sign that is not established by convention, but by the knowledge of a recurrent natural phenomenon. There is a relationship of contiguity between the sign (smoke) and the phenomenon it stands for (fire). Based on the belief that "if smoke, then fire," a person seeing smoke can infer that it might come from a nearby fire. The smoke does not "stand for" the fire the way in which the word *fire* might be used in telling a story about a past event. The actual smoke is connected, spatio-temporally and physically, to another, related, phenomenon and acquires "meaning" from that spatio-temporal, physical connection.[12] Starting from similar observations, the American philosopher Charles Peirce called the smoke an index and distinguished it from completely arbitrary signs (symbols) and signs that try to reproduce some aspect of their referent (icons) (see section 6.8). Indices (or **indexes**, as most scholars prefer today) are signs that have some kind of existential relation with what they refer to (Burks 1949). This category can be easily extended to linguistic expressions like the demonstrative pronouns *this*, *that*, *those*, personal pronouns like *I* and *you*, temporal expressions like *now*, *then*, *yesterday*, and spatial expressions like *up*, *down*, *below*, *above*. The property of these expressions has been called **indexicality** and has been shown to extend to much of linguistic communication.

---

[12] The philosopher Paul Grice (1957/1971) called this kind of meaning "natural" and the meaning established by convention "unnatural." For Grice, unnatural meaning is characterized by intentionality (see section 7.3.2).

Language use is full of examples of linguistic expressions that are connected to or point in the direction of aspects of the sociocultural context.

> In a topological image, indexicality is by definition what I call a radial or polar-coordinate concept of semiotic relationship: indexical sign-vehicles point from an origin that is established in, by and "at" their occurring as the here-and-now "center" or tail, as it were, of a semiotic arrow. At the terminus of the radial path, or arrowpoint, is their indexical object, no matter what the perceptual and conceptual dimensions or properties of things indexed. Strictly by virtue of indexical semiosis, the "space" that surrounds the indexical sign-vehicle is unboundedly large (or small), characterizable in unboundedly many different ways, and its indexical establishment (as having-been-brought into being) almost limitlessly defeasible. (Silverstein 1992: 55)

Thus, an expression like *this table* includes an imaginary arrow[13] to something recognizable, most likely something perceptually available to both the speaker and the addressee. Such availability, however, needs not be immediate. For example, a word or expression can be used to index a past or future experience. Code switching is often used as an index of this sort. By uttering a word in another language, speakers might point to another time or place, where either they or their addressee have been or will be. In bilingual communities, where language switching is a daily affair, the choice of a particular language over another may index one's ethnicity or a particular political stance toward the relation between language and ethnicity. This is the case, for example, in Quebec, Canada (Heller 1982, 1995). In the following telephone conversation, for example, the use of French by a patient who is calling the appointments desk in a hospital is interpreted as an index of the patient's preference for French over English:

(1) CLERK: Central Booking, may I help you?
     PATIENT: Oui, allô?
     CLERK: Bureau de rendez-vous, est-ce que je peux vous aider?[14]
                                                    (from Heller 1982: 112)

Because of its political implications, however, the offer of a choice between the two languages might be resisted, as it is the case in the following example:

---

13 Sometimes the "arrow" is not that imaginary given that the use of demonstratives like *this* are often accompanied by gestures.

14 In a footnote, Heller points out that this expression, as common in language contact situations, appears to be a word-by-word translation of the English formula *may I help you?* rather than a corresponding French expression to achieve the same effect.

(2) WAITER: Anglais ou français, English or French?
     2 BILINGUALS: Bien, les deux ...
                     "Well, both ..."
     WAITER: No, mais, anglais ou français?
                     "No, but, English or French?"
     2 BILINGUALS: It doesn't matter, c'est comme vous voulez.
                     "whatever you want."
     WAITER: (sigh) OK, OK, I'll be back in a minute.
                                         (from Heller 1982: 116)

These examples show that indexes range from apparently innocuous inquiries (can you speak French?) to political commitments (which side are you on?). For this reason, it is important to distinguish among different kinds or degrees of indexicality. For example, Silverstein (1976b) suggested that the index *this* simply presupposes the existence of an identifiable referent. The pronoun *you*, on the other hand, does something more than imply the existence of an addressee, it actually makes the social category of "addressee/recipient" happen or at least puts it on record. A person is not officially an addressee until he or she is addressed as *you* (whereas the table is already next to the speaker before he says "this"). Languages that have socially differentiated second-person pronouns (e.g. the classic T/V type of distinction of many European languages, French *tu/vous*, Spanish *tu/Usted*, German *du/Sie*, and Italian *tu/Voi* or *tu/Lei*) further exploit the indexical properties of personal pronouns by using them as pointers toward contextually relevant social coordinates of equality/inequality, solidarity/ power (Brown and Gilman 1960). These are indexes that Silverstein (1976b) called "maximally creative or performative." The ways in which we define the world around us is part of the constitution of that world. It is this creative and performative aspect of indexicality that is used by speakers in the construction of ethnic and gender identities (Gumperz 1982a, 1982b; Hall and Bucholtz 1995). To say that words are indexically related to some "object" or aspect of the world out there means to recognize that words carry with them a power that goes beyond the description and identification of people, objects, properties, and events. It means to work at identifying how language becomes a tool through which our social and cultural world is constantly described, evaluated, and reproduced. According to Gumperz, this interactional work is performed through a vast range of **contextualization cues**, a subclass of indexical signs which let people know what is going on in any given situation and how interaction is expected to proceed (see section 6.8.2.2). Since contextualization cues are unequally dis-tributed in any given population, indexicality is an important aspect of how power relations and power dynamics are played out in institutional encounters where a minority group is confronted with a new set of indexes:

> Contextualization practices diffuse in accordance with
> institutionalized networks of relationship and their acquisition is
> constrained by the economic, political, and ideological forces that
> serve to minoritize large sectors of the population. This mismatch
> becomes particularly important as formerly isolated populations
> become absorbed into modern nation states ...
>
> (Gumperz 1996: 402)

We should now be able to see the strong connection between indexicality and performance. Such a connection is made even more apparent in the discussion of the third notion, participation.

1.4.3 Participation

As mentioned earlier in this chapter, linguistic anthropologists share with other social scientists a concern for speakers as social actors. This means that speaking is seen above all as a social activity involving always more than linguistic expressions. This epistemological stance is well captured in the following statement, which was originally written by Hymes as a criticism of Chomsky's notion of competence:

> We have ... to account for the fact that a normal child acquires
> knowledge of sentences, not only as grammatical, but also as
> appropriate. He or she acquires competence as to when to speak,
> when not, and as to what to talk about with whom, when, where, in
> what manner. In short, a child becomes able to accomplish a
> repertoire of speech acts, to take part in speech events, and to
> evaluate their accomplishment by others. This competence,
> moreover, is integral with attitudes, values, and motivations
> concerning language, its features and uses, and integral with
> competence for, and attitudes toward, the interrelation of language
> with the other code of communicative conduct.
>
> (Hymes 1972b: 277–8)

One of the main points in this passage is the recognition of the fact that to be a speaker of a language means to be a member of a speech community. The latter, in turn, means having access to a range of activities and uses of language. To be a competent speaker of a language means then to be able to do things with that language as part of larger social activities which are culturally organized and must be culturally interpreted. The notions of communicative event, speech event, and speech activity are some of the notions used in the past to capture this basic idea. The concept that is currently used to capture the fact that speaking is part of larger activities is **participation**. This notion stresses the inherently social, collective, and distributed quality of any act of speaking. To speak a language means to be able to use sounds that allow us to participate in interaction with others by evoking a world that is usually larger than whatever we can see and touch at any given moment. The connection through this larger world, whether real or imaginary, is partly produced through the ability of words to do things – their performative power (see section 1.4.1 above) –, which is, in turn, partly possible thanks to their ability to point to something beyond themselves – through their indexical properties (see section 1.4.2 above).

Participation assumes cognition to manage the retrieval of information and the prediction of others' action necessary for problem-solving. It also assumes a corporeal component, a live body that interacts with the environment not only physically (for instance, by touch) but also meaningfully. To be a human being means to be engaged in a continuous process of interpretation of our spatial and temporal relations to the world around us (*Umwelt*). Such a world includes material objects – tools and artifacts – as well as other live bodies (C. Goodwin 1981, in press; Goodwin and Goodwin 1996; Hanks 1990; Heidegger 1962; Merleau-Ponty 1962). Participation implies the sharing of material and ideational resources (languages included), but it does not assume an equally shared knowledge or control of such resources. One of the reasons to explore the notion of participation in the study of cultural practices has been the differentiation that characterizes any community or group of people (see chapter 2). Finally, participation as an analytical concept replaces old dichotomies like speaker-hearer or sender-receiver. As we will learn in the rest of this book (especially in chapter 9), any text can simultaneously represent several authors; meaning is often constructed by the juxtaposition of different voices, each of which is achieved through the use of different languages, dialects, and styles of delivery.

1.5 Conclusions

In this chapter I have introduced the discipline of linguistic anthropology by focusing on some of its main theoretical notions and concerns. I stressed the importance of looking at language as a set of cultural practices and the need to understand linguistic anthropology as fundamentally an interdisciplinary enterprise that draws from a variety of approaches within the humanities and the social sciences and yet presents its own unique views of the nature of speaking and its role in the constitution of society and the interpretation of culture. Among the other linguistic sciences, linguistic anthropology is the closest to sociolinguistics. As it will become clearer in the following chapters, linguistic anthropologists share an interest in speakers as members of speech communities and in the social distribution of linguistic forms, repertoires, and speech activities.

Whereas sociolinguists tend to view formal grammarians and historical linguists as their main interlocutors, linguistic anthropologists are concerned with maintaining a dialogue with the the social sciences in general and the other subfields of anthropology in particular. Such a dialogue is made possible through the development of areas of research which are centered around a number of key concepts. Among them, I have introduced three: performance, indexicality, and participation. I will return to these concepts in the next chapters, but of the three, participation is the one that will be more fully developed (see chapter 9). This is due to the fact that I see it as a potentially useful link between several important trends of research within and outside of linguistic anthropology. In proposing different units of analysis for the study of language, units of participation will emerge as a promising attempt to study linguistic structures without losing track of the rich social fabric in which they are used.

2

Theories of culture

If the premise of linguistic anthropology is that language must be understood as cultural practice, our discussion of the field must include a discussion of the notion of culture. This task is particularly challenging at the moment. Never before has the concept of culture been so harshly scrutinized and attacked from all sides. In recent years, the concept of culture has been criticized as an all-encompassing notion that can reduce sociohistorical complexities to simple characterizations and hide the moral and social contradictions that exist within and across communities. Many social scientists – including some anthropologists – have argued that the notion of culture is so identified with a colonialist agenda of intellectual, military, and political supremacy on the part of western powers toward the rest of the world that it cannot be used without assuming a series of naive and misleading dichotomies such as "us" and "them," "civilized" and "primitive," "rational" and "irrational," "literate" and "illiterate," and so on. "Culture" is what "others" have, what makes them and keeps them different, separate from us. In the nineteenth century culture was a concept used by Europeans to explain the customs of the people in the territories they came to conquer and populate (in Africa, North and South America, Australia, the Pacific Islands, Asia). Today, culture is used to explain why minorities and marginalized groups do not easily assimilate or merge into the mainstream of society. A criticism of such uses is valuable, among other things, in making us aware of the role of academic discourse in the production and legitimation of marginalization; a role that academic personnel engage in often without an awareness of it (e.g. Bhabha 1994; Fox 1991; Said 1978). At the same time, new generations of students of human social conduct need to have a historical understanding of our root metaphors and concepts, if they want to attempt new theoretical elaborations and syntheses. Whatever problems earlier concepts of culture might have had, they are small compared with the danger of avoiding defining the concept that can help us understand similarities and differences in the ways in which people around the world constitute themselves in aggregates of various sorts.

Rather than systematically reviewing the different theories of culture that have been proposed over the last century by anthropologists,[1] I will limit myself here to six theories of culture in which language plays a particularly important role. These theories are by no means uncontroversial and one of them is based on a paradigm – Vygotskian psychology – that is certainly not part of mainstream anthropology. My choice should be seen as instrumental to the main goal of this book, the discussion of language from an anthropological perspective. For each theory of culture, I will highlight the concept of language either explicitly or implicitly embedded in the theory.

2.1 Culture as distinct from nature

A common view of culture is that of something learned, transmitted, passed down from one generation to the next, through human actions, often in the form of face-to-face interaction, and, of course, through linguistic communication. This view of culture is meant to explain why any human child, regardless of his genetic heritage will grow up to follow the cultural patterns of the people who raised him. A child separated from his blood relatives and brought up in a society different from the one in which he was born will grow up to be a member of the culture of his adoptive parents. Largely through language socialization, he will acquire the culture (language included) of the people he lives with.

> In anthropology a culture is the learned and shared behavior
> patterns characteristic of a group of people. Your culture is learned
> from relatives and other members of your community as well as
> from various material forms such as books and television programs.
> You are not born with culture but with the ability to acquire it by
> such means as observation, imitation, and trial and error.
>
> (Oswalt 1986: 25)

Despite the acknowledgment made in textbooks like the one just mentioned of the need for an "ability to acquire" culture, the view of culture as learned is often understood in opposition to the view of human behavior as a product of nature, that is, as an endowment which is passed down from one generation to the next through the principles of genetics. The "nature/nurture" dichotomy has divided scholars who are in fact interested in the same question: what makes humans special? The answer of this question must lie at the crossroads of biology and culture, inheritance and acquisition. No better example could be found than language. There is no question that humans have a capacity to acquire a language. Hearing children all over the world, when exposed to the sounds of the language spoken by those around them will be able in a relatively short time (two, three

---

[1] Useful reviews of theories of culture are provided in Keesing (1974) and Ortner (1984).

years) to start processing first and then producing complex messages with complex ideas. The capacity to learn a language is in fact independent of the ability to hear sounds, as shown by the spontaneous use of sign language by deaf people. When exposed to an environment in which people systematically use gestures to communicate, deaf children easily adopt those gestures and use them just as efficiently as hearing children use linguistic sounds (Monaghan 1996; Padden and Humphries 1988; Sacks 1989; Lane 1984). What is clear at this point is that in the acquisition of language, nature and culture interact in a number of ways to produce the uniqueness of human languages.

The idea of an opposition between culture and nature was brought to American anthropology by scholars like the German-born Franz Boas,[2] who was influenced by the philosophy of Immanuel Kant as well as by nineteenth-century idealist philosophers. From Kant, Boas certainly took the idea that our intellect is a major force of our understanding of the world. In 1798, Kant had published a book based on a course he had given in the last thirty years called *Anthropologie in pragmatischer Hindsicht* (Anthropology from a pragmatic perspective), in which he defined anthropology as the study of what a human being does because of his free spirit, as opposed to the natural laws that govern human physiology. This definition of anthropology follows from Kant's view of culture (German *Kultur*) as the ability to set arbitrary (i.e. non-natural) ends, a necessary condition for human freedom (*The Critique of Judgment*, §83). This view is further articulated in G. W. Hegel's *Phenomenology of the Mind*, where people are said to be different from animals not only for their ability to control their instincts, but also for their capacity to overcome their idiosyncracies by sharing needs and accepting standards that are more universal. For Hegel, culture is a process of *estrangement* from (in German *Entfremdung*) or "getting out of" (*Entäußerung*) the "natural" or biological self. It is part of this "natural" self to be self-centered. Culture means the ability to step out of our own, limited ways of seeing things and take someone else's perspective. This process makes it possible to have knowledge of oneself (*Selbstbewusstsein*) as well as knowledge of the Other. Such knowledge is always a theoretical way of thinking. The word that Hegel uses for culture is instructive: *Bildung*, that is, formation (echoing the Latin *formatio*) or shaping (of matter or thought). According to Gadamer ([1960] 1975), this concept originates in eastern mysticism and is strongly associated not only with the idea of humans carrying in their soul the image of God but also with a

---

[2] "Culture may be defined as the totality of the mental and physical reactions and activities that characterizes the behavior of the individuals composing a social group collectively and individually in relation to their natural environment, to other groups, to members of the group itself and of each individual to himself. It also includes the products of these activities and their role in the life of the groups" (Boas 1911/1963: 149).

universal ethics, a struggle to control human instincts and thereby rise toward pan-human values. The process of socialization, of which the acquisition of language is such an important part, is aimed at shaping the child's mind and behavior toward ways of thinking, speaking, and acting that are acceptable to a community that is larger than the child's own family (Mauss 1935).

In this perspective, language is part of culture. More specifically, languages categorize the natural and cultural world in useful ways. They are rich systems of classification (taxonomies) that can give important clues about how to study particular cultural beliefs or practices. Such systems of classification are arbitrary – how to explain, otherwise, the differences in vocabulary and semantic domains across languages? We know, for instance, that where one language may group all components of a given set under the same label (e.g. English *we*), another language may make several, more subtle, distinctions within the same set (e.g. many languages have several different ways of translating the English *we*, depending on whether or not there are more than two parties or on whether or not the hearer is included) (see pp. 305–6). Properties of objects or persons that are irrelevant to one system of classification may be crucial for another. Linguistic anthropologists in the past have documented innumerable examples of such language-specific classifications (see Cardona 1985 for a review of relevant literature). Lounsbury (1962/1969), for instance, showed that in Seneca (an Iroquois language of western New York State), unlike English and many other languages, a crucial distinction is made in terms of patrilineal vs. matrilineal kin, with the term *haʔnih* covering one's father, father's brother, father's mother's sister's son, father's father's brother's son, etc. and the term *hakhnoʔsēh* applying to mother's brother, mother's mother's sister's son, mother's mother's brother's son, etc. (Lounsbury [1962]1969: 195). These examples show that linguistic labels can give cultural anthropologists important clues about the type of social distinctions that are relevant for a given group. This is true not only of what a language has but also of what it does not have. The fact that some languages do not have a translation for the English word *privacy*, for instance, might indicate that the concept of "privacy" is not present or it is conceptualized in ways that do not allow for a single word to represent it.

Similar considerations can be made about how verbs in different languages classify actions and agents. In English, for instance, the same verb *die* is used for both humans and animals (and sometimes metaphorically extended to machines and objects that seem to have a "life," e.g. batteries, engines). In Samoan, on the other hand, a distinction is made between the dying of people (*oti*) and that of animals (*pē*) – with machines being treated like animals, e.g. `ua pē le ta`avale "the car is/has broken, lit. has died." Does this mean that the relationship between humans and animals is felt to be different by Samoan and English speakers?

These are the kinds of questions that those investigating linguistic relativism have been interested in (see chapter 3).

Attention to lexical distinctions of this sort was very much part of the structuralist program in linguistics, as exemplified in Europe by the work of Trier (1934) and Hjelmslev ([1949]1961)[3] and in the United States by the proponents of **componential analysis** (Conklin 1962/1969; Goodenough 1956; Lounsbury 1956). In these studies, language is seen as a system of "abstractions" that identifies classes of objects (mostly typically through nouns), classes of actions (through verbs), classes of properties (through adjectives), classes of relationships (through prepositions or postpositions), classes of events (through verb phrases), classes of ideas or thoughts (through full sentences [Boas 1911: 21]).

2.2 Culture as knowledge

If culture is learned, then much of it can be thought of in terms of knowledge of the world. This does not only mean that members of a culture must know certain facts or be able to recognize objects, places, and people. It also means that they must share certain patterns of thought, ways of understanding the world, making inferences and predictions. In a famous statement that sums up what we might call the *cognitive view* of culture, Ward Goodenough wrote:

> ... a society's culture consists of whatever it is one has to know or
> believe in order to operate in a manner acceptable to its members,
> and do so in any role that they accept for any one of themselves.
> Culture, being what people have to learn as distinct from their
> biological heritage, must consist of the end product of learning:
> knowledge, in a most general, if relative, sense of the term. By this
> definition, we should note that culture is not a material
> phenomenon; it does not consist of things, people, behavior, or
> emotions. It is rather an organization of these things. It is the forms
> of things that people have in mind, their models for perceiving,
> relating, and otherwise interpreting them.
>
> (Goodenough [1957] 1964: 36)

There is a linguistic homology at work here. To know a culture is like knowing a language. They are both mental realities. Furthermore, to describe a culture is like describing a language. Hence, the goal of ethnographic descriptions is the writing of "cultural grammars" (see Keesing 1972: 302 and section 6.3.2).

---

[3] See Lehrer (1974) for a discussion of the theory of semantic fields in lexical analysis. Tyler (1978) contains detailed discussions of different models of lexical analysis within linguistics.

In the cognitive view of culture, the body of knowledge necessary for competent participation in a community includes both **propositional knowledge** and **procedural knowledge**.

Propositional knowledge refers to beliefs that can be represented by propositions such as *cats and dogs are pets*, *smoking is bad for your health*, and *newborn babies cannot crawl*. These are the "know-that" types of statements ethnographers often try to elicit from informants. Procedural knowledge is the "know-how" type of information that must often be inferred from observing how people carry on their daily tasks and engage in problem-solving. To drive a car we not only need to know what different parts of the cars do, e.g. a certain pedal if pressed increases the speed or stops the car (propositional knowledge); we also need to actually know when and how to use that information. We need to know the "procedures," that is, the specific sequences of acts, through which a given goal, for instance, accelerating or stopping, can be achieved. We also need to recognize whether a situation requires a certain action.

In the 1960s cognitive anthropologists became interested in terminological systems as a way of tapping into the cognitive world of a given group of people:

> To the extent that cognitive coding tends to be linguistic and tends to be efficient, the study of the referential use of standard, readily elicitable linguistic responses – or *terms* – should provide a fruitful beginning point for mapping a cognitive system. And with verbal behavior we know how to begin. (Frake [1962]1969: 30)

Language in this case is understood as a set of propositions about what the speaker (as a member of a society/speech community) knows (or believes). Such propositions must all be reduced to the form: Subject + Predicate, e.g. *this plant* (Subject) *is a strawberry bush* (Predicate), *John* (Subject) *is Mary's father's brother* (Predicate), *a hibiscus* (Subject) *is a kind of flower* (Predicate). Such propositions can then be connected to larger sets through rules of inference like the following:

> John is Mary's father's brother
> x's father's brother is x's uncle
> _____
>
> John is Mary's uncle

Cognitive anthropologists rely then on the knowledge of linguistic categories and their relationships to show that to be part of a culture means (minimally) to share the propositional knowledge and the rules of inference necessary to understand whether certain propositions are true (given certain premises). To this propositional knowledge, one might add the procedural knowledge to carry out tasks such as cooking, weaving, farming, fishing, giving a formal speech, answering the phone, asking for a favor, writing a letter for a job application.

In more recent work on culture and cognition, the task of finding cultural "rules" on the model of linguistic rules has been abandoned in favor of models that are said to be less dependent on linguistic formalism and linguistic analysis (Boyer 1993a; Dougherty 1985). Psychologists, philosophers, and anthropologists have argued that there are categorical schema (or schemata) that are readily available to the human mind and these form **natural kinds**, categories about which people seem to be able to make inferences without having an explicit "theory" or "model" of such concepts. The approach earlier advocated by ethnosemanticists like Frake or Goodenough does not seem to work because people are not able to provide the propositions (or the features) that describe the necessary and sufficient conditions for what constitutes a "dog" or a "shaman," but they consistently show that they have an intuitive understanding of what these concepts imply. Even young children can easily infer that something that was referred to as a dog eats food, sleeps, and looks at things, whereas an object like a hammer cannot engage in any of those activities. One of the most commonly mentioned example of a natural kind is "living kind" (Atran 1987, 1990; Atran and Sperber 1991; Sperber 1985). The fact that children seem to easily acquire an understanding of living-kind terms without being taught and with very little direct experience has been used as evidence that there are "innate expectations about the organization of the everyday biological world." (Atran 1993: 60) According to Atran, one of these expectations is that living kinds have an essence whereas artifacts are defined by functions.

This theory about innate ability to make categorial distinctions has been variously used by symbolic anthropologists interested in ritual and religious life (Boyer 1990; Boyer 1993b). Bloch (1993), for example, utilizes Atran's hypothesis about the naturalness of the living-kind category for a rather complex argument about how the Zafimaniry of Madagascar can conceptualize the transformation of human beings into artifacts (the houses they used to inhabit). After the death of the couple who built it, a house is seen as the couple and becomes a "holy house" (*trano masina*), a source of blessing for the descendants (Bloch 1993: 115). To understand this symbolic transformation, Bloch argues, we must take into consideration the fact that before becoming "wood," the material with which the house was built was trees. "This passage from people to trees was possible in the mind because it is premised on the unity of the domain of living kinds" (Bloch 1993: 119). The further passage, from living kind (trees) to artifact (house), is however more problematic or less natural for the human mind and therefore, Bloch argues, needs material symbols, including massive decorated wooden planks which replace, over time, the flimsy parts of the house (woven bamboos and mats) used by the original couple. The central posts and hearth become then the permanent replacement of the ancestors and it is these artifacts that the descendants address when seeking a blessing.[4]

Although this new generation of cognitive anthropologists claim to be less dependent on linguistic analysis than their predecessors, the shift of focus from the description of separate cultural systems to the universal bases of human cultures reproduces the shift from behaviorist to innativist theories of language in the last thirty years. Chomsky (1965, 1968) argued for innate principles for language acquistion based on the fact that children do not have sufficient input to be able to produce the type of generalizations they need to acquire the fundamentals of language in a relatively short time (two to three years). Similarly, contemporary cognitive anthropologists argue that for certain types of cultural concepts, there is not sufficient evidence in people's experience. For example, religious symbolism tends to involve implicit principles – principles that are rarely fully articulated – and vague statements. Hence their acquisition would not be possible "without having certain principles that make it possible to go further than the material given" (Boyer 1993: 139). Such principles consist of the application of assumptions about natural kinds to a non-natural domain. According to Boyer, much of religious practice is made possible by the con-struction of such "pseudo-natural kinds." This simply means that many cultural categories (e.g. what constitutes a shaman, a poet, or anyone who has some special, undefinable characteristic) are used "either directly as natural-kind names, or as a predicate which implies the existence of a natural kind" (Boyer 1993: 132).

2.2.1 Culture as socially distributed knowledge

Recent work by anthropologists and cultural psychologists (Lave and Wenger 1991; Resnick, Levine, Teasley 1991; Suchman 1987) on how people think in real life situations has provided another perspective on culture as knowledge. For these researchers, knowledge is no longer something exclusively residing in a person's mental operations. As succinctly stated by anthropologist Jean Lave (1988: 1), when we observe how people problem-solve in everyday life, we find out that cognition is "distributed – stretched over, not divided – among mind, body, activity and culturally organized settings (which include other actors)." To say that cultural knowledge is *socially distributed* means to recognize that (i) the individual is not always the end point of the acquisition process, and (ii) not

---

[4] One of the complications here is that the Zafimaniry have the same word (*hazo*) for tree (living thing) and wood (non-living thing), but see Bloch's (1993: 116) way out of this apparent puzzle.

everyone has access to the same information or uses the same techniques for achieving certain goals. The first point implies that knowledge is not always all in the individual mind. It is also in the tools that a person uses, in the environment that allows for certain solutions to become possible, in the joint activity of several minds and bodies aiming at the same goal, in the institutions that regulate individuals' functions and their interactions. This is the position taken by cognitive anthropologist Edwin Hutchins, who, by studying navigation as practiced on the bridge of a Navy ship, came to the conclusion that the proper unit of analysis for talking about how cognition takes place must include the human and material resources that make problem-solving possible.

> The proper unit of analysis for talking about cognitive change includes the socio-material environment of thinking. *Learning is adaptive reorganization in a complex system.* It is difficult to resist the temptation to let the unit of analysis collapse to the Western view of the individual bounded by the skin, or to let it collapse even further to the "cognitive" symbol system lying protected from the world somewhere far below the skin. But, as we have seen, the relevant complex system includes a web of coordination among media and processes inside and outside the individual task performers. (Hutchins 1995: 289)

Such diversity in the distribution of knowledge across participants and tools does not only concern the more esoteric, technical, or specialized fields (e.g. medicine, navigation, arts and crafts, public speaking); it also permeates everyday domains and activities. This perspective on knowledge and learning implies that what a person needs to know or do in order to be a competent member of a given group cannot be easily represented by a set of propositions. The idea that one might learn how to do something from a set of explicit instructions is daily challenged by anyone who has ever tried to learn to cook from a cookbook or to use a computer program following a manual. More often than one might suspect, there is a moment when one gets stuck or the unexpected happens. It is then that we realize the invaluable experience of having been previously exposed to an expert's actions, the need of having been *in the task* before being able to reproduce it on our own, the degree to which words alone can reproduce the context in which a transformation called learning takes place. Individual change is difficult to produce when it is the individual alone that is in charge. It is not by accident that the most common way of transmitting knowledge in the world is apprenticeship. It is a system that limits participation in the task and yet allows a person to feel involved in the whole task. The novice can watch the experts at work and is slowly let into the task. This means that at each stage of learning the learner already has an image of what the next step should be like. This kind of learning is quite different from the learning that is fostered in schools, where the learner is continuously exposed to a set of instructions on how to do something without having had the experience of watching experts at work for a while and without knowing why something is needed.

The idea that knowledge is distributed affects our notion of what it means to be a member of a culture. In the western popular view, all members of a culture are considered to have the same knowledge. But this is clearly not the case. People from different parts of the country, different households within the same community, or sometimes even individuals within the same family, may have quite different ideas about fundamental cultural beliefs (e.g. the identity or existence of God), different expertise in mundane cultural practices (e.g. cooking and eating), and different strategies for interpreting events and problem solving. Edward Sapir seemed quite aware of this property of culture when he stated that "Every individual is, then, in a very real sense, a representative of at least one sub-culture which may be abstracted from the generalized culture of the group of which he is a member" (Sapir 1949a: 515).

In some cases, people may not even be aware of the degree of diversity expressed in their own community – one could in fact argue that linguistic practices are important ways in which a homogeneous view of culture may be perpetrated. Languages provide ready-made categorizations and generalizations that are accepted as given. We speak of "Americans," "Italians," "Japanese," as if they were monolithic groups. We use expressions like *in this country we believe in freedom* or *English prefers short sentences*, despite the fact that the notion of "freedom" is not something shared by all members of society and the notion of "short sentence" is quite context-specific and often violated by the best writers. Language, not only as a system of classification, but also as a practice, a way of taking from and giving to the world, comes to us with many decisions already made about point of view and classification. Although this does not mean that when two individuals use the same expression they are necessarily sharing the same beliefs or the same understanding of a given situation, stereotypes are routinely reproduced through the unreflective use of linguistic expressions that presuppose gender, race, or class differentiation.

Although communities vary in terms of the range of diversity represented in them, diversification is the norm rather than the exception. Within anthropology, it was Anthony Wallace's theoretical writings on culture and personality that first introduced the alternative view of culture as an *organization of diversity* (see Wallace 1961: 28). According to Wallace, what characterizes people who share the same culture is not uniformity but "their capacity for mutual prediction." Whether or not prediction is a factor, we know that communities are successful, that is, they survive with a manageable degree of internal conflict, not when everyone thinks the same (something that seems impossible), but when different points of view and representations can co-exist. Racial, ethnic, and gender discrimination as well as violence are manifestations of problems people have accepting as meaningful other ways of being, including their ways of speaking. The work done by John Gumperz and his associates on the use of language in multilingual communities highlights the specific ways in which language can be a barrier to social integration (Gumperz 1982a, 1982b; Jupp, Roberts, and Cook-Gumperz 1982).

2.3   Culture as communication

To say that culture is communication means to see it as a system of signs. This is the semiotic theory of culture. In its most basic version, this view holds that culture is a representation of the world, a way of making sense of reality by objectifying it in stories, myths, descriptions, theories, proverbs, artistic products and performances. In this perspective, people's cultural products, e.g. myths, rituals, classifications of the natural and social world, can also be seen as examples of the appropriation of nature by humans through their ability to establish symbolic relationships among individuals, groups, or species. To believe that culture is communication also means that a people's theory of the world must be communicated in order to be lived.

2.3.1   *Lévi-Strauss and the semiotic approach*

One of the earliest examples of the view of culture as communication is found in the work of the French anthropologist Claude Lévi-Strauss. According to him, *all cultures are sign systems* that express deeply held cognitive predispositions to categorize the world in terms of binary oppositions (Leach 1970; Lévi-Strauss 1963a, 1963b, 1978; Pace 1983). Lévi-Strauss starts from the assumption that the human mind is everywhere the same and cultures are different implementations of basic abstract logical properties of thinking which are shared by all humans and adapted to specific living conditions. In his view, which is partly a reaction to and a criticism of earlier conceptualizations of "primitive thought," there is no basic cognitive difference between thinking about the world in terms of abstract concepts such as algebraic expressions or binary numbers and thinking in terms of totemic names (e.g. eagles vs. bears, earth vs. sky, upstream vs. downstream) taken from the natural world (physical surroundings, plants, and animals). The differences between the ways of thinking of so-called "traditional" societies (hunters and gatherers, for instance) and western, technologically advanced people have to do with the resources they use in building their theories. "Primitive thought" constructs myths by using a limited number of already existing characters, metaphors, and plots.[5] Western science, on the other hand, constantly creates new tools and new concepts; for instance, doctors and engineers have instruments specifically designed for their work and their work only. But myth and science work alike, they both use signs and work by analogies and comparisons.

The view of culture as communication is particularly evident in Lévi-Strauss's use of concepts taken from linguistic theory for explaining the relationships between different cultural categories. For instance, Lévi-Strauss extended the Russian linguist Roman Jakobson's theory of the acquisition of sounds to the distinction between culture and nature. Jakobson argued that children start to make sense of the sounds they hear by constructing a system of oppositions that has a binary distinction between vowels and consonants on the one hand and a trinary distinction among the three maximally distinct vowels (i, a, u) and the three maximally distinct consonants (p, t, k) on the other. For Jakobson, the triangles of maximal distinction among vowels (figure 2.1) can be described by means of two basic oppositions in acoustic properties of sounds, namely, between what he called **compact** and **diffuse** and between what he called **grave** and **acute** sounds:[6]

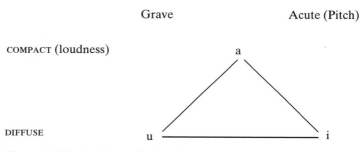

Figure 2.1. Jakobson's vocalic triangle

---

[5] Lévi-Strauss used the French term *bricolage* to refer to the use of whatever is at hand to build or construct something. A "bricoleur" is "someone who works with his hands and uses devious means compared to those of a craftsman" (Lévi-Strauss 1966: 17). "Primitive people" would be those who work like bricoleurs, rearranging elements already found somewhere else.

[6] The distinction between "compact" and "diffuse" is based on the shape of the acoustic signal as shown in a spectogram, depending on whether it shows a higher vs. a lower concentration of energy in a relatively narrow, central region of the spectrum, accompanied by an increase vs. decrease of the total amount of energy. "Grave" and "acute" refer to a concentration of energy in the lower vs. upper frequencies of the spectrum. See Jakobson, Fante, and Halle (1963), Jakobson and Halle (1956), Hyman (1975: 35).

Lévi-Strauss saw in this triangle a *method* for talking about cultural transformations of nature, including the universal activity of cooking. He adapted Jakobson's triangle of maximally distinct vowels to a *culinary triangle* (Lévi-Strauss 1965) in which the sounds are replaced by properties of food and the oppositions between acoustic features are replaced by the opposition between culture and nature and between elaborated and unelaborated:

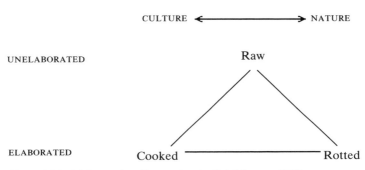

Figure 2.2. Lévi-Strauss's culinary triangle (Lévi-Strauss 1965)

The binary distinction between "unelaborated" and "elaborated" is used to represent the tranforming action of both culture (cooking) and nature (rotting) on food. The category "raw" is in between culture and nature because raw foods are typically admitted in culinary traditions (as when raw fruit or vegetables are served on a plate during a meal) but are not as elaborated or transformed by culture as cooked ones.[7]

The issue then becomes the extent to which the same types of combinations or substitutions are found in a variety of different cultures. If they are found in historically unrelated societies, the anthropologist may see in these associations *universal categories of human thought*. In this method notions taken from linguistic theory can be used in cultural analysis because culture is understood as a system which communicates itself through social actors. Lévi-Strauss believed that it is not people who communicate through myths, but myths that communicate through people. The best statement about this position is found in a comment he wrote about his own writing.

> You may remember that I have written that myths get thought in
> man unbeknownst to him. This has been much discussed and even
> criticized by my English-speaking colleagues, because their feeling

---

[7] Lévi-Strauss's original formulation introduces more subtler distinctions such as the distinction between roasted and smoked and roasted and boiled (see also Leach 1970: 28–31).

is that, from an empirical point of view, it is an utterly meaningless sentence. But for me it describes a lived experience, because it says exactly how I perceive my own relationship to my work. That is, my work gets thought in me unbeknown to me. I never had, and still do not have, the perception of feeling my personal identity. I appear to myself as the place where something is going on, but there is no "I," no "me." Each of us is a kind of crossroads where things happen. The crossroads is purely passive; something happens there. A different thing, equally valid, happens elsewhere. There is no choice, it is just a matter of chance. (Lévi-Strauss 1978: 3–4).

In this paradigm, the concrete human being, the historical being who is not only the site of sensations, thoughts, and feelings, but also the source and origin of actions, vanishes in a transcendental, non-cultural, non-historical subject (Mannheim 1991: 150–1). We need to get to Geertz and interpretive anthropology in order to rethink of human beings as sociohistorically located, *interpreting* subjects (section 2.3.2) and to Bourdieu and practice theory (section 2.5) to fully realize that there is more than decoding in interpretation (Moore 1994: 74).

2.3.2   *Clifford Geertz and the interpretive approach*

Culture is communication also for Clifford Geertz, who, in contrast to Lévi-Strauss, does not see cultural differences as variations of the same unconscious human capacity for abstract thought. Rather than striving to understand underlying similarities among cultures, Geertz is more interested in developing a method of inquiry that stresses the never-ending interpretive process characteristic of human experience – this perspective he shares with philosophical hermeneutics (Gadamer 1976). His goal is to find ways of understanding human cultures rather than trying to explain them by means of causal theories that use general laws of behavior:

> The concept of culture I espouse ... is essentially a semiotic one.
> Believing, with Max Weber, that man is an animal suspended in
> webs of significance he himself has spun, I take culture to be those
> webs, and the analysis of it to be therefore not an experimental
> science in search of law but an interpretive one in search of
> meaning. (Geertz 1973: 5)

For Geertz, the "webs" out of which culture is made must be uncovered through careful ethnographic investigations and reflections which might bring out different points of view on what seem to be the same event. The concept of *thick description* – borrowed from Gilbert Ryle – is a leading metaphor in Geertz's theory of culture: an ethnographer goes back to the same materials and adds "layers" – this would be the sense of "thick" as in a *thick pile* – as well as density, concentration – like in a *thick soup*. Geertz's view of culture focuses on culture as a product of human interaction – "culture ... is public ... it does not exist in someone's head ..." (ibid.). Human beings both create culture and must interpret it. To say that culture is not in someone's head means to emphasize the fact that culture is out there, both produced by and available to humans for interpretation. In this perspective, cultural manifestations are acts of communication. When we observe people engaged in a public debate, participating in a funeral, going to a soccer match, or watching a cock fight, we see people engaged in coordinated behaviors which not only imply but also produce worldviews, including local notions of *person* (or *self*), a concept that is central to Geertz's work as well as to much of cultural anthropology. To be standing in a line to get into a theater not only implies a set of assumptions (and hence knowledge) on how to get access to a seat for a public performance – a theme that would be foregrounded by cognitive anthropologists –, it also communicates notions of public order, individual rights, and social cooperation. It communicates a certain notion of person while bringing it into being. For the same reasons, to refuse to be in a line is also a communicative act which publicly asserts defiance of public norms and criticism of the rights and duties implied by those norms.

2.3.3   *The indexicality approach and metapragmatics*

More recent versions of the view of culture as communication have been informed by work on indexicality (see sections 1.4.2 and 6.9.2). This is particularly the case in Michael Silverstein's expansion on Peirce's and Jakobson's theoretical work. In this new perspective,[8] the communicative force of culture works not only in representing aspects of reality, but also in connecting individuals, groups, situations, objects with other individuals, groups, situations, and objects or, more generally, with other contexts. In this view, meaning (of messages, acts, situations) is made possible not only through conventional relationships between signs and their contents – e.g. the word *desk* means a certain type of material object at which people sit and carry out certain tasks – but also through signs-activated connections between selected aspects of the on-going situation and aspects of other situations. Communication is not only the use of symbols that "stand for" beliefs, feelings, identities, events, it is also a way of pointing to, presupposing or bringing into the present context beliefs, feelings, identities, events. This is what is sometimes called the *indexical meaning* of signs.

[8] See Silverstein (1976b; 1981; 1985a; 1985b; 1987; 1993), Hanks (1990; 1996), Lucy (1993), Mertz and Parmentier (1985), Parmentier (1994), Wertsch (1985a).

In this type of meaning, a word does not "stand for" an object or concept. It rather "points to" or "connects" to something "in the context" (see section 1.4.2). What it points to is either "presupposed" or entailed (that is, "created").

This means that communicative forms (linguistic expressions, graphic signs, gestures, live performances) are vehicles for cultural practices to the extent to which they either presuppose or establish some contextual features (for example, who is the recipient of what is being said, the relative social relation between speaker and hearer) that are not necessarily "described" by the message (or its denotational meaning), but are nevertheless understood. This type of meaning covers not only the so-called **deictic terms** like *here, there, now, yesterday, I, you,* etc., which must be interpreted vis-à-vis the conventionalized spatio-temporal context of the utterance in which they are used. It also includes highly ideological aspects of language and culture such as the establishment of authorship and recipientship (through the use of pronominal forms and reported speech) and the relative status of the participants (through special lexical or morphological choices) (see section 6.8.2). In this framework, a language, through its indexical uses of its elements, provides a theory of human action, or a **metapragmatics** (Silverstein 1985a, 1985b, 1993).

2.3.4   Metaphors as folk theories of the world

Finally, the considerable body of literature on metaphors can also be considered as another case in which culture is seen as transmitted through linguistic forms and hence as communication, although the study of metaphors has been particularly attractive to anthropologists who subscribe to the cognitive view of culture (Keesing 1974) (see also section 3.2.2).

From the functional view of metaphors as ways of controlling our social and natural environment (Sapir and Crocker 1977) to the more recent cognitive theories that see metaphors as processes "by which we understand and structure one domain of experience in terms of another domain *of a different kind*" (Johnson 1987: 15),[9] figurative language has always attracted anthropologists, linguists, and philosophers interested in how the specific form and content of our speech can be seen as a guide to our experience of the world (see chapter 3). The cognitive study of metaphors as cultural schemata (or as expressions dependent upon schemata) is closely associated with the idea that we understand the world, language included, in terms of prototypes, which are simplified, generalized views or folk theories of experience (Rosch 1973, 1978). Prototype theory is opposed to any "checklist theory," which tries to define membership to a class (or words, acts, events) in terms of a discrete set of features or properties – for example, a

---

[9] This concept is discussed in Lakoff and Johnson (1980). See also Lakoff (1987).

bachelor is described in terms of the following features: (i) male, (ii) adult, and (iii) unmarried. Prototype theorists explain the difficulty in applying the word *bachelor* to certain unmarried men by postulating a folk theory of the world in which people marry at a certain age and only one time (Fillmore 1977b). In the more complex, real world, there are people who cannot marry (priests) and people who are too young or old or who have been married and divorced too many times to be seen as real bachelors. Along similar lines, Sweetser (1987: 44) argued that the meaning of the word *lie* "is inherently grounded in a simplified or prototypical schema of certain areas of human experience." Such simplified schema includes moral principles such as (i) Try to help, not harm, and (2) Knowledge is beneficial. Life of course is more complicated and there can be cases of conflict between the two principles. When informing might hurt people, speakers might resort to withholding information or even lying (for example, for politeness).[10]

2.4   Culture as a system of mediation

> The common use of a language takes place at the same level as the common use of all of the objects which surround us in the society in which we were born and in which we live. (Rossi-Landi 1970: 521)

Tools are by definition mediational objects. They are objects that come in between the user and the object of his work. This view of tools goes all the way back to Marx's notion of "instrument of labor," as shown by the following quote:

> An instrument of labour is a thing, or a complex of things, which the labourer interposes between himself and the object of his labour, and which serves as the conductor of his activity. He makes use of the mechanical, physical, and chemical properties of some substances in order to make other substances subservient to his aims. ... The earth itself is an instrument of labour, but when used as such in agriculture implies a whole series of other instruments and a comparatively high development of labour. (Marx 1906: 199)

In this view, "instruments of labor" are whatever humans use to control the environment and produce resources. By definition, such instruments are always "between." They are between people and their food (e.g. a fork), people and the weather (e.g. an umbrella), people and physical matter (e.g. an ax), people and other people (gestures, utterances), people and their own private thoughts (private speech, mental representations).

---

[10] For folk theories as cultural models, see the essays in Holland and Quinn (1987) and D'Andrade and Strauss (1992).

Figure 2.3 offers a preliminary representation of the mediating role played by tools.

HUMAN ——————— TOOL ——————— ENVIRONMENT

Figure 2.3 Tools mediate between humans and the environment

In figure 2.3, tools and artifacts produced by human labor stand between humans and their environment, viz. mediate the interaction with the physical or social world. Culture organizes the use of tools in specific activities, such as hunting, cooking, building, fighting, remembering the past and planning the future. In each case, people's ability to appropriate, exploit, or control nature or their interaction with other human beings is augmented or simply modified by the use of tools. Our relation with the world, however, needs not always be mediated. If it starts raining while we are sitting in a park and our hair and face get wet, the relation between us and nature becomes less direct, less mediated (we still have our clothes and our thoughts). If we pull out an umbrella, however, by trying to control nature's impact on part of our body, we modify the potential consequences of a natural phenomenon to fit our needs or limitations. In this case, our relation with nature is mediated by a specific tool, the umbrella, which, in this case, represents culture. This double possibility of human experience, as either direct or mediated, is represented in figure 2.4 through a triangle (see Vygotsky 1978: 54).

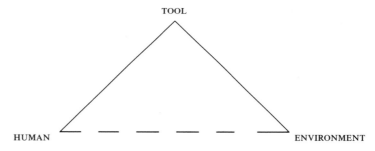

Figure 2.4 Tools as a mediating alternative between humans and the environment

This model includes the possibility of both material cultural objects, e.g. umbrellas, and non-material or ideational objects, e.g. symbols – the use of an intermittent line for representing the relationship between humans and the environment foreshadows doubts about the empirical reality of such an unmediated relationship (see below). For instance, our relationship with nature, rain included, can be mediated by a theory of rainfall – is rain good or bad, or even a sign of achieved communication with God? What matters in figure 2.4 is that the mediated relationship (straight lines) is an alternative to the unmediated relationship with the environment (intermittent line). We can get someone to leave our room by pushing him out, e.g. by using our hands and arms, or we can get him to do the same thing by utilizing symbols, e.g. by pointing to a sign on the wall that says "no visitors" or by asking him to leave. When we use our body to achieve our goal, our relation with the "intruder" is not necessarily (or completely) mediated by culture. When we use symbols, it is always mediated.

In this view, culture includes material objects such as the umbrella and ideational objects such as belief systems and linguistic codes. Both material and ideational structures are instruments through which humans mediate their relationship with the world. Although in some cases people attempt to control the environment through direct, physical intervention, at other times, they are equally if not more powerfully able to control their environment by means of symbolic tools. Thus, culture includes adzes, arrows, hammers, saws, chairs, buildings, paper, pens, transistors, disk drives, bicycles, and cars, as well as theories about God (religion), the Earth and the universe (cosmology), the human body (medicine), human emotions, tools such as natural-historical languages (e.g. English, Arabic, Malagasy), and artificial languages (e.g. musical notations, computer languages). Cultural products include conversations, declarations of friendship and love, letters to the editor, phone calls to our parents, as well as plays, radio announcements, movies, and music videos. Culture includes small as well as complex "objects," that is, whole languages and specific expressions or code words we use in our everyday life (e.g. *how are you?; hi; we should get together one of these days; have I ever met you before?*, etc. – to know what each of these expressions really means we need to know how to use them). All of these products are ways of representing and dealing with the world. They are interpretations of the world and interpretations are themselves tools to act within the world.[11]

Mediation is a fairly neutral concept in which neither the Subject/User nor the Tool/Mediating Object is given prominence. It is however a model that needs further development and refinement in a number of areas. First, it does not say much about the internal organization of each of the elements in the triangle. In particular, for linguistic anthropologists, it does not say enough about the theory of language structure that should be pursued. Second, it leaves out the methodological issue of the kinds of material we would be looking for, and how they should be analyzed. Finally, it still assumes that there is an experiential dimension of unmediated, or natural relationships with the environment. This, as cultural anthropologists have been arguing for some time, is a questionable claim,

[11] For a criticism of the tool-metaphor and its political and economic implications, see Baudrillard (1975) and Sahlins (1976).

given that even when we stand naked in the middle of the rain forest or swim in the middle of the ocean, we have our culture with us. We stand (or swim) in culturally defined ways and we think and represent ourselves in that environment through conscious thought, which has been shaped by culture-specific socialization practices, including practices defining our relationship with the forest and the ocean.

Once we start thinking about culture as a set of related but different systems of mediation that rely on communicative and cognitive tools of various kinds, the unity of the notion of culture starts to be seriously questioned. It becomes, in other words, more difficult to talk about "a" culture, although it is still possible to use the adjective "cultural" in discussing systems of mediation that are used by particular groups in particular types of activities. The term culture however loses its power to sweepingly represent an entire population or group. This deconstruction of the notion of culture is further developed in the next theory I will be introducing, namely, the view of culture as a system of practices.

The theory of culture as a mediating activity between people and the world they inhabit (mentally and physically) is but an extension of the notion of language as a mediating system. It is based on the similarity of tools and signs (words included) and builds on that metaphor, especially on the idea that language is a historical product and hence something that must be understood in the context of the process that produced it (Rossi-Landi 1973: 79). The instrumental view of language implies the theory of language as a system of classification since it recognizes that linguistic expressions allow us to conceptualize and reflect upon events while giving us the means to exchange ideas with others. But it also assumes that linguistic expressions are not just representations of an external reality; they are very much part of that reality and instruments of action in the world. To speak of language as a mediating activity means to speak of language as tool for doing things in the world, for reproducing as much as changing reality. It is through language that we make friends or enemies, exacerbate or try to solve conflict, learn about our society and try to either conform to it or change it. The theory of language as a mediating system and speaking as a mediating activity is close to the theory of language presented by speech act theorists (see chapter 7). In both cases, language is an instrument of action (with representation or informing being kinds of action), a tool that is available and that, like all tools, is both enabling and constraining. This concept of language is thus very close to Sapir's, as shown by the following quote:

> ... if I shove open a door in order to enter a house, the significance
> of the act lies precisely in its allowing me to make an easy entry.
> But if I "knock at the door," a little reflection shows that the knock

in itself does not open the door for me. It serves merely as a sign
that somebody is to come to open it for me. To knock on the door is
a substitute for the more primitive act of shoving it open of one's
own accord. We have here the rudiments of what might be called
language. A vast number of acts are language in this crude sense.
That is, they are not of importance to us because of the work they
immediately do, but because they serve as mediating signs of other
more important acts. (Sapir 1949a: 163–4)

What are these other "more important acts"? Probably the fashions of speaking,
the ways of being in the world suggested by the ways we speak of and in the
world. Language is a "guide" to social life because it stops us from acting in a certain way (e.g. opening a door by shoving it), that is, it suggests and implements
alternative ways of relating to objects and people (see section 3.2).

2.5 Culture as a system of practices

The notion of culture as a system of practices owes a great deal to that intellectual movement known as poststructuralism. In the late 1960s and early 1970s, a
number of European scholars started to question some basic assumptions of the
structuralist paradigm, including the idea that there is a one-to-one correspondence between a meaning and its expression. Generalizations about entire cultures and abstractions based on symbolic oppositions – like the ones used by
Lévi-Strauss (see section 2.1.3) – were criticized as "essentialist" or "metaphysi-
cal" and there was more interest in the moment-by-moment and dialogic construction of interpretations. The interest in the stable aspects of cultural systems
was replaced by a return to diachrony and historicity. The search for societies
where one might still find "primitive" forms of organization and thought intact
was replaced by a widespread recognition of the fluidity of cultures, their inherently contaminated nature. The same ideas motivated contemporary interest in
multiculturalism and transnational communities.

It is not by accident that poststructuralism originates in France, especially in
the writings of scholars like Lacan, Foucault, and Derrida (Sarup 1989). Postwar
French intellectuals had been strongly influenced by Martin Heidegger's philosophy and this philosophy can be seen as at the heart of the poststructuralist agenda,
regardless of its different versions and beyond its criticism of Heideggerian
thought.

In the late 1920s, Heidegger (1962, 1985, 1988, 1992) argued that what philosophers and scientists so easily identify as the "objects" of their study are not the
most basic entities of our experience. The rational thinking Subject identified by
the great philosophers of Modernity – Descartes, Kant, and Husserl – is not the

exclusive or privileged source of our understanding of the world. Our abstract, conceptual, "theoretical" understanding of the world is not primary but derived from other existential premises including our being immersed in an environment where objects are encountered as pragmatically useful, situations are experienced in the context of particular attitudes or "moods," and people are beings to be-with. These relationships with the world cannot easily be represented with the analytical tools used by social scientists who are experts at isolating elements out of their context. The extension of Heidegger's reasoning to contemporary social science brings the realization that binary oppositions and propositional knowledge are no longer the conditions or causes of our experience of the world, but generalizations and representations that presuppose other, more fundamental dimensions of human experience, including historicity (Dilthey [1883] 1988) and what Heidegger called *Befindlichkeit* "affectedness" or "disposition" (Dreyfus 1991; Heidegger 1962).

Despite Bourdieu's criticism of Heidegger's philosophy,[12] practice theory is a good example of a poststructuralist paradigm that builds on some of Heidegger's intuitions about the existential roots of human knowledge and human understanding of the life-world. For example, Bourdieu stresses the inextricable relationship between knowledge and action-in-the-world, past and present conditions (Bourdieu 1977, 1990). For him, social actors are neither completely the product of external material (e.g. economic or ecological) conditions nor socially conscious intentional subjects whose mental representations are self-sufficient:

> The theory of practice as practice insists, contrary to positivist materialism, that the objects of knowledge are constructed, not passively recorded, and, contrary to intellectualist idealism, that the principle of this construction is the system of structured, structuring dispositions, the *habitus*, which is constituted in practice and is always oriented towards practical functions. (Bourdieu 1990: 52)

As a unit of analysis, Bourdieu introduces the notion of *habitus*, a system of dispositions with historical dimensions through which novices acquire competence by entering activities through which they develop a series of expectations about the world and about ways of being in it.[13]

> The *habitus* – embodied history, internalized as a second nature and so forgotten as history – is the active presence of the whole past of which it is the product. As such, it is what gives practices their

---

12 See especially Bourdieu (1988) and Bourdieu and Wacquant (1992: 150–6).
13 For an earlier use of the term *habitus* as socially transmitted habits, see Mauss ([1935] 1979: 101).

relative autonomy with respect to external determinations of the immediate present. (Bourdieu 1990: 56)

This approach is an attempt to overcome the subjectivist/objectivist dichotomy in the social sciences by emphasizing the fact that the Subject or human actor can culturally exist and function only as a participant in a series of habitual activities that are both presupposed and reproduced by his individual actions. Such reproduction must not, of course, be thought of as completely predictable, otherwise we would have another form of determinism, which Bourdieu, like all poststructuralist, post-Marxist theoreticians, is trying to escape. For him, culture is neither something simply external to the individual (e.g. in rituals or symbols handed down by older members of the society) nor something simply internal (e.g. in the individual mind). Rather, it exists through routinized action that includes the material (and physical) conditions as well as the social actors' experience in using their bodies while moving through a familiar space.

Social theorists like Bourdieu have emphasized the importance of language not as an autonomous system – as proposed by structuralists (see section 6.1) – but as a system that is actively defined by sociopolitical processes, including bureaucratic institutions such as schools (Bourdieu and Wacquant 1982, Bourdieu, Passeron, and de Saint Martin 1994). For Bourdieu one cannot discuss a language without taking into consideration the social conditions that allow for its existence. It is, for instance, the process of state formation that creates the conditions for a unified *linguistic market* where one linguistic variety acquires the status of *standard language*. A language only exists as a linguistic *habitus*, to be understood as recurrent and habitual systems of dispositions and expectations. A language is itself a set of practices that imply not only a particular system of words and grammatical rules, but also an often forgotten or hidden struggle over the symbolic power of a particular way of communicating, with particular systems of classification, address and reference forms, specialized lexicons, and metaphors (for politics, medicine, ethics) (Bourdieu 1982: 31). Although Bourdieu's emphasis on the social meaning of alternative forms or stylistic variations (Bally 1952) is a classic topic of sociolinguistic inquiry (cf. Ervin-Tripp 1972), his reflections force variationists and pragmaticians to look beyond specific linguistic exchanges. What is often forgotten by those linguists and philosophers who stress the power of words to do things (see chapter 7) is that a certain linguistic expression can perform an action (e.g. a request, offer, apology) only to the extent to which there is a system of dispositions, a *habitus*, already shared in the community (Bourdieu 1982: 133). Such systems are, in turn, reproduced by daily speech acts, organized and given meaning by institutions such as the school, the family, the work place, which are not only established to exclude others, but also to keep those who are in them under control, to make sure that the acts they perform and the meanings they attribute to such acts remain within an acceptable range.

These reflections are important because they link individual acts to larger frames of reference, including the notion of community, a concept that has been at the center of much debate within sociolinguistics and linguistic anthropology (see chapter 3).

2.6   Culture as a system of participation

The idea of culture as a system of participation is related to culture as a system of practices and is based on the assumption that any action in the world, including verbal communication, has an inherently social, collective, and participatory quality. This is a particularly useful notion of culture for looking at how language is used in the real world because to speak a language means to be able to participate in interactions with a world that is always larger than us as individual speakers and even larger than what we can see and touch in any given situation. Words carry in them a myriad possibilities for connecting us to other human beings, other situations, events, acts, beliefs, feelings. This is due to the ability that language has to describe the world as well as to its ability to connect us with its inhabitants, objects, places, and periods; each time reaffirming a socio-historical dimension of human action among others. The indexicality of language is thus part of the constitution of any act of speaking as an act of participation in a community of language users. We might come into a situation assuming a common language to later realize that it is through acts of speaking that such a language is constituted, challenged, and changed.

If the world is held together by communicative acts and connected through communicative channels, to speak means to choose a particular way of entering the world and a particular way of sustaining relationships with those we come in contact with. It is then through language use that we, to a large extent, are members of a community of ideas and practices.

Any system of participation requires a cognitive component to manage the retrieval of information and the prediction of others' action necessary for problem-solving, and a corporeal component, which accounts for our ability to function in a physical environment which is full of material objects as well as live bodies. Participation also requires the explicit sharing of existing resources (belief systems, languages, the built environment, people) and their implicit assessment for the task at hand. But it does not assume an equally shared knowledge or control of such resources. In fact, if we start from the notion of participation, it is easier to approach variation, given that we can maintain a sense of the different parties involved while recognizing the fact that they exist socially as part of a larger unit. Participation will be further developed in chapter 9, as we discuss its usefulness in defining a valid unit of analysis for the study of linguistic practices.

2.7 Predicting and interpreting

A basic distinction among different theories of culture as well as among different theories of language – some of which we will examine in more detail in the next chapters – is the extent to which theorizing means providing **predictions** of individual occurrences of phenomena as opposed to an **interpretation** of individual events, performances, dialogues, speech acts, utterances, and even individual sounds.[14] The tension between these two approaches is not unique to anthropology and continues to permeate much of the current metatheoretical debate within the social sciences. Such a tension, of course, is not new. The very inception of such fields as sociology and anthropology in the nineteenth century was characterized by a debate about the extent to which doing a science of people should follow the methods of a science of the physical world. Can we predict human behavior in the same way in which we can predict the motion of solid bodies in physics? Should we be more concerned with what is unique about a group of people or with the features of their language or culture that make them part of the larger human species? Can we speak of scientific "laws" when we are dealing with human actions? Each of the anthropologists mentioned above (Boas, Malinowski, Goodenough, Lévi-Strauss, Geertz, etc.) has his or her own more or less original answer to these questions. I have of course my own preferences, which will become more apparent in the rest of the book as we move into other, more specific topics of discussion. Before concluding this chapter, however, I want to offer a few general principles implicitly or explicitly assumed by most contemporary social scientists thinking and writing about language and culture:

1. Social actors themselves, and hence speakers, must have ways of making predictions in their daily life, otherwise they would be living in a state of constant chaos and uncertainty that would be too unstable to ensure their well being. People make predictions such as which language or dialect is appropriate to speak in a given situation, that a question is likely to be followed by an answer, and that people will laugh at their jokes if they are friendly.

2. Social actors, however, are complex beings who participate in complex systems. This means that there is always the possibility that people will behave in unpredicted (if not generally unpredictable) ways (e.g. not speak at all when

---

[14] I am leaving out the issue of the particular method to be used in either one of these two enterprises. Thus, I am not discussing the merits or problems of, say, deductive vs. inductive methods. Either method can be used to pursue the universalistic or the particularist interest.

questioned or not laugh at a good joke). In particular, it is possible that certain behaviors will not be easily interpretable (either by the actors or by the analyst). Rather than seeing these cases as anomalies, the student is advised to treat them as the manifestations of the not fully predictable (not pre-determinate) nature of human conduct, an important component of the meaning-making mechanisms that characterize human social life (both Geertz and Bourdieu, among others, have stressed this point). In addition to being open to the possibility of different interpretations (by different people, at different times, in different languages or styles), we must actively engage in the suspension (or "bracketing") of the most obvious interpretation, an act that phenomenological approaches have often seen as a crucial step for the rational understanding of the world. As students of human behavior, we must realize that what might appear "natural" about any one interpretation may in fact be extremely "cultural" and hence that confessions of ignorance or uncertainty are just as important as the reasonable explanations provided by our favorite consultant or our favorite theorist.

3. Regardless of whether or not one uses statistical methods, it is important to give other researchers a sense of how common or recurrent a given phenomenon is or, rather, how frequently it appears in our data. How often something happens (is said, heard, written, done) is important in people's life.

4. The extent to which a given phenomenon is seen as an occurrence of a more general category is partly due to our interpretive frame. This is true of individual sounds and words, which are never pronounced exactly in the same way (see chapter 6), as well as of types of speech exchanges or verbal performances. This means that we always have two choices: look for the general in the particular or the particular in the general. The theoretical question is always also an empirical question: what is the ground for our generalization? Where did we get our categories? Where did we look for evidence?

5. Social actors themselves are involved in the work of making their actions and their interpretations fit into particular "models." An actor-oriented approach tries to understand those models through an analysis of the participants' specific actions. The following chapters are about the ways in which such an analysis can be done.

6. In general, metaphors are good to think with, but they should not get in the way of new ways of thinking about a problem. This applies to formal representations as well. Formalization is a tool and like all tools is designed for a certain job. More generally, as researchers, we must understand the advantages and limitations of the analytical procedures we employ. We must monitor our own procedures. This does not mean, however, that we should make such monitoring the exclusive or principal subject of our work.

7. Finally, all theories are mortal.

2.8 Conclusions

Culture is a highly complex notion and a much contested ground within contemporary anthropological theory. Many of the basic assumptions that guided anthropological research only a few decades ago have been critically assessed by new generations of researchers. Current theories have tried to avoid an all-encompassing notion of culture in favor of more context-specific and context-dependent practices or forms of participation. In all theories of culture presented here, however, language always plays an important part. For the notion of culture as learned patterns of behavior and interpretive practices, language is crucial because it provides the most complex system of classification of experience. Language is also an important window on the universe of thoughts that interest cognitive scientists (see section 2.2). As psychologists and linguists have been saying for several decades, linguistic and cognitive development are closely connected and a complex communicative system – whether spoken or signed – is a prerequisite for a rich intellectual life. Human languages are also powerful metalanguages (see section 9.3), communicative systems that can be used to talk about other communicative systems, themselves included (as demonstrated by any linguistic textbook!). Furthermore, languages imply or express theories of the world and thus are ideal objects of study for social scientists.

So much of our social life is conducted, mediated, and evaluated through linguistic communication that it should be no surprise that social scientists like Lévi-Strauss used concepts developed within linguistics as tools for the study of culture (see section 2.3). Language also provides us with a useful link between inner thought and public behavior. Even when we articulate our thoughts in our own mind we are only partly doing something "private." We are also relying on a set of cultural resources (including categorizations, theories, and problem-solving strategies) that probably belong not only to us but to a community. The public nature of language is what allows ethnography to exist (see chapter 4). An ethnographer uses language both as a resource for knowledge (what people say, what people say they think, what people say they do, what they do by saying, etc.) and as a tool for the representation of such knowledge (see chapters 4 and 5).

Language is also the prototypical tool for interacting with the world and speaking is the prototypical mediating activity. Control over linguistic means often translates into control over our relationship with the world just as the acceptance of linguistic forms and the rules for their use forces us to accept and reproduce particular ways of being in the world (see section 2.5). Finally, the view of language as a set of practices emphasizes the need to see linguistic communication as only a part of a complex network of semiotic resources that carry us throughout life and link us to particular social histories and their supporting institutions.

Each of the theories presented so far highlights a particular aspect of linguistic systems. In this sense, each theory contributes to our understanding of culture as a complex phenomenon and points toward a different set of properties that can be studied. Each theory implies a different research agenda, but all of them together form a broad mandate for the study of culture and for the analysis of language as a conceptual and social tool that is both a product and an instrument of culture. The chapters to follow will examine in more detail some of the methodological and theoretical foundations of such a research agenda.

3
Linguistic diversity

Linguists have always been concerned with linguistic diversity. But, depending on the theoretical approach and research interest of the scholars involved, the goals and methods for looking at differences across languages have varied considerably. Generative grammarians like Noam Chomsky and his students have devoted their professional lives to explaining phonological, morphological, and syntactic differences across languages by means of a few general principles. They developed a theory of Universal Grammar, a set of rules and conditions on rules that should allow us to describe the grammar of any language and could hence be used to hypothesize the innate interpretive strategies that allow children to acquire any human language. In their endeavor to describe and account for differences between languages, formal grammarians have tended to ignore differences within the same language. Their research strategy has been to assume homogeneity rather than diversity within the same speech community. Sociolinguists have criticized this strategy and chosen the opposite route. They have started from the empirical observation that there is a considerable amount of differentiation within any given speech community in terms of how people pronounce words, construct and interpret utterances, and produce more complex discourse units across social contexts. On the basis of this observation, sociolinguists have devised methodologies for the systematic study of linguistic variation and its relation to contextual factors (including social class, gender, age, setting, style). This research dealt with a number of issues usually ignored by formal grammarians, like, for instance, the challenging goal of defining the boundaries of speech communities and the type of knowledge that is necessary for being a competent member of any such community. Linguistic anthropologists have been concerned with similar issues, but they have also faced the complex question of the relation between language and thought or what has been known as the "linguistic relativity hypothesis." More recently, language diversity has been recast as one of the dimensions of what has been called "language ideology." This chapter will introduce linguistic diversity by drawing from these various traditions.

3.1 Language in culture: the Boasian tradition

To understand how the issue of linguistic diversity arose in North American scholarship, we must go back to when linguistic anthropology was conceived as part of the "four fields approach" in anthropology. Starting with the founding of the American Ethnological Society in 1842 and the American Anthropological Association in 1902, which was launched by members of Section H of the American Association for the Advancement of Sciences (AAAS), anthropology in the United States was conceptualized and in many respects practiced as a **holistic** discipline that studied the physical (now "biological"), linguistic (first referred to as "philological"), cultural, and archaeological records of human populations. In contrast to Europe, where **ethnologists** had their own departments, separate from archaeologists, paleontographers, and philologists (the earlier incarnation of today's "linguists"), in the United States anthropology students were required to have some knowledge of all four fields, in addition to an in-depth knowledge of their own field of specialization. The scholar who more than anyone else represented in theory and practice this holistic view of anthropology was Franz Boas.

3.1.1 *Franz Boas and the use of native languages*

One of the founders of American anthropology, the German-born Boas (1858–1942) was attracted to the study of language by his experience among the Eskimos and the Kwakiutl Indians of the Northwest Coast.[1] He argued that one could not really understand another culture without having direct access to its language. Such a need for linguistic study was not only a practical one, but, he insisted, a theoretical one, due to the intimate connection between culture and language:

> In all of the subjects mentioned heretofore, a knowledge of Indian
> languages serves as an important adjunct to a full understanding of
> the customs and beliefs of the people we are studying. But in all
> these cases the service which language lends us is first of all a
> practical one – a means to a clearer understanding of ethnological
> phenomena which in themselves have nothing to do with linguistic
> problems ... It seems, however, that a theoretical study of Indian
> languages is not less important than a practical knowledge of
> them; that the purely linguistic inquiry is part and parcel of a

---

[1] For discussions of Boas's role in the development of the field of anthropology in general and in the US in particular, see Hatch (1973: 37–73), Langness (1987); on Boas's views on language, see Hymes (1964b), Lucy (1992a), Stocking (1974).

thorough investigation of the psychology of the peoples of the world. If ethnology is understood as the science dealing with the mental phenomena of the life of the peoples of the world, human language, one of the most important manifestations of mental life, would seem to belong naturally to the field of work of ethnology.

([1911]n.d.: 52)

Boas's interest in American Indian languages was transmitted to his students, some of whom, like Edward Sapir, went on to make important contributions not only to American Indian linguistics but to the study of language in general (see below). More importantly, however, Boas's view of the necessity of language for human thought and hence for human culture became a basic thesis of American cultural anthropology in the first half of this century, as shown in this passage by another of his students, A.L. Kroeber ([1923]1963: 102):

In short, culture can probably function only on the basis of abstractions, and these in turn seem to be possible only through speech, or through a secondary substitute for spoken language such as writing, numeration, mathematical and chemical notation, and the like. Culture, then, began when speech was present; and from then on, the enrichment of either meant the further development of the other.

Methodologically, this view of the role of language in culture meant that linguistic systems could be studied as guides to cultural systems. In Boas's case, his fascination with language led to the publication of numerous volumes of ethnography almost exclusively based on recorded "texts," that is, transcriptions of what (usually bilingual) key informants would recall about past traditions, including ceremonies, art, etc. These transcriptions were sometimes done by Boas himself, at other times directly by his key informant (see Sanjek 1990c: 107; Stocking 1974). Many, for example, were done by his Kuakiutl collaborator George Hunt who learned Boas's transcription techniques (Boas 1966: 4–5; Sanjek 1990b: 199).

Transcribing native descriptions of ceremonies and other aspects of traditional culture was part and parcel of the "salvaging anthropology" practiced by Boas and had obvious implications. Like other anthropologists of his time, Boas was concerned with the rapid disappearance or dramatic alteration of Native American languages and cultures and wanted to preserve them by documenting them while there were still people who spoke the languages fluently and could describe their cultural tradition. A positive side of this process was the realization that many of the ideas about "primitive languages" found in the literature were empirically unsound, including the claim that in American Indian languages sounds were not pronounced as accurately as in European languages. This view, Boas showed, was based on the limitations of the observers who had difficulties recognizing sounds that were uncommon in European languages (Boas 1911). A less positive consequence was that, by concentrating on narratives about the past, the method used by Boas created an **ethnographic present** that was empirically questionable (Fabian 1983). Ethnographers concentrated on informants' recollections of past customs and ignored a century or more of European contact, even when such contact had quite striking consequences in the life of the people they were studying. Furthermore, the texts were often produced by one "key informant" and were not checked against other sources or versions (see chapter 5 for a discussion of transcription).

Despite these limitations, however, Boas's methods became a landmark of what became linguistic anthropology. He insisted on the publication of verbatim native accounts of ceremonies and other aspects of their cultural heritage. Publications of the texts used by the ethnographers in formulating their accounts should allow readers to have access to some of the sources from which the ethnographies were based. This is the same logic that is used today in providing detailed transcription of verbal interaction (see chapters 5 and 8). Readers can see with their own eyes what the discussion is based on. Although not all information can be shown on a transcript, there is in it much more than can be found in descriptions that offer no textual sources. When participant-observation (see chapter 4) was introduced and accepted as a standard method in ethnography, it replaced the so-called "armchair anthropology." Direct experience of cultural practices – "being there" (Geertz 1988) – became the source of most descriptions and the collection. At the same time, however, the practice of publishing texts with the informants' accounts was largely abandoned. Paradoxically, although participant-observation was meant to be a more empirical method for collecting information on a community's customs, once ethnographers started to give their own descriptions of the social life of the people they studied, the empirical validation of fieldwork experience suffered a considerable blow: readers no longer had access to the textual sources of such descriptions (Tedlock 1983).

While transcribing native texts and translating them, Boas became fascinated by the different ways in which different languages classify the world and the human experience. He used this observation as another argument in favor of **cultural relativism** – the view that each culture should be understood in its own terms rather than as part of an intellectually or morally scaled master plan, in which the Europeans or those of European descent tended to be at the top.[2]

Boas used his knowledge of American Indian languages to show that the way languages classify the world is arbitrary. Each language has its own way of building up a vocabulary that divides up the world and establishes categories of experience. What in English might be represented by different words (water, lake, river, brook, rain, etc.), in another language might be expressed by the same word or by derivations from the same term (Boas 1911/n.d. 19). It is in this context that he mentioned what is now the famous example of the different words for "snow" in Eskimo:

> It seems important ... to emphasize the fact that the groups of ideas expressed by specific phonetic groups [read "words" or "morphemes"] show very material differences in different languages, and do not conform by any means to the same principles of classification. To take again the example of English, we find that the idea of WATER is expressed in a great variety of forms: one term serves to express water as a LIQUID; another one, water in the form of a large expanse (LAKE); other, water as running in a large body or in a small body (RIVER and BROOK); still other terms express water in the form of RAIN, DEW, WAVE, and FOAM. It is perfectly conceivable that this variety of ideas, each of which is expressed by a single independent term in English, might be expressed in other languages by derivation from the same term.
>
> Another example of the same kind, the words for SNOW in Eskimo, may be given. Here we find one word, *aput*, expressing SNOW ON THE GROUND; another one, *qana*, FALLING SNOW; a third one, *piqsirpoq*, DRIFTING SNOW; and a fourth one, *qimuqsug*, A SNOWDRIFT.

As shown by Laura Martin (1986), the "words for snow in Eskimo" became a standard reference in the popular and scientific discusssions of the relationship among language, culture, and thought, with the number of words escalating from

---

[2] It is important to understand Boas's cultural relativism in the context of the types of evolutionary models of societies common at the time. It is also important to remember that culture for him was a mental or psychological concept. Hence, he was especially a relativist with respect to intellectual achievement (he criticized the view that there were living people who were less intelligent than others) and moral standards (he ridiculed the use of the term "savages" when talking about people, like the American Indian tribes he studied, who in many respects, like, for example, hospitality, seemed to Boas much more gracious than "civilized" Europeans).

five to the hundreds.[3] Whereas there would be nothing special about the fact that a language has more words than another for a particular area of experience, Boas was aiming at the more general point that there might be a cultural motivation for the development of lexical distinctions. This intuition was later modified by Sapir and by Whorf who argued that if a language encodes a particular experience of the world, its use might predispose its speakers to see the world according to the experience encoded in it. Before examining some of the implications of this intuition, I need to introduce some of Sapir's and Whorf's ideas which are relevant to this discussion.

3.1.2 *Sapir and the search for languages' internal logic*

Edward Sapir (1884–1939), probably the most famous scholar in the history of linguistic anthropology, continued and expanded Boas's interest in languages by paying more attention to linguistic structures and emphasizing the ways in which each language is a complete and perfect system that must be understood in its own terms (Darnell 1990). He saw language as a prerequisite to the development of culture and continued in the Boasian tradition of harsh criticism of any attempt to classify certain languages as "primitive" or more "limited" than others.[4]

> No tribe has ever been found which is without language and all
> statements to the contrary may be dismissed as mere folklore ...
> language is an essentially perfect means of expression and
> communication among every known people. Of all aspects of
> culture it is a fair guess that language was the first to receive a
> highly developed form and that its essential perfection is a
> prerequisite to the development of culture as a whole.
>
> (Sapir 1933: 155)

Sapir's fascination with the internal logic of each linguistic system is well illustrated by his enthusiasm for the notion of **phoneme**, an abstract unit of linguistic analysis to which we will return in later chapters. Sapir was well aware of the potential psychological consequences of the idea that languages have their own internal logic . What came to be later known as the "Sapir-Whorf hypothesis" or the "linguistic relativity hypothesis" is partly an outcome of his views on the socializing and uniformizing force of human languages. At the same time, Sapir

---

[3] Martin shows that all the "Eskimo" words mentioned by Boas are actually derived from two roots – she also points out that there is no "Eskimo" language, but a number of related language varieties belonging to either the Yupik or Inuit-Inupiaq branches (see Woodbury 1984). This means that "Eskimo" has as much differentiation as English, which distinguishes between snow and flake (Martin 1986: 422f).

[4] For a more recent criticism of the work on "primitive" languages, see Wierzbicka (1994).

was also an advocate of the importance of **individuality** in culture. He saw culture as the symbolic interplay between individuals and society. He used to say that anthropologists "believe in a world of discrete individuals but a oneness and continuity of culture" (Sapir 1993: 141). His distinction between "genuine" and "spurious" cultures (Sapir 1924) is a theoretical warning against the dangers of a society – such as the industrialized western society in which Sapir lived – that does not properly recognize the needs of its individual members. A genuine culture is one in which there is harmony between societal and individual needs – as in the traditional American Indian societies Sapir came into contact with during his fieldwork. A spurious culture instead is one in which the individual is forced into frustrating and spiritually meaningless tasks in the name of higher efficiency. In a genuine culture, "[t]he major activities of the individual must directly satisfy his own creative and emotional impulses, must always be something more than means to an end" (1924: 316). Sapir's interest in poetry and aesthetic functions of language was part of his efforts to make sense of the struggle of individuals against what he saw as the constraints (or "tyranny") of the symbolic system (e.g. language) they must use to express themselves. As pointed out by Jane Hill (1988b), Sapir's position on how tight each linguistic system is changed over time. We must thus be careful to assign to Sapir either a deterministic stance on the language-thought relation (i.e. "language determines thought") or a pre-structuralist view of language as a closed system (i.e. "we cannot explain language structure through non-linguistic factors"). For instance, it is questionable whether he really believed that any "language is an essentially perfect means of expression and communication" (see quote above). After all, it is in his book *Language* that he makes the famous statement: "Unfortunately, or luckily, no language is tyrannically consistent. All grammars leak" (Sapir 1921: 38). In the next chapters, we will occasionally return to Sapir's work to examine or draw from his contributions to specific areas of study within linguistic anthropology.

3.1.3 *Benjamin Lee Whorf, worldviews, and cryptotypes*

Benjamin Lee Whorf (1897–1941) was a chemical engineer who managed a double career as a successful insurance agent and as a linguist. His interest in languages arose out of his concern, in his adult life, for the potential and actual conflict between religion and science. But even as a boy, according to his biographer John B. Carroll (1956: 6), Whorf had been an avid reader of Middle America prehistory and Maya archaeology. Whorf later studied Hebrew in order to read the Old Testament and became fascinated by a book by an early nineteenth-century French dramatist, philologist, and mystic, Antoine Fabre d'Olivet, entitled *La langue hébraïque restituée*. Fabre d'Olivet had proposed a theory of interpretation in which each letter of the Hebrew alphabet was associated with a specific meaning. These meanings could be used as keys to what the author saw as the hidden meanings of the book of Genesis. Such an approach, on more scientifically solid but not less original grounds, was later extended by Whorf to the study of grammar. As he became motivated to read more widely on languages and linguistics, Whorf approached the subject of American Indian languages. In a few years, he was presenting papers at the International Congress of Americanists and publishing papers in professional journals. His meeting with Sapir in 1928 and his consequent studies at Yale put him in contact with new intellectual resources and sharpened his understanding of grammatical theory and analysis.

Whorf's most famous contribution to linguistic theory is his focus on the relationship between language and worldview. He believed that the structure of any language contains a theory of the structure of the universe, which he at times called "metaphysics." Such a structure becomes particularly evident when one examines languages and cultures that are quite different from one's own:

> I find it gratuitous to assume that a Hopi who knows only the Hopi language and the cultural ideas of his own society has the same notions, often supposed to be intuitions, of time and space that we have, and that are generally assumed to be universal. In particular, he has no general notion or intuition of TIME as a smooth flowing continuum in which everything in the universe proceeds at an equal rate, out of a future, through a present, into a past; or, in which, to reverse the picture, the observer is being carried in the stream of duration continuously away from a past and into a future.
>
> (Whorf 1956a: 57)

> Thus, the Hopi language and culture conceals a METAPHYSICS, such as our so-called naïve view of space and time does, or as the relativity theory does; yet it is a different metaphysics from either.
>
> (Whorf 1956a: 58)

For Whorf, the goal of linguistic analysis is to describe such worldviews. Since they cannot be inferred from direct questioning of informants, who are often not aware of their choices and habits, they must be studied on the basis of systematic observations of grammatical patterns and, in particular, on the basis of comparison between languages that are radically different, such as, for instance, English (or other European languages) and Hopi (or other American Indian languages). The systematic study of patterns of language – Whorf also used the term "**configurations**" – can reveal not only explicit or **overt categories** (also called **phenotypes**) but also implicit or **covert categories** (also called **cryptotypes**). In English, for instance, the plural of nouns is an overt category because it is either marked by the suffix -*s* or by other features of the phrase or sentence they occur with (e.g. form of the verb, the use of the article). A noun like *fish* for instance does not inflect in the plural (remains *fish*), but its number may be reflected in the shape of the verb (*the fish are in the tank*) or in the presence or absence of the article (*fish appeared*). Intransitive verbs in English are instead a covert category because they do not have a particular suffix or marker that distinguishes them from other types of verbs. "The classification of the word is not apparent until there is a question of using it or referring to it in one of these special types of sentence, and then we find that this word belongs to a class requiring some sort of distinctive treatment, which may even be [a] negative treatment," (1956f: 89) that is, the fact that certain rules cannot apply. Only by applying certain kinds of rules do we realize that certain English verbs like *go*, *lie*, *sit*, *rise*, *gleam*, *sleep*, *arrive*, *appear*, *rejoice* behave alike and differently from other verbs (e.g. from transitive verbs like *cook*, *push*, *see*, *seat*, *take*, *show*). For instance, we cannot use intransitive verbs in passive sentences. We do not say *it was being gone* or *it was arrived*.

The recognition of covert categories is an important intuition for a number of reasons. First, it shows that languages make distinctions not only in terms of what words look like or can do, but also in terms of what they do not or cannot do – this insight was further developed by Noam Chomsky in his use of unacceptable sentences in linguistic argumentation (see below). The notion of covert category or cryptotype can also be seen as a precursor of the notion of **deep structure** (Chomsky 1965) – a level of linguistic categorization that is not directly visible or audible but nevertheless necessary to explain why a language behaves in a certain way (see chapter 6). Second, the belief in cryptotypes meant that languages that may appear rather "simple" at the superficial level (e.g. languages that have no overt gender or number distinctions) might actually be quite complex at a more abstract, covert level (Whorf 1956b: 83). This was one of the ways in which Whorf linked his research to his moral and political views. He was committed to reducing the European sense of superiority and with promoting a "brotherhood of thought" (Carroll 1956: 27). A careful linguistic analysis allows us to appreciate the complexities of linguistic systems that at a superficial level might seem simple. Finally, the systematic identification of overt or covert patterns in a given language makes it possible to form empirically verifiable hypotheses about the limits of awareness that native speakers can have about their own use of language, a theme more recently explored by Silverstein (1981), Lucy (1992a) and others (Lucy 1993) (see section 6.8).

The relationship between language and worldview, which is such a central part of Whorf's program, has continued to be an important part of linguistic anthropology (Hill 1988a; Koerner 1992). But our notions of language and worldview have changed and so have our ideas about their relationship (Gumperz and Levinson 1991, 1996; Hill and Mannheim 1992). This has meant not only that the range of phenomena investigated under the rubric "linguistic relativity" has been modified and partly expanded, but also that we can no longer take for granted some of the assumptions on which Sapir's and Whorf's work were based. The notion of worldview used by Whorf (as well as by Sapir and Boas) is tied to a particular theory of culture, namely, culture as knowledge (see section 2.2). It is also tied to a particular theory of language, one that pre-dates the work of sociolinguists and other researchers devoted to the empirical study of variation within communities as well as within individuals. Before introducing some of these more recent contributions, we need to review some of the implications of the classic view of linguistic relativity.

3.2 Linguistic relativity

One of the strongest statements of the position that the way in which we think about the world is influenced by the language we use to talk about it is found in Sapir's 1929 article "The status of linguistics as a science" where he states that humans are actually at the mercy of the particular language they speak:

> It is quite an illusion to imagine that one adjusts to reality essentially without the use of language and that language is merely an incidental means of solving specific problems in communication or reflection. The fact of the matter is that the "real world" is to a large extent unconsciously built up on the language habits of the group. No two languages are ever sufficiently similar to be considered as representing the same social reality. The worlds in which different societies live are distinct worlds, not merely the same world with different labels attached. (Sapir [1929] 1949b: 162)

This position was echoed a decade later by Whorf, who framed it as the "**linguistic relativity principle**," by which he meant "that users of markedly different grammars are pointed by the grammars toward different types of observations and different evaluations of extremely similar acts of observation, and hence are not equivalent as observers but must arrive at somewhat different views of the world" (Whorf 1956c: 221). As mentioned earlier, for Whorf, the grammatical structure of any language contains a theory of the structure of the universe or "metaphysics." He articulated this view in a number of examples on how different languages classify space, time, and matter. Perhaps the most famous English example he ever gave is the use of the word *empty* referring to drums that used to contain gasoline. In this case, he argued, although the physical, non-linguistic situation is dangerous ("empty" drums contain explosive vapor) speakers take it to mean "innocuous" because they associate the word *empty* with the meaning "null and void" and hence "negative and inert" (1956d: 135). The relationship among these different meanings and levels of interpretations is well captured in figure 3.1.

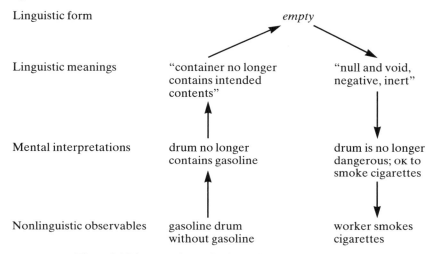

Linguistic form   *empty*

Linguistic meanings   "container no longer   "null and void,
                           contains intended   negative, inert"
                           contents"

Mental interpretations   drum no longer   drum is no longer
                           contains gasoline   dangerous; ok to
                                                        smoke cigarettes

Nonlinguistic observables gasoline drum   worker smokes
                           without gasoline   cigarettes

Figure 3.1 Diagram of one of Whorf's fire-causing examples

(Lucy 1992a: 50)

These ideas generated a considerable debate within anthropology and psychology, including a fair number of empirical studies aimed at either confirming or disproving the linguistic relativity hypothesis (Hill and Mannheim 1992; Koerner 1992; Lucy 1992a). Whorf's ideas remain attractive even after studies that show that some of his specific claims about the Hopi language are empirically questionable or simply inadequate. Malotki (1983), for example, showed that Hopi verbs do have tense inflection (present, past, future) (Whorf 1956d: 144) and that the Hopi language does use spatial metaphor for talking about time.

Despite some of the empirical problems encountered by Whorf's linguistic analyses, the issue of whether or not, or to what extent, language influences thought is likely to remain an important topic within linguistic anthropology, especially as a new generation of scholars find themselves attracted by new ways of testing Whorf's intuitions about how "grammatical categories, to the extent that they are obligatory and habitual, and relatively inaccessible to the average speaker's consciousness, will form a privileged location for transmitting and reproducing cultural and social categories" (Hill and Mannheim 1992: 387). This is an attractive idea for many reasons, including the fact that it deals with epistemological themes that are quite central to the study of cultural practices.

3.2.1 Language as objectification of the world: from von Humboldt to Cassirer

Sapir and Whorf were not the first ones to articulate the view that language might influence thinking. A century earlier, the German diplomat and linguist Wilhelm von Humboldt (1767–1835) wrote the treatise *Linguistic variability and intellectual development*, published posthumously by his brother Alexander, which presents the first systematic statement on language as worldview (German *Weltanschauung*). This book, although not always consistent in its argumentation, does anticipate the basic formulation of linguistic relativity, as shown in the following statement:

> Each tongue draws a circle about the people to whom it belongs, and it is possible to leave this circle only by simultaneously entering that of another people. Learning a foreign language ought hence to be the conquest of a new standpoint in the previously prevailing cosmic attitude of the individual. In fact, it is so to a certain extent, inasmuch as every language contains the entire fabric of concepts and the conceptual approach of a portion of humanity. But this achievement is not complete, because one always carries over into a foreign tongue to a greater or lesser degree one's own cosmic viewpoint – indeed one's personal linguistic pattern.
>
> (von Humboldt [1836] 1971: 39–40)

By being handed down, then, language is a powerful instrument that allows us to make sense of the world – it provides categories of thought –, but, at the same time, because of this property – constrains our possibilities, limits how far or how close we can see. Embedded in these existential themes, there lie several important assumptions about the nature of language and the relationship between language and the world.

First, the conceptualization of language as an objectification of nature, and hence the evolutionary step toward the intellectual shaping of what is considered as an otherwise unformed, chaotic matter, is at the basis of the philosophical assumptions that guide a linguist like Ferdinand de Saussure and a philosopher like Ernst Cassirer. The roots of these assumptions can be found in Kant's view of the human intellect as a powerful device that allows people to make sense of an otherwise unordered or incomprehensible universe. We can interpret experience thanks to *a priori* principles such as time and space – we learn about the world from perceiving objects in our environment, but we can experience them only through the *a priori* concepts of time and space. When we examine the neo-Kantian perspective represented by Cassirer's philosophical work on language, we find something that Humboldt had in fact already done, namely, the replacement of Kant's cognitive categories (the transcendental knowledge that allows humans to make sense of experience) with linguistic categories.

> Like cognition, language does not merely "copy" a given object; it rather embodies a spiritual attitude which is always a crucial factor in our perception of the objective. (Cassirer 1955: 158)

This substitution of cognitive categories with linguistic categories, however, comes with a price. Whereas the categories of human thinking can be at least in principle conceived as shared and hence universal, the categories of human languages immediately present themselves as highly specific, as shown by the inherent difficulties of translating from one language into another and by the attempts to match linguistic patterns across languages. For instance, the "cases" or inflections of nouns in Latin do not easily match the surface distinctions made in languages with very little nominal morphology, like English or Chinese. Similarly, the gender distinctions found in European languages (masculine, feminine, and, sometimes, neuter) are too crude for the distinctions made by Bantu languages, which can have more than a dozen of gender (or "noun class") distinctions (cf. Welmers 1973: ch. 6). If we read these problems as evidence of the fact that different languages classify reality in different ways, we are faced with the question of freedom of expression. In other words, if a language gives its speakers a template for thinking about the world, is it possible for speakers to free themselves of such a template and look at the world in fresh, new, and language-independent ways? For Cassirer, like for Kant before him, humanity solves this problem partly through art, which allows an individual to break the constraints of tradition, linguistic conventions included. The true artist, the genius for Kant, is someone who cannot be taught and has his or her own way of representing the world. This uniqueness is a partial freedom from the constraints of society as they exist in language and other forms of representation.

Language – which is understood by Cassirer as an instrument for describing reality[5] – is hence a guide to the world but is not the only one. Whereas individual intuitions can be represented by art (Cassirer [1942] 1979: 186), the group's intuitions can be represented by myth, which sees nature *physiognomically*, that is, in terms of a fluctuating experience, like a human face that changes from

---

[5] This is what linguists and philosophers of language refer to as the "denotational function" or property of linguistic expressions (see 6.1).

one state to the opposite, "from joy to grief, from elation to depression, from mildness and benevolence to anger or fury" (Cassirer [1942] 1979: 174).

For Cassirer, these are ways of escaping the "prison of language." Both art and myth, in their own specific ways, have a life of their own, independent from *logos*, the rational thought articulated through language. Thanks to art and myth humans have a way of representing, as well as perceiving, understanding, and acting out, aspects of their psychosocial being that may not be objictified in language. Although Cassirer makes too sharp a division between the language of myth, art, and the language of logic and ends up reducing language (as opposed to myth and art) to logical and context-independent thinking,[6] his ideas are helpful because he attempts what most linguists avoid, namely, the discussion of linguistic forms and functions within the more general category of human expressive behavior.

3.2.2   Language as a guide to the world: metaphors

Another version of the Sapir-Whorf Hypothesis is represented by the recent contributions to the study of metaphors, which have been analyzed as providing conceptual schemata through which we understand the world. George Lakoff and Mark Johnson (1980) suggested that (i) our everyday language is much richer in metaphors than we might suspect, (ii) metaphors are means of viewing one kind of experience in terms of another, and (iii) metaphors imply certain theories (or "folk theories") about the world or our experience of it. For example, the concept "theory" is understood in English through the metaphorical concept THEORIES ARE BUILDINGS (Lakoff and Johnson 1980: 52), as shown by the following expressions that can be used in talking about theories: foundation, support, shaky, stand, fall, collapse, framework (ibid. p. 46). Another conceptual metaphor is UNDERSTANDING IS SEEING (or IDEAS ARE LIGHT SOURCES), as in: "I *see* what you're saying. It *looks* different from my *point of view*. I've got the *whole picture*. That's an *insightful* idea. That was a *brilliant* remark. The argument is *clear*. Could you *elucidate* your remarks?" (ibid. p. 48).

These generalized metaphorical concepts allow us to make connections across experiential domains and to find coherence between unrelated or not necessarily similar events. What Lakoff and Johnson call "structural metaphors," for example, can "induce similarities" (1980: 147). For example, the IDEAS ARE FOOD metaphor establishes similarities across two domains (thinking and eating)

---

[6] For a criticism of Cassirer's distinction between mythic and logical thought, see Tambaiah [1968]1985: 33–4). Tambaiah himself, however, ends up making a similarly questionable distinction when he categorically opposes language to non-verbal action (1985: 53).

which are not otherwise necessarily linked in a person's experience and is, in turn, based on some more basic metaphors, including the MIND IS A CONTAINER metaphor, which represents a strong theory of the nature of the human mind. According to Lakoff and Johnson, a metaphor is acceptable as a characterization of our experience partly because it fits with other, more general metaphor concepts and forms with them a coherent whole. This paradigm is particularly appealing to cultural anthropologists who see culture as a system of knowledge (see sections 2.2 and 2.3.4).

3.2.3   *Color terms and linguistic relativity*

One of the strongest criticisms of linguistic relativity came from researchers who studied color terms crosslinguistically. Berlin and Kay (1969) reported results based on the empirical study of color terminology in twenty languages and the consultation of the literature of an even larger number (78 according to Kay and McDaniel 1978: 610) and argued that there are universal constraints on (i) how languages encode and organize basic color terms and (ii) how languages change over time by adding new basic color terms to their lexicon.[7] They discovered that there are eleven universal perceptual categories organized according to the following implicational hierarchy illustrated in figure 3.2 below – where the expression "a <b" means that b implies a, that is, "*a* is present in every language in which *b* is present and also in some language in which *b* is not present" (Berlin and Kay 1969: 4).

$$\begin{bmatrix} \text{white} \\ \text{black} \end{bmatrix} < [\,\text{red}\,] < \begin{bmatrix} \text{green} \\ \text{yellow} \end{bmatrix} < [\,\text{blue}\,] < [\,\text{brown}\,] < \begin{bmatrix} \text{purple} \\ \text{pink} \\ \text{orange} \\ \text{grey} \end{bmatrix}$$

Figure 3.2 Implicational hierarchy of basic color terms

(Berlin and Kay 1969)

The same eleven categories in the same ordering can be interpreted temporally, in terms of an evolutionary scale which goes from a system that has only white and black to the more differentiated system with more basic color terms.

---

7 Berlin and Kay present a number of criteria for the identification of a color as "basic." The criteria include the following characteristics: (i) the term is monolexemic, that is, the meaning is not derived from the meaning of its parts, (ii) its meaning is not included in any other kind of color term, (iii) its application should not be restricted to a narrow class of objects, and (iv) it must be psychologically "salient" for informants (Berlin and Kay 1969: 8).

Kay and McDaniel (1978) later explained these findings – with some minor modifications – on the basis of human neurophysiological processes of perception. They also reiterated the claim that the basic color terminology discovered around the world in genetically unrelated languages provided strong empirical evidence against either the strong or weak versions of the Sapir-Whorf Hypothesis. Whorf's statement that "the world is presented in a kaleidoscopic flux of impressions which has to be organized by our minds – and this means largely by the linguistic systems in our minds" was interpreted by Kay and McDaniel (1978: 610) as saying that "each language imposes on the individual's 'kaleidoscopic flux of impressions' its own idiosyncratic semantic structure." This seems to be invalidated by the universal regularities identified by the research on basic color terms.

This work has generated a considerable number of follow-up studies, some supporting and other ones criticizing the original design and its results (Maffi 1991). Some critics of Berlin and Kay's work argued that (i) they misread Whorf and (ii) linguistic categorization does seem to matter for certain types of psychological task. For example, Lucy and Shweder (1979) not only argued that language matters in recognition memory, but also that Whorf did not say that the world is *perceived* in a "kaleidoscopic flux of impressions" but simply that the world *presents* itself as such and that the work of language is to organize such a flux. In this version, Whorf's point was about logical necessity (or lack thereof). He believed that all things "are equally alike and equally different, that is, the number of true things one can say about any two things (the number of predicates that apply) are equal, and perhaps infinite." (Lucy and Shweder 1979: 602) There is no implication that language is the independent variable and categorization the dependent one. Rather, language includes perceptual categorization (although, in some cases, it might choose to ignore it). More recently, Lucy (1992a: 178) pointed out that linguistic relativity – at least in Whorf's version – does not rule out the possibility of discovering semantic universals.

Beyond the specific claims made about basic color terms, Berlin and Kay's research contained a number of important hypotheses and research agendas. By discovering a "natural" tendency to name certain color distinctions, they were undermining the notion of the arbitrary (i.e. conventional) nature of linguistic signs made popular by de Saussure. If genetically unrelated languages come up with similar classification systems, there must be principles of linguistic encoding that are language independent (this hypothesis is at the basis of Berlin's work on sound symbolism, see section 6.8.1). Furthermore, the lexicon, as displayed by color terminology, does not seem to be organized in discrete categories to be represented by binary features, as proposed by generative semanticists like Jerrold Katz (1964), but as continuous functions. Kay and McDaniel (1978) argued that fuzzy set theory and prototype theory are better equipped for handling these data. Whereas in standard set theory (and in feature analysis of the lexicon) an element either *is* or *is not* a member of a given set, in fuzzy set theory and prototype theory, an element is a member *to a certain degree* (Lakoff 1972; Kay and McDaniel 1978; Rosch 1973, 1975; Zadeh 1965, 1971). These ideas later contributed to Kay's collaboration with Charles Fillmore and Mary O'Connor to devise a "construction grammar" where syntactic configurations are linked to semantic and pragmatic interpretations (Fillmore 1996; Fillmore, Kay, and O'Connor 1988). Similar ideas are found in George Lakoff's (1987) notion of "idealized cognitive models," which he developed around the notion of metaphor (see above).

3.2.4 Language and science

The issue of linguistic relativity speaks to the core of the anthropological enterprise because it touches upon the possibility of a science of humans as entities that are more than biological beings. If indeed language (in a broad sense of the term) is (or can be) really constraining, how can we use it to describe what we or others do, believe, think, and feel?

If language itself represents a particular way of looking at the world, a pair of glasses that we are given at birth and keep wearing without being conscious of it, how can we see what others, wearing different glasses, see?

[margin annotation: good!]

There are a number of answers to this question. None of them is in itself completely satisfactory, but all of them together constitute the tools of trade that allow us to engage in anthropological research.

First, inspired by Cassirer's theory, we could accept his challenge and try to turn into artists. This means that we need to act as creative beings who are not afraid of violating expectations while moving within still predictable canons of communication. There is no question that in science, like in art, many ideas are born out of sudden intuitions, epiphanies that are difficult to reconstruct in an accurate manner. There is an art of discovery just like there is an art of presenting an idea to the public. At the same time, like in the artists' world, in science as well new ideas can only be generated and sustained when they do not go too far from what is already accepted. Like artists, researchers live in a *market* of ideas, where cultural capital is produced and rules of success are constantly evaluated (Bourdieu 1982, 1985; Rossi-Landi 1970, 1973).

The second solution implicitly proposed by Cassirer is to study cultural products, like myths, that reveal certain truths about a community that the members themselves might not be aware of or might not be willing to openly recognize. This is one of the central concerns of symbolic anthropology (see Dolgin, Kemnitzer, and Schneider 1977). The assumption is that a culture communicates in a myriad ways beyond the descriptive statements produced by natives when interviewed by the ethnographer (see the discussion in section 2.1.3 about culture as communication). This is also an extension of Freud's intuition that dreams are smarter than dreamers and that in dreams we are able to make new connections, recognize problems, and even find solutions. A group of people might not be able to articulate what they really care about or why they behave the way they do, but their stories, performances, and everyday expressions might reveal their inner motivations.

A third solution is to study the conditions under which a language or, better, its speakers can overcome the limits of their own worldview or metaphysics. This is, for instance, what suggested by Silverstein's work on metapragmatics (see sections 1.4.2 and 6.8). For Silverstein, given our use of language to study cultural phenomena, we need to test the extent to which a language and its speakers are able to recognize certain distinctions and give us crucial hints on how to find generalizations. A theory of indexicality provides the analytical tools for such an investigation. In this perspective, the "prison of language" is a hypothesis that must be tested by comparing statements that native speakers make about their own language usage with hypotheses based on actual usage.

Another solution is to rethink the very concept of language and combine our discoveries about grammatical categories and their implications with our understanding of linguistic communication as a practice that implies the simultaneous cooperation and collusion of several distinct codes, modes of communication, and participants (see chapter 9). In this sense, whatever "limits" might exist in one of the components of the communicative event could be overcome through the qualities of other components. A language is more than a set of phonological, morphological, syntactic, or lexical categories and rules for their use. A language exists in the context of cultural practices which, in turn, rely on a number of other semiotic resources, including the representations and expectations provided through the participants' bodies and movements in space, the built environment in which they act, and the dynamic relations established through recurrent ways of doing things together.

Whichever route we choose, we must recognize that some kind of linguistic relativity affects in principle any scientific enterprise. Any theorizing – e.g. making hypotheses, isolating phenomena, providing general principles – needs a language and implies a perspective, a point of view. Such a recognition, however, should not be seen as the end of science, but simply as the end of a simple-minded notion of science. Science always lives in a tension between two poles or forces, sometimes called **subjectivism** and **objectivism**. Subjectivism starts from the assumption that any phenomenon is partly created, co-constructed by the person (i.e. subject) who "discovers" it or simply describes it. Historicism is but a particular version of this approach: all phenomena are historically located; they exist in relation to other phenomena that give it meaning, whether or not we are aware of it. Language, of course, enters into such a historical context at different levels and in different ways. Objectivism is the theoretical perspective which purposedly ignores the sociohistorical grounding of interpretations and claims the possibility of a universal, context-independent set of criteria for the description of a given phenomenon. When we talk about "sentences," "complements," "prepositions," "inflection" or individual sounds, we ignore – for the purpose of analysis – their sociohistorical and psychological grounding in particular speech acts and speech activities produced by particular subjects at a particular time, in a particular place.

The difference among different approaches to the study of cultural phenomena, speech included, lies in the extent to which researchers operate within one set of assumptions or the other. Researchers also vary in the extent to which they try to move in and out of these two different modes. Formal linguists, for instance, tend to live in an objectivist world of phenomena, where sentences and meanings have lost their connection to particular situations and are examined for their supposedly universal properties. They step out of such a world only to gather more data, i.e. examples for further analysis. Linguistic anthropologists, on the other hand, try to devise ways of maintaining a connection between linguistic forms and its producers. Both groups, however, work with theoretical constructs. The notion of "speech event" used by ethnographers of speaking (see chapter 9) is just as theoretical as the notion of "verb" used by grammarians or the notion of "adjacency pair" used by conversation analysts (see chapter 8). In the world "out there," there are no verbs, no speech events, and no adjacency pairs. There are particles of matter moving around in certain recurrent and yet not fully predictable patterns. We interpret such experiences as and through symbolic means, including linguistic expressions. That's what it means to be human. The anthropological study of language aims at clarifying the factors that go into the production of such representations, including their similarities and differences. Such a study, however, cannot proceed without reexamining the very notion of "language." Despite its routine use by social scientists, the term "language" is often left unanalyzed. I will continue this discussion of linguistic diversity by returning to the meaning of "language" and proposing to replace it with a number of alternative notions, including linguistic varieties, repertoire, and speech community.

3.3 Language, languages, and linguistic varieties

It is important to distinguish between "language" and "*a* language." The former refers to the human faculty to communicate using particular types of signs (e.g. sounds, gestures) organized in particular types of units (e.g. sequences) and the latter refers to a particular sociohistorical product, identifiable with a label such as "English," "Tok Pisin," "Polish," "Swahili," "Chinese," "American Sign Language," "Sign English." Although sociolinguists (and linguistic anthropologists) routinely use the term "language" in the first, general sense, much of the research in sociolinguistics in the last four decades has shown that the identification of "*a* language" as the linguistic system used by a given group of people can be quite problematic. Every time we subject *a* language (e.g. "English," "Swahili," etc.) to systematic investigation, we discover that it displays a considerable variation across speakers and situations. This means that we cannot be sure that what we are describing for a few speakers or even for an entire group of people will have a social distribution larger than that group. Not only are there places, for instance, in Melanesia, where several different "languages" are recognized within a relatively small territory – Papua New Guinea is supposed to have more than 750 languages –, but even in large urban settings where speakers might consider themselves speakers of the "same language," there might in fact be rather different forms and rules for their interpretation. Just like a group of teenagers hanging out at the same intersection every afternoon might have their own special style of speaking, different from the style used by their parents and maybe even from their older siblings, members of a profession will have their own lexicon and assumptions about how to describe a problem or prescribe a solution. This means that in our investigations we need to be aware of variation and be prepared to use or devise methods that allow us to get a sense of the relationship between the group of people we study and the larger **networks** in which they operate (L. Milroy 1987; Milroy and Milroy 1992). In the past, linguistic anthropologists have been skeptical of some of the theoretical assumptions implicit in the quantitative methods necessary for assessing intragroup variation, but they have been dealing mostly with small groups or relatively small data sets. As more linguistic anthropologists extend their work to urban environments, they will have to reassess their evaluation of quantitative sociolinguistics and face the challenge of a confrontation with its methods and theoretical assumptions.

Sociolinguists have also taught us that we cannot always trust members' characterization of linguistic differences and groupings. What people call "a language" as opposed to "a dialect" might simply be due to social stigma or to the political decision to give one particular dialect the status of standard language. For these reasons, sociolinguists prefer the term *variety* (also *linguistic variety* or *variety of language*), to be thought of as a set of communicative forms and norms for their use that are restricted to a particular group or community and sometimes even to particular activities. Sociolinguists' varieties might cover what other researchers call languages, dialects, registers, or even styles (Andersen 1990; Biber and Finegan 1994). The advantage of using the term variety is that it does not carry the usual implications associated with words like "language" and "dialect" and can cover the most diverse situations, including "all the languages of some multilingual speaker, or community" (Hudson 1980: 24).

In addition to the notion of social distribution, the term "variety" also implies the concepts of *linguistic repertoire* and *speech community*, both of which are central for a clarification of "language" as the object of our study.

3.4   Linguistic repertoire

Linguistic repertoire is a concept originally introduced by Gumperz (1964: 137) to refer to "the totality of linguistic forms regularly employed in the course of socially significant interaction." The assumption in this case is that speaking a language means to be involved in a continuous process of decision-making, although not necessarily a conscious one (see also Ervin-Tripp 1972). Repertoire is thus a concept that can apply to either groups or individuals (Platt and Platt 1975). Whether an individual's repertoire can ever be the same as the repertoire of his community is partly an empirical question. It can be ascertained through detailed investigation of the speech of individuals matched against the range available in their community. But it also depends on our choice of the constituting elements of repertoire (or units of analysis) and the boundaries of the community in which the repertoire is found. If we only concentrate on phonological variation and a small community, for instance, it might be easier to find individuals whose repertoire coincides with the repertoire of their community. If we include larger units (e.g. lexical choices, speech genres) and we widen the boundaries of the community, it will be unlikely that individuals would be able to match the repertoire of their community.

The notion of repertoire then raises a number of issues. The first is the issue of variation. Does the study of repertoire give us a sense of the extent to which variation is pervasive in a given speech community? Can it shed light on how important variation is? The second is the issue of meaning. Once we ascertain the existence of a range of possible choices (phonological, syntactic, lexical, etc.), can we also tell whether a decision with respect to one of the alternative forms has implications for individual speakers? The third issue concerns the social and cultural organization of a repertoire. What are the criteria by which individual speakers make choices within a given repertoire? Can we trace such choices to individual, situational, institutional factors? How important is the type of social organization in which a repertoire is assessed? Most of the work on sociolinguistic variation is done in communities where social differences can be framed in terms of social classes. Do other kinds of social systems (e.g. small egalitarian communities, caste or feudal types of systems) treat repertoire differently? The fourth question has to do with individual freedom and change. To what extent do individual speakers have real options in adopting one variant over another (e.g. dropping the postvocalic /r/ in NYC, using honorific language in those communities that recognize it as a "special" or "separate" register)? To what extent does the behavior of an individual reflect group expectations? Do some individuals (e.g. community leaders, famous artists) have the power to affect the linguistic choices of their community?

As shown by these questions, the notion of repertoire forces researchers to think about a range of issues that are central to the role of language in social life. Although repertoire is different from what is usually understood as "grammar" it makes similar assumptions about norms and expectations. One of its advantages is that it does not have the same presuppositions about "speaking proper." A repertoire is something that all speakers have, regardless of where they went to school or for how long. At the same time, it is obvious that one's life experience, including schooling, is a crucial element of one's repertoire. For researchers, concentrating on repertoire means to select a range of linguistic features, a set of situations, and a speech community.

3.5 Speech communities, heteroglossia, and language ideologies

> The conventional wisdom of the Tower of Babel story is that the collapse was a misfortune. That it was the distraction or the weight of many languages that precipitated the tower's failed architecture. That one monolithic language would have expedited the building, and heaven would have been reached ... Perhaps the achievement of Paradise was premature, a little hasty if no one could take the time to understand other languages, other views, other narratives. Toni Morrison (1994: 19)

As it will be made clear in the discussion of ethnographic methods in chapter 4, linguistic anthropologists typically do not just work *on* a language variety but on the language variety (or variet*ies*) spoken *in* a particular community. In other words, linguistic anthropologists start from the assumption that any notion of language variety presupposes a community of speakers. Such a community is a point of reference for the individuals who use a given variety as much as for the researcher who is interested in documenting such usage.

3.5.1 *Speech community: from idealization to heteroglossia*
Linguistic anthropologists share with sociolinguists the concern for a definition of speech community as a real group of people who share something about the way in which they use language. This concern yields an approach that differs from the one proposed by most formal grammarians, who start from the assumption that the community they work in is homogeneous (Chomsky 1965: 3).

Homogeneity is an idealization common (although by no means universal) in science: investigation starts with the assumption of order and uniformity. Variation is usually put aside as "exceptions to the rule" or "insignificant." Locating himself in this tradition, Chomsky assumes that there must be a property of the human mind that allows "a person to acquire a language under conditions of pure and uniform experience" (Chomsky 1986: 17). Only after having established the rules and principles governing such an idealized community, should more complex conditions be introduced and studied. The idealized type of experience mentioned by Chomsky is studied by investigating native speakers' (often the linguist's own) intuitions about whether or not a given linguistic form or sentence is acceptable, that is, roughly speaking, whether it "sounds right" (this is different from whether it would be judged acceptable by a school teacher). The English sentences below are an example of this method at work. Three verbs that can take a complement clause – marked by square brackets – starting with *what* are examined by imagining possible sentences in which they might occur. The examples preceded by an asterisk (*) are the unacceptable ones (from Chomsky 1986: 88):

(1)   I asked [what time it is]
(2)   I wondered [what time it is]
(3)   I (don't) care [what time it is]
(1)'   it was asked what time it is
(2)'   *it was wondered what time it is
(3)'   *it was cared what time it is

Acceptability judgments provide the basis for the generalizations made by the linguist about particular grammars. For instance, the fact that only the sentence with the verb *ask* can be made into an acceptable passive sentence with the verb *be* (*it was asked ...*) is used to show that the relationship between the main verb (*ask*, *wonder*, and *care*) and the following complement clause (*what time it is*) is different for *ask* as opposed to *wonder* and *care*. Whereas *ask* is a transitive verb, *wonder* and *care* are not and therefore the embedded clause starting with *what ...* cannot become the subject of the passive verbs *was wondered* and *was cared*.[8] Such generalizations, in combination with hypotheses about the "underlying" or "deep" structures that might describe such phenomena,[9] are used to posit

---

[8] Sentences (1)'-(3)' in fact are not standard passives, otherwise the "subject" clause [what time it is] would be before the main verb, as in
    (1)"   [what time it is] was asked
This is however a bit odd in English and another rule has been applied to "move" the subject to the end and replace it with the "empty" pronoun *it*.

[9] See chapter 6.

principles that should apply to all languages (what Chomsky calls "Universal Grammar").

As shown by the development of formal linguistics from the 1960s on, the use of intuitions on how different words fit into the same pattern has been a very powerful method for quickly producing rules and generalizations about syntactic regularities. But this method encounters some problems when adopted as the main source of information about what it means to know a language or even a small part of it. Labov (1972b: ch. 8) articulated a number of these problems, including the limited range of data available by working on only one's own or a few informants' intuitions, the difficulty of having intuitions about variation and its meaning for the speakers, and the theoretical limitations of assuming that differences in intuitions can be resolved by attributing them to different "dialects." Looking at it from an anthropological perspective, Hymes (1972b) pointed out that the very definition of acceptability is problematic given that to know a language means not only to know what is grammatically acceptable. It also means to know what is socially and culturally acceptable. Again, this kind of information is difficult if not impossible to gain by simply imagining examples or situations. To these objections, formal grammarians often reply that there is a fundamental misunderstanding in this debate. They are talking about a different kind of "language" from the one that is studied by sociolinguists and anthropologists. What formal grammarians are interested in is not a sociopolitical product or process but an abstraction, constructed by the linguist to make hypotheses about the human mind. Chomsky (1986) uses the term "Internalized language" (or "I-language") for this kind of construct and distinguishes it from the "Externalized language" (or "E-language) studied by those interested in language use.

It is important to stress that from a sociological and anthropological perspective, the problem with this approach is not idealization per se, but some of its implications and consequences. I will mention here only two problematic areas. The first is the connotations of linguistic purism that a linguistic theory exclusively based on idealization carries. Chomsky (1986: 17) explicitly says that a speech community in which people use a mixture of two languages, e.g. French and Russian, would not be "pure" enough to be an ideal object of study for theoretical linguistics. But this assumption could mean the exclusion of most if not all real communities in the world. All speech communities that have been studied systematically show *some* degree of linguistic, sociological, and cultural differentiation. Sociolinguists and linguistic anthropologists believe that there is always some "mixing" whether in the form of two very different varieties (French and English) or in the form of "dialectical" or "stylistic" differentiation (see below the discussion of heteroglossia). Without getting into the negative connotations of the use of the term "pure," the idealization program in practice means that at least for now we should not be studying any community where we perceive a considerable degree of "mixing" or "impurity." Although this kind of approach is presented as the most rational method, what is left for "later" might *never* be studied, if all the existing human resources continue to be used for testing and revising models of "pure" communities rather than for considering whether these models can be extended to real life situations where "impure" mixing is the norm. This is indeed what has happened to theoretical linguistics as developed by Chomsky and his students. In forty years of intense research by a group of innovative and highly productive scholars, very little if anything has been said about how to relate the abstract knowledge of the idealized members of "pure" communities to the concrete acts of linguistic performance by people who live in real communities.

It is in the context of this discussion that I see Toni Morrison's statement (quoted above) as a powerful reminder of the origins of the myth of linguistic purity. Why don't we use our theoretical stance, our scientific wisdom, to abandon the belief that it would be better and easier if we all spoke the same language, the same dialect, or in the same style? Why don't we embrace instead the idea that variety is part of human cultures and human nature? Why don't we accept that there always are contrasting forces in any human aggregate and even within the same individual? Such a recognition would define a different kind of program for the study of humanity, including language. We would start from the assumption that variation is the norm and we would look for ways of documenting it in order to understand language as part of the human condition.

This is what is suggested by the work of many contemporary theorists, including the ones inspired by the work of the Russian linguist, philosopher, and literary critic Mikhail Bakhtin, who argued that the linguistic homogeneity assumed by most linguists, philosophers, and philologists is an ideological construction, historically tied to the development of the European states and the efforts to establish a national identity through a national language to be called by one name: German, French, Russian, Italian. Such a unified notion of *a* language has no necessary relation to real language use. In the reality of everyday life (as well as in the careful work of great artists such as some of the novelists studied by Bakhtin), the speech of any one person is filled by many different *voices* or linguistically constructed personae, a quality that Bakhtin called *raznorecie*, a term translated in English as *heteroglossia*:

> At any given moment of its evolution, language is stratified not only into linguistic dialects in the strict sense of the word ... but also – and for us this is the essential point – into languages that are socio-ideological: languages of social groups, "professional" and

75

> "generic" languages, languages of generations and so forth. From this point of view, literary language itself is only one of these heteroglot languages – and in its turn is also stratified into languages ... (Bakhtin 1981b: 271–2)

The many social, cultural, cognitive, and biological factors responsible for heteroglot language or what sociolinguists call linguistic variation conspire toward a continuous tension between what Bakhtin called the *centripetal* and the *centrifugal* forces of language.

The centripetal forces include the political and institutional forces that try to impose one variety or code over others, e.g. Quechua in Peru in the sixteenth century (Mannheim 1991), English in Scotland in the twelfth and sixteenth centuries, the Tuscan dialect in Italy in the fourteenth century (De Mauro 1976: 23–4), Spanish in the Indian communities in Mexico and other parts of Central and South America, and so on. These are centripetal because they try to force speakers toward adopting a unified linguistic identity.[10] The centrifugal forces instead push speakers away from a common center and toward differentiation. These are the forces that tend to be represented by the people (geographically, numerically, economically, and metaphorically) at the periphery of the social system.

Linguistic anthropologists have looked at such alternative norms as strategies for the construction of social or ethnic identity. By virtue of their resistance to the official, standard, majority language or variety, speakers maintain alternative, often parallel identities.[11]

3.5.2   Multilingual speech communities

Among the Arizona Tewa community studied by Paul Kroskrity (1993), three centuries of contact, including intermarriage, with their more numerous Hopi neighbors have not eradicated the Tewa language, although there are signs of language loss among the younger members of the community. Despite the fact that there are times when the Arizona Tewa identify themselves as Hopis (especially with respect to the outside world), "they reserve an identity for themselves which is unavailable to the Hopi and uniquely their own" (Kroskrity 1993: 7). The language brought by the ancestors of the Arizona Tewas from the Rio Grande Pueblos almost 300 years ago is the most important symbolic vehicle of this identity. Although most members of the Arizona Tewa speech community

---

[10] By no means should this statement be interpreted as implying that speakers have no roles in defining the future of a particular linguistic variety. See Kulick (1992) for a discussion of the role of local beliefs in the adoption of Tok Pisin in Papua New Guinea.

[11] The notion of *covert norm* in sociolinguistics tries to explain the preference of non-standard linguistic features by certain speakers (see Trudgill 1974, 1978).

have some knowledge of at least three languages (Tewa, Hopi, and English), the Arizona Tewa language has a special status for the Tewas, as shown by the ways in which they try to protect it. Paradoxically, the special status of Tewa as symbol of ethnic identity is what makes it also particularly vulnerable, given that it cannot be transmitted to or by people considered to be outsiders.

Kathryn Woolard's (1989) study of the use and prestige of Catalan in Barcelona provides another interesting case where one can see how a minority language can survive as a symbol of ethnic identity and a measure of personal prestige. Despite centuries of political control by the central Spanish government and the gradual imposition of the language of the Spanish state, Castilian, as the language of school instructions, Catalan has survived as the first language of a large part of the population while maintaining a high status in Catalonia.

How is it possible that the Castilian political dominance has not been able to secure linguistic prestige for its speakers? This is due, according to Woolard, to the fact that in Catalonia there is a reversal of the usual power relation between majority and minority languages. The "minority language," Catalan is not the "low prestige" language, but the language of the economically dominant bourgeoisie. Castilian, on the other hand, is the language of the immigrant workers from Andalusia and other, less prosperous areas of the country. This means that the centrifugal forces in Catalonia are represented by a native population that is wealthier than the population of immigrants for whom Castilian is their first language.

> It is who speaks a language rather than where it is spoken that gives it its force. Authority is established and inculcated most thoroughly not in schools and other formal institutions, but in personal relations, face-to-face encounters, and the invidious distinctions of the workplace and residential neighborhoods. (Woolard 1989: 121)

In another sociohistorically oriented study of a bilingual community, Jane and Kenneth Hill (1986) discuss the fate of Mexicano – also known as Aztec or Nahuatl –, the modern descendant of the language of the Aztecs, Tlaxcalans, and many other peoples of Mexico and Central America. They show that for hundreds of years the people of the Malinche Volcano communities in Mexico borrowed extensively from Spanish by taking from it grammatical and lexical features such as suffixes (e.g. the adverb-forming *-mente* or the nominal plural marker *-es*), complementizers (e.g. *que*, which also acquires an evidential function), and full clauses with main verbs (e.g. *yo creo que* "I believe that" and *parece que* "it appears that"). Spanish and Mexicano are woven into one another in such a way that Hill and Hill prefer to speak of a "syncretic language" rather than "language mixing." Mexicano speakers, for instance, have reanalyzed certain Spanish forms and adapted them in creative ways to Mexicano syntax or morphology. Until recently, Mexicano speakers had managed to control ideologically the force of Spanish by restricting its fuller use "to the sphere of the elevated, the distance between strangers, the realm of inauthenticity, as opposed to the domestic, intimate, authentic voice of Mexicano speaking in everyday uses" (Hill and Hill 1986: 402). But the strategy of syncretism is under attack. Today Spanish is replacing Mexicano, which is passing out of use in many towns and becoming a secret language – or "anti-language" in Halliday's sense (1976). Not only is Mexicano used for a much restricted range of communicative functions and situations (e.g. for "passwords" or obscene challenges to outsiders), but the attitudes toward its use have undergone a radical shift. There is a real devaluation of Mexicano as spoken today – its syncretism – and a resurgence of purism. Given the lack of institutional support for the re-establishing the older variety of Mexicano, such a devaluation is equivalent to the rejection of Mexicano altogether, which has become an "oppressed language" (Albó 1979). This trend in language use and language attitudes is part of a wider trend to abandon an Indian or "indigenous" identity in favor of a "Mexican" identity. Such a larger trend is manifested in the way in which people dress, the kinds of houses they build and the like, and the kinds of products they consume. But the struggle is not over. There are people who learn Mexicano as adults as a way of participating in local networks of reciprocity, instantiated in ritual and religious activities. Furthermore, Spanish still has a "distancing" function for most speakers. Although many Malinche towns are divided between *mexicanos* (Mexicano-dominant speakers) and *castellanos* (Spanish-dominant speakers), some speakers are starting to recognize the possibility of a shared ethnic identity that accepts both kinds of speakers. This allows for members of the same family not to be divided over linguistic issues. It also grants indigenous people the authority to make choices, including linguistic ones, instead of being mere passive victims of centripetal forces and dominating ideologies. Toward the end of their book, Hill and Hill eloquently summarize their attitude toward these complex issues:

> As linguists and anthropologists, we celebrate human diversity. We are awed by the power through which human beings construct an infinite variety of symbolic universes, each so intricately detailed and delicately organized that our sciences cannot comprehend them, yet so responsive to change that a way of speaking like Mexicano, for 500 years under the most ferocious attack, can respond and change and meet the attack through nothing more than the everyday linguistic struggle expressed in the talk of humble people. These symbolic universes of language constitute

the principal treasurehouse of the human intellect, and when one is lost – as Mexicano may be lost if nothing is done – we are all deprived. (Hill and Hill 1986: 446)

They proceed to propose a number of possible steps to counteract the discourse of purism, recognize the changing, heteroglot nature of any speech community, and defend the cultural heritage contained in indigeneous languages. Anticipating the words of Toni Morrison quoted at the beginning of this section, Hill and Hill conclude with a homage to language diversity and the responsibility of "the people of the world" to contain cultural imperialism and allow for the preservation of historical-natural languages as treasures that belong to humanity as a whole.[12]

3.5.3 Definitions of speech community

It is in the context of this kind of enterprise that the notion of speech community (or what Gumperz called "linguistic community," see below) becomes an extremely important notion for the anthropological study of linguistic phenomena. In this section, I will review some of the issues involved in its definition and propose a working definition to which I will return in the final chapter.[13]

The idea of the inherently variable nature of any language or speech community is nothing new, as shown by the following quote from the American structuralist linguist Leonard Bloomfield "The difficulty or impossibility of determining ... exactly what people belong to the same speech-community, is not accidental, but arises from the very nature of speech-community. ... no two persons – or rather, perhaps, no one person at different times – spoke exactly alike" (1935: 45).

Whereas the realization of such variability convinced formal grammarians to ignore it by establishing an idealized homogeneity of homogeneity, sociolinguists decided to face variability and make it the subject matter of their investigation.

In Labov's (1966, 1972a, 1972c) important studies of linguistic variation in New York City, speech community was first defined "by participation in a set of shared norms" (Labov 1972c: 120). These are norms for the use of language as well as for the interpretation of linguistic behavior.

> That New York City is a single speech community, and not a
> collection of speakers living side by side, borrowing occasionally
> from each others' dialects, may be demonstrated by many kinds of
> evidence. Native New Yorkers differ in their usage in terms of
> absolute values of the [sociolinguistic] variables, but the shifts

---

[12] For different views on the role of linguists in helping preserve indigenous languages, see Hale et al. (1992), Ladefoged (1992), Dorian (1993).

[13] For a useful review of the debate up to the late 1980s, see Hudson (1980: 25–30). More recent discussions will be mentioned in the rest of this section.

between contrasting styles follow the same pattern in almost every case. Subjective evaluations of native New Yorkers show a remarkable uniformity, in sharp contrast to the wide range of response from speakers who were raised in other regions.

(Labov 1966: 7)

For Labov, participation in the same speech community is defined on the basis of shared patterns of variation or evaluation of linguistic behavior. As long as speakers who have different patterns of use understand and evaluate the different linguistic forms in the same way, we can say that they belong to the same speech community.[14] If their evaluation varies, however, we can no longer say that they belong to the same speech community.

As pointed out by some critics of this approach (Dorian 1982; Romaine 1982), this evaluative measure may exclude speakers who perceive themselves to be part of the same community even though their linguistic norms or evaluations of speech forms may differ. For instance, in her study of descendants of Gaelic-speaking fisherfolk in eastern Sutherland, Dorian (1981) discusses what she calls "semi-speakers," that is, "individuals who have failed to develop full fluency and normal adult proficiency in East Sutherland Gaelic, as measured by their deviation from the fluent-speaker norms within the community" (Dorian 1982: 26). Despite the fact that their speech is quite different from the speech of the fluent bilingual and they are insensitive to many breaches of grammatical norms, these semi-speakers consider themselves part of the Scottish Gaelic speech community. Their self-perception is supported by their ability to understand what is said and how to interact in Gaelic:

Low-proficiency members of these networks, unlike the linguist-guest, were never unintentionally rude. They knew when it was appropriate to speak and when not; when a question would show interest and when it would constitute an interruption; when an offer of food or drink was mere verbal routine and was meant to be refused, and when it was meant in earnest and should be accepted; how much verbal response was appropriate to express sympathy in response to a narrative of ill health or ill luck; and so forth.

(Dorian 1982: 29)

To account for these kinds of situations Dorian prefers definitions of speech

---

[14] "… it seems plausible to define a speech community as a group of speakers who share a set of social attitudes towards language. In New York City, those raised out of town in their formative years show none of the regular pattern of subjective reactions characteristic of natives where a New York City variable such as the vowel of *lost* is concerned" (Labov 1972a: 248, footnote 40).

community that do not make reference to either norms or evaluations. One solution favored by Dorian is Corder's (1973: 53) definition: "A speech community is made up of people who *regard themselves* as speaking the same language; it need have no other defining attributes." This notion of speech community is close to the notion of *imagined community* introduced by Anderson (1983).

Another solution is to abandon altogether the criterion of either norms or expectations and look at what speakers do in their daily life, who they interact with. Gumperz's earlier definition of "linguistic community" avoided norms and expectations and concentrated on social contact:[15]

> [a linguistic community is] a social group which may be either monolingual or multilingual, held together by frequency of social interaction patterns and set off from the surrounding areas by weaknesses in the lines of communication. Linguistic communities may consist of small groups bound together by face-to-face contact or may cover large regions, depending on the level of abstraction we wish to achieve. ([1962: 29] 1968: 463)

This definition is more appropriate for those situations where speakers who live in close contact speak different languages. The literature on multilingualism abounds of cases where within the same village or family speakers of different age, gender, or social status have differentiated competence in different language varieties. One of the most complex cases ever reported is Sorensen's (1967) and Jackson's (1974) discussion of the Vaupés territory of southeast Colombia, where over twenty exogamous patrilineal descent units are identified with a corresponding number of mutually unintelligible languages. Since language is the main criterion for exogamy (people must marry someone who speaks a different language), there is always multilingualism within each village, longhouse, and family. Given demographic factors, marriage patterns, and patrilocal residence, there can be up to four different father-languages represented by the in-married women within the same longhouse (Jackson 1974: 56). Although there is one language, Tukano, which is used as a lingua franca, in certain situations people may use a language that is not understood by everyone.[16]

---

[15] Gumperz's later definition, however, includes the notion of "a shared body of verbal signs" ([1968] 1972: 219). An attempt to implement the notion of "contact" within a variationist framework is provided by Milroy's (1980) use of the unit "network."

[16] Although sometimes politeness might dictate the choice of a language (e.g. on the basis of the the addressee's father's language), other times code shifting is described by Jackson as simply motivated by the pleasure of using a different variety: "I have been with women who said, 'Let's speak Tukano' and did so for a period of time, even though none of them had Tukano as a father-language and all spoke [two other languages] as well as Tukano" (Jackson 1974: 59).

This system allows for a fluidity of code shifting and adaptation to variation that is puzzling to anyone brought up in a monolingual community, but has a ring of familiarity to most multilingual speakers. Linguistic variation is in fact not as rare as monolingual speakers or some theorists would like to believe. Even within monolingual communities – as demonstrated by several decades of sociolinguistic empirical research – differentiation and shifting of codes may be more pervasive than usually believed. What in some communities might result in a shift from one language to another (e.g. from English to Spanish, from a local vernacular to a pidgin), in some other communities might result in a shift from one style or register to another (e.g. from authoritarian to egalitarian, from distant to familiar, from ritual to casual). Even within monolingual communities, in other words, different groups and different individuals within a group may use or switch between what Hymes (1974) called different *ways of speaking*, a term inspired by Whorf's *fashions of speaking*. A great deal of linguistic anthropological research is about such different ways of speaking, their distribution, their function, and the ideologies associated with their use, including an increasingly rich body of work on gender differences in language use (e.g. Hall and Bucholtz 1995; Philips, Steele and Tanz 1987; Tannen 1993a).

I propose that we take a speech community to be *the product of the communicative activities engaged in by a given group of people*. This definition takes the notion of speech community to be a point of view of analysis rather than an already constituted object of inquiry. It recognizes the constitutive nature of speaking as a human activity that not only assumes but builds "community." According to this definition, to engage in linguistic anthropological research means, first of all, to look at a group of people's daily dealings with one another from the point of view of the communication they exchange and the communicative resources they employ. This definition is inspired by Rossi-Landi's (1973) definition, but it avoids his assumption of the existence of an already defined "language":

> The totality of the messages we exchange with one another while speaking a given language constitutes a speech community, that is, the whole society understood from the point of view of speaking.
> (Rossi-Landi 1973: 83, translation mine)

Another aspect of Rossi-Landi's theory that deserves consideration is the intuition that the linguistic forms and contents used by members of a community have a value just like goods have values in the context of a market. To study a speech community for Rossi-Landi means to study the circulation of linguistic signs seen as products of human labor that satisfy certain needs while at the same time suggesting or imposing new ones. As articles of consumption, words have power over their speakers; they presuppose a worldview just like commodities presuppose certain desires in the potential users. Through the view of the speech community as a market, Rossi-Landi reframes in Marxist terms – that is, as **linguistic alienation** – one of the most important concerns of linguistic anthropologists, namely, the relationship between individual speakers and the language system they use, an issue that is at the core of Sapir's and Whorf's legacy. To what extent are individuals in control of the linguistic resources they use in communicating? To what extent can speakers impose their own meaning and interpretations on the messages they produce? How do we assess authorship in speaking (or writing)? How expressive is language? How shared is it? What does linguistic communication teach us about the tension between autonomy and sociability? These questions are at the core of the issue of the relationship between linguistic code and ideology that informs the current debate on linguistic relativity as it resurfaces through the work on language and identity.

3.6 Conclusions

In this chapter, I have examined a number of basic theoretical issues centered around the notion of "language" and "language diversity." I have argued that the notion of language diversity ties together the earlier discussions of linguistic relativity and the more recent discussions of language contact and language mixing. The study of language from the point of view of the differentiation presupposed or brought about by linguistic options and linguistic choices commits linguistic anthropologists to a notion of language that builds on the assumption that variation is the norm rather than the exception. In making this assumption, linguistic anthropologists share sociolinguists' program for a socially minded linguistics. At the same time, due to their historical roots, linguistic anthropologists are more directly involved in the study of language ideology with the wide range of issues that such a complex notion implies (see Silverstein 1979; Woolard and Schieffelin 1994). To study language in culture means something more than the ways in which cultural categories are reflected in language or the ways in which linguistic taxonomies are guides to the worldview of those who employ them. An anthropologically minded study of language means the recognition of the complex interplay between language as a human resource and language as a historical product and process. Such an interplay must be approached with a number of theoretical tools, including the concepts introduced in this chapter. It also needs sophisticated methods for the documentation of the ways in which linguistic communication enters into and sustains our social life. The next two chapters will be dedicated to the latter goal.

4

Ethnographic methods

This chapter and the next will present a critical review of the more common data-collection techniques and analytical procedures currently practiced by professional linguistic anthropologists.[1] With the exception of occasional references to practical questions, this chapter will emphasize the logic of research habits and procedures rather than the technical solutions needed to solve common research problems. In a few cases, I will briefly discuss what I consider some of the most innovative and interesting ways of documenting the role of communication in the constitution of culture. A more specific discussion of the practice of transcription will be done in chapter 5.

Linguistic anthropologists use traditional ethnographic methods such as participant-observation and work with native speakers to obtain local interpretive glosses of the communicative material they record. They also use elicitation techniques similar to those employed by typological linguists interested in grammatical patterns. Recently, these methods have been integrated with new forms of documentation of verbal practices developed in such fields as urban sociolinguistics, discourse analysis, and conversation analysis. The advent of new technologies for the electronic recording of sounds and actions has broadened the range of phenomena that can be studied, increased our analytical sophistication, and, at the same time, multiplied the number of technical, political, and moral problems that a fieldworker must confront. As we enter this new technological era, it is imperative to develop a discursive arena in which to examine the pros and cons of the new tools within a general discussion of methodology for the study of human communicative behavior.

4.1 Ethnography

If the goal of linguistic anthropology is the study of linguistic forms as constitutive elements of social life, researchers must have ways of connecting linguistic forms

---

[1] Within the related field of sociolinguistics, Stubbs (1983) is an introductory textbook to discourse analysis that is particularly sensitive to the methods used for collecting conversational data. See also Milroy (1987).

with particular cultural practices. Ethnography offers one valuable set of techniques for such a goal. For this reason, the integration of ethnography with other methods for the documentation of speech patterns is one of the most important distinguishing qualities of linguistic anthropologists as compared to other researchers interested in language or communication. In this section I will provide a brief discussion of the basic features of what constitutes an ethnographic inquiry and suggest ways in which such features can be an integral part of the study of language.[2]

4.1.1 What is an ethnography?

As a first approximation, we can say that an ethnography is the written description of the social organization, social activities, symbolic and material resources, and interpretive practices characteristic of a particular group of people. Such a description is typically produced by prolonged and direct participation in the social life of a community and implies two apparently contradictory qualities: (i) an ability to step back and distance oneself from one's own immediate, culturally biased reactions so to achieve an acceptable degree of "objectivity" and (ii) the propensity to achieve sufficient identification with or empathy for the members of the group in order to provide an insider's perspective – what anthropologists call "the **emic** view" (see section 6.3.2).

A few words should be said here about the use of the term "objectivity," which has been harshly criticized in recent writings about the ethnographic experience (Kondo 1986; Rosaldo 1989) and, more generally, in current debates in and about the social sciences (Manicas 1987). With respect to ethnography, the problems with the term "objectivity" arise from its identification with a form of positivistic writing that was meant to exclude the observer's subjective stance, including emotions, as well as political, moral, and theoretical attitudes. Such an exclusion, in its more extreme or "purest" form, is not only impossible to achieve, it is also a questionable goal, given that it would produce a very poor record of the ethnographer's experience (De Martino 1961). How would one be able to say what people are doing without at least a minimal identification with their point of view? One would end up saying things like "people squat on the floor, grab their food with their hands and bring it to their mouth – and this, they call 'eating'." As it is obvious from this example, rather than being "objective" and impartial, accounts of this kind can easily be read as implying a negative evaluation of local practices.

---

[2] What follows is by no means a full-scale introduction to ethnographic methods, but a brief discussion of what I consider some of the central issues pertaining to the process of practicing ethnography and producing ethnographic descriptions. For more informed descriptions of current ethnographic methods in cultural anthropology and related fields, see Agar (1980), Spradley (1980), Jackson (1987), as well as the critical appraisals in Clifford and Marcus (1986), Geertz (1988), Rosaldo (1989), Sanjek (1990a).

Equally implausible is a description that completely identifies with the native perspective and does not, in some fashion, reflect the researchers' perception of the described events, including their own sociohistorical awareness of pecularities (or, alternatively, predictability) of such events and hence their value for comparative purposes. What matters, however, is the attempt to control or put between brackets one's value judgment. Although this might be seen as a step that anthropologists share with phenomenological philosophers like Husserl and interpretivist sociologists like Weber, the practice of refraining from thinking the obvious is an important part of doing any kind of science. The problem, of course, is that it is not sufficient. A science of people, a human science, cannot but also exploit the researchers' ability to identify, empathize with the people they are studying. This implies that there exists in ethnography a certain playful element which consists of changing the familiar into the strange and, vice versa, the strange into the familiar (Spiro 1990) (see also section 2.1 on Hegel's notion of culture).

Given that there are different degrees of distance from or closeness to a given ethnographic reality, descriptive adequacy for most ethnographers lies somewhere in the middle. Geertz (1983) adopted the psychoanalytic contrast between "experience-near" and "experience-distant" to illustrate this point:

> An experience-near concept is, roughly, one that someone – a patient, a subject, in our case an informant – might himself naturally and effortlessly use to define what he or his fellows see, feel, think, imagine, and so on, and which he would readily understand when similarly applied by others. An experience-distant concept is one that specialists of one sort or another – an analyst, an experimenter, an ethnographer, even a priest or an ideologist – employ to forward their scientific, philosophical, or practical aims. "Love" is an experience-near concept, "object cathexis" is an experience-distant one. "Social stratification" and perhaps for most people in the world even "religion" (and certainly "religious system") are experience-distant; "caste" and "nirvana" are experience-near, at least for Hindus and Buddhists ... The real question ... is what roles the two sorts of concepts play in anthropological analysis. Or, more exactly, how, in each case, ought one to deploy them so as to produce an interpretation of the way a people lives which is neither imprisoned within their mental horizons, an ethnography of witchcraft as written by a witch, nor systematically deaf to the distinctive tonalities of their existence, an ethnography of witchcraft as written by a geometer.
>
> (Geertz 1983: 57)

The "balance" between being insensitive and turning into a witch is simply the realization that writing ethnography implies the understanding of several, sometimes contradictory, sometimes complementary points of view. A successful ethnography, then, is not a method of writing in which the observer assumes *one* perspective – whether "distant" or "near" –, but a style in which the researcher establishes a dialogue between different viewpoints and voices, including those of the people studied, of the ethnographer, and of his disciplinary and theoretical preferences. This is indeed the style of the best ethnographies we have. They are a composite of a number of viewpoints, including the observer's and the observed. They combine the sense of awe at what the ethnographer might see or notice for the first time with a genuine attempt at finding out how such practices are made "ordinary" for the participants – or, conversely, how something that is taken for granted by the ethnographer appears exceptional or incomprehensible to the people being studied.

What is, however, often missing in most ethnographies is an explicit discussion and documentation of the dialogical practices out of which descriptions are born. As Dennis Tedlock (1983) points out, despite the fact that most of what we learn in the field is the product of live dialogue – between ourselves and the "natives" as well as among the natives themselves –, one sees very little if anything of that dialogue in published ethnographic accounts. Tedlock's criticism of what he calls **analogical anthropology** and his proposal for a **dialogical anthropology** articulates the contribution of linguistic anthropological methods to the study of culture. Rather than replacing native discourse with the observer's monologic narrative (whether in the first or third person), as typical of analogical anthropology, dialogical anthropology promotes native talk to the position of prominence so as to give readers more direct access to how members represent their own actions as well as how they deal with fieldworkers and comply with their demands.[3] The practice of **transcription** (see chapter 5) and its embedding in ethnographic description is an essential element of this process as investigators make explicit the sources from which they derive their understanding of a given cultural phenomenon.

The criteria for identifying a community as suitable for an ethnography can be quite varied, including political, geographical, racial, theoretical, and methodological considerations. The complex of features required for thinking about a

---

[3] "In the classic ethnography, the informants, collectively, speak occasional isolated words in a totally exotic language; in confessions or reflections, on the other hand, where contact between individuals and between cultures is an undeniable reality, informants are allowed occasional complete utterances, but these are likely to contain or even to consist entirely of words from contact languages. In any case, the dominant mode, even of the confession, is the monologue" (Tedlock 1983: 326).

number of individuals as forming a "community" also vary, ranging from shared living space to affiliation with the same political, religious, or educational institution. We have thus ethnographies of people who live or work in the same town, village, island, building, and factory, and ethnographies of those who spend a certain period of time together, such as the participants in a class, a political confrontation, a religious movement, a ceremonial exchange.

4.1.1.1 Studying people in communities

The initial assumption that the people studied form a "community" must be sustained by systematic observations. This means that ethnographers expect to find certain commonalities among the members of the group, certain shared or mutually intelligible habits, social activities, ways of interacting and interpreting social acts. Language is of course an important indication of membership in a community; variation in linguistic patterns such as a frequent switching between languages, dialects, or registers (see chapters 1 and 9) is an index of possible internal subdivision within the same community. In general, the focus on one group should not be seen as implying cultural homogeneity in the group. The more we study different societies and especially complex multiethnic, post-industrial societies like the US the more we realize that the homogeneous community where everyone speaks the same language (or dialect) and knows everything there is to know for daily survival is either a romantic idealization of small-scale societies or a collective construct that is at the heart of nationalism (Anderson 1991). Despite this recognition, however, ethnographers are still in constant search for **patterns**, that is, recurrent configurations in people's behaviors, descriptions, interpretive procedures, uses of natural resources, and production and handling of tools and artifacts. Whether or not an ethnographer will be attracted more by similarities than by differences among members of the community will be, in large part, determined by his theoretical preferences. This is why the notion of culture he adopts is so very important in the process of producing an ethnography. If the ethnographer assumes, following Wallace's (1961) suggestion, that a culture is an organization of diversity, she will look for the ways in which members are able to coordinate their actions and goals, *despite their differences* (see section 2.1.2). In other words, the ethnographic account will try to describe not only how a particular group of people are kept together by their similarities but also how they are united despite or on account of their differences. If, on the other hand, the ethnographer is oriented toward a view of culture as something shared more or less in equal measure by all members, he will concentrate on commonalities and will tend to ignore differences, claiming that they are irrelevant variations of a basic, underlying pattern.

Ethnographers assume that the information they need is somehow available through particular types of data-collection techniques. In this sense, ethnographers do not differ from other human scientists, such as psychoanalysts, for instance, who believe that it is possible to arrive at hidden psychological conflicts through the examination of overt behavior such as oral narratives, drawings, or physical reactions. What differentiates ethnographers from other students of human conduct is that they try to come as close as ethically appropriate to their subjects' cultural experience (the American Anthropological Association has guidelines that can be consulted). Rather than acquiring knowledge of the reality they want to study from oral or written reports, ethnographers live for an extended period of time with the people whose way of life they want to understand, watching them work, eat, play, talk, laugh, cry, be angry, sad, happy, satisfied, frustrated. The **observation** of a particular community is not attained from a distant and safe point but by being in the middle of things, that is, by **participating** in as many social events as possible. It is this often difficult but necessary combination of modalities of being with others and observing them that is referred to as **participant-observation**, a building stone of anthropology's contribution to our understanding of human cultures (Malinowski 1935, vol. 2: 3–4).

In this sense, before being a product, that is, a written text, ethnography is an experience or a process (Agar 1980: 1). It is the experience of participating in the social life of a given group as a way of understanding how they constitute each other into a collectivity, what makes them at the same time unique and predictable.

As it becomes obvious from the exemplary anecdotes that ethnographers like to tell about their fieldwork, their experience is for them rich with meanings that go well beyond the satisfactory completion of the research project as originally envisioned. Fieldwork has important consequences for the ways in which a researcher will, from that point on, think about his work and, at a more personal level, his own personal life. For the apprentice, however, all of the talk about transformations and understanding is often too vague. For anyone who has never tried it before, it is difficult to imagine exactly how one engages in ethnographic work. The first questions anthropology students ask are about the kinds of phenomena they should look for once in the field. Answers such as "an ethnographer is interested in everything" or "anything can be the object of inquiry for an ethnographer, it depends on his or her interest" are not much help to the novice. Non-exhaustive but extensive lists like the one in table 4.1 might be more useful as a first approximation.

Table 4.1 *Topics of ethnographic study*

Ethnographers are interested in:

– what people do in their daily lives (e.g. the activities they engage in, how they are organized, by whom and for whom)
– what they make and use (artifacts)
– who controls access to goods (land products) and technologies
– what people know, think, feel
– how they communicate with one another
– how they make decisions (e.g. what is right or wrong, what is permissible, what is strange, unusual, what is true)
– how they classify objects, animals, people, natural and cultural phenomena
– how the division of labor is organized (across genders, ages, social classes, ranks, etc.)
– how the life of the family/household is organized, etc.

The general issue behind these themes is a concern with the **constitution of society and culture**. Ethnographers gather information in order to answer two basic questions: (1) how is social order constituted (created, managed, reproduced), that is, what makes this particular group of people a functioning unit of some sort? and (2) how do individuals make sense of their way of living, that is, how do they explain (to themselves first) why they live the way they do and differently from others (sometimes even their neighbors)?

In collecting information that might help them answer these questions, ethnographers are expected to respect analytical, methodological, as well as ethical standards that have been established over the years by a long series of documented individual experiences. Here are some of these rules as seen by British anthropologist Raymond Firth, one of Malinowski's most acclaimed successors:

> Over the last fifty years social anthropology has developed a fairly sensitive technique of fieldwork. Rules have been worked out for securing as accurate information as possible. The fieldworker is encouraged to have maximum contact with the people he is studying, as by living in their midst. He is expected to use the vernacular, not only to avoid the misconstructions of an interpreter, but to be able to reinforce his set questions with material picked up by listening to ordinary conversation between the people themselves. He is expected not to rely on single informants for all significant data, but to indulge in a thorough process of checking. The opinions he obtains from individuals are not to be taken as

objective statements of the social reality, but as reflections of the
position and interests of the people who give them. Above all,
generalizations about local institutions are not expected to be
framed solely upon verbal data collected from informants, but to be
backed up at every turn by the field-worker's own observations of
the actual behaviour of the people. (Firth 1965: 3)

As revealed by this eloquent and succinct statement, a major preoccupation for
ethnographers is the reliability of the information they collect. They must not
only develop ways of ascertaining the accuracy of what people tell them but also
ways of assuring their readers that their descriptions are accurate. This means
that ethnographers have to deal with two types of interlocutors: the subjects of
their studies and their future readers. The recognition of these two, often con-
flictual, allegiances unveils a profession that is constantly dealing with issues of
"power, resistance, institutional constraints, and innovation" (Clifford 1986: 2)
during fieldwork and after. There is no way of turning away from these questions
and responsibilities. There are, however, ways of incorporating into the research
and its public (re)presentation the tension created by the ethnographer's intru-
sion into the world of Others who (by definition) have different ideas and standards from the ethnographer's. This means that in addition to the issue of access
(to people, resources, information), ethnographers have become sensitized to
the question of their role in the community where they work. More and more
have ethnographers become concerned with how they are perceived, what they
are expected to do, and the extent to which their individual research agenda as
well as their representation of such an agenda is the by-product of several, sometimes complementary, sometimes conflicting forces and allegiances.

4.1.2 *Ethnographers as cultural mediators*

Ethnographers thus have started to recognize that they operate as **cultural mediators** between two traditions: one established by their discipline and their particular theoretical orientation and the other represented by the people they study
and live with, who have their own understanding of what the fieldworkers should
be doing and how they should conduct themselves. In recent ethnographies, the
role of members in influencing the ethnographer's research agenda has been
made more explicit. Here is an example from the introductory chapter of Fred
Myers's ethnography of the Pintupi, an Aboriginal people from the Western
Desert in Australia:

As Margaret Mead once said, anthropology has informants, not
objects of study. People teach us. The condition of my living in
Pintupi communities has always been my participation as a

> "relative." Their acceptance has never been based on my research, which they have never been much interested in once they decided I was a friend (despite my sincere and lengthy attempts to explain my work). Rather, what they expect from me is my human commitment to them as fellow people. This condition has set the tone of my whole research. Since the Australian government's policy of "self-determination" began, the Pintupi have insisted that those who live in their communities must "help Aboriginal people."
>
> Their willingness to provide me instruction in Pintupi culture has followed a similar course in making me part of their lives. The Pintupi I know have emphasized my learning through participation and have been reluctant to submit to the sort of "white room" formal sessions of inquiry of which, in frustration, I have occasionally dreamed. It is neither polite nor productive to ask a lot of questions. When individuals have sponsored me with their help, we have worked by my spending a day in participant-observation, waiting for opportune moments to ask questions. In this way I learned gradually to identify certain Pintupi symbolic constructs with realms of action, not just as objects of analysis, but also in making myself understood. My experience of Pintupi culture, then, conforms to Wittgenstein's dictum not to ask what a thing means, but to look to its use. (Myers 1986: 15)

As implied by Myers's remarks, being an ethnographer means first of all learning to look and to listen. While in the field, there are all kinds of interactions and transactions around us, the majority of which is (fortunately) not just caused by our mere presence. In order to describe these interactions, we must first learn to recognize them as of the same "kind." This means that the repetitiveness of everyday life is a crucial element in our ability to learn to detect patterns. As participant-observers, we acquire expectations and learn to make predictions about what a given act (including words) produces and where or how it might have originated. In the process of learning to make these predictions, we must locate ourselves in time and space. We must choose *where* to sit (or stand) and *when* to be present. Such choices are not without consequences. We know this and, as Myers reminds us, the members of the group we study know it too. People often have strong ideas about where an outsider/visitor/guest (plus or minus other identities we might have acquired during our stay) should be and what he or she should be doing. They also have strong ideas about which public persona should be presented to the fieldworker. For these reasons, fieldwork is nothing but a long series of negotiations and compromises between our expectations and standards and those of our hosts. An emblematic example of such negotiations is provided by Elinor Ochs in the introduction to her ethnographic study of language acquisition and socialization in Western Samoa:

> When I first began recording Samoan children and their caregivers in the summer of 1978, I encountered a serious methodological problem. Instead of engaging in the usual range of everyday household activities and interactions, the children would sit very properly on mats near my own mat and either wait for me to tell them what to do or perform at the command of an older sibling, parent, or other relative. Worse for the poor researcher, instead of conversing in the register typical of most social interactions in the village (the register Samoans call "bad speech"), caregivers and children appeared to use only the register Samoans call "good speech," characteristic of written Samoan and of Samoan spoken in school, church, and certain business settings and to foreigners who know Samoan. "Please," I would say over and over to members of the household, "just go on doing what you usually do and do not pay attention to me." I hoped somehow that this formula would magically create the context for the "spontaneous" talk of children and caregivers that is characteristic of longitudinal studies of child language in other societies. How else would I be able to bring back "comparable" data? The failure of my magic and the prospect of loss of face in the world of developmental research led me to a full-scale analysis of the basis of this problem. (Ochs 1988: 1)

Ochs's solution to her problem was to readjust her intellectual focus and reframe her interest in language development within a larger setting that included, among other features, the social organization of space in a Samoan household. In her case, the behavior of the children and adults she was observing and recording forced her to reconsider not only the effect that her presence in the house might have but also the boundaries of her analytical framework. If, as she discovered, people's verbal behavior changes in different parts of the house and depends on where the researcher is sitting, the very notion of "language" as the object of inquiry must be reconsidered to include in its scope the interplay between sounds and spatial orientation, speech acts and bodily acts (see chapters 3 and 6).

Myers's and Ochs's experiences illustrate how the process of ethnography always involves ways of learning from the people one studies (Spradley 1980: 1). This learning is often seen as part of the ethnographer's strategy "to grasp the native's point of view, his relation to life, to realize *his* vision of *his* world," according to Malinowski's now classic definition of the goal of ethnography (1922: 25). But this view is only partly accurate. In the Malinowskian tradition, the ethnographer is portrayed as a novice, treated by the natives as a grown-up child who still needs attending as well as constant reminding of what is appropriate and what is inappropriate in any given situation. Ethnographers routinely sustain this perception by putting themselves in situations in which they are clearly incapable of competent behavior. This is done sometimes unknowingly and other times strategically, to see how people react to one's blunders, given that error-corrections may offer an opportunity to hear explicit definitions of social norms and rules of etiquette.

Beyond the representation of ethnographers as naughty children or culturally impaired adults lie other sometimes complementary sometimes contrasting realities. Ethnographers' relationships with the people they study are by no means simply those of subordinate novices to superordinate experts. Their humility to be detected in some of their attitudes is part of a professional posture that, whether or not subjectively intentional, is expected to pay off in the long run. The ethnographer's interest in people's lives and their problems is often similar to the lawyer's interest in his clients' complaints and the therapist's interest in his patients' conflicts. It is sympathetic but detached. In listening to people's stories, especially the more dramatic ones, the ethnographer's interest is often not only for the tellers and their personal drama, but for the plot behind their stories, not for the individuals involved in those dramas but for the dramatis personae they represent, not necessarily for the ways in which a conflict might be resolved but for the logic implicit in that conflict. In their conversations with their subjects, ethnographers have an awareness of professional goals that projects them beyond the here-and-now and into the realm of academic writing and professional quests. This does not mean that real interest in human dramas or real friendships is not there to start with or cannot develop during or after the fieldwork experience. It just means that as ethnographers we cannot pretend to be what we are not: one of "them." There is a need for honesty with others as well as with ourselves in terms of our very special forms of participation in people's lives and dramas. As suggested by Narayan (1993: 672), "what we must focus our attention on is the quality of relations with the people we seek to represent in our texts: are they viewed as mere fodder for professionally self-serving statements about a generalized Other, or are they accepted as subjects with voices, views, and dilemmas – people to whom we are bonded through ties of reciprocity and who may even be critical of our professional enterprise?"

The view of the ethnographer as the child-novice is inaccurate because ethnographers are professional adults who usually come from powerful foreign nations and institutions that have economic and military superiority over the people they are studying. These researchers act and are usually perceived as wealthy and powerful individuals who have only a temporary and in many respects very limited interest in the community they study and live in. Beyond ethnographers' intentions, motivations, or awareness, there are political and global processes that enter into the relationships they establish in the field. Anthropologists have just started to investigate these relationships and their potential and actual consequences, especially now that a new generation of ethnographers have gone to study their own community or the community of their parents (e.g. Abu-Lughod 1991; Appadurai 1991; Kondo 1990; Mani 1990; Narayan 1993; Said 1989). At the same time, one should not overestimate the power of researchers over their subjects or informants. As pointed out by Harvey (1992: 75), "the relationship between researcher and researched cannot be depicted as a straightforward hierarchical one in which the researcher simply imposes an agenda." It is simply patronizing or racist to think of the people we study as innocent victims of our own academic and scientific plans. They have their own ideas, plans, and goals. We must fit into their lives just like they need to fit into ours.

The view of ethnographers as cultural mediators emphasizes the fact that no matter how "close" or "distant" ethnographers act, feel, or think, their interpretations as well as their actions are always embedded in larger processes and more complex dialogues. Part of the work done in and through ethnography must thus include an understanding of such dialogues, regardless of the extent to which individual researchers decide to devote their research and publications to a discussion of such an interpretive process. Just as it would be naive to characterize ethnography as always a genuine and selfishless quest for knowledge, it would also be misleading to see it as an unavoidable and unmediated act of domination where ethnographers and the people they study simply act as puppets on the stage of a human theater totally controlled by more powerful and hidden agents. An ethnography is an interpretive act and as such should be turned on itself to increase the richness of descriptions, including an understanding of the conditions under which description itself becomes possible. Linguistic anthropologists' contribution to the ongoing definition of ethnography, its goals, conditions, and outcomes is an emphasis on the need to let our subjects speak, as much as possible, with their voices and their bodies, to tell the stories they normally tell in their daily life. The process of transcription discussed in the next chapter must be understood in the context of such an enterprise.

4.1.3 How comprehensive should an ethnography be? Complementarity and collaboration in ethnographic research

When Malinowski started to promote ethnography in its modern sense, that is, as participant-observation, he was thinking of ethnographies as total, comprehensive accounts of a given people. The ethnographer had one or two years to become acquainted with the language spoken in the community and (at the same time!) describe every possible aspect of social life and material and symbolic culture he or she could document.

> An Ethnographer who sets out to study only religion, or only technology, or only social organisation cuts out an artificial field for inquiry, and he will be seriously handicapped in his work.
>
> (Malinowski 1922: 11)

This condemnation of partial descriptions and endorsement of *total* ethnographies produced some remarkable accounts but also well-known oversimplifications. There were always certain aspects of the culture that were either ignored or taken for granted, sometimes with the assumption that they were either fairly straightforward or in no need of special investigation. Language was often one of those cultural aspects placed in this residual category. Ethnographers could not do without it, but they would rarely give it the necessary systematic attention. It was an instrument for other, theoretically more important topics such as the social organization, the kinship system, and, in some cases, the interpretation of myths and legends. The sixth edition of the *Notes and Queries on Anthropology* produced by the Royal Anthropological Institute of Great Britain and Ireland (1951), for instance, dedicates a chapter to "Language"; its best advice to the prospective ethnographer is either to get hold of already existing linguistic descriptions or get trained in linguistics. In eleven pages, the reader is introduced to gestures, sign language and spoken language, including sections on phonology, grammar, and semantics. The next chapter is on material culture, which occupies one hundred and eighteen pages!

Contemporary anthropologists have come to accept the fact that one person cannot cover the culture of a group *in all its aspects*, as originally prescribed by Malinowski (1922), and that different researchers will emphasize different aspects, according to their expertise and theoretical interest. We have now ethnographies of particular groups (e.g. weavers, tailors, drug addicts, doctors), activities (classroom interaction, musical performances, spirit possession, rites of passage), events (trials, political meetings, marriage ceremonies, gift exchanges), and social processes (socialization, acculturation, hospitalization, marginalization, institutionalization of certain practices). The ethnographic description of languages is no exception. Linguistic anthropologists adopt ethnographic methods to concentrate on the ways in which linguistic communication is an integral part of the culture of the groups they study. While participating in the broader social life of a community, the linguistic anthropologist documents communicative behaviors across a range of interactions (including casual conversation, political and ceremonial events, theatrical representations, singing, mourning) and among particular groups of people (women, men, children, chiefs, commoners, priests, orators, doctors, etc.). Through the selection and classification of social activities on the basis of language use, linguistic anthropologists are able to produce more accurate accounts of language structure and use than those provided by cultural anthropologists with only limited training in linguistic methods and models.

The danger of a too restricted understanding of the social life of a community – a danger seen mostly through the lenses of verbal codes and verbal performances – must be compensated for by relying on direct or indirect collaboration with other researchers, who may be studying the same group with different research foci. Such collaboration has produced some of the best linguistic anthropological studies of the last few decades. For instance, Bambi B. Schieffelin's (1990) ethnographically informed study of language socialization among the Kaluli people of Mount Bosavi in Papua New Guinea and Steven Feld's (1982) portrait of the interpenetration of sounds, feelings, and social relations among the same people clearly benefited from each other. Furthermore, they both crucially relied on Edward Schieffelin's (1976) earlier work on the cultural organization of sentiments (anger and appeal in particular) in the same community. Genevieve Calame-Griaule's (1965) much celebrated study of the linguistic ideology of the Dogon (in Mali) was made possible by the massive number of previous ethnographic studies, including the seventy or so publications by her father, French anthropologist Marcel Griaule. His work provided a solid foundation on which she could present a complex series of hypotheses about how language works both as a metaphor and a connecting element in the Dogon cosmology and philosophy of everyday life.

These projects, among others, have shown us that the image of the lone fieldworker traveling to a foreign land never visited by an anthropologist before and then writing single-authored papers and monographs is an anachronism, perhaps nothing more than a mixture of romantic humanistic ideals with methodological solipsism.

The criticism of isolated projects or the praising of collaboration should not be interpreted as an imperative to write only co-authored papers and open up all one's notebooks and files for anyone to see; there are still many issues, including those of privacy and the protection of the people who allowed us to witness their daily lives, that need to be reckoned with. But an increased awareness of the dialogic nature of any epistemological search is certainly in the air, accompanied by a renewed sense of the importance of the connection between knowledge and power, access and responsibility. As a new generation of students from a wide range of ethnic, racial, and national backgrounds enters the western academic arena, our descriptions are bound to be affected; our discourse of the Other will never be the same. The grandchildren of the "primitives" described by the founding fathers (Boas, Malinowski, Radcliffe-Brown) and mothers (Benedict, Mead, E. C. Parsons) of anthropology are not just reading our books, they are also sitting in our classes, assessing our descriptions, and, hopefully, getting trained to ask new questions and propose new answers. Authorship and cooperation are bound to have a new meaning in future ethnographic works. These issues have been to a great extent brought to light by the contributions of feminist anthropologists who have forced anthropologists and other social scientists to deal with the gendered nature of so-called objective accounts and with the situatedness of any ethnographic description (Haraway 1991; Harding 1986; Spivak 1985).

4.2 Two kinds of field linguistics

Linguistic anthropologists are not the only ones who travel long distances to go and live within a community of speakers with the goal of describing their language. Linguists have been doing it for a long time as well and field methods courses are an important part of any linguist's training, at least in the United States. There are however, some important differences between the ways in which linguistic anthropologists and most linguists work in the field. The practice of ethnography I just outlined is one such difference. For linguists exclusively or mostly interested in grammar, the reason to travel to a distant location and live within a community of speakers is usually to have the luxury of virtually unlimited access to speakers of different ages, gender, and social status, who can provide a much more reliable and varied data base than the one produced by meeting with one or two native speakers in a research office inside the walls of a western academic institution. Although they may occasionally participate in the life of the community, being on site is not seen by most field linguists as an occasion to capture speakers' use of the language with one another. Instead, the field experience is an occasion to train a number of native speakers to become **language consultants**, who learn to use their **intuitions** to provide judgments of acceptability of different grammatical forms. "Can you say – ?" the linguist says; the native speaker's reaction to the proposed expression is noted down and the next structure is presented, "How about – ?", followed by a series of other questions: Which one is better? What's wrong with this one? How would you say it instead? And so on. These techniques are important for uncovering regularities in the linguistic system and for getting access to forms that might not be very common in everyday usage. At the same time the exclusive use of such methods systematically avoids getting into what makes language a social institution and a cultural practice.

Linguistic anthropologists, on the other hand, make extensive audio and video recording of everyday encounters. These forms of documentation are complemented by participant-observation and a number of related field techniques for the study of verbal performance, including ethnographic notes, drawings, maps, interviews, and still photography. Such techniques are used with the aim of revealing local verbal practices as well as local conceptualizations of such practices and their place in the social organization of the community (see table 4.2).

Table 4.2 *What linguistic anthropologists are interested in*

– The basic organization of the relationship between sounds and meanings as revealed by actual language use in a variety of social activities and (if grammatical descriptions are already available) the extent to which previous grammatical descriptions reflect actual language use or only special, e.g. literacy-bound, uses
– local conceptualizations of what constitutes "language," including characterizations of newborns' and outsiders' speech
– the spatial distribution of language uses (e.g. is there a central place for public verbal performance, like the *marae* in Ancient Polynesian societies or the "gathering house" among the Kuna? Are there differences in the ways language is used in different parts of a house?)
– the features and cultural significance of what is understood as ritual or ceremonial language vis-à-vis everyday speech
– the social distribution of different styles, genres, and speech events (e.g. what are the ways in which different social groups mark themselves off through special linguistic registers or verbal performances?)
– the extent to which local theories of language structure and language use relate to local cosmologies
– the role of language socialization in the shaping of notions of person, mind, and social relations
– the interpenetration of different codes (e.g. speech, gestures, clothes) in the constitution of messages and their interpretation.

The general theme behind these questions is the different ways in which language as an abstract system of classification (of the natural and cultural worlds) and as a mode of social interaction provides the material out of which a group of people recognize themselves as a community.

4.3 Participant-observation

There are different modes of participant-observation, from *passive participation*, in which the ethnographer tries to be as unintrusive as possible to *complete participation*, in which researchers intensively interact with other participants and might even get to participate in and perform the very activity they are studying (Gold 1969; Spradley 1980: 58–62; Williamson et al. 1982: ch. 8). In the case of linguistic fieldwork, complete participation means being able to interact competently in the native language and even perform the verbal genres one is studying. This might not necessarily be a voluntary choice by the researcher. In Samoa, for instance, when I was sitting on the side of the house where orators sit, I would be expected to perform if the occasion arose. Local experts acted as teachers, advisers, and sympathetic supporters. The expectation that I should speak competently in public was not due to my declared interest in language and verbal art but to my acquired social identity as "chief" and spokesperson (Duranti 1994a: 23). Being the only adult male in our research team,[4] I was the most suitable candidate for verbally representing what was considered my "extended family." Any time someone would address our group with a ceremonial speech, the other participants would turn toward me, their faces conveying the expectation that I would speak next. In these situations, it was much more difficult for me to keep track of what was going on around me, run a tape recorder, or have time to scribble down notes. At the same time, these experiences gave me insights into the pathos of performance that I could have never gained from observation or interviews.

Complete participation, when possible and ethically appropriate, gives researchers a great opportunity to directly experience the very processes they are trying to document. Though it is by no means equivalent to entering the mind and body of a native speaker, performing gives a researcher important insights into what it means to be a participant in a given situation and suggests hypotheses and further questions. The epiphany produced by entering the activity one is studying is well captured by Feld's recounting of his experience of among the Kaluli:

> While there were many things I was able to understand about
> Kaluli ideals of sound expression as a result of traditional
> participant observation, I don't think I really began to feel many of
> the most important issues, like ... the construction of a song climax,
> until the day I composed a song about [E. Schieffelin] and Bambi
> [Schieffelin]'s leaving Bosavi that brought tears to the eyes of
> Gigio, one of their oldest and closest friends. I wept, too, and in
> that intense, momentary, witnessing experience, I felt the first
> emotional sensation of what it might be like to inhabit that aesthetic
> reality where such feelings are at the very core of being human.
>
> (Feld 1982: 236–7).

[4] This does not mean that women in Samoa never deliver ceremonial speeches or engage in complex negotiations; I have encountered and heard very gifted female orators. There is however a strong preference for men, especially titled ones (*matai*), to be the spokespersons on most occasions. This preference does not apply to activities that are organized and run by women.

At the same time, the preoccupation with one's own performance implies an attention to one's role and one's perception by others that can be very absorbing and, from the point of view of documenting what is going on, extremely distracting. For this reason, ethnographers must often restrain themselves from being complete participants. They learn to assume the strange status of accepted **by-standers** or professional **overhearers** (see also section 9.3.2). This sometimes implies finding what amounts to a **blind spot** in the scene, that is, the least intrusive place where to sit or stand. For Ochs studying Samoan children's language, this meant sitting in what is considered the "back" region of the house, where she would *not* be treated with all the honors of high status guests (see section 9.5). For anyone studying the order of servings in a ceremony, the blind spot is the place where one would not be served. For someone recording a conversation, the blind spot is the place where the participants would not feel obliged to include him. For an ethnographer studying a classroom, the blind spot might be a seat where one would not be in the continuous visual gaze of the majority of the students; one would want to stay away from the boards on which teachers write or the place where children stand to give oral presentations. In general, it is much harder to find the right place to be in more informal and intimate settings than in public, formal ones. Participant-observation inside a house occupied by a large family might be one of the biggest challenges an ethnographer might encounter. Leichter provides a striking portrait of the problems encountered in such situations in her description of an observer's dilemmas in trying to learn about a family's literacy practices:

> On entering a home with the intention of learning how the family handles literacy, the observer is immediately faced with such practical problems as where to sit or stand, what areas of the home to attempt to observe, and which family members to watch and talk with. Even with a focus as definite as television-viewing, the observer is faced with numerous decisions about how to focus observations. Sitting beside family members while they watch television, for example, makes it impossible to observe their eye-gaze direction. Since more than one activity is generally going on simultaneously in most households, the observer must continually face the question of where to focus his or her attention. These decisions are made more difficult by the realization that watching one activity frequently means missing another. (Leichter 1984: 43)

In addition to finding the appropriate place, researchers must also find the right demeanor for a given place. Sometimes this means that they must be immobile so as not to draw attention; other times, it means that they have to keep busy.

For instance, one might be writing notes on a book or attending to some object or tool (the tape recorder, the camera) that requires one's unconditional attention.

The underlying rationale for finding the blind spot and trying to be as unintrusive as possible is not to pretend that one is not there, but to get as close as possible to what it is like to be a marginal participant. While it is not ethically appropriate and practically feasible to completely hide one's presence, at the same time it is very limiting to collect data solely on participants' response to *our* presence on the scene. Although such data have been shown to be instructive (Duranti 1990; Haviland 1986, 1991; Howe and Sherzer 1986), they should not constitute the bulk of our corpus.

There are also times when the most appropriate behavior is to accept being treated as a guest or being the center of attention (this is especially true during the first days in a community or the first few visits to a particular site). For this reason, there are no absolute rules about how one should conduct oneself while engaged in participant-observation. Questions of social sensibility must determine in each case what is the most appropriate response to our hosts' expectations. This is an area where mistakes are common, often unavoidable, but usually not fatal, although there have been cases in which the disrespectful behavior of earlier ethnographers has caused a ban on any future research. A guiding general principle here is that respect for our hosts' sensitivity should always override our desire for "good" data and the thrill of documenting something exemplary for our research goals.

Overall, it is safe to say that a variety of modes of participation is necessary for a rich description of any event or social situation. This means that ethnographers must routinely alternate between moments of high involvement and moments of low involvement in the activities that surround them.

4.4 Interviews

Interviews, in the loose sense of the term, are a common form of interaction during fieldwork. Ethnographers are continuously asking questions and many of the questions they ask are about topics and issues they are trying to make sense of. In this sense, ethnographers' questions are never as naive or as useless as they might sound, given that any answer, even what might appear the most guarded or the least informative, might be quite informative for the researcher – if not at the time, sometimes later. There are however specific times when the researcher sits down (often with a note pad in his hands or the tape recorder running) and presents a series of more or less structured, partly preplanned questions to a member of the community who is believed to be particularly knowledgeable about a specific area of expertise. For linguistic anthropologists, the interview might be a time to obtain background cultural information that is crucial for understanding particular speech exchanges they are studying. For some researchers who follow sociolinguistic methods (Labov 1972a, 1972b), the interview might be an occasion for getting a linguistic corpus for studying grammatical forms, stylistic variations, and attitudes toward the language (Hill and Hill 1986). In these cases, the linguist is not looking for "experts" but simply for "speakers" and one of the main concerns is how the speech produced during the interview is representative of the speaker's usage. Such a concern is part of a more general issue regarding the appropriateness of the interview situation for gaining access to local knowledge and local communicative practices. For William Labov (1984: 29), for instance,

> *[f]ace-to-face interviews are the only means of obtaining the volume and quality of recorded speech that is needed for quantitative analysis.* (italics in the original)

Most linguistic anthropologists do not agree with this general principle and believe that, although at times useful, interviews can rarely provide the richness of information needed for a culturally informed linguistic analysis. There is no substitute for the observation and recording of actual interactions among native speakers involved in everyday tasks, whether private and mundane or public and institutionally oriented. Presently available audio and video technologies allow for a high level of accuracy even when speakers are not speaking directly into a microphone while sitting in a quiet environment in front of the researcher. When interviews are considered necessary or unavoidable, a number of caveats must be kept in mind in order to know what to expect and how to handle an interview situation.

4.4.1   The cultural ecology of interviews

Reactions to the researcher's questions will vary, depending on a number of factors, including the extent to which the interview format fits into local practices of obtaining information (see below) or the nature of the topics discussed. Questions might be directed to a domain of knowledge that is recognized as valuable in the culture, as it is typically the case for public speaking and certain kinds of specialized (sometimes esoteric) knowledge (medicine, magic, genealogies), or an area that may not be seen as a worthy domain of expertise such as, for instance, activities involving children (e.g. verbal games, children's songs, socialization routines, speech errors made by children).

In some communities, access to certain topics and events might simply be forbidden to an outsider. This is known to be the case with Australian aborigines' rituals pertaining to the Dreaming and with some Native American religious ceremonies. When fieldworkers are allowed to participate in or witness what is considered a sacred ceremony with limited access (e.g. only for adults or only for initiated males), they must be very careful not to violate the trust that has been placed in them. Any reporting about such events must be weighed carefully and negotiated with members of the community.

Fieldworkers must be aware of the fact that each community has its own ways of conceptualizing what an "interview" is. When, as is often the case, a culture does not have such a speech event in its repertoire, local notions of giving out information or learning must be taken into consideration for understanding members' reactions to the researcher's attempt to conduct an interview. In Madagascar, for instance, as reported by Elinor Ochs Keenan (1974; 1976), information is considered a *scarce good* and people are reluctant to provide both insiders and outsiders with what might be considered "news." Like in many other societies in the world, genealogies are often jealously protected and the fieldworkers who are interested in them might have to wait months or years before finding anyone willing to discuss the subject in some detail. In Samoa, it is not appropriate to ask questions about people's personal motivations. Questions like "why did he do it?" for instance often produce either a standard generic refusal to commit oneself (*ta`ilo* "[how would poor] me know?") or in cases of deviant behavior, "(he was) drunk" (*ōnā*) – an answer that does not presuppose factual knowledge about the alcohol intake of the person spoken of. Any further inquiry is not likely to produce many more details or insights. Not only do Samoans not like to venture into psychological explanations or speculations about individuals' inner states of mind, but the request to engage in such interpretive practices by the researcher can be seen as inappropriate and even dangerous. For instance, the reconstruction of past events to be presented as causally linked to a present crisis can reopen old wounds and get people emotionally drained. This is made clear in formal occasions such as the village council (*fono*) where participants are urged to look forward rather than to reintroduce into the discussion conflicts that happened in the past and were considered resolved (Duranti 1994a: 97).

One should also never forget that getting information out of people might leave them with the feeling that something precious is being taken away. Paying someone an informant's fee might not be sufficient for compensating the sense of loss an individual might experience when something he might have mentioned in a moment of intimacy or as a gesture of friendship toward the fieldworker is turned into a piece of data to be potentially shared by thousands of people around the world.

Researchers also need to study the local **ecology of questioning**. In other words, fieldworkers need to find out who is allowed to question who, when, and how. In western societies questioning is expected and permitted during the early stages of the learning process (especially in the context of school activities) but in many places in the world asking questions is not seen as an appropriate activity for a novice. In many societies, novices are expected to observe and imitate what experts do rather than bothering them with questions (Lave 1990; Rogoff 1988). Thus, when Charles Briggs tried to learn about carving in a Mexicano community in Northern New Mexico by using interviews, he was faced with all kinds of "procedural problems" (1986: 43). People either did not answer his questions directly or provided very limited or apparently contradictory information. Fortunately Briggs recorded his attempts over time and from a careful study of his own questions and his consultants' answers, he gained a new understanding of the process of interviewing that can help other researchers who might find themselves in similar situations.

> This material provides insight into some of the communicative blunders I committed in research with Mexicanos ... I simply assumed that a knowledge of Standard Spanish, a research project that proved acceptable to the couple and their community, and the development of a friendship would enable me to begin interviewing. I similarly believed that interviews would provide the best means of gaining social-cultural and sociolinguistic competence ... Because I was ignorant of the community's oral traditions and lacked command of any of the requisite pragmatic skills, the elders had no choice but to regain control of the interaction by breaking the interview frame. (Briggs 1986: 64)

Briggs discovered that in order for him to learn about carving and tradition, he would have to enter the role of a traditional apprentice. His hosts' preferred mode of instruction was to hand him a piece of wood and a penknife and help him learn how to carve. Only in that context was Briggs able to obtain more detailed information on the carvings and their socio-cultural meaning.

> I then found myself in the position of being able to gain additional information by repeating one of their statements, followed by a tag question: "So your father used to be a great joker, did he?" Thus, once I had grasped the appropriate means of learning and had gained a minimal level of competence, the Lópezes were quite willing to provide me with information on the carving art. Fortunately, the couple allowed me to turn on my tape recorder at such times. This not only provided a wealth of background noise for my initial recordings, but it provided me with data on the way the Lópezes were teaching me to learn. (Briggs 1986: 65)

As this passages indicates, one needs a considerable level of analytical sophistication to detect from the transcripts of the interviews both where miscommunication occurs and which specific linguistic mechanisms are being used by the interviewer and interviewees to convey the respective understanding of the event.

4.4.2   Different kinds of interviews

Although linguistic anthropologists tend to rely on spoken interviews rather than on interviews based on written questionnaires, they do prepare written material to plan and guide their oral interviews with a member of the community. In such contexts it is important to gain an understanding of the local implications associated with using and producing written records. Depending on the history of the community, members may have distrustful attitudes toward interactions and documents that may have socioeconomic or legal implications (e.g. filling out a form). The same considerations apply to taking notes and audio or video taping while talking to people (see below).

Different considerations apply depending on whether one is conducting a few occasional interviews or numerous interviews that are expected to produce comparable data. Urban sociolinguists have developed several methods for collecting dozens or even hundreds of structured interviews. One of these methods is a **standardized questionnaire**. It is designed for use by different fieldworkers and can be adapted to a variety of situations, including subjects' different class or ethnic background. Shuy, Wolfram, and Riley (1968) used standardized questionnaires in their Detroit Dialect Study, which was developed to guide educational policies by surveying the various English speaking subcultures of the city. Fieldworkers dealt with approximately 700 speakers, of four age groups from a wide variety of social and ethnic backgrounds. Despite the researchers' commitment to the notion that "[t]he informality of the interview was a crucial factor in obtaining data on casual speech" (p. 40), the requirement of high quality sound needed for phonetic analysis produced what for most linguistic anthropologists would be considered a very formal context:

> The framework of the interview was simple and standardized. The fieldworker would hook up the microphone around the informant's neck, start the tape, which had already been threaded onto the machine, and ask the informant to give his name and count to ten. This gave a recited list, one of the more formal styles we wished to obtain, and served as a further identification on the tape in case it should be mixed up with others. The fieldworker would then proceed with Parts I through IV of the questionnaire ... (Shuy, Wolfram, and Riley 1968: 41)

In Parts I through IV, the fieldworker was instructed to ask questions such as "What kinds of games do you play around here?", "What are your favorite TV programs?", "Do you have a pet? Tell me about it."

Although these techniques were very effective in eliciting a large data set of linguistic forms that could be compared with one another and submitted to statistical analysis, their goal was limited to eliciting speech forms in various styles rather than elucidating the relationship between each speech style and the context of its use. Furthermore, the fact that most of the questions were pre-planned guaranteed a certain uniformity and continuity from one interview to another, but limited the development of topics that were of interest to the informants and might have suggested new questions for the interviewer (see also Wolfson 1976).

Linguistic anthropologists' interviews tend to be less structured than the ones organized around a standardized questionnaire, but they can be equally focused on some specific topics, including linguistic forms. The main difference between sociolinguistic methods and linguistic anthropological methods is that most linguistic anthropologists do not use interviews as their main technique for collecting speech samples, but as occasions for eliciting native interpretations of speech already collected in other situations, mostly in spontaneous interactions. In some cases, linguistic anthropologists might ask native speakers to produce certain linguistic forms and even engage in lengthy performances – which might produce stories, myths, magical formulae, oratorical speeches, polite expressions, and a number of grammatical forms –, but such occasions are usually designed to complement or clarify information collected in non-interview situations.

A typical question-answer type of focused interaction between the fieldworker and the native speaker is centered around the transcription of tapes previously recorded (see section 5.7). Another common type of interview is one that centers around the compilation of native taxonomies of speech genres. Such taxonomies are useful because they give researchers a way of getting a sense of the range of linguistic phenomena – or **repertoire** (Gumperz 1972) – that are possible/available in the community (see section 3.4). The knowledge of such a repertoire helps researchers decide how representative a certain style of speaking is, how it is related to other styles, and how it is seen by the people who perform it and their audience. One of the most extensive and complex taxonomies of speech genres ever described was collected by Gary Gossen (1974) in his study of Chamula oral tradition (see figure 4.1).

Gossen (1974: 52–55) offers an informative description of the methods he followed in collecting the taxonomy; from such a discussion we learn not only how he collected his data, but also the rationale for the choices he made in selecting his informants and pursuing certain themes revealed in their answers:

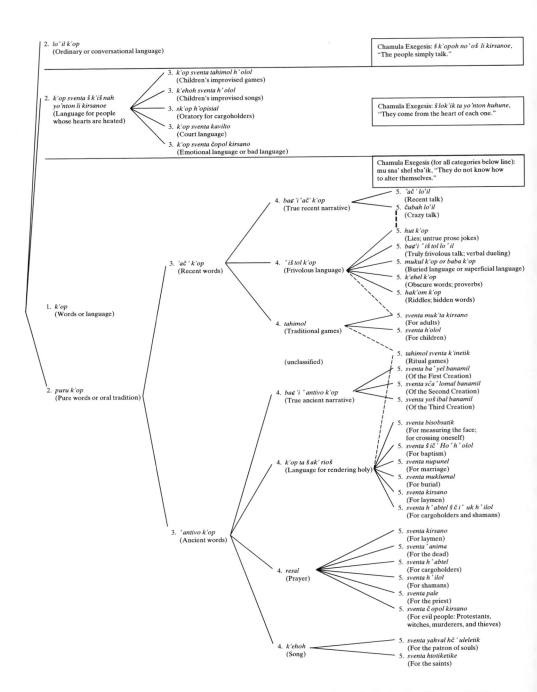

Figure 4.1 A folk taxonomy of Chamula verbal behavior (Gossen 1974)

108

A complete taxonomy of Chamula folk genre ... was elicited at intervals over a period of one year essentially from six male informants ranging in age from eighteen to sixty years. The same informants provided the majority of the texts that are included as genre examples and as an appendix to this book. Five informants came from two contiguous hamlets; the sixth lived in the nearby ceremonial center. They were selected from this limited territory so that it would be possible to control for spatial data in their texts. Both formal question frames and informal discussion were used to elicit the categories of the taxonomy. The two methods were complementary in that formal interviewing (for example, "How many kinds of – would you say there are?") produced a taxonomy and genre labels that could be used informally to identify and talk about types of texts after they had been recorded or transcribed. A typical question asked countless times was, "Is this a – ?"

The taxonomy was useful in that it provided explicit native genre labels for organizing the collection of texts and also helped to assure a more comprehensive coverage of the forms of verbal behavior recognized by the Chamulas ... the design of the field work depended in large part on the initial information that was obtained from the taxonomy. (Gossen 1974: 53)

Gossen also mentions the places in the taxonomic scheme which represented "fairly general agreement" and those that "were not given as consistently by all informants" (1974: 54). Such statements are important not only factually – they let other researchers know how to weigh the information displayed in the chart –, but also methodologically, because they alert readers not to overemphasize the psychological as well as phenomenological reality of the classification. This means that a taxonomy like the one reproduced in figure 4.1 above is *one* of the possible ways of organizing the information provided by several native speakers. One should also be reminded that classifications of this sort are of little use without a documentation of actual performances of the speech genres. In my work on Samoan oratory, for instance, I found that orators differed in some of their statements about different parts of a traditional ceremonial speech. Some of those differences, however, could be explained in terms of variations and constraints on the speeches during real-life situations. The recreation of those genres in separate contexts (e.g. exclusively for the researcher's tape recorder) failed to produce the modifications necessary to accommodate to a knowledgeable, demanding, and interactive audience (Duranti 1994a). Similarly, Tedlock (1983: 292) discovered that the version of a story told in the presence of a tape recorder might be not as explicit as the one told among family members and in front of the fieldworker without his tape recorder.

These events tell us that researchers must counteract the likely **variation in performance** of any speech form with a **variation in types of participation**, including alternating between passive and complete participation and between the presence and the absence of an electronic recording device. Although asking questions is a professional habit for researchers, sometimes, as Myers reminded us (see above), simply listening to what is going on around us is the best strategy for learning. This of course implies that the fieldworker is able to understand what people are saying.[5]

4.5 Identifying and using the local language(s)

In isolating a language to be used for an ethnographic study, it is also important not to create a "gap" in what Gumperz called the "**communication matrix**," namely, the totality of communication roles within a society (Gumperz 1968: 464). This means that we should not exclude English from a study of an urban community in India, just as it would not be methodologically sound to exclude Spanish in the study of the English of the Hispanic population in Southern California or Texas. The relevance of a code at a particular moment in an interaction is of course an empirical matter that must be decided on the basis of investigation. But the method for collecting data is a theoretical choice. This is why it is important not only to conduct interviews with native speakers about speech genres and speech styles, but also to get a more direct sense of the range of events in which members of the community participate (see section 9.2).

There is no question that fieldworkers should try their best to become familiar with the language(s) used by the people they study. This is important not only for the ability to conduct interviews without interpreters, but also, and most importantly, for understanding what is going on. As eloquently stated by Witherspoon,

> The greatest value of learning the language of another people
> does not come from being able to interview informants without
> interpreters or from providing native terms in ethnographic
> writings; it comes from being able to understand what the natives
> say and how they say it when they are conversing with each other.
> (Witherspoon 1977: 7)

---

[5] See Mead (1939) and Lowie (1940) for a debate about the use of native languages as ethnographic tools. See Owusu (1978) and section 4.5 for a discussion of the use of translators in fieldwork and the problems generated by ethnographers' lack of familiarity or fluency in the languages spoken by the population they want to study.

However clumsy and inadequate ethnographers' attempts to speak the local language might sound, they symbolize a commitment, and show respect and appreciation for the cultural heritage of the people they study. When, for sociohistorical reasons, the people themselves have a low opinion of their own language or dialect, the use of their language or dialect by fieldworkers might be resisted. In this as in other circumstances, the use of a particular language or dialect becomes a political statement that can have long-term consequences for personal as well as public relations between people.

Unfortunately, many early classic anthropological studies were done by researchers who had only a very limited knowledge of the native languages. Writing about work done in the African continent from the point of view of a scholar and a "native," Maxwell Owusu (1978: 327) remarked:

> ... one may very well ask how many Euro-Americans know our language beyond the usual literal dictionary translations that inevitably make a caricature of native terms and idioms and confuse local meanings and expressions? I have not met one yet, certainly not among our esteemed ethnographic "experts" and critics. And what is even more disturbing about their general attitude is that they continue to produce "authoritative" monographs and essays on African cultures without seriously worrying about the degrading effects of their language deficiencies on the quality of the data. Publishing editors often cannot ensure or do not care whether the native terms are even spelled correctly.

Realistically speaking, it is often difficult for a researcher to be already fluent in the local language before arriving at the field site. This means that the most common situation (for those who work outside of their own community) is one in which the ethnographer knows *something* about the language (for linguistic anthropologists this is likely to be, minimally, information about the typological and structural characteristics of the language – or languages – spoken in the area), but is not a fluent (or even a minimally functional) speaker. The most typical situation is then that of trying to rely at first, as much as possible, on bilingual speakers who are able to speak either our native language or a language we already speak with some fluency. Jane and Kenneth Hill (1986), for instance, in their study of **linguistic syncretism** (a term replacing the more judgmental "language mixing")[6]

---

[6] "The term 'syncretic' [in speaking about Mexicano] is a more appropriate choice than the word 'mixed,' partly because the people of the Malinche take a negative view of mixing in language, and partly because by its very technicality the term 'syncretic' suggests something of the work and creativity of the Mexicano speakers of the Malinche" (Hill and Hill 1986: 1).

among Mexicano speakers in Central Mexico, relied on a literate sixteen-year-old native speaker of Mexicano for all of their interview data, which were based on a standard questionnaire (see also section 4.4.2). The same person was also responsible for the first transcription of all interviews. Hill and Hill (1986: 67–89) discuss at length the contexts of the interviews and the role played by the interviewer, giving readers a good sense of both the advantages and the limitations of such a method.

In situations in which a pidgin is common in the area – as is the case for instance in East Africa or in Papua New Guinea and other parts of Melanesia –, researchers can begin their work by using the pidgin and then slowly move into the use of the local language. The experience of several researchers I have spoken to over the years suggests that this is an efficient research strategy for the first few weeks or months, but it should be only a momentary or complementary part of the interpretive process in the field. The researcher's goal should be to move quickly to interacting as much as possible with monolingual speakers (when they constitute the majority of the population) or in the language that is the most commonly used, typically, the language that children are expected to speak – things get more complicated when a community has more than one native language or when children are not learning the same language their parents learned as children (see Kulick 1992). One should also be wary of relying too much on bilingual speakers. Except for communities in which almost everyone is bilingual, there are usually important reasons for certain individuals to know a second language; that is, they are often people who have lived and worked outside of the community for a certain period of time or have relatives from another area or country. This means that they are more capable of taking the point of view of the researcher and understanding his needs, but at the same time, that they are probably not the most typical individuals in the community. This is one of the paradoxes that field researchers must live with, namely, that the people who understand us the best and are most easily understood by us are usually the ones who are the closest to the way we are (Duranti 1996). One of the difficulties of fieldwork is to be able to take advantage of the insights that such people can provide without exclusively indulging in their accessibility at the expense of our attempts to communicate with other members of the community.

As we shall see in the next section, linguistic anthropologists try to overcome some of these problems by relying on direct recording of spontaneous interaction not only between them and their subjects but also, and mainly, between the subjects themselves. Electronic recording and play-back allow the researcher to employ members of the local community to transcribe and help translate linguistic interaction at its normal speed and are an invaluable means for training the researcher's ear to the subtleties of the local ways of speaking.

4.6 Writing interaction

> Meaningful action is an object for science only under the condition of a
> kind of objectification which is equivalent to the fixation of a discourse by
> writing. (Ricoeur 1981: 203)

Although writing is not the only thing that an ethnographer does, there is no
ethnography without writing (Geertz 1973). This is true from before fieldworkers arrive at their site (they must first convince advisers, colleagues, funding
agencies, and local authorities of the worth of their project) to the moment when
they hand over the final draft of a manuscript with the result of their work. What
interests us in particular here is the parts in between these two moments.

One of the distinguishing features of linguistic anthropologists is their reliance
on recording machines, especially tape recorders and camcorders (video cameras that can also play back the recorded tape) – technologies that can be conve-
niently used to capture and analyze spontaneous interactions. Contemporary
research complements – without claiming to completely replace it – the use of
ethnographic notes with additional, especially electronic, recording devices.
This section introduces the readers to the specific properties of some of these
devices and to the ways in which the information stored in them is transformed
for analytical purposes.

The concept of "writing interaction" presents problems from the very start.
Regardless of how good we are as writers, we know that if our goal is to have the
most accurate record of a given interaction, writing is a very poor technology for
describing the richness of the experience of either *being* in an event or *witnessing*
it as an observer. There is no question, for instance, that a good quality video
recording or a film with a sound track of an event is going to have a lot more
information than a written description of it. At the same time, it is also true that
(i) we cannot make visual and sound records of everything – for a variety of reasons that include ethical as well as economic, practical, and even theoretical considerations –, (ii) even if we could approximate such a total audio-visual documentation, it would still never be the same as the experience of "being there,"
and (iii) as I will discuss below, there might be situations for which a written
record might be more revealing than a visual one.[7]

In order to deal with the inherently problematic nature of the use of writing
in describing interaction in general and verbal interaction in particular, we must

---

[7] I am quite aware of the fact that the dichotomy between "written" and "visual" is potentially misleading given that writing, after all, is a visual medium. What changes in the
two recording modalities discussed here is the relative degree of arbitrariness, and,
more precisely, the relative iconicity of the medium.

start from the following assumption: *any process of documentation is, by definition, partial, that is, it assumes a point of view and it is selective* – this implies that we will never have a "perfect" recording device that would reproduce the exact context of the recorded event. Such a recording device would have to be a time-machine that would be able to bring us (and everyone else involved) back to the time of the event. Since in order to leave everything exactly the way it was we would need to be there without a memory of having been there, this research strategy would create an infinite loop; we would keep going back to the same interaction and we would never come up with an analysis of it.

Once we accept such a partiality, however, we also realize that it is part and parcel of our goal, namely, analysis. In other words the selective nature of any kind of description gives it its analytical properties. An **analysis** is, after all, *a selective process of representation of a given phenomenon with the aim of highlighting some of its properties.* An analysis that tried to reproduce a perfect copy of its object would not be an analysis, it would give it back to us the way it was. *Analysis implies transformation*, for some purpose. This applies to using a thermometer to check our body temperature as well as to writing down on a piece of paper a word we heard for the first time. In both cases we are using a tool (a thermometer, pencil and paper) to mediate our interaction with a certain object or phenomenon (our body, people interacting in front of us). In both cases, we are doing this with an interest in seeing certain properties – and certain properties only – of the phenomenon. Only in a different moment of the documentary process will we be concerned with integrating the information gathered with supplementary information. The strength of the thermometer as a tool is precisely that it can ignore everything except the temperature. The strength of the scribbled note is that it allows us to focus on that one word and ask someone about it at another time or look for it in a dictionary. Of course the word is not everything that went on at that particular time, but it is something; it can point us in other directions; it can help us learn about other words, other meanings, other interactions.

The advantage of seeing things this way is that we don't have to engage in the hopeless search for the perfect recording tool or the perfect description. At the same time we don't have to spend our energies complaining only about the deficiencies of the tools we have at our disposal. What we need to do instead is to understand the specific properties of such tools. Once we know the specific limitations and advantages of each tool, we are in a better position to know how to integrate technology to provide richer descriptions and more comprehensive analyses of complex sociocultural phenomena. We know now that, when used properly, tape recorders, video recorders, and computers *can* be used to our advantage, including producing more accurate analyses of people's interactions. A tape recorder, for instance, is certainly a more suitable tool to store a complete conversation than our memory, no matter how good we think we are at listening and remembering. A photograph can allow us to see details of a scene that we might have missed with our naked eyes. It might also work at refreshing our memory about who was present and where that person was located. The same can be said of films and video recordings, which have – like tape recorders – the additional property of having a temporal dimension and hence of storing information about movement. With these tools we have the tremendous advantage of being able to see, over and over again, how auditory and visual access are exploited by members in constructing meaningful interactions. In fact, a video tape has a richness of information that is well beyond our present analytic abilities. Although at this point a video tape is, albeit limited, the best type of record we can have if we are interested in the integration of speech with body movements and, more generally, with visual communication, we are still trying to learn how to take advantage of such a tool. New directions in computer technology can offer new solutions to this problem. More generally, the invention of new tools that can be used for storing, replaying, manipulating, and reproducing information about human interaction not only offers new solutions to old problems, it also opens up the possibility of new analytical questions (see the Appendix on practical tips for recording human interaction).

4.6.1   Taking notes while recording

The discussion of new tools and especially electronic devices should not be interpreted as the end of the traditional ethnographic notes. Ethnographic notes can add dimensions of description that cannot be captured on tape, not even on video tape. First, there is an experiential, subjective dimension of "having been there" that is not quite visible or audible on a tape – although tapes can reveal important aspects of how our being there was enacted, perceived, and negotiated. Second, the notes can be used to document information about the participants in an interaction, including their cultural background, their profession or social status, age, previous knowledge of one another, their relationship with us. All of these and many others bits of information, which can be collected by simply talking to people, add a depth of knowledge about events and people that cannot be seen by simply watching a tape. We never know what kinds of questions we will be asking later on. For this reason, it is important to collect as much information as possible about whatever seems potentially relevant. The fact that we will not be able to know *everything* is not a reason to know *nothing*. Our curiosity is always triggered by our interests and we develop a sense of what we like to know about people and situations. At the same time, it is important to follow intuitions and the directions indicated to us by others. Third, we do want to be able to be more than just the "cameraperson" in each interaction we participate in. It is important for a researcher interested in how people communicate with one another to assume different roles (from passive to active participant, for instance) and along different degrees of visibility in the scene. Having a little notebook with us allows us to scribble down a few notes, sometimes just a word, or to make a sketch of a situation, indicating in it where people are seated or who is moving in which direction. It also allows us to note down what is happening that is not being recorded (people moving behind the camera or leaving to go somewhere else). We might be suddenly struck by an idea, a connection we never made before and feel the urgency of writing it down (that's the way most of us have been trained to deal with new ideas!) rather than waiting until later when we are alone. When we go back home, at the end of the day, those short sentences and sketchy drawings will prove very useful in our attempt to put together a descriptive narrative of what we experienced during the day. It is not uncommon that even a few hours later our memory will have already started to act so selectively (and so analytically) that the notes can be very useful in correcting our shaky recollections. It is thus imperative for researchers to look over their notes as soon as possible after the recording session and write down extensive fieldnotes based on those notes. I have found that fieldnotes contain crucial information which helps me contextualize what I recorded on tape.[8]

4.7 Electronic recording

> Looking ahead, it appears that a future science of language and communication, both visible and acoustic, will be made possible, in all probability, not by refinements in notational systems but by increasing sophistication in methods of recording, analyzing, and manipulating visible and auditory events electronically.
>
> (Armstrong, Stokoe, and Wilcox 1994: 354)

The introduction of recording machines such as the tape recorder and the video camera (or camcorder) among the field researcher's tools has a number of advantages over the traditional method of participant-observation based on the researcher's skills at listening, seeing, and (most importantly) remembering – whether or not aided by written notes. The ability to stop the flow of discourse or the flow of body movement, go back to a particular spot and replay it allows us to concentrate on what is sometimes a very small detail at the time, including a particular sound or a person's small gesture. Recent work based on audio and visual

---

[8] A very basic form of note taking which turns out to be very helpful is the writing of the date of the recording and the names of the participants on the tape label. For audio tapes, the researcher can give information about the situation into the microphone before starting to record and for video tapes, date and time can be displayed either throughout the recording or at the beginning and after any "cut" or interruption.

recordings has shown that participants are in fact sensitive to the most minute details of an interaction, including the quality of a single sound and the direction of a very brief glance. Since such sensitivity is usually not at the conscious level, it cannot be investigated by simply asking informants about it. Once a "phenomenon" is identified and selected by the researcher, however, members – as well as other "experts," including the researcher's colleagues – will have a chance to assess it in their own terms,[9] in some cases confirming in other cases throwing doubts on the researcher's hypothesis. Through such an experience, others can add their reactions and evaluations to the researcher's. As a larger number of people enter the interpretive process and the researcher's interpretation becomes more vulnerable, the quality of the hypotheses made increases.

4.7.1 *Does the presence of the camera affect the interaction?*

Invariably, every time I discuss an interaction with the aid of a video tape, there is someone in the audience who asks: "Didn't the presence of the camera affect the interaction?" Video images seem to trigger this question more than, say, verbal descriptions of a given situation in the field or transcriptions of stories told by informants into a tape recorder. One could make an argument that the presence of the tape recorder and of the researcher's notebook also affect the situation. Carried to its logical consequence, the "impact" question could be used to argue that it would be better *not to be there* at all. This could be realized in two ways: (i) by *not* studying people or (ii) by not letting the participants know that their interaction is being recorded. The first option is self destructive and hopefully unacceptable to anyone who has made it so far in this book. It implies that we should not try to improve our understanding of what it means to be human and have a culture (including a language) simply because we cannot find the ideal situation for naturalistic-objective observation. The second proposal is first of all unethical and, second, impractical under most circumstances outside of laboratories with two-way mirrors. Some researchers try to circumvent some of these problems by giving the camera to a member of the community. This method has the advantage that it offers a different perspective from the ethnographer's – the categories whereby something is selected for recording might be different[10] – but it does not really solve the ethical problems given that members might feel entitled to intrude much more than outsiders in the lives of their family and neighbors and this might create even more ethical dilemmas.

---

[9] Despite the fact that the framing of a phenomenon already directs future listeners and viewers to hear and see in a selective way, there is room for a certain level of independent judgment that is not possible when researchers simply state what they observed.

[10] This was what Sol Worth was interested in when he gave cameras to the Navajos so that they would make their own movies (Worth and Adair 1972).

In fact, the camera-effect is only one special case of what is usually called the **participant-observer paradox**: to collect information we need to observe interaction, but to observe interaction (in ethically acceptable ways) we need to be in the scene; therefore, any time we observe we affect what we see because others monitor our presence and act accordingly. If we think a moment about this logical loop we realize that it is not only part of doing research. It is part of being a social being, a member of a society and a producer/consumer of cultural interpretations. Being a social actor, a participant in *any* situation and in *any* role, means to be part of the situation and hence affect it (see section 4.1.2). Is there a solution to this paradox? Life itself is an attempt to resolve the participant-observer paradox. So-called neutral observation, where the observer is completely separated from the observed is an illusion, a cultural construction. This does not mean that we should ignore the paradox, but that we should deal with it with the awareness of its unavoidability. In the social sciences, dealing with the paradox means to *understand the different ways in which the presence of certain types of social actors (e.g. ethnographers) or artifacts (e.g. cameras, tape recorders, notebooks, questionnaires) play a role in the activity that is being studied, and the different kinds of transformations that each medium and technique produces*. For example, there is no question that our presence as observers is more intrusive in some situations than in others. There is a difference between walking with a camera in our hands into a room where two people are having a conversation and bringing a camera to a public event that involves dozens of people. At the same time, the way we present ourselves, what we do as well as what our hosts are occupied with have a lot to do with the impact of our presence and the camera on the observed. Video recording (or filming) raises some of the same questions raised by other documentary techniques such as interviewing (see section 4.4.1 above). We must develop ways of evaluating how what we see around us changes when we bring into a situation a video camera or any other type of recording device. At the same time, it should be kept in mind that, perhaps with the exception of obvious **camera behaviors** (e.g. certain types of camera-recognitions or salutations like staring into the camera and smiling), people usually do not *invent* social behavior, language included, out of the blue. Rather, their actions are part of a repertoire that is available to them independently of the presence of the camcorder. One might even argue that the presence of the camera may be used as an excuse for certain types of social actions that might have been done anyhow, like when people point to the camera to provide a reason to be polite or be generous. I believe that most of the time people are too busy running their own lives to change them in substantial ways because of the presence of a new gadget or a new person. As shown by many researchers over and over again, even with a lens aiming at them, participants still manage to argue with one another, be overrun by emotions, reveal intimate aspects of their private lives, or engage in lengthy evaluations of the private lives of other people (including the fieldworker!).

An understanding of the impact of the camera on a given context also implies an understanding of the kind of information represented by it. A tape contains a filtered version of whatever happened while the tape was running. It has, however, the power to capture social actions in unique ways. Thus, as I discussed earlier (section 4.6), cameras have the power to keep a record of an interaction that maintains some of its temporal and kinesic characteristics.[11] Such a record can be viewed by different people and subjected to analysis in ways that are quite different from the ways in which a narrative by an observer of the same event would allow. As with any other recording device, rather than blindly rejecting the use of a camera because it might influence people or embrace its use as a technology that can produce the ultimate objective accounts, we must work at understanding what a camera can offer for our theoretical and methodological goals.

4.8   Goals and ethics of fieldwork

> Qu'est-on est venu faire ici? Dans quel espoir? A quelle fin?
> Lévi-Strauss, *Tristes Tropiques*

The *Anthropology Newsletter* published monthly by the American Anthropological Association is full of ethical dilemmas. More and more writing within and outside of anthropology has been focusing on ethical and political issues implicit in the practice of studying human beings. Within linguistic anthropology, Penelope Harvey (1992) and Niko Besnier (1994) have recently addressed ethical problems in tape recording interaction. In a frank and intriguing discussion of a very difficult subject, Harvey risked taking an unpopular position defending clandestine tape recording while recognizing its ethical implications. She argued that without tape recording drunken speech, she would have not been able to understand some important aspects of the relationship between language and power in the Peruvian Andean community she studied. The ethical problem about not sharing our goals with our informants, she argues, comes from the nature of representation and authorship in anthropology. We cannot "be entirely open about exactly what data are being collected, since it is only at the stage of writing that the collection of memories, impressions, notes and recordings become 'data' by going on record" (Harvey 1992: 82).

Besnier (1994) wrote about the unforeseen consequences of exposing recorded interaction to members of the community who were not present at the time of

---

[11] There are many aspects of a situation that not even a camera can capture, including smell, a dimension of context that has been vastly underestimated in the study of human conduct despite its most obvious effects such as the activation of memories.

the recording – like when, for instance, we ask a third party to help us transcribe a recorded tape. Like Harvey, he argues that the ethics of fieldwork are more complex than the principle of informing participants that one is recording their actions or not allowing someone to listen to what other members of their community said when they were not present. Besnier elaborates on some of Harvey's points and turns the discussion of the ethical problem he faced into an occasion for a criticism of the implicit wisdom of participant-observation without audio or video recorders:

> I would like to take Harvey's point further, suggesting that
> anthropological methods that base ethnographic analyses on
> *impressionistic re-creations* of what is said during a drunken episode
> or a gossipy moment are more abusive of scientific authority than
> methods based on the microscopic analysis of a transcript of what is
> said, without ignoring, of course, the ethnographic authority
> embedded in the transcribing process (see Tedlock 1983).
>
> (Besnier 1994: 27)

Poststructuralist and postmodernist critiques of the role of the researcher in visiting foreign places and making claims of authority have certainly made these discussions more frequent in recent years, but such issues have been in the minds of anthropologists for quite some time, as shown by the above quote from Lévi-Strauss's autobiographical *Tristes tropiques*. His questions "What have we come to do here? With which hope? For which goal?" succinctly capture one of the main issues in ethnographic work. What is behind the ethnographer's quest for knowledge of the Other? Are there hidden, unwritten motivations, sometimes within, sometimes without the researcher's conscious motivation for fieldwork experience? What are we looking for? What do we want to find? Who sent us?

There is no question that travels of discovery, in the name of science, have often been travels of conquest (Reill and Miller 1996). For these reasons, the age of naiveté in anthropology is over. What replaces that age must be negotiated through theoretical and empirical attempts to deal with the conflicts that accompany any search for other ways of being, doing, and saying. There are many different solutions, none of which is the ultimate one. The Italian anthropologist Ernesto De Martino, who worked half a century ago on what he saw as oppressed subcultures in the south of Italy, suggested that ethnographic research should start from "a commitment to tie our traveling to the explicit recognition of an actual passion, connected to a vital problem in our own society" (1961: 20, translation mine). It is the goal of the researcher to explain how such a passion is translated into an ethnographic account, with an awareness of the complexities I have hinted at. There is however no way of escaping the responsibility we have as researchers towards the people we study. This does not mean that we should always and only write what we think they will like, but that whatever we decide to say publicly and publish should be informed by our awareness of the potential consequences of our research (the American Anthropological Association offers some guidelines on the ethics of fieldwork, but they by no means exhaust the possible issues and situations encountered during fieldwork). We need to develop a theoretical understanding of our position and positioning in engaging in ethnographic methods. The concept of ethnographers as cultural mediators discussed above is one way to come to terms with the complex reality of anthropological fieldwork. Ignoring the problems or deciding to stay home are not viable solutions.

4.9 Conclusions

In this chapter I have shown how, by drawing from different fields dedicated to the study of human interaction and communication, linguistic anthropology provides a unique blend of recording techniques and analytical dimensions for our understanding of human cultures. In the next chapter, I will explore how the information recorded through the methods discussed in this chapter is transformed into texts and other forms of visual representations that can help us improve our analytical understanding of language as a cultural practice.

An important aspect of the linguistic anthropological methods discussed in this chapter is the integration of traditional participant-observation methods with new recording techniques that allow for a different kind of access to the ethnographer's experience. In the next chapters I will refer to a number of other disciplines and approaches (in linguistics and sociology in particular) that make use of similar recording devices and ultimately produce what appear to be similar types of documents (texts, transcripts). Since these other disciplines have something to offer to our understanding of the ways in which language enters the constitution of social action, it is important to maintain an open and informed attitude toward them. There is also no copyright on methods in the social sciences. One should feel free to use what seems to work for one's goals. Experimenting with new techniques (e.g. video, computers) can provide insights and reveal phenomena that had been previously ignored or left unanalyzed. At the same time, new technologies also bring new ethical and political problems. A discipline that is concerned with the issue of representation must grow by maintaining a vigilant eye on the pros and cons of new methods of documentation while developing a critical understanding of the pros and cons of the old ones.

5

Transcription: from writing to digitized images

Boas and Malinowski were both concerned with standards of field research and empirical methods and believed that showing the linguistic sources of their ethnographic descriptions, that is, informants' verbal accounts, was a very important part of an anthropologist's task. Since they did not have the luxury of a machine that could record and then play over and over again what the informant said, transcription meant writing down in a systematic and careful fashion informants' answers to questions regarding traditional knowledge and various aspects of the social organization of their community. The transcription of an actual conversation among native speakers or any other kind of verbal performance at the normal rate of speech was beyond the technological reach of early ethnographers. To capture information about language use, they were forced then to rely on two kinds of techniques. One was to try to catch a word or phrase as it was used in the course of an interaction, make a mental or written note about it, and then wait for an opportunity to ask an informant about it:

> When an exceptionally good phrase [about botany or gardening]
> occurred I would make a brief note of it, mental or written, and
> then lead my informant to repeat it, not necessarily as I had first
> heard it, but so as to reproduce the information it contained and its
> linguistic character. (Malinowski 1935, vol. 2: 5)

Another technique was to elicit narratives about a given topic and transcribe them. This method relied on native speakers' ability (and patience) to speak clearly and slowly, and their willingness to adapt to the ethnographer's limited understanding of the local language. Ordinary talk, whether formal or casual, was of course a real problem, as reported by Boas himself in a letter to Ruth Benedict in 1930 (Boas was seventy-two):

> I am worrying now about the style of oratory because I do not yet
> know how to get it down. Anyway I have my troubles with ordinary
> conversation. Narrative I can understand quite well, if they talk

distinctly, but many have the Indian habit of slurring over the ends
of their words – whispering – and that makes it difficult.

(quoted in Mead 1959: 43)

Things have changed considerably in the last few decades. With the invention of
tape recorders first and video recorders more recently,[1] new research methods
have been developed. Linguistic anthropologists in particular have been quick
to capitalize on these technological advances. Most linguistic anthropologists
have adopted electronic recording of natural speech as a standard practice in their
research methods. The introduction of these new media has fostered higher standards of accuracy and an interest in interactional details that would have been
overlooked in the past.[2] Linguistic anthropologists have become particularly keen
on producing transcripts of stretches of native discourse recorded during spontaneous interactions, ranging from ceremonial events to casual conversations.

In this chapter, I introduce different units of analysis of spoken language and
the logic that underlies their use. I dedicate several sections to the "word" as a
unit of analysis because it has been so important in both linguistics and anthropology. I then launch into discourse units and the different formats and conventions
that have been introduced for their transcription. I also discuss transcription
tools other than writing, including drawings and digitized images. Finally, I discuss
translation and various formats for its representation.

5.1 Writing

Writing systems have been important for the development of linguistic analysis
for at least two reasons: they have been crucial for our understanding of how linguistic sounds change over time (historical linguistics) and for the segmentations

---

[1] Film, of course, was available much before video technology was perfected to allow for
portable cameras and camcorders. With some notable exceptions (e.g. Connor, Asch,
and Asch 1986), however, ethnographic filming has run its own parallel course and
ethnographers have rarely incorporated film in their analyses. This is partly due to the
forbidding cost of film and the technical expertise required, not to mention the common
field condition of not having electricity to recharge batteries, high humidity, etc. In addition, however, there has always been in western academia a higher value given to words
over images. With the exception of a few visual anthropology programs, anthropology
graduate students and junior faculty are usually encouraged to publish printed material
rather than spend their time producing films or figuring out how to integrate the two
media.

[2] Within different disciplinary traditions such as human ethology and social psychology
there is a more established tradition of detailed empirical studies of visual communication (e.g. Argyle 1969, Argyle and Cook 1976; Eibl-Eibesfeldt 1968, 1970, 1974; Ekman
1982; Kendon 1977, 1980, 1990). In sociocultural anthropology, Bateson and Mead
(1942) were among the first to encourage fieldworkers to use photography and film but
even today most ethnographers do not engage in detailed analysis of audio-visual
recordings.

of meaningful strings of sounds into units of analysis such as sentences and these, in turn, into words and their components (morphemes, phonemes) (see below and chapter 6). Written records have allowed linguists to have access to earlier stages of languages (Ancient Egyptian, Hittite, Sanskrit, Old Turkish, Ancient Mayan). By comparing those early records with existing languages – the so-called "daughter languages" of the older, dead ones –, in the eighteenth- and nineteenth-century linguists were able to develop hypotheses about how languages change over time and across space (Bynon 1977; Lehmann 1973; Keiler 1972). The theories developed on the basis of such written records have been then used to reconstruct earlier stages (what linguists call "proto- languages") of currently spoken languages that had no indigenous writing tradition.

But writing systems contain a number of assumptions about language structure. One of the best case studies to make this point is Mark Aronoff's (1985) analysis of the orthography developed by the Masorets for Biblical Hebrew between AD 600 and 800. Aronoff shows that the conventions introduced to mark stress are based on a syntactic analysis of the text that resembles, in some respects, the formalization adopted by modern structuralist and generative syntacticians.

Writing – more specifically alphabetic writing – was essential to the notion and practice of transcription as originally developed by Boas for "salvaging" rapidly disappearing Native American languages and cultures (see section 3.1). Given that writing down the sounds of a language makes us face important decisions on linguistic structures and the organization of a given linguistic system, Boas and his American Indian consultants were not only making a record of the past, they were also presenting an analysis of the language they were transcribing.

Writing is a powerful form of classification because it recognizes certain distinctions while ignoring others. For instance, in English we use the letter "s" for representing the plural of words despite the fact that when we do so we are in fact conflating distinct sounds: the *s* of *cats* is not the same as the *s* of *dogs* (see section 6.3). Native speakers of English "know" this difference, although they might not be aware of it, while literate non-native speakers are often confused by the the fact that same letter is used for what are in fact different sounds.

Writing down a language that has never been written before constitutes a first *description* of that language. By allowing us to see what we hear, that is, by transforming an acoustic phenomenon into a visual one, writing allows for a different type of manipulation of linguistic signals, for different kinds of abstractions, for new types of connections. But like any other powerful analytical tool, writing not only highlights certain properties (Goodwin 1994), it also hides some others (Irvine and Gal in press). First, visual representation in the form of orthographic conventions of any sort (whether alphabetic or syllabic, for instance) reproduces an ideology of interpretation whereby we believe that we know what something means by a one-to-one match between individual words and individual meanings. This is indeed the theory of interpretation represented by past and present extensions of propositional logic to natural languages. As I will discuss below and in later chapters, this theory presents some problems, especially when faced with speech as used in actual interaction and not under controlled conditions.

Second, since any writing system contains a partial theory of the sounds and units of the language it purports to represent, when we write down the sounds of a language that has never been transcribed before, we bring to it a history of ways of thinking about what linguistic sounds are like and what they are for. Writing is also associated with particular grammatical traditions. Thus, the early missionaries in Africa, Asia, North and South America, and Oceania used the distinctions found in Latin grammars as their guiding principles for grammatical description. This meant that they imposed morphological distinctions such as nominal cases (nominative, dative, ablative, vocative) even on languages in which the noun did not change depending on its place in the sentence (Anderson 1985a: 197–8; Cardona 1976: 37–42).

Writing down a language also establishes a particular dialect or register among the several in use at any particular time as the **standard language**. Such a practice has important consequences not only for the destiny of local dialects that are different from the one chosen as the standard, but also for the type of idealization made by students of language (Finegan 1980; Morgan 1994). Until the birth of urban sociolinguistics in the 1960s, issues of orthographic representations in the West were mostly restricted to the interest of fiction writers who wanted to reproduce (or just give a feeling for) non-standard dialects, usually in dialogue. With the exception of phoneticians and phonologists, western grammarians (syntacticians, semanticists) working on their own language did not seem to have doubts as to how to represent the examples they were creating for their argumentation. Even now, if one opens up a linguistic textbook or a journal of formal linguistics, one discovers that syntacticians working on English assume that there is no problematic relationship between the graphic representation of sentences on a page and their spoken counterpart. In other words, standard orthography is implicitly associated with the idealization of speech that is central to contemporary formal theories of grammar. The uncritical adoption of a particular system of representation is therefore not simply a theoretical stratagem (e.g. we need to assume some basic abstract system to explain language acquisition and shared semantic interpretations), but also an ideological ploy that ends up reinforcing hegemonic assumptions about what any speaker *should* be saying. This means that although writing offers us great opportunities for analysis, it also constrains the range of phenomena we are likely to study and taints them with particular ideological implications. It is therefore crucial that we critically appraise the use of orthographic representation in linguistic analysis, so that we can exploit writing as an analytical tool while stretching the analytical boundaries established by its past uses.

Finally, recent experiments have suggested that familiarity with a writing system (the practice of reading in particular) might be crucial for developing the ability to segment speech into separate sounds (phonemes) or larger units (morphemes) (see chapter 6). We cannot assume, for instance, that any speaker of English would be able to separate the sounds that linguists see as forming a word like *fly* or *bite*. In a series of so-called *phoneme deletion* experiments, in which subjects are asked to delete a particular sound of an existing word, most non-literate adults could not perform the task. Reviewing the existing literature and their own work on this faculty, Scholes and Willis write:

> Speakers of English are able to manipulate phonemes only if they can read. The acquisition of the alphabetic representation of language enables the language knower to transfer this way of representation (i.e. sequences of discrete sublexical elements) to speech. In short, we know about phonemes because we know about letters. (Scholes and Willis 1991: 220)

The hypothesis that writing has an impact on speakers' ability to perform linguistic analyses on their own or on other people's speech is part of an attempt to link the introduction of literacy to cognitive as well as social changes in individual members of particular speech communities. This is a topic of great controversy given that the role of literacy in linguistic analysis has been underestimated if not altogether ignored by grammarians as well as by philosophers of language, who have been assuming that the type of analysis they engage in is an adequate idealization of cognitive abilities that any speaker of a language (and not only linguists) can make.[3] Although many formal linguists today recognize that what they might be studying is the grammatical competence of an idealized group of speaker (viz. the tacit knowledge of language by an average university professor), they do not readily admit that their culture, including the culture of literacy and the importance that reading and writing have in their daily life, might in fact have an impact on the type of analysis they propose.

5.2 The word as a unit of analysis

Alphabetic writing was particularly important for the identification of the word as a basic unit of analysis in linguistics. Although linguists have been searching for writing-independent criteria for establishing the boundaries of words in different languages around the world, there is little doubt that the first impulse for assuming

---

[3] On Sapir's analytical use of intuitions by speakers of unwritten languages, see section 6.3.1.

the word as a basic unit of analysis in linguistics must have come from alphabetic writing conventions. Among the criteria currently used to isolate words in consistent ways are: pausing, stress, and certain morphological processes or constraints that seem to apply to words but not to larger units (Anderson 1985b).

Languages display a considerable variation in length and shape of words, especially when we use pausing as a criterion for defining word boundaries. Whereas in some languages, one seems to be able to pause after each syllable (Vietnamese is said to be such a language), in other ones, most typically Native North American languages, pauses are allowed only after what appear as full sentences. Another criterion used to distinguish word units is permutability of word order. Words can often be moved in different positions within a sentence (although languages as well as types of words within the same language vary considerably in this respect), but parts of words (morphemes) cannot as easily be moved around. Thus, whereas in Latin sentences like (1) below we can change the order of units such as *lupus*, *vulpem*, and *arguebat* and still produce meaningful sentences (Latin is particularly flexible with respect to word order), the same cannot be said of the meaningful parts of each word.

(1)	Lup-us	vulp-em	arguebat
	wolf-Subject	fox-Object	accuse+Past
	"The wolf was accusing the fox"		
(1)'	vulpem	lupus	arguebat
(1)"	arguebat	lupus	vulpem
(1)'''	lupus	arguebat	vulpem
(1)''''	vulpem	arguebat	lupus
(1)'''''	arguebat	vulpem	lupus

Thus, we cannot move the ending of lupus (*-us*) or the ending of vulpem (*-em*) to produce **uslup* or **emvulp*. Similarly, we cannot move the part of the verb (*-ebat*) that conveys the information about temporal relations.

Traditional orthographies are not always consistent in the ways in which they recognize words and analysts must develop their own understanding of the status of a particular morpheme or combination of morphemes. This is especially the case with categories like pronouns and tense or aspect markers, which are sometimes treated as separate words and other times as affixes and hence part of larger word units. This is the case, for instance, with so-called "clitic pronouns." They are typically unstressed, unemphatic, short morphemes that do the work of referring to participants in the immediate context (linguistic or otherwise). For these reasons, then, they do not seem to qualify as independent words. Orthographic traditions, however, vary. In written Bantu languages, for instance, clitic pronouns are typically treated as part of the verb. When the full nouns in (2), from

Haya (in Tanzania), are replaced by anaphoric pronouns, as in (3), they are shown to be part of what Bantu specialists call the "verb complex," a string of morphemes that includes subject-verb agreement, tense and aspect markers, causative or instrumental infixes, and other types of syntactic and semantic markers:[4]

> (2) *Kat' á-ka-siig-is'   ómwáán' ámajút' ékitambâla*
> Kato 3sg-Pst-smear-Instr child   oil   handkerchief
> "Kato smeared oil on the child with the handkerchief"

> (3) *Kat' á- ka-ki-ga-mú-siig- isa*
> Kato 3sg-Pst-pro$_i$-pro$_{ii}$-pro$_{iii}$-smear-Instr
> "Kato smeared it on him with it"   (i=handkerchief; ii=oil; iii=child)

In this case, then, no difference is made between the subject-verb agreement (*á-*) which must always appear on the verb – notice that it is present even though the Subject is expressed by a full noun (*Kato*) – and the pronouns referring to the various other nominal arguments (Object, Goal, and Instrument) in the sentence, which are there when the full nouns are not present.

The orthography of Romance languages, on the other hand, typically treats clitic pronouns as separate words in sentences with finite verbs and as suffixes in sentences with infinitival verbs. This is shown in the Italian examples (4) and (5) below, where the third person singular masculine pronoun *lo* is in one case a separate word and in the other a suffix to the verb *chiamare* "call":

> (4) A; Sai dov'è Mario?
> know:2ndsing where is Mario
> "Do you know where Mario is?"
>
> B; No, ma **lo** vedo   domani.
> no but him see:1stSing tomorrow
> "No, but I see **him** tomorrow."

> (5) A; dove posso trovare Mario?
> "where can I find Mario?"
>
> B; puoi chiamar**lo** a casa verso le tre.
> can:2ndSg call-him at home around the three
> "you can call **him** at home around three."

Should *lo* be thought of as a word? It depends. The pronoun *lo*, like other clitic pronouns (*mi, ti, la, li,* etc.) typically participates in the intonational unit of the verb

---

4 In these examples the apostrophe indicates that the final vowel of a word is deleted, e.g. the "o" of the name *Kato*, when the next word starts with a vowel; the acute stress indicates a high tone, the circumflex a rising and falling tone, and the absence of stress a low tone (see Duranti and Byarushengo 1977: 63).

with which it co-occurs and does not carry primary stress (*lo-védo* and *chiamár-lo*). Furthermore, clitic pronouns can participate in assimilation processes that indicate a tendency to become part of larger units. Thus, as shown in (5) above, when the pronoun *lo* co-occurs with an infinitive form (*chiamar-lo*), the verb loses its final vowel (becoming *chiamar* instead of *chiamare*). Similarly, when the clitic pronoun precedes a word that starts with a vowel, it tends to lose its final vowel, e.g. *Mario lo imita* (lit. "Mario him imitates") –> *Mario l'imita*. These phenomena show that clitic pronouns can enter the structure of another word and it might make sense to think of them as part of larger word units. At the same time, if we take pausing as a criterion, things do not appear so straightforward. Italian speakers can stop after each of the words in a sentence like *lo vedo domani* (although, again, this ability might be due to writing practices). Furthermore, if there is ambiguity, the clitic pronoun *can* be stressed for emphasis (*la vedi? No, ló vedo* "do you see her? No, I see *him*").

The decision about whether an expression should be granted the status of "word" usually reflects how seriously a researcher has taken the task of analyzing a language and showing the relationships among its different parts. Decisions about word units become particularly important whenever linguists are involved in either revising or establishing orthographies (Romaine 1994; Schieffelin and Doucet 1994). In these cases, a consistent analysis might make a difference for the accessibility of the orthographic conventions to native speakers, children in particular. Furthermore, an understanding of what constitutes an individual word can enter the discussion of the nature of linguistic classifications, especially for anthropologists interested in the evolution of those classifications across time and space.

5.2.1 *The word as a unit of analysis in anthropological research*

The word as a unit of analysis has been particularly important in anthropological research. Key notions in anthropological theory such as the concepts of *potlatch*, *totem, mana, taboo*, and many others are actual words taken from a particular language and raised to symbols of universal or quasi-universal types of human activities, relationships with the supernatural, and individual or group characteristics. The most important part of traditional social anthropology, namely, the study of kinship systems, is based on the ability that humans have to use individual words to identify social relations among people. But kinship charts are just one well-known example of the interest that ethnographers have always had in native classifications. Lists of names for plants, animals, tools, and places have always formed an important part of fieldworkers' notebooks, reflecting the western view that the first step in knowing something is the ability to write down its name, hence the identification of individual words is crucial. This is demonstrated in an exemplary way by **evolutionary studies** of color terminology (Berlin and Kay 1969) and ethnobotanical nomenclature (Berlin 1992). In these cases, the extent to which the names for different colors, animals, or plants are derived from the same word has been seen by evolutionists as evidence for how human groups might expand their vocabulary over time.

> In the ethnobiological lexicons of all languages, one is immediately struck by the structural uniformity of expressions that linguistically characterize man's recognition of the basic objective discontinuities of his biological world. These expressions are, for the most part, unique "single words" that can be said to be semantically unitary and linguistically distinct. Examples of such semantically unitary names in English folk biology would be oak, pine, and maple. Primary terms of this sort appear to represent the most commonly referred to concepts of the botanical world and can be referred to as "generic names." (Berlin 1975: 66)

Berlin argues that simple words naming generic classes are the first items in the ethnobotanical lexicon of all languages. The next stage consists of names produced by analogy (by means of expressions meaning "like" or "related to") and after that come processes such as the addition of modifiers (e.g. the adjective "true" or "genuine") with distinctions that are eventually lexicalized and lose the connection with the original generic name. In this kind of evolutionary study the word is the starting point as well as the goal of linguistic classification.

5.2.2 *The word in historical linguistics*

Another area of study that has been largely based on the word as unit of analysis is **historical linguistics**, that is, the study of how languages change over time, including the development of different languages from a common ancestor. The **comparative method**, a technique by which sound similarities and differences across languages are systematically examined and laws are proposed to explain those similarities and differences, started out as a way of matching lists of words. Despite the reluctance many linguists feel about centering their work on words, the comparative method has been very successful in historical reconstruction:

> Linguists have commonly been uneasy about relying on vocabulary. They consider vocabulary to be the least significant part of a language. It may be very unstable and vary widely from speaker to speaker and situation to situation. Phonology and grammar [=morphology, syntax] are more central. Yet there are certain crucial advantages of vocabulary over other sectors of language for comparative work. 1. Vocabulary items are relatively easily found and easily stated. 2. There can readily be obtained a sizeable

sample of word-pairs (or glosses that will produce word-pairs) which come close to being independent of each other. [...] 3. Gloss lists can be selected in such a way as to bias our results in certain desirable ways. For example, word resemblances due to language universals are particularly common in a few specific meanings (e.g. child words for parents) and apparently negligible elsewhere. By eliminating such glosses, this source of resemblances can be minimized to the point of insignificance, and hence be safely overlooked in preliminary comparative work. (Gleason 1972: 4–5)

Starting with William Jones's 1784 lecture on the relationship between Sanskrit (an ancient language of India) and European languages and continuing with the work of the European historical linguists of the nineteenth century (Bopp, Rask, Schlegel), the comparison of word lists across languages has been used again and again not only to identify language groups (called "families") but also to reconstruct the origins of certain human groups or races.[5] The comparative method was used, for instance, to posit a southeast Asian origin of the Polynesian people before convincing archaeological evidence was available (Kirch 1984: 42). Examples of the relationship among different Austronesian languages is given in table 5.1, where groups of cognate terms in four modern languages (Tagalog, Malay, Fijian, and Samoan) are derived from the same reconstructed form in an ancient hypothetical language called "Proto-Austronesian." Figure 5.1 illustrates the relationship among some of the main subgroups of Proto-Austronesian.

Table 5.1 *Some proto-Austronesian terms and their related forms in four modern languages (Pawley 1974: 486)*

	Proto-Austronesian	Tagalog	Malay	Fijian	Samoan
two	*Duwa	dalawa	dua	rua	lua
four	*e(m)pat	apat	empat	vā	fā
five	*lima	lima	lima	lima	lima
six	*enem	anim	enam	ono	ono
bird	*manuk	manok	manu	manumanu	manu
eye	*mata	mata	mata	mata	mata
road	*Zalan	daan	jalan	sala	ala
pandanus	*panDan	pandan	pandan	vadra	fala
coconut	*niuR	niyog	nior	niu	niu

[5] See Irvine (1995) for a critique of the ideology implied in the use of the notion of "family" for genealogical classification, especially as it applies to nineteenth-century studies of African languages.

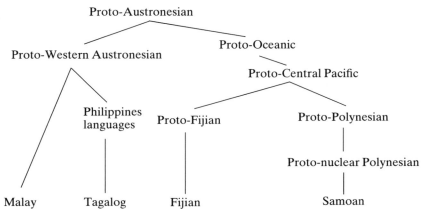

Figure 5.1 A tree-structure (also called "family tree") representing
hypothesized relationship among four Austronesian languages
(Pawley 1974)

The use of word lists from different languages is a powerful method for reconstructing relationships between different languages. The "family trees" produced
from these comparisons, however, do not necessarily represent true historical
states or events (Bynon 1977: 67–75). They also ignore variation within the same
speech community (Weinreich, Labov, and Herzog 1968) and the possibility of
language contact and spread of linguistic forms across linguistic family boundaries (Nichols and Peterson 1996; Trubetzkoy 1939; Weinrech 1953). Unfortunately, the assumption of uniformity and regularity necessary for this kind of
reconstruction risks perpetrating the view of the meaning of a word as context-
independent. As we shall see, in fact, any word acquires its meaning in the context of larger units such as sentences (chapter 6), speech acts and language
games (chapter 7), sequences of turns (chapter 8), speech events and participant
frameworks (chapter 9). Finally, what we call a word may in fact be expressing
different kinds of "signs." Historical reconstructions tend to be based on one
particular type of sign, namely, "symbols" (see section 6.8).

5.3 Beyond words

Despite the great advances in our understanding of linguistic structures and
language change on the basis of the word as a unit of analysis, linguists and
logicians have long recognized that words only have meaning within the context of
a sentence (or a proposition). The "cognitive revolution" of the 1960s included an
irreversible shift from the study of sounds and words to the study of full sentences.
Especially due to the work of Noam Chomsky and his students, phonology and
morphology were replaced by syntax as the most important area of research. At

the same time, researchers in a variety of fields interested in language processing and language use began to explore units larger than sentences. In the 1970s many students of language discovered that there were linguistic phenomena that should be studied in the context of discourse units rather than by looking exclusively at isolated sentences. A particularly active group of typological linguists mostly working in California rediscovered the earlier work on the informational structure of sentences by Prague School linguists and by M. A. K. Halliday and started to apply discourse notions such as "topic" and "theme" to the study of syntax (Givón 1979; Li 1974, 1976, 1978). There was also a renewed interest in language universals based on actual comparison among languages rather than on innate abstract principles (Greenberg 1963; Greenberg et al. 1978; Hawkins 1979; Keenan and Comrie 1977; Edward Keenan 1972, 1976).[6] This research inspired some linguists to look at texts of various sorts to establish the basic word order in a language and its relation to other syntactic and discourse phenomena. More or less at the same time, a group of sociologists soon to be known as "conversation analysts" became interested in the sequential aspects of conversational exchanges as the loci where the constitution of the social order could be studied without what they saw as the pitfalls of classical normative sociology, namely, without the *a priori* acceptance of such concepts as social role, social class, social situation (see chapter 8). Conversation and discourse analysts showed that, contrary to what was argued up to that point by formal grammarians working on isolated sentences, it was possible to engage in a systematic study of the language of conversational interaction.

Within psycholinguistics, language acquisition studies had often been based on discourse and interactional exchanges between children and adults, but this method was seen more as imposed by the circumstances (it was difficult if not impossible to do experiments on very young infants) than as a conscious and happy choice among researchers. In the 1970s, however, child language researchers also became influenced by conversation analysis and began to investigate new types of units, including certain types of interactional routines for grabbing the floor (e.g. *you know what?*, *look!* in English, *¡mira!* in Spanish), maintaining a topic, and building coherence (Ervin-Tripp 1973, Ervin-Tripp and Mitchell-Kernan 1977; Garvey 1984; McTear 1985; Ochs and Schieffelin 1983). It was in this new intellectual climate that discourse analysis gained a momentum and was established as a legitimate field of inquiry, giving birth to several symposia, collections of articles, and journals. Although linguistic anthropologists, given their interest in native texts, narrative, and performance, had been doing discourse analysis all along, they had done so mostly in a theoretical vacuum. This became an occasion

---

[6] For a more recent collection of articles on language typology, see Shibatani and Bynon (1995).

for some of them to reenter the mainstream of linguistic research without losing their identification with language as part of culture.

In later chapters, I will discuss some of these contributions to our understanding of language as a cultural practice. In what follows I will concentrate on the issue of how stretches of discourse can be collected and represented.

5.4 Standards of acceptability

Given linguistic anthropologists' interest in lengthy, spontaneously produced verbal exchanges, the issue arises as to how to collect samples of lengthy exchanges. A linguist interested in collecting grammatical forms, for example, might elicit **monologic discourse** – that is, a narrative performed by a native speaker for the linguist in front of a tape recorder – or **imagined interactional exchanges**. Although such imagined exchanges may be useful for certain types of linguistic analysis, they cannot be used as hard evidence of actual interactional strategies or, more generally, of patterns of language use. We have sufficient experience with spontaneous verbal interaction now to know that we cannot trust speakers' ability to *imagine* what they would say in a given situation nor can we expect them to *remember* exactly what they said in the past. Social scientists have shown again and again that memory is extremely selective and shaped by the future as much as by the past. Even the most skilled observers may miss or misinterpret what might turn out to be important properties of an exchange. In asking a native speaker to produce an imagined exchange, we are likely to get an **idealized exchange**, which might be accurate in some respects but unreliable in others.

In their analysis of different levels of respect in Nahuatl, Hill and Hill (1978) showed that reported conversations offer poor models of how speakers may show respect to one another. In one of the interviews they collected, a priest reporting what he had said to the president of his community kept alternating among level I ("intimate"), II ("distant"), and III ("honorable") in his use of address forms (pronouns, personal names, titles) and verbal agreement:

> This may in fact be what happens when an ordinary parishioner is
> transformed into a person of high status; but we have never
> observed this kind of random variation in actual conversations,
> which almost always display a very stable level of usage, with any
> deviation being fairly easy to explain on contextual grounds.
>
> (Hill and Hill 1978: 132)

There are also certain types of features of an interaction that simply cannot be reproduced during elicitation or in a report about an exchange in which the speaker participated. Examples of such phenomena are **pauses** and **overlaps**, which are absent in idealized exchanges.[7] As has been convincingly shown by conversation analysts, pauses and overlaps are interactionally important phenomena (Sacks, Schegloff, and Jefferson 1974). Their exact place of occurrence and their relative length provide information that is used by participants to interpret what is going on, decide whether to produce further talk, and, if so, of what nature (see chapter 8). Equally important are the re-starts, cut-offs, and other corrections that speakers make of their own talk. A transcript that reflects so-called **false starts** and other apparent "mistakes" may reveal a recurrent organization of such phenomena that is relevant for participants' understanding of each other's past actions and their expectations for future actions (Goodwin 1981). Thus, for instance, Schegloff (1979b) has shown that people regularly correct themselves (he uses the term **self-repair** for this phenomenon) when they introduce a new topic in conversation. The position of the **corrected** (or **repaired**) item is typically at the word that keys the **new topic**. Here are two examples:[8]

(6) B: That's too bad ((very quiet))
    A: hhh!
      (0.5)
-> B: (I `unno) `hh Hey do **you** see V- (0.3) fat ol' Vivian anymouh?
    A: No, hardly, en if we do:, y'know, I jus' say hello quick'n `hh
          y'know jus' pass each othuh in the ₍e hall(way).₎ still handing
    B: [Is she   ]
        aroun' (with) Bo:nny?

(7) B: `hh But it's not too bad, `hh
    A: That's goo₍d, ((very quiet))
-> B: [Diyuh have any-cl- **You** have a class with Billy this
        te:rm?
    A: Yeh he's in my abnormal class.
    B: mn Yeh ₍ how-]
    A: [Abnor]mal psy-ch

The recording of actual conversations and the careful transcription of the utterances exchanged during such conversations reveal regularities that deserve analytical attention. How are corrections organized? Why are they recurrent in certain types of discourse environments? How common are they crossculturally? These

---

[7] For example, overlaps cannot occur when a dialogue is performed by one speaker.
[8] The relevant segments, with the new topic being introduced are the following (in simplified form):
    (6)' B: Hey did you see V- (0.3) fat ol' Vivian anymore?
    (7)' B: Did you have any cl- You have a class with Billy this term?

same questions can be asked about other interactional phenomena such as overlaps and silences (see chapter 8). Their theoretical importance in understanding human interaction across social contexts cannot be evaluated without a good documentation of their occurrence.

The work of conversation analysts with audio and video recordings of ordinary English conversational interactions in the last three decades has introduced new **standards of acceptability** not so much for what a transcript should look like – their conventions are certainly not immune to criticism (see below) – but for the kind of evidence that researchers need to substantiate a claim about patterns of language use. Studies exclusively based on recollections or occasional observations of speech patterns seem no longer acceptable. New standards must apply to old studies as well. Scholars who quote earlier studies should review the research methods used by the authors they cite to establish whether the evidence presented in the past would hold up in the present. Unfortunately, not everyone who writes about conversational exchanges is careful about reviewing the research methods used by the authors they quote. A careful examination of many of the now classic studies of face-to-face communication published in the 1970s will reveal that for some time, linguistic anthropologists, like many of their colleagues in other branches of anthropology and linguistics, did not feel obliged to give information on how they collected the data discussed in their published work (or perhaps editors and publishers found this information trivial and not worth occupying printed pages). Even in those few cases in which authors openly discuss their methods, such discussions were not adequately attended to by readers and colleagues. For instance, despite the fact that in her influential study of greetings among the Wolof, Judith Irvine states at the very beginning of the article that she was unable to record greetings on tape,[9] most of the colleagues I talked to about the article believed that Irvine had audio tapes of the greetings. They had simply *assumed* that she did.

Without implying that one should throw away several decades of observations and speculations about face-to-face encounters that did not have the luxury of magnetic or electronic recording, it is imperative that new generations of researchers learn to read past contributions in the light of current standards of acceptablity. Particular attention should be given to passages in which fieldworkers describe the conditions under which the study was conducted. When such information is not available, one should try to contact the writer. If this is not possible, extreme care should be exercised in generalizing from descriptions

---

[9] "It proved difficult to persuade informants to act out hypothetical greeting situations for my benefit, and difficult ever to record greetings on tape (hence the 'typical' greeting I have illustrated on p. 171 is a construct of my own experience rather than a recorded text)" (Irvine 1974: 168).

that are not accompanied by a discussion of the methods used in collecting the information presented in the article.

5.5 Transcription formats and conventions

I will hereafter use the term *transcription* for the process of **inscribing** social action and *transcript* for the finished, although by no means definitive, product of such a process. Following Ricoeur's formulation (1971), I will consider inscribing a process whereby some of the characteristics of an action in real time and space (e.g. something someone said) are fixed into a record that will outlast the fleeting moment of real-life performance.

> In living speech, the instance of discourse has the character of a fleeting event. The event appears and disappears. This is why there is a problem of fixation of inscription. What we want to fix is what disappears. (Ricoeur [1971]1981: 198)

Although transcription has been largely used for fixing vocal sounds into graphic representations, in a transcript there are no *a priori* reasons to favor speech over other forms of communication. As I will show later, the more we learn about representing other aspects of communicative behavior, the more we realize how important it is to develop ways of integrating the analysis of speech with other codes and other modes of communication.

Any kind of inscription is, by definition, *an abstraction in which a complex phenomenon is reduced to some of its constitutive features and transformed for the purpose of further analysis.*[10] This applies to alphabets as much as to photographs, X-rays, or any kind of measurement. What changes in each medium is not only the instrument used but also the relationship between the form of representation (writing, black-and-white images, numbers on a scale) and the phenomenon that is being represented through the inscription technology. Thus, when we write on a piece of paper a phrase that someone just said, we are creating a record of his live action of speaking (for a purpose and for an audience) exclusively as a linguistic token, which can be later examined and compared to other similar linguistic tokens either in the same or in different codes. In so doing, we are performing two important analytical operations involving different levels of abstractions:

a) *Selection.* We are concentrating only on a very small subset of the actions the speaker performed. Thus, we are leaving out other aspects of what the speaker was doing, for instance, with his body (eyes, mouth, hands, etc.). We are also ignoring the prior, simultaneous, or subsequent acts that he and the other

---

[10] The reason for speaking of "*further* analysis" is that transcription is itself a form of analysis.

participants in the scene performed, including further talk that might be relevant to the one segment we decided to make a record of.

b) *Simplification.* We are simplifying the speaker's performance by ignoring certain features of his speech and presenting an abstraction of it that is theoretically informed (some like to call it "biased"). Thus, when we look at an utterance as represented by a spectrogram, we realize that sounds are not as separate as they appear when we write them down. Typically, in casual conversation, there are no spaces (or pauses) between most words that form the same utterance. Linguists have thus been relying on intonation as one of the indicators of discourse units – Chafe (1987), for instance, has introduced the term **intonational units**. Furthermore, the features of what we consider one sound may spread over several sounds, making it difficult to say where one sound starts and where it ends.

The issue here, as always in representation, is the relevance of the information we decide to reproduce on a piece of paper or on a computer disk for a particular purpose. As Ochs (1979) reminds us, the choices we make in preparing a transcript are always influenced by theoretical as well as pragmatic considerations – e.g. readability (see my rendition of Schegloff's example in footnote 8 above). In addition to the goals of the research agenda – a transcript should carefully represent what is of theoretical interest to the author –, there are what we might call aesthetic considerations. A transcript should not have too much information, otherwise it becomes too unpleasant to read and defies one of its purposes, namely, being accessible to others (Ochs 1979: 44–45). A transcript should be inviting, that is, it should make readers feel like they want to read it. Visual display and conventionality have, for this reason, an important part in transcription. Transcripts done according to conventions that are unknown to most people or seem unintuitive do not look appealing and readers are more likely to skip them. This possibility always lingers over the choice between conventional orthography and phonetic symbols. The advantage of using conventional orthography is that it is accessible to a much larger audience. The problem with it is that it comes with a set of prescriptive assumptions about what a language should be like and makes it difficult to represent how it is actually spoken. If one looks at a transcript like the one given in (8) below, it is difficult to imagine what the speaker sounded like, but it is very readable given that there are only a few extra conventions that a reader must learn, mostly about pauses (between square brackets or with two periods) and lengthened sounds (the symbol "–"):

(8) Okay. The movie seemed very [.25] sound oriented [.4] Even
though there weren't [.6] there was no dialogue. [3.5] [1.5] A–nd
[1.3] the first [.75] thing I noticed ... was ... the sound of the man
picking ... pears. (Chafe 1980: 304)

There is, however, a major problem in using standard orthography, namely, that it serves best speakers of the standard dialect – which is after all the variety that the writing system is designed to represent. Speakers of other varieties are implicitly characterized as deviant, proportionally to the number of modifications necessary to represent their speech. Thus, the most used convention in the next transcript – from an interview with a Black teenager – is the apostrophe (') to signal that a sound expected in Standard English is missing.

> (9) LARRY: You know, like some people say if you're good an'
> shit, your spirit goin' t'heaven ... 'n' if you bad,
> your spirit goin' to hell. Well, bullshit! Your spirit
> goin' to hell anyway, good or bad.
> INTERVIEWER: Why?
> LARRY: Why? I'll tell you why. 'Cause, you see, doesn'
> nobody really know that it's a God, y'know, 'cause
> I mean I have seen black gods, pink gods, white
> gods, all color gods, and don't nobody know it's
> really a God. An' when they be sayin' if you good,
> you goin' t'heaven, that's bullshit, 'cause you ain't
> goin' to no heaven, 'cause it ain't no heaven for
> you to go to. (Labov 1972c: 194)

Given the potential implications of using modified standard orthography, sociolinguists like William Labov who work on non-standard dialects must constantly stress that what they are transcribing is just *another language* and not an impoverished one. After the passage reproduced here in (9), Labov (1972c: 194) goes on to write: "Larry is a paradigmatic speaker of nonstandard Negro English (NNE) as opposed to standard English (SE)." Needless to say, the issue of what a given dialect or language is called can be highly controversial. This can be quite an issue in some cases, for instance, in Native America, where people might insist on a nomenclature that is not attested in previous literature (Jane Hill, personal communication).

Another problem with standard orthography is that it does not do justice to certain paralinguistic phenomena, including **sound play**,[11] and in this way precludes the possibility of generalizations on such phenomena (Ochs 1979: 45).

Alphabets that have been developed by phoneticians have the advantage of building on traditional orthography but favoring actual pronunciation. In

---

[11] "The use of standard orthography is based on the assumption that utterances are pieces of information, and this, in turn, assumes that language is used to express ideas. In sound play, the shape rather than the content of utterances is foregrounded and the function of language is playful and phatic ... rather than informative" (Ochs 1979: 45).

principle, they do not come with preconceptions about which particular pronunciation is the standard or unmarked one. One such alphabet is the one developed
by the International Phonetic Association (IPA), which has enough symbols to
systematically cover the total range of linguistic sounds found in natural languages (Pullum and Ladusaw 1986). Anyone who is familiar with the IPA symbols
should be able to read them, without having to know anything about the language
that is being transcribed.[12] Computer technology with different fonts available
on the same screen has made it easier to have access to such alphabets, but their
use is still limited to people who have had an extensive training in phonetics or
linguistics. As shown in example (10), the knowledge of the Latin alphabet or
English orthography is not sufficient (although it helps!) to guess what the symbols
represent (Ladefoged 1975: 161).

> (10)   æplslɛmənsəntʃɛriz

Once we are told that (10) represents something that in English orthography
would be written *apples, lemons, and cherries*, things start to get a bit clearer. If
we try to make it easier by separating the phonetic symbols into "words," we
encounter a classic problem of transcription, namely, the need to make decisions
that seem arbitrary at first. In this case, for instance, it is difficult to decide on
pre-theoretical grounds where to break the sequence əntʃɛriz "and cherries,"
given that the sound "t" in a sense belongs to both "and" and "cherries" – one
could either say that the "d" of *and* has become "t" for assimilation to the next
sound (tʃ) or say that it just disappeared. The final choice should be determined
by our phonological theory, that is, the kind of phonological processes we consider common in languages in general and in one language in particular.

> (10)'   æpls   lɛməns   ən   tʃɛriz
>   apples   lemons   and   cherries

To avoid some of these problems, most people working on spontaneous interaction end up adopting the compromise of adapting traditional orthographies to
their descriptive and theoretical needs. There are, however, different ways of
doing this, from very conservative to experimental. For instance, in conversation
analysis, English orthographic conventions are adapted to reproduce some stylistic and vernacular properties of the participants' speech:

> (11)   KEN: Hey yuh took my chair by the way an' I don't think that was
>   very nice.

---

[12] This does not mean that from the symbols alone a reader would be able to sound like a
native speaker or like the person whose speech is being represented. There are still considerable limitations to the amount of information that can be encoded on alphabetic
representations of sounds.

AL: *I* didn' take yer chair, it's *my* chair.

(from Sacks, Schegloff, and Jefferson 1978: 28)

The problem encountered in (10) with the word *and* is resolved in (11), just like in (9), by writing *an'*, a convention that most speakers (and readers) of English are likely to understand. In some cases, however, the adaptations of English orthography are harder to interpret for those who are not practitioners of this method. Thus, the forms *yuh* and *yer*, two forms that are often used by conversation analysts, represent fast vernacular pronunciations of "you" and "your" respectively that are not so obvious to most readers of English. Things get more obscure with words like *does* and *was*, which are often transcribed by conversation analysts as *dz* and *wz* respectively. In this case, readers must guess that the letters "d" and "z" have syllabic value [d̥z̩] otherwise the sequence would be interpreted as a voiced alveolar affricate (e.g. the first sound of the Italian word *zebra* [dzebra] or in the last sound of the English *lads* [lædz]). Although a native English speaker may at times guess what conversation analysts' choices mean, the lack of internationally available conventions make these renditions much less accessible to readers who are non-native speakers of English. In transcripts like the one in (12) below, the adaptation of English orthography to phonetic transcription is carried to an extreme by marking as special pronunciations those that are quite predictable, such as *iz* for *is* or *he'z* for *he's*. Since the "s" of *is* is typically pronounced voiced ([z]) – see chapter 6 – by native speakers, it is hard to understand the reason for changing its ordinary spelling. The question here is whether a phonetic feature that is predictable from general rules of the orthography should be marked (cf. Edwards and Lampert 1993; Macaulay 1991a; 1991b: 24).

(12)   F: 'hh how iz our fri::end
        N: Oh: he'z much better I'm, 'fraid –
              ⌈hh h h h
        F: ⌊Well uh that's *mar*verlous   (Pomerantz 1984: 96)

Although for most readers these transcripts are still more accessible than those in IPA format, they require familiarity with their mostly implicit conventions.[13] Usually they turn out to be excellent mnemonic devices for those who have listened to the transcribed interaction a sufficient number of times to imitate them, but they are baffling to everyone else.

One of the issues in this as well as in other transcription systems is the

---

[13] For a list of conventions used by conversation analysts, see Atkinson and Heritage (1984:ix–xvi), M. H. Goodwin (1990:25–6). These lists do not provide hints on how to read the phonetic conventions.

audience for whom the transcript is produced (Haugen 1980; Macaulay 1991b: 24). Since a transcript is going to be quite different depending on who is seen as its primary audience, we must make conscious and consistent choices. This does not mean that once we opt for one system we cannot change our mind later on. What is important is to follow a criterion that is consistent with our priorities and that can be understood by our readers. Thus, if we are concerned with the ability of native speakers and other people who know the language (especially other social scientists who do not have a linguistic training) to read our transcripts, we might opt for adapting standard orthography to our needs. At the same time, we must be aware that the choice of standard orthography may also cut out some readers or misguide them. This is particularly so for languages that are not likely to be known by most of our readers. My decision, for instance, to follow Samoan orthography in my transcripts and use the letter "g" for the velar nasal ŋ, which is otherwise written "ng" in most orthographies, has meant that almost no one among my colleagues or students remembers that the word written *lāuga* ("ceremonial speech") is pronounced [la:uŋa] – everyone keeps saying [lauga]. The fact that I always have a footnote or paragraph explaining Samoan orthographic conventions in my publications does not seem sufficient, even with linguistically sophisticated readers. Rather than blaming my readers, I should probably rethink the ways I have been trying to communicate with them. I mention this piece of personal history to stress the fact that *the process of transcribing implies a process of socialization of our readers to particular transcribing needs and conventions.* We must decide what is important for us to communicate in our transcripts and devise effective strategies to such ends. For this reason, a transcript that is devised for personal use only will be different from one that we plan to present at a conference or publish. In publishing a transcript, we might need to amplify a certain type of information while simplifying in other areas. The ephemeral character of any version of a transcript is made more apparent in those cases in which researchers move over time to investigate different aspects or different levels of the same exchange. We might then get not only different versions of the same transcripts in different subsequent publications, but also different versions within the same article. This is for instance the case in Goodwin and Goodwin's (1992a) discussion of assessments, where the different layers of interactional complexity of a brief exchange are made evident through slight modifications of the same transcript. I will reproduce here the first four versions (there are a total of eight in the article):

(13)　　(Version I, Goodwin and Goodwin 1992a: 161)
　　　　DIANNE:　　**Jeff** made en asparagus pie
　　　　　　　　　　it wz s::**so: goo**:d.

(13)'   (Version II, ibid., p. 163)

    D I A N N E: **Jeff** made en asparagus pie

                it wz s::**so**[: **goo**:d.

    –> C L A C I A: I love it.

(13)"   (Version III, ibid., p. 166)

    D I A N N E: **Jeff** made en asparagus pie

                it wz s::**so**[: **goo**:d.

    C L A C I A: I love   it.

                  L____| L_|

                ((nod   nod))

(13)'"   (Version IV, ibid., p. 168)

                    ((lowers   *((nod with*

                    upper   *eyebrow*

                    trunk))   *flash))*

                    __|____   __|___

    D I A N N E: it waz s : : **so**[:   **goo**:d.

    C L A C I A: I love   it.

                  L____| L____|

                ((nod   nod))

Although this technique would not be practical for transcripts that cover several minutes or hours of conversational interaction,[14] it does offer a powerful representation of the analytical process the researchers went through while examining different aspects of the information made available to them in the recording (in this case a video tape).

For transcripts of long stretches of interaction, gestures can be incorporated by extending the use of the bracket originally introduced by conversation analysts for overlapping talk. Such a technique has been used by Ochs, Jacoby, and Gonzales (1994) in transcripts such as the following:

(14) S T U D E N T: [And let me tell you (0.2) there's something (.)

                  [((*moves toward board; adjusts glasses*))

                  mo:re I can say: mtsk is [that that (0.2) those gu-

                                        [((*points to j*))

---

[14] At least not in traditional print. It becomes more feasible with the help of computer technology.

143

that dynamics starts (0.5) not at the moment you
[read this point (0.5)   [but   [at the moment
[((*points to b, looks at PI*))   [((*looks at board*))
                                      [((*points to a*))

(Ochs, Jacoby, and Gonzales 1994: 153)

As Ochs (1979) points out, the visual display of a transcript has important implications and consequences for the way in which readers will process the information and assess the importance of different elements.

The traditional bias in favor of speech and against non-verbal behavior – reflected in the term itself with its negative definition (non-verbal is anything that is *not* verbal) – is something that has become more and more apparent with the increased use of video technology and the richness of the audio-visual display. Researchers are learning to integrate in their representations information available to the interactants but earlier on only grossly recorded in their fieldnotes.

5.6   Visual representations other than writing

Although in face-to-face encounters talk often dominates interaction, a transcript that only shows what people have been saying may leave out some important aspects of what was happening at the time among the participants. However, the kinds of transcripts I have been discussing so far were designed to represent speech and not other forms of communication or social action. Anyone who has tried to represent on a page what people actually do in a stretch of face-to-face interaction knows that traditional orthography is indeed a very poor medium for representing visual communication, not to mention the physical surroundings of the interaction. Verbal descriptions of what people do rarely capture the meaningful subtleties of human action. Furthermore, by transforming non-talk into talk, verbal descriptions reproduce the dominance of speech over other forms of human expression before giving us a chance to assess how non-linguistic elements of the context participate in their own, unique ways, to the constitution of the activity under examination. In many cases, it is still true that a picture is worth a thousand words. Students' reactions to slides and footage of a landscape or social event often reveal how misled they had been by printed words. For instance, there is a big difference between describing what the outside or the inside of a house looks like and seeing an image of it. In some cases, previous ideas about what an event might look like prevent readers from accurately processing what an author might have written. Until they saw a video tape of a Samoan *fono*, some of my students believed that the chiefs would be standing around during such a meeting. To see everyone seated along the periphery of the house was a shock to them.

Several methods have been used by social scientists over the years to visually enhance the printed rendition of fleeting moments of interaction. Each method is grounded in a different tradition and reveals different theoretical interests. I will here briefly concentrate on two traditions: the representation of gestures and the representation of participants' visual access to each other and to their surrounding environment.

5.6.1 Representations of gestures

> Actio quasi sermo corporis.
> Cicero, *De oratore* 3, 222[15]

At least since Darwin's interest in human gestures as a source of insights into human evolution (Darwin 1965), anthropologists, human ethologists, and other social scientists have been fascinated with the issue of the universality vs. cultural relativity of gestures and expressions (Bremmer and Roodenburg 1992; Eibl-Eibesfeldt 1970; Polhemus 1978). Anthropologists have been drawn to this discussion for a number of reasons, including the need to provide an accurate description of communicative events.

Sociocultural and linguistic anthropologists have long been aware of the need to complement traditional ethnographic accounts based on naked-eye observation with more precise and detailed descriptions based on more reliable forms of documentation. Gregory Bateson, for instance, in his "Epilogue 1936" to *Naven* – an ethnography of the Iatmul people of New Guinea that has since become a classic of social anthropology – regretted that he had been forced to use vague and inadequate descriptions of the expressive behavior or "tone," as he called, of social actors: "Until we devise techniques for the proper recording and analysis of human posture, gesture, intonation, laughter, etc. we shall have to be content with journalistic sketches of the 'tone' of behaviour" (Bateson 1958: 276).

Thanks to the work of visual anthropologists, ethnographic filmmakers, ethologists, and visually oriented linguistic anthropologists, the recording and analysis of human gestures have lately become more and more common in anthropological studies.

It is now universally accepted that in face-to-face interaction what humans say to one another must be understood vis-à-vis what they do with their body and where they are located in space (e.g. Birdwhistell 1970; Farnell 1995; Goodwin 1984; Goodwin and Goodwin 1992a, 1992b; Hall 1959, 1966; Kendon 1973, 1977, 1990, 1993; Kendon, Harris and Key 1975; Leach 1972; Schegloff 1984; Streeck 1988, 1993, 1994; Streeck and Hartge 1992). This means that one of the greatest challenges in representing gestures is not just to reproduce a particular posture

[15] "Delivery (is), in a way, the language of the body" (see Graf 1992: 53).

or movement, which can be done with a series of drawings, but how to visually maintain on a page the connection with co-occurring talk. The recurrent inter-penetration of verbal and visual communication in everyday interaction has been at the center of some of the work recently done by linguistic anthropologists working with audio-visual records.

In an attempt to extend the boundaries of conversation analysis beyond verbal communication, Goodwin (1979, 1981) introduced a series of conventions that were explicitly designed to integrate information on eye-gaze patterns with sequences of turns at talk. In the following segment, for instance, Goodwin (1979, 1981: 131–3) tries to visually capture the relationship between the reshaping of an utterance as the speaker's eye gaze moves from one participant to another.

(15)   (Goodwin 1979, 1981)

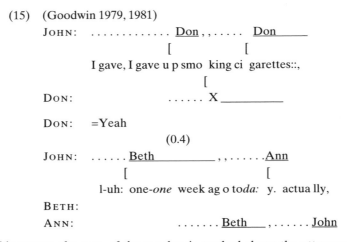

In this system, the gaze of the speaker is marked above the utterance and the recipient(s) below it. Dots mark movement of one party's gaze from one partici-pant to another. A solid line indicates gaze by one party toward the other. Commas indicate the withdrawing of gaze. By means of these conventions, Goodwin is able to show how the utterance produced by John (*I gave up smok-ing cigarettes one week ago today actually*) is shaped by (a) whether the selected recipient makes eye contact with the speaker (John changes the utterance in moving from one recipient to the next and finally adds an adverb *actually* which allows enough time for Ann to gaze back at him) and (b) the extent to which and the manner in which the recipient knows the event reported by the speaker (Beth is John's wife and already knows about John's attempt to give up smoking, hence his attempt to make the announcement into an anniversary by saying *one week ago*).

In his comparative study of the symbolic structuration of space and movement by members of two different speech communities, Haviland (1996) uses a combination of transcription, verbal description of gestures, and figures to illustrate how, in telling a story, Guugu-Yimithirr speakers keep track of cardinal points – this ability and practice make their orientation system more "absolute" than "relative" (Haviland 1996: 285).

. . . . ! . . . .

mathi   *past-manaathi*
rain + ABS past-become-Past
"The rain had passed over."

     right hand: palm out, pulled towards E then
          push out W, slight drop.

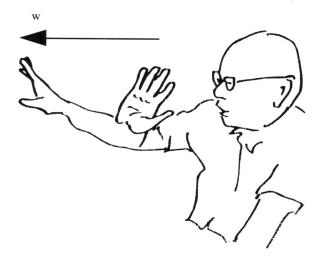

Figure 5.2 Text and picture of storytelling episode (I)
(Haviland 1996: 310)

...!..................................

and yuwalin   *nguumbaarr*   *guthiirra*   *nhaathi*
    beach-LOC   shadow + ABS   two + ABS   see-PAST
                             gadaariga
                         come + RED-PAST-SUB
"and (he) could see two shadows coming along the beach."
              right-hand: pointing with straight arm W,
                    moving S to rapid drop to lap.

Figure 5.3 Text and picture of storytelling (II) (Haviland 1996: 311)

In these and other cases, linguistic anthropologists have been particularly interested in the unique ways in which gestures that accompany or replace talk contribute to the flow of interaction and rely on the participants' shared knowledge. In her study of Plains Indian Sign Talk and other gestures that are an integral part of Nakota (or Assiniboine) narratives, for example, Brenda Farnell characterized the use of the lips in place of the pointing index – a gesture that is common among many Native American communities (e.g. Sherzer 1973) – as a gesture that provides participants in an exchange with a sense of intimacy and shared history:

> The performative value of this gesture lies in its potential for discretion as a smaller and less obvious gesture, often serving to preserve a degree of intimacy between speaker and addressee that would be lost if a finger-pointing gesture or speech were used instead. (Farnell 1995: 158)

To capture the complex and yet systematic relation between speech, gestures, and space, Farnell uses the Laban script (or Labanotation), a complex system of symbols invented by Rudolph Laban (1956) to describe dance movements. This system of transcription allows Farnell to match words (on the left column) with actions on the right column.

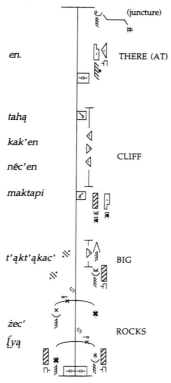

ĺyą   žec',   t'ąkt'ąkac' maktapi néc'en   kak'en tahą, en.
Rocks   there   big cliffs [cut edge] this   over there   at
"There are large rocks that form a cliff, over there."

Figure 5.4 Transcription in the Laban script of Plains Indian Sign talk
(Farnell 1995: 94)

Another transcription system for body motion and for prosodic and paralinguistic aspects of talk was devised by Birdwhistell (1970), a pioneer in kinesics, the study of how humans use their body for communicating. These graphic conventions are particularly valuable to the analysts for seeing patterns in their data but remain difficult to decode for the reader without intense training and practice.

As frequently lamented by those who work on gestures, the relatively little attention that gestures have had compared to speech in the study of human communication continues a tradition of research that identifies the basic structure of communicative acts with grammatical units. This is only partly due to technological limitations or to the recognized centrality of speech in human societies. It is also a consequence of an ideology of communicative events that takes writing (and hence texts) as the highest form of human communication and iconic representations as less sophisticated (Farnell 1995: ch. 2). Writing (especially alphabetic writing), however, is more adequate for the structural analysis of segmentable sound sequences (see section 5.1) than for other forms of communication, especially gestures.

5.6.2   Representations of spatial organization and participants' visual access
Video and computer technologies are rapidly making the task of analyzing and documenting the interplay of speech and gesture much easier. For example, it is possible now to represent the spatial organization of an interaction and the participants' visual access to one another by transfering to the page (or the computer screen) a video image. This can be done by digitizing a frame taken from a video tape. Figures 5.6 and 5.7, for instance, show very different forms of participation in the same narrative event. In 5.6, the man on the left (M) is a **peripheral participant** – a term I am borrowing from Lave and Wenger (1991) –, who listens to the story being told by the woman at the table (R) but is not directly involved in the narration. In 5.7, on the other hand, we can see R the narrator (on the left, smiling) directly address and get sympathetic response from the woman on the far right, D, whom she identifies as her primary recipient by her gaze and body position (she is facing and addressing her among the various participants).

Figure 5.5. The man standing on the left (M) listens to R's story as a peripheral participant

Figure 5.6. A funny line gets a laugh from the story's primary recipient (D)

5.6.3   Integrating text, drawings, and images

Despite their power to communicate the feeling of a fleeting moment in ways that an audio recording or linguistic transcript could never do, images like the two above still do not have in them much of the information that is available to the participants and that researchers might find relevant to their analysis. For instance, camcorders do not record people's names or social relations unless the participants themselves refer to them in their talk. They also do not show a 360° view of the setting and where everyone in the scene is located with respect to one another. In addition to frames like the two above, then, it can be useful at times to display for the reader a diagram with some of the information that is not available in the video or on the sound track. Figure 5.7 shows an example of how a computer graphic program can be used to represent the seating arrangement of the participants around the table and the kinship relations among them (for a similar technique, see Goodwin and Goodwin 1992b).

When we match the information in figure 5.7 with the visual record and the transcript of what is being said – a narrative about R's first encounter with her mother-in-law some thirty something years earlier –, we are in a better position to make sense of the organization of this event. I, for instance, is often integrating R's story with comments and clarifications, which he addresses to P, right across from him. He also anticipates some of what R is about to say. Once we put together the information that I and R are husband and wife with the theme of R's narrative, for instance, we can better understand the ways in which I participates in the event. He is the only one in the scene who had independent access to the events and characters R is telling about in her story. In some moments, in fact, he is one of the characters of R's narrative. These features warrant his participation as an ideal *co-narrator* but not as a *primary recipient* – he already knows the story (see chapter 9).[16] We can also see some differences between D and P, on the one hand, and D and M on the other that might help us make sense of R's choice of D as her primary recipient. D is R's only female affine in the scene. This means first of all that she is less likely than P to have already heard R's story. Furthermore, her structural position is similar to R's position in her own story. D is a young woman who married into R's family. It might thus be easier for her to identify with R's position or perhaps better appreciate R's reactions to the treatment she received from her mother-in-law.

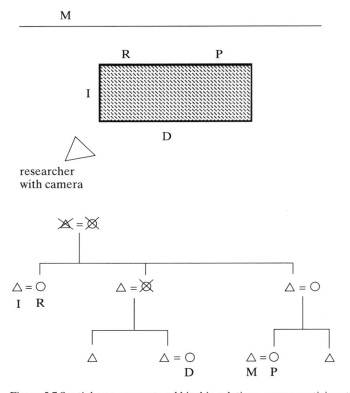

Figure 5.7 Spatial arrangement and kinship relations among participants in event shown in figures 5.5 and 5.6 above.

In performing this kind of analysis it is important to remember that whether or not certain facts about the participants will be relevant to whatever we have to say about what they say is not something that can be decided *a priori*. We cannot say once and for all that kinship is *always* important in social interaction or that

---

16 This does not mean that people do not tell each other stories they already know, because they do at times, but that when this happens the story is framed differently.

gender is (see section 8.3.2). There are moments when kinship (or some other social attribute such as gender, social class, ethnicity, profession) might not be relevant to what is going on. The relevance of different attributes or background knowledge participants have of one another is an empirical question that must be addressed on each occasion. At the same time, it should be obvious that having access to such background knowledge about the social actors in a scene opens up for the analyst a wealth of interesting questions which allow for more complex (or, in Geertz's terms, "thicker") accounts (see section 2.3.2). For one thing, new hypotheses are possible that could not be thought of before. This is indeed the strength of linguistic anthropology with respect to other approaches to the analysis of discourse: its commitment to finding appropriate ways of integrating the information on a transcript with other kinds of knowledge that is being shared or accessed by the participants.

Of course, when more ethnographic information is revealed about a particular context, we grow hungrier, that is, we want more. We are thus faced with the fact that unveiling cultural knowledge about the participants becomes a potentially endless process. Geertz was hinting at this aspect of doing ethnography when he told the by now famous "turtles" story:

> There is an Indian story – at least I heard it as an Indian story – about an Englishman who, having been told that the world rested on a platform which rested on the back of an elephant which rested in turn on the back of a turtle, asked (perhaps he was an ethnographer; it is the way they behave), what did the turtle rest on? Another turtle. And that turtle? "Ah, Sahib, after that it is turtles all the way down."
>
> Such, indeed, is the condition of things. ... Cultural analysis is intrinsically incomplete. (Geertz 1973: 28–9)

This property of cultural analysis is seen by some as discouraging. If we can never get near to the bottom of things, what kind of science are we engaged in? But this is precisely the distinctive feature of human life, namely, that there is a potentially infinite number of layers of meaning in what we do. In fact, if our science is to look into such layers, our science is included in what we study – it is intrinsically reflexive (Luhmann 1981) – and therefore our science is just as infinite as the object of our study. The issue is not how to avoid getting into the potentially infinite layers, but how to find order in them, sometimes an order that is similar to the one proposed by the participants themselves, some other times a different order, that would be alien or even appalling to them. Once more, the difference among different approaches to social interaction lies in the ways in which each discipline moves along the different interpretive paths. Rather than

restricting their analytic boundaries to specific forms (as grammarians and conversation analysts often do) or to specific contents (as psychologists often do),
linguistic anthropologists are interested in exploring ways of integrating information made available through a *variety of interpretive procedures*, including
traditional participant-observation and fieldnotes, drawings, digitized images,
transcripts with translations, and kinship charts.

5.7 Translation

> Let me start with the apparently paradoxical and yet perfectly plain and
> absolutely true proposition that the words of one language are never
> translatable into another. (Malinowski 1935, vol. 2: 11)

Most linguistic anthropologists work on languages other than their native language and must present what is recorded on a tape to an audience who is not likely
to know the language spoken by the participants in the interaction. This means
that for many linguistic anthropologists an important part of preparing a transcript consists of **translating**. This activity involves more than going from one
language to another. It implies a long series of interpretations and decisions that
are rarely made apparent in the final product, which might just look like another
line of text. In fact, as Malinowski theorized a long time ago (1923), translation
assumes an ability to match words with the context in which they were uttered. It
is an activity that for anthropologists is intimately linked to ethnography. It
implies an understanding not only of the immediate context but also of more
general assumptions, such as a people's worldview, including their ways of relating the use of language with social action. If we conceive of translation as the
mere exercise of matching words or phrases in one language with those of another,
we are likely to miss one of the main contributions of the anthropological study
of language, namely, the idea that for anthropologists the activity of translating
is intimately related to ethnography, to the contextualization of words within the
activity and the larger sociopolitical and cultural systems in which their speakers
participate.

Translation starts in the field, when the linguistic anthropologist works at producing an **annotated transcript** (Schieffelin 1979, 1990). The annotated transcript not only contains contextual notes written during the recording sessions
(see chapter 4), but all kinds of interpretative statements made during the transcription process. In preparing the transcripts of 83 hours of spontaneous speech
between Kaluli children and their mothers, siblings, relatives, and other villagers,
Schieffelin soon discovered that the mothers' comments on the tapes, including
their laughter at situations they found humorous, constituted an important
source of information on how they saw the situation. These comments, accompa-

nied by the interpretation produced by a male assistant who had not been present during the recording, were integrated in a transcript that had a lot more
than the words that had been exchanged among participants. It is transcripts of
this sort that provide the basis for future translations. Several techniques are
now available for keeping track of these on-going commentaries. The interaction with the knowledgeable participant/informant/research assistant can be
recorded on tape, hand notes can be written on the side of the transcription
pages, or (when a computer is being used) footnotes can be added to the text.

There are several formats for presenting transcripts with translation. All of the
formats I will present here are currently adopted by linguistic anthropologists and
each of them has different implications and consequences. The reason for discussing each one of them is to give readers an opportunity to judge which method
is best suited to their needs. There is no such a thing as a *perfect* transcript, but
there are transcripts that are *better* than others for certain specific needs!

Format I: Translation only.

The first format is to give the translation only. This is usually done when the
researcher wants to concentrate on the content of what was said or feels that the
original text might be unimportant or distracting. Here is an example from a
transcript of a segment of a Kuna ritual greeting between a chanting "chief"
(CC) and a responding "chief" (RC) inside the "gathering house":

(16) CC: Yes you appear as always.
      RC: Indeed.
      CC: In truth.
            You still appear.
            In good health.
      RC: Indeed.
      CC: In truth evil spirits.
            In truth I do not want.
            I utter.
      RC: Indeed.
      CC: Powerful evil spirits, see.
            Then I do not want them to enter.
      RC: Indeed.
      CC: Now I am still in good health, say.
            In truth still this way.
      RC: Indeed.   (Sherzer 1983: 75)

What is made apparent in this example is that even when only a translation is
provided the visual display of the text is still important in conveying a number of

important assumptions about how the material should be interpreted. In this case, the format assumes a notion of **line** and a notion of **verse**. As discussed by Sherzer in a separate chapter, "lines are marked grammatically by means of an elaborate set of line initial and line final affixes, words and phrases" as well as by syntactic and semantic parallelism and intonational patterns (Sherzer 1983: 41). Verses are identified – in Kuna as in American Indian oral narratives in general – "not by counting parts, but by recognizing repetition within a frame, the relation of putative units to each other within a whole" (Hymes 1981: 318). In other words, texts like the one in (16) above presuppose a fairly complex theory of local poetics, which the researcher must find ways to make explicit, whether in the same text or elsewhere. In some cases, linguistic anthropologists have been experimenting with printing conventions to convey in the translation some of the prosodic features of the original oral performance. Thus, Tedlock (1983) used capitals to mark what was said in a loud voice (a convention also used in other traditions), long dashes or repeated vowels to indicate lengthening, and different heights to convey tonal structure, with "spilling letters" indicating a glissando:

(17) The girl went inside and PUT MORE WOOD ON, the fire was really
      blazing, then it came CLOSER.
      It came closer
      calling
      hooooooooooooooooooooooooooohaaaaaaaaaaaaaaaaaa
                                                   a
                                                    a
                                                     a
                                                      a
                                                       y it said.
      The girl heard it very clearly now.   (Tedlock 1983: 84)

Although there is no question that having only the translation makes reading easier, one of the disadvantages of not having the text in the original language is that other researchers are not given an opportunity to validate or question the author's decisions in the translation process. This is the reason for most linguistic anthropologists to go against the wishes of journal editors and printing presses and argue for the need to present both the text in the original language and the translation. There are several ways of doing this.

Format II. Original and subsequent (or parallel) free translation.
This format is designed to maintain the unity of the text in each language. In (18), for example, the two versions are placed next to each other, with an attempt to maintain an horizontal parallelism.

(18) (Dispute at board meeting)
      Disputant:

1.	Lo que se NECESITA ...	What is NEEDED ...
2.	Yo soy de ese opinión.	I am of this opinion.
3.	A mí no me importa	It doesn't matter to me
4.	quien es usted,	who you are,
5.	de comisión o como	a board member or whatever
6.	quiera que SEA.	you want TO BE. (Briggs 1986: 78)

The use of line numbers helps the reader to compare the original text with the translation. An additional convention for long poetic lines is that of utilizing indentation, as proposed by Joel Kuipers in his transcription of Weyewa ritual speech:

(19)

oruta koki	gather the monkeys	1
ta kalunga	in the field	2
ka ta mandi'i teppe,	so that we can sit on the mat,	3
wandora-na wawi	summon the pigs	4
ta maredda	in the meadow	5
kai terrena pa-mama;	so that you get the quid;	6
	(Kuipers 1990: xvi)	

In this variation on this format, "lines one through three and four through six are each part of a single poetic line" (ibid.).

These formats continue to assume the notion of a "line" (see above) and are more apt for poetic and ritual speech, but awkward or more arbitrary for ordinary speech. Things are also made more complex by those cases in which the original is in a language with polysyllabic words and complex morphology. In these cases, translators are forced to split words arbitrarily and cannot maintain the parallelism between left and right side of the page:

(20) **S76:** Neh, solamente nimo-yōlcocoa para cē, para cē demanda, para cē crreclamarōz cē cosa īhuāxca, quihtōz, 'Pos xiquitta ōnēchcuilihqueh in noāx-noh.' 'Pos ¿quēn ōmitzcuilihqueh?' Pos ih-quīn huān ihquīn, [etc.]

As for me, I am sad only for such a, such a demand, for one who would claim something of his own, who will say, "Well look, they took away my donkey." "Well how did they take it away from you?" Well like this and like this, one is sad in his soul because they took it [etc.]

(Hill and Hill 1986: 86)

Transcription: from writing to digitized images

The logic here is that the authors want the readers to see the original text but are not expecting them to pick out which word is which just from the transcript. When they want to achieve such a goal, they must shift to a different format.

Format III. Parallel free translation and morpheme-by-morpheme[17] gloss under the original.

Hill and Hill use this format when they discuss specific grammatical processes. In the following example, for instance, it is important to see that the word *tlaxcal* "tortilla" has become part of the verb, that is, it has undergone the grammatical process called *noun-incorporation* (Mithun 1986; Sadock 1980):

(21)	ni-tlaxcal-	chīhua	"I am making tortillas"
	I TORTILLA	MAKE	(Hill and Hill 1986: 251)

In this case, the left side of the page gives the original text and, on a different line, a literal, in this case morpheme-by-morpheme translation, and the right side gives the free translation. The distinction between the two is important not only because the morpheme-by-morpheme translation may use different words from the free translation, but also because the words in the original language might have a different order from, in this case, English and might make a decoding based on word-by-word translation difficult. When the text is more than one line long, the parallel format becomes awkward and yet another format is advisable.

Format IV. Original, interlinear morpheme-by-morpheme gloss, and free translation.

This format utilizes three lines, one on top of the other, as shown in the following Samoan example:

(22) 523 *Mother:* `ua uma na `ē `ai?
    Pst finish Comp you eat
    "Have you finished eating?"

524 *Son:* ((nods))

525 *Mother:* alu ese lā`ia ma igā.
    go away then from there
    "Then get away from there."

526 *Son:* `o lea e sau e avaku le mea lea.
    Pred this TA come Comp take-Dx Art thing this
    "I've come here to take this thing."

(Duranti 1994: 156, slightly modified)

---

[17] For a discussion of morphemes, see section 6.4.

The words on the first line (with the original text) can be spaced in such a way to allow for a one-to-one match with the interlinear glosses on the second line. This format is particularly appropriate when the author wants readers to follow the translation process more closely. It is the standard format for most linguistics journals. Its only drawback is that it crowds the page with lots of written material and requires some time to get used to reading it.

The last two examples also show that word-by-word glosses imply a minimal level of grammatical description; they force the linguist to assign particular grammatical, functional, or denotative meanings to each morpheme in the text. Abbreviations such as "Pst" for "past tense," "Comp" for "complementizer," "Art" for "article," and "Dx" for deictic particle assume a theory of Samoan grammar that may not be the focus of the discussion but needs to be attended to before providing the glosses.

The exposure to these different formats is a necessary part of any linguistic anthropologist's training not only because students should get used to the different conventions, but also because in their work they need to be aware of the need for a format that, while meeting the current standards of the research community, can also fullfil their expository needs. In some cases, a *range of transcription formats* might be necessary within the same article or book, depending each time on the specific point made by the author(s). In some cases, if the researcher only wants to identify a morpheme or a word on a line of transcript, there might be no reason to gloss every word and attention to the linguistic form can be achieved by underlining or boldfacing. An example of this method is provided in (23) from a transcript of Tzotzil conversation in which the author, John Haviland, is examining the use of the particle *a`a*:

(23)   p: xlok' ono nan **a`a** yu`van
            Indeed there will be enough, of course.   (Haviland 1989: 45)

In this case the use of boldface points to the only linguistic feature the author wants the reader to focus on.

Other times, researchers might be faced with a situation that requires new conventions. In his study of language socialization in a multilingual village in Papua New Guinea, Don Kulick (1992) devised conventions that would make clear which language was being spoken at any given time. He used italics for words in Tok Pisin, italics and single underlining for the local vernacular, Taiap, and roman for the English translation. Underlining of the roman helps the reader keep track of which variety is being spoken by only following the English translation.

(24) Sopak: *Sia. ŋa ruru sɛnɛ ia*   Sia [exclamation]. <u>These two</u>
                 kirwmbri wakarɛ. ɛnd-   <u>poor kids I just don't know.</u>
                 ɛ karɛ, ɛndɛkarɛ [turns   <u>Hungry, hungry.</u> [turns to
                 to Mas] *mm. Masito.*   Mas] Mm. Masito.
                 Kisim spun i go givim papa   Take the spoon and go give it
                 [hands Mas a spoon] *Spun.*   to Papa. [hands Mas a spoon]
                                            Spoon.

                                                               (Kulick 1992: 203)

5.8 Non-native speakers as researchers

The question is at times raised outside of anthropology, especially among formal linguists working on their own language and conversation analysts working in their own society, about the feasibility of working on a language of which the researcher is not a native speaker and hence of the validity of generalizations made about meaning by non-native speakers. Although these doubts seem at first quite legitimate, they often start from the wrong assumptions.

One of the reasons to reject work that is not done by native speakers on their own language stems from the methodological preferences of the different researchers. Thus, for linguists working on native speakers' intuitions, it would seem very suspicious that a non-native speaker would make hypotheses on meaning. To this objection, there are two answers: (i) much of the work of linguistic anthropologists is *not* based on intuitions and introspection but more likely on correlations (tendency, for instance, for certain forms to appear in certain contexts); (ii) linguistic anthropologists rely heavily on native speaker's intuitions and judgment in preparing their transcript, that's what the concept of annotated transcript (see above) is about. Finally, it should be said that the assumption that a researcher–native speaker is the ideal condition is itself suspicious. It assumes that a native speaker has privileged access to theory building, hypotheses, and thick description. Although this might sometimes be the case, it goes against one of the tenets of anthropology, namely, the idea that one of the ways to describe culture is to look at it from both the inside and the outside. Whereas it is hard (and often impossible) for non-members to see things from the inside of the culture, it is equally hard for members to see things from the outside. The problem with many sociologists' view that one needs ethnography only or *especially* when working in another culture is based on the fact that when working on one's culture and within one's society one can leave much knowledge implicit (see chapter 8).

5.9 Summary

Here are some of the main points made in this chapter:

  (i) transcription is a *selective* process, aimed at highlighting certain aspects of the interaction for specific research goals;

 (ii) there is no *perfect* transcript in the sense of a transcript that can fully recapture the total experience of being in the original situation, but there are *better* transcripts, that is, transcripts that represent information in ways that are (more) consistent with our descriptive and theoretical goals;

(iii) there is no *final* transcription, only *different, revised* versions of a transcript for a particular purpose, for a particular audience;

 (iv) transcripts are *analytical products*, that must be continuously updated and compared with the material out of which they were produced (one should never grow tired of going back to an audio tape or a video tape and checking whether the existing transcript of the tape conforms to our present standards and theoretical goals);

  (v) we should be as *explicit* as possible about the choices we make in representing information on a page (or on a screen);

 (vi) transcription formats vary and must be evaluated vis-à-vis the goals they must fulfill;

(vii) we must be critically *aware* of the theoretical, political, and ethical implications of our transcription process and the final products resulting from it;

(viii) as we gain access to tools that allow us to integrate visual and verbal information, we must compare the result of these new transcription formats with former ones and evaluate their features;

 (ix) transcriptions change over time because our goals change and our understanding changes (hopefully becomes "thicker," that is, with more layers of signification).

We must keep in mind that a transcript of a conversation is not the same thing as the conversation; just as an audio or video recording of an interaction is not the same as that interaction. But the systematic inscription of verbal, gestural, and spatio-temporal dimensions of interactions can open new windows on our understanding of how human beings use talk and other tools in their daily interactions.

6
Meaning in linguistic forms

Like other social scientists, linguists are very inventive at creating new terms for the mere purpose of description. This makes their work authoritative and at the same time impenetrable to those who are outside of the field of linguistics. In this chapter, I will introduce some of the units of analysis employed by grammarians in the formal study of the structure of natural languages (phonemes, morphemes). After introducing some basic principles of structuralist linguistics, I will discuss how events and participants' roles are marked through nominal and verbal morphology. In particular, I will illustrate how the differentiated treatment received by different types of referents across languages is related to contextual features such as animacy, person, and level of involvement. Grammatical structures and choices will be shown to be related to a number of parameters, including the nature of action and the extent to which information is foregrounded or backgrounded. I will then introduce the notion of metalinguistic awareness and show that certain aspects of meaning that cannot be captured by studying speakers' intuitions can be captured when we examine spontaneous language use, especially conversational discourse. The relation between language and gender will be illustrated through the notion of indexicality, a property of a particular type of signs.

6.1 The formal method in linguistic analysis

Most of the linguistic analyses of what I identify here as "linguistic forms" have been based on a **formal method** of inquiry (Carnap 1942) according to which the properties of linguistic expressions are studied without paying too close attention to the non-linguistic correlates of those expressions. The linguist concentrates on linguistic forms without trying to connect them to events and objects in the world they describe (what philosphers call "designata"). In general, phonologists, morphologists, and syntacticians are more interested in the relationship among different elements of the linguistic system (sounds, parts of words, phrases and sentences) than in the relationship between such elements and the "world out there" that such a system is meant to represent. In the formal method, linguistic signs are taken out of their natural context – as part of acts of communication and hence social acts – and examined as part of an abstract formal system. This method is based on a number of assumptions.

One assumption is that linguistic forms are shared by a particular group of speakers. No consideration is usually given however to the cultural and political processes that make such sharing possible or necessary (Bourdieu 1982: 26). For the purposes of their analysis, structuralist and generative linguists alike act as if form-content relationships remain constant across time, space, and speakers – this is part of the **synchronic approach** to linguistic description – and that social, cultural, or psychological implications or consequences for a linguistic choice are not relevant to such a description. A new version of this approach is the autonomous view of syntax assumed by many contemporary formal linguists, Chomsky and his students in particular.

In engaging in structural analysis, grammarians look at words, sentences, and their components as symbolic elements that can be readily manipulated (that is, modified and combined in various ways with other elements of the system) to establish the rules that govern their understanding and use by speakers. Such techniques presuppose a view of language as predominantly an instrument for informing or describing the world (for a different view, see chapter 7). In other words, although grammarians are concerned with meaning, they usually focus on what logicians and semanticists call **referential** or **denotational** meaning (Lyons 1969, 1977), that is, respectively, the property of linguistic expressions to identify particular objects in the world (e.g. use of the expression *the red guitar* in the utterance *John wants the red guitar*) or a particular class of objects, properties, events (e.g. the use of *guitar* in the sentence *John just bought a guitar*).[1] Usually grammarians do not make any claim about other aspects of meaning, variously called social, affective, emotive, indexical, all of which are of primary interest to linguistic anthropologists and sociolinguists (see Romaine 1984; Silverstein 1979, 1985b). They also assume that, with the exception of indexical expressions such as *I, you, here, now,* etc. (see sections 1.4.2 and 6.8.2), denotational meanings are shared, that is, they remain constant across speakers and over time and space. Finally, the formal method of analysis is based on the assumption (introduced by the German logician Gottlieb Frege) that the meaning of a proposition is made up out of the meaning of its constituent words (Dummett 1973: 4).

As we shall see later in this chapter, the inclusion of other types of meaning in

[1] The distinction between reference and denotation is also known as a distinction between *reference* (German *Bedeutung*) and *sense* (German *Sinn*) or *extension* and *intension* (see also Allwood, Andersson, and Dahl 1977; Chierchia and McConnell-Ginet 1990; Frege [1892]1952).

the study of grammatical units allows linguistic anthropologists and discourse analysts to unveil a new set of linguistic phenomena.

6.2   Meaning as relations among signs

One of the major contributions of linguistic analysis in the last century has been the idea that the basis of meaning lies in the kinds of relations that signs – words, conventional gestures, street signs, traffic signals, etc. – have with one another in a particular system. The Swiss linguist Ferdinand de Saussure, considered by many the founder of modern linguistics and the inspiration for the European intellectual movement known as **structuralism**, believed that certain objects (marks on paper as well as sound waves in the air) acquire meaning, that is, become **signs**, in two ways: (i) by being temporally or spatially connected to other (similar) elements and (ii) by being understood in opposition to other (similar) elements that could have been used but were not. Saussure called the first type of relations **syntagmatic** and the second type **paradigmatic** (psychologists sometimes talk about the same relations in terms of **horizontal** and **vertical** relations). Saussure defines syntagmatic relations as relations of contiguity (or *in presentia*). In a sentence, words acquire meaning by being *next to* other words. This becomes immediately apparent when we consider words that can have quite different meanings. For example, the word *line* in examples (1)–(4) conveys different concepts and refers to different objects in the world. The meanings of *line* is each time recoverable by looking at the other words it co-occurs with.

(1)   I can't draw a straight *line* without a ruler

(2)   People must form a *line* if they want to be served

(3)   I can't remember a single *line* of that poem

(4)   What is the *line* of argument you're following?

In (1) and (2), the meaning of *line* is defined by the verb that precedes it – *draw* in (1) and *form* in (2). In (3) and (4) the meaning of *line* is defined by the rest of the nominal phrase to which it belongs – *of that poem* and *of argument* respectively. The structuralist notion of syntagmatic relations in this case captures the idea often articulated by philosophers and logicians (Frege, Wittgenstein) that words only make sense within the context of a sentence.[2]

Paradigmatic relations are *oppositional* relations (Saussure used the Latin term *in absentia*). They are defined by what something is *not*, that is, the range of alternative signs within the same system.

---

[2] For example, Wittgenstein in his *Tractatus Logico-Philosophicus* says: "3.3 Only propositions have sense; only in the nexus of a proposition does a name have meaning" (1961: 14). The English term *proposition* is here, as elsewhere in the logico-philosophical literature of the period, a translation of the German term *Satz* (see Willard 1972).

In the following sentence, for instance, the word *big* must be understood in contrast to the other possible words that can be used in its place.

(5)   Paul is a big man.

If I am trying to look for Paul in a group of people, I will be able to exclude those who look *small* or *tall but thin*. The structuralist idea is that the meaning of what we use is partly given by what we do not use. The choice of *big* must be seen not only in contrast with its opposite, *small*, but also with words that are closer and yet distinct, like *great*. Structuralists would say that to understand what *big* means we must take into consideration the fact that the system (i.e. the English lexicon) also has the word *great*. When we use the word *big*, we are not just doing that, we are also not using the word *great*. We know that *a great man* is different from *a big man*. Hence the importance of what is *not* said (Tyler 1978).

As Lévi-Strauss understood when he introduced structuralist methods in cultural anthropology, this notion of meaning-by-opposition and possible variations within a class can be applied to any system of classification and especially to those systems that can be characterized by dualism or binary oppositions: male and female, blood relations and affines, nobles and commoners, gods and mortals, citizens and slaves, sea animals and earth animals, dead and live beings, raw and cooked foods (see chapter 2). In each case, the meaning of one member is given by its opposition to the other. It is the fact that there are people who are *not* nobles (i.e. commoners) that gives nobles their special status. In a structuralist account, any relation of domination is not only imposed from the top (e.g. by force or laws); it is also sustained from the bottom, by those who act as "inferiors." Such an account purposely ignores the sociohistorical conditions that brought about the present situation and emphasizes the element of choice that is implicit in any system of classification.

More generally, the structuralist view of meaning is potentially relevant to anyone interested in how people interpret their environment, including other people's actions. If we substitute "words" with "acts," we can apply the structuralist view of meaning in language to meaning in any human encounter. We can for instance analyze the presentation of a gift, which may or may not be accompanied by language, as an act that must be interpreted both syntagmatically (sequentially) and paradigmatically (in opposition to other possible acts). An offer of food made as soon as the food is brought to the table is interpreted differently from an offer made later, after other people have been served already. Furthermore, the meaning of the act of offering might also depend on the range of foods available. If the table is full of different plates with warm foods and we are offered the contents of a can, we might find the offer not sufficiently generous or even offensive. Such a reaction would be based however on the assumption that we know what the participants value the most and what the local rules are in treating guests at a table. In this case, in order to really know how to interpret the meaning of *when* an offer is made and *what* we are offered, we need to know the relevant distinctions for the people who are making the offer, what matters for them. For instance, canned food, when imported and more expensive, might be considered more valuable than fresh food (this is usually the case, for example, in Western Samoa). To better illustrate the structuralist point that any act of interpretation must take into consideration what matters within a given system of choices, we need to look at how individual sounds are used to convey meaning. As we will see, the principles originally developed within the study of sound systems were later expanded to the study of human behavior (see section 6.3.2).

The concept of meaning as relations among signs (*in presentia* and *in absentia*) has been used for the study of all kinds of communicative systems, especially within the field of semiotics (Barthes 1968; Eco 1976). Jakobson (1956, 1968), for example, saw syntagmatic and paradigmatic relations as the basis for understanding a wide range of phenomena, including aphasia, verbal art, realistic novels, paintings, and films. He suggested that in Russian lyrical songs, for example, artists prefer to explore paradigmatic relations and therefore tend to favor metaphoric constructions, whereas realistic authors like Tolstoy used syntagmatic relations in employing metonymic figures like the synecdoche (part for the whole): "In the scene of Anna Karenina's suicide Tolstoy's artistic attention is focused on the heroine's handbag; and in *War and Peace* the synecdoches 'hair on the upper lip' or 'bare shoulders' are used by the same writer to stand for the female characters to whom these features belong" (Jakobson 1956: 78). In painting, cubism favored metonyms and surrealism favored metaphors. In film, close-ups are metonymic because they allow the use of a detail for the whole while parallel editing is metaphoric because it juxtaposes the actions of two characters and hence forces the audience to think of one character by means of the actions of the other.[3]

6.3 Some basic properties of linguistic sounds

Humans' ability to produce and perceive linguistic sounds is due to a combination of physiological, neural, cognitive, and contextual factors. Physiologically, humans' speech is afforded by a larynx of a particular shape and size and a supralaryngeal vocal tract of a particular shape and length, which acts as a filter for the air coming from the lungs. Since the human larynx is not as efficient for respiration as that of non-human primates and other animals, researchers

---

[3] For an exploration of the role of metaphorical and metonymic relations in grammaticalization, see Heine, Claudi, and Hünnemeyer (1991).

speculate that it must have developed for extra functions such as the production of speech.

The air tract of an adult human is also quite different from that of a newborn child or a chimpanzee (Lieberman 1975: 108–9). A few months after birth, the anatomy of infants starts developing to allow for the production of the full range of sounds produced by adults. By the age of two, a child has an adult-like supralaryngeal vocal tract.

From a neurological and cognitive point of view, humans must be able to control and move their vocal organs at a fairly high speed to produce linguistic sounds.

> Human speech is the result of a source, or sources, of acoustic energy being filtered by the supralaryngeal vocal tract. For voiced sounds, e.g., sounds like the English vowels, the source of energy is the periodic sequence of puffs of air that pass through the larynx as the vocal cords (folds) rapidly open and shut. The rate at which the vocal cords open and close determines the fundamental frequency of phonation. Acoustic energy is present at the fundamental frequency and at higher harmonics. (Lieberman 1975: 10)

Humans must also be able to tune into and analyze, at a fairly high speed, the particular types of sounds that another speaker is producing. Humans can decode linguistic sounds typically produced at a rate of 20 to 30 segments per second despite the fact that the human ear usually cannot identify sounds at a rate higher than 7 to 9 segments per second (Liberman 1970) and sounds that are transmitted at a rate of 20 segments per second or higher are heard as an undifferentiable "tone" (Lieberman 1975: 7). Linguistic sounds "glide" into one another, affecting and being affected by the surrounding sounds. This is what phoneticians call **coarticulation**. What is considered the same consonant can be quite different depending on the following vowel. The /k/ sound of the word *car* is articulated much further back in the mouth than the /k/ of *key*. All three consonants in the word *spoon*, /s/, /p/, and /n/ acquire lip rounding, one of the defining features of /u/, the only vowel in the word (Daniloff and Hammarberg 1973). Hearers use several different cues, acoustic and contextual, to analyze into discrete units sounds that are in fact not rigidly separable, either in terms of their acoustic signal or in terms of the way in which they are articulated.

Lieberman and other phoneticians use these properties of linguistic sounds to suggest that hearers do a terrific (and largely unconscious or automatic) job at **unscrambling** the linguistic signal (Lieberman 1975). Such a job would require hearers to idealize or regularize a rather variable input. Variation in fact seems to be the norm in sound production, not only because the same speaker never pronounces a word *exactly* the same way, but also because there is variation in the ways in which individual speakers configure their own repertoire of linguistic sounds. Phoneticians have shown experimentally that sounds that have different acoustic properties can be used to convey the "same" linguistic sound by two different speakers. What for one speaker is used to produce the sound [ɛ] for another speaker might represent the sound [ɪ] (Lieberman and Blumstein 1988: 177). This means not only that different speakers might use different parts of the vocal tract to produce what is perceived as the same sound, but that hearers routinely adjust to such variations, as long as certain parameters and differentiations are roughly maintained constant.[4] Linguists have hypothesized that speakers-hearers must rely on theoretical, that is, abstract units that can be easily adapted to the specific qualities of the sounds produced by a particular speaker. Linguists call these units **phonemes**, classes of sounds such as /t/, /i/, /p/, /θ/, that can be combined in a sequence to form larger, meaningful units such as /tɪp/, /pɪt/, and /tiθ/ (spelled *tip, pit, and teeth*).[5]

6.3.1 The phoneme

The notion of phoneme was introduced in linguistics to capture the fact that not all variations in how a given sound is pronounced produce differences of meaning. In English, for instance, whether we say /p/ or /b/ can make a difference as shown by the following list of words (from Hyman 1975: 61).

/p/	/b/
pin	bin
rapid	rabid
rip	rib

Phonologists say that despite the fact that /p/ and /b/ share the same **place of articulation** – they are both **bilabial** (both lips are at work to stop the the air and produce the sound) – and some aspects of their **manner of articulation** – they are

---

[4] "Human speakers do not attempt to produce the same absolute formant frequency values for the 'same' vowels. They instead produce a set of formant frequencies that is frequency-scaled to their approximate supralaryngeal vocal tract length" (Lieberman and Blumstein 1988: 178–9).

[5] It is not clear yet whether thinking of words as sequences of distinct units like phonemes captures the ways in which speakers actually perceive linguistic sounds. Fowler (1985) has pointed out that if we think in terms of distinct segments, each of which has its own (ideal) position, most of talking involves *getting to* them. Armstrong, Stokoe and Wilcox (1994) used this argument to propose that articulating sounds might not be too different from articulating gestures in signed languages. Perhaps the ability to think in terms of such units is not so much a universal feature of language processing but a fairly sophisticated way of analyzing speech based on an exposure to theoretical constructs such as alphabetic writing systems (see section 5.1).

both produced by first stopping the air flow (they are thus called **stops**) –, /p/ and /b/ do not share the way in which the vocal cords are used. In /b/ the vocal cords vibrate (for this reason it is called a **voiced** sound) whereas in /p/ they rest (in which case a **voiceless** sound is produced).[6] Whereas the use of the vocal cords is considered by phonologists to be the crucial feature – the **distinctive feature** – that makes /p/ and /b/ separate phonemes, there are other features that /p/ and /b/ exhibit (or acquire) in certain contexts that are not considered relevant to making them separate phonemes. Thus, for instance, /p/ in English is aspirated[7] at the beginning of a word (but not at the end of it) so that the word *pin* is actually pronounced [pʰin] whereas the word *rip* is pronounced [rip] (and not [ripʰ]). But since the aspiration of *p* does not produce a word with a different meaning ([ripʰ] is just an unusual pronunciation that might even pass unnoticed), phonologists treat [p] and [pʰ] as belonging to the same class, the phoneme /p/. This is a classification that makes sense, however, only within a particular system, namely, the sound system of the English language. There are other languages in which the aspiration of a bilabial stop does make a difference in meaning. For instance, in Korean, *pul* and *pʰul* are not variations of the same word, but two different words with two different meanings, "fire' and "grass" respectively. In such cases, phonologists would consider p with aspiration and p without aspiration as two different phonemes: /pʰ/ and /p/ respectively (see Finegan and Besnier 1990: 66–8).

The phoneme as a unit of analysis is meant to capture the distinction between linguistic variations that matter and variations that do not matter – or between features that are distinctive and features that are non-distinctive. When we perform an analysis of the ways in which the various oral organs move when sounds are produced or the ways in which the sound waves produced by a particular articulation are formed (as can be done by studying a spectogram, see Ladefoged 1975), we find that there are innumerable variations from one instance to the other of what speakers might perceive as the same sound. From the point of view of the denotational meaning of those sounds, however, many variations can be ignored, including variations in volume, pitch (in non-tonal languages like English),

---

6 For those who are not familiar with the distinction betweed voiced and voiceless sounds, the best way to experience it is to articulate two other sounds, /z/ and /s/, which are distinguished by the same opposition – voiced/voiceless – but are produced by a continuous flow of air, which makes it easier to hear the difference: cover your ears with your hands and pronounce the two words *eyes* and *ice* stretching out the last sound of each word; you will be able to feel the vibration in the *s* of *eyes* because it is phonemically a *voiced* sibilant, /z/, but not in the *-ce* of *ice* because it is a *voiceless* (or unvoiced) sibilant, /s/.

7 This means that there is a stronger puff of air coming out of the mouth after the /p/ of *pin* than there is after the /b/ of *bin*. Phoneticians analyze aspiration as an extended period of voicelessness after the articulation of the stop and before the following vowel (Ladefoged 1975: 43 and 124).

breathy voice, or emphatic lengthening of sounds. Some variations, such as the one between unaspirated and aspirated voiceless stops in English (for instance, [p] vs. [pʰ]) can be ignored because they are predictable, that is, they depend on the surrounding sounds and do not alter the denotational meaning of the word in which they occur.

The concept of phoneme is extremely attractive to anyone interested in how human minds process the flow of events and phenomena in which they participate. Particularly in the first half of this century, anthropological linguists and cultural anthropologists traded arguments in finding justifications for the general principle that there are abstract patterns or forms that may be psychologically real but difficult to see or hear. Sapir felt that the need for abstract classes to accommodate concrete cases of sounds produced by native speakers was strongly supported by his fieldwork experience with unwritten languages. He believed that native speakers of such languages had a hard time transcribing nuances of sound differences that they did not perceive as meaningful. When asked to divide up words, they would often produce forms that would be closer to abstract representations or etymological reconstructions than to what they had just said a few seconds earlier in the context of an entire word or phrase. It is on such grounds that Sapir argued in favor of the **psychological reality of the phoneme**. An example will illustrate his reasoning. While trying to teach his Southern Paiute informant, Tony Tillohash, to write his language phonetically, at one point Sapir selected the expression *pa:ßaʰ* "at the water," formed by a sequence of: voiceless bilabial stop ([p]), stressed long *a* [a:], voiced bilabial spirant ([ß]), unstressed short *a* ([a]), and final aspiration ([ʰ]).

> I asked Tony to divide the word into its syllables and to discover by careful hearing what sounds entered into the composition of each of the syllables, and in what order, then to attempt to write down the proper symbol for each of the discovered phonetic elements. To my astonishment Tony then syllabified: *pa*, pause, *paʰ*. I say "astonishment" because I at once recognized the paradox that Tony was not "hearing" in terms of the actual sounds (the voiced bilabial *ß* was objectively very different from the initial stop) but in terms of an etymological reconstruction: *pa* "water" plus postposition **-paʰ* "at." The slight pause which intervened after the stem was enough to divert Tony from the phonetically proper form of the postposition to a theoretically real but actually nonexistent form. (Sapir 1949d: 48–9)

The "theoretically real" form for Sapir is the one with the phoneme /p/, which is realized in Southern Paiute in four different ways depending on where it occurs in a word or phrase, with [β] being the form that it assumed after a long voiced vowel, hence the form *pa:βaʰ* . The alternation between [p] and [β] in Southern Paiute is similar to phonological processes found in other languages. For instance, in Spanish the sound [b] becomes [β] when it occurs between two vowels. In the following example the first sound of the word *banca* "bench" changes when the word is preceded by the article *la* "the (feminine)" that ends with a vowel (from Hyman 1975: 62):

(6) *banca* [baŋka] "bench"
(7) *la banca* [la βaŋka] "the bench"

What happens in (7) is a typical case of **assimilation**: the first sound of *banca* acquires some of the properties of its surrounding sounds, that is, *assimilates* to the sounds that are next to it. Rather than closing the vocal organs (in this case the lips) completely to articulate a voiced stop [b], native Spanish speakers extend the feature of continuous air flow that characterizes vowels (the preceding [a] of *la* and the following [a] of *banca*) to the intervening consonant. The result is that instead of a stop (where the air stream is momentarily blocked), the sound produced is a **fricative** ([β]), that is, a sound that is produced by letting the air out of the mouth through a narrow passage (in this case between the lips). This creates a "friction" effect. The two sounds, [b] and [β] in Spanish are said to be in **complementary distribution**. This means that they never appear in the same environment, that is, [b] never appears between vowels and [β] never appears when it is not preceded by a vowel. In a phonemic analysis of these two sounds in Spanish, [b] and [β] are thus considered two **allophones** (that is, two variants) of the same phoneme (there are theoretical reasons for choosing /b/ over /β/ as the symbol for the more general, abstract unit). What is different between the Spanish and the Southern Paiute example is that whereas in Spanish what we posit as the abstract unit, the phoneme /b/, does appear in certain phonological contexts (e.g. when the sound is not preceded by a vowel), in Southern Paiute, the sound /p/ of the morpheme *-paʰ* never appears because, being part of a suffix, the /p/ of *-paʰ* always follows some other sound that affects its articulation. It is in this sense that *-paʰ* is a "theoretical form." It is an abstraction rather than something that speakers actually ever say. To convey this idea, Sapir wrote **-paʰ*, using the asterisk, a convention commonly used in historical linguistics for reconstructed but unattested forms (the form **pəte:r* is given as the Proto-Indo-European reconstructed form for what is now the English word *father* because we have no way of really knowing what Proto-Indo-European people used to say). The fact that a native speaker of Southern Paiute could articulate the form *-paʰ* when dividing the word *pa:βaʰ* gave Sapir an argument in favor of his belief in the psychological reality of the forms that linguists postulate on the basis of distributional factors. Similar arguments were later used by generative linguists to argue for abstract or "deep" structures to represent certain types of relations between different elements of a sentence (Chomsky 1957, 1965).

6.3.2   Emic and etic in anthropology

When a sound difference between two words produces a meaning difference, linguists say that there is a *phonemic* difference between the two words. When a sound difference between two words does not produce a meaning difference, we say there is a *phonetic* difference. As shown above, the role of aspiration in English is phonetic whereas in Korean it is phonemic. In Korean, aspiration has an effect on the referential or denotational meaning of a word, but in English it does not. From this distinction, Kenneth Pike (1954–56, 1966, 1971) introduced the terms *emic* and *etic* for talking about behavior that is significant and behavior that is not significant for the people who engage in it.

> It proves convenient – though partially arbitrary – to describe behavior from two different standpoints, which lead to results which shade into one another. The etic viewpoint studies behavior from outside of a particular system, and as an essential initial approach to an alien system. The emic viewpoint results from studying behavior as from inside the system. (Pike 1971: 37)

This distinction became very important in anthropology in the 1960s, when field-workers were encouraged to distinguish between an emic and an etic perspective in their descriptions. The emic perspective is one that favors the point of view of the members of the community under study and hence tries to describe how members assign meaning to a given act or to the difference between two different acts. The etic perspective is one which is instead culture-independent and simply provides a classification of behaviors on the basis of a set of features devised by the observer/researcher. **Etic grids** are lists of features of a given phenomenon that can be used in comparative work. Not all features might apply to all situations or communities. Hymes's model of the components of a speech act – Situation, Participants, Ends, Act sequences, etc. (see section 9.2) – is an example of an etic grid.

As pointed out by Keesing (1972), there are different versions of the emic/etic distinctions. Emic is sometimes seen as equivalent to "mental" or "ideational" and hence not directly accessible while etic is identified with behavioral and hence with visible acts. Other times, emic is simply the point of view of the members of a group and etic is the point of view of the observer. If the observer is an anthropologist who has studied or read about other communities, the observer's perspective is likely to include a list of likely features – sometimes cast as a set of potential universals of human culture.

Different approaches within anthropology have tended to favor one perspective over the other. In the "New Ethnography" School, which included Goodenough's and Frake's notion of a *cultural grammar* (see section 2.2), the goal of ethnography is to describe a culture in emic terms. For example, in his work on Subanum cultural activities, Frake (1964) argued that we cannot rely on a crosscultural (i.e. etic) list of criteria to find out what counts as "religious behavior" for a particular group. We must instead find out how certain behaviors are interpreted and conceptualized by the members of the group. Cultural materialists like Marvin Harris argued against this position by recasting the distinction between emic and etic in terms of participants' vs. observers' categories.

> If behavioral events are described in terms of categories and relationships that arise from the observer's strategic criteria of similarity, difference, and significance, they are etic; if they are described in terms of criteria elicited from an informant, they are emic. (Harris 1976: 340)

Some of the problems with the emic/etic distinction have to do with the fact that it relies on two problematic homologies, one between language and culture and the other between anthropological goals and methods and linguistic goals and methods, especially those developed by formal grammarians.

Language is part of culture but definitely not all of it. How a woman feels about her children and how she conceives of her relationship with her husband can be certainly talked about but includes more than the verbal strategies through which such feelings and relationships are represented or negotiated. The sense of "respect" implicit in a man's behavior toward certain individuals in his community includes a range of acts, stances, and beliefs of which language is only a part. The products of human labor, including the artifacts that are such an important part of the definition of what a person thinks of "home" or "workplace" or "temple" are a fundamental component of the cultural context through which lives are lived and meanings are assigned to them. And yet such artifacts have a life that is often complementary to and certainly not identical with linguistic expressions. As we start to think about the relation between language and culture, we realize that what we say depends on our notions and theories of what language and culture are (see chapters 2 and 3). Nevertheless, the two domains are not identical and any homology between the two must take into consideration such a lack of identity.

Grammarians tend to assume a considerable number of shared principles and rules across languages. Whether or not one accepts Chomsky's notion of

Universal Grammar and the specific claims he makes about innatism, most formal linguists today, especially in the US, are committed to the study of the universal properties of human languages. Anthropologists do not talk about a Universal Culture and are divided over the extent and nature of a "universal human character" that would be at the basis of all cultures (but see the discussion of cognitive views of culture in section 2.2).

The object of investigation for formal linguists is native speakers' intuitions of acceptability (e.g. "Can you say this sentence? Does it mean the same as this other one?"), not native speakers' theories about why language behaves the ways it does. Anthropologists, instead, not only spend a considerable amount of time asking people what they think about things, events, and relationships, they also take members' conceptualizations as local theories in need of explanation. Linguists differ as to the extent to which actual speech behavior is considered relevant for linguistic descriptions and linguistic theory. Formal linguists tend to look at only a subset of the phenomena one might call "language" – the ones that can be studied under the assumption that language is a property of the human mind. For such phenomena, the study of speakers' intuitions is judged sufficient and even optimal. Anthropologists do not usually draw sharp boundaries around the notion of culture and do more than ask questions of informants. They also observe and describe a fair amount of public behavior, rituals in particular. This means that anthropologists are, by definition, into a realm of human activity linguists would call "performance" (see section 1.4.1).

These and other factors make it difficult to decide the extent to which the emic/etic distinction originally drawn on a homology between linguistic sounds and human behavior can be applied in a generalized way across situations and cultures.

6.4   Relationships of contiguity: from phonemes to morphemes

As mentioned earlier, in addition to relations of opposition, signs, including linguistic sounds, typically enter into relations of contiguity with other signs. When phonemes are combined together in sequences, they form **morphemes**, the smallest sequences of sound to carry independent meaning. For example, the sounds /p/, /i/, and /n/ have no meaning of their own but when combined in the sequence /pin/ they produce the English word *pin*. The sounds /i/ and /ŋ/ make up the ending /iŋ/(spelled -*ing*) of verbs, like in *liv-ing* or *jok-ing*. The individual sound /s/ conveys the meaning of "plural" when added to *book*, *seat*, *lip*.

To isolate a morpheme, a grammarian must be able to establish that a particular sound or sequence of sounds *regularly* conveys a particular meaning. Morphologists usually ignore the problems one encounters when trying to accurately describe such a meaning and feel satisfied when native speakers intuitively recognize a given form as "roughly meaning the same" across different words – e.g.

un- in *unorthodox* or *unusual*, or *-ism* in *Marxism* and *Cubism*. Native speakers' intuitions can sometimes contradict historical records and point to similarities between parts of etymologically unrelated words, like, for example, the *-ust* of *must*, *rust*, *crust*, *fust*, and *dust* – meaning roughly "surface formation" (Bolinger 1950: 120). Similarly, the word *ambush* is heard by speakers as suggesting that someone is hiding in the bushes (ibid. p. 128). Linguistic theories vary in the extent to which such intuitions are recognized in the morphological analysis.

With the same type of arguments used for talking about allophones (section 6.3.1), morphologists talk about **allomorphs**, that is, variants of what can be considered as the same basic form. A classic example is the plural ending in English, which can have three different phonetic realizations, as shown by the following examples:

(8) books /buks/
     dogs   /dogz/
     glasses /glasəz/

The three endings, /s/, /z/, and /əz/ respectively, are considered realizations of the same morpheme, which morphologists usually represent as *-Z*, to distinguish it from the phoneme /z/ (Spencer 1991: 6).

The notion of morpheme is important in the study of speech because it makes the analyst particularly attuned to the role that different parts of words or phrases play in conveying a particular meaning. Just as no description of a language is possible without an understanding of the basic sound distinctions made by native speakers, no in-depth understanding of a language can be reached without a careful analysis of the ways in which words are formed and different linguistic elements are combined together to form larger, meaningful units.

Linguistic anthropologists have often been attracted to the study of morphological phenomena because they have found that natural languages are quite rich in the ways in which they use variations in the shape of a word to signal changes in context and interpretive frame.

For instance, in many languages, social features of the situation or the relationship among participants are marked through special morphemes that convey respect for the addressee, the occasion, or even bystanders (Agha 1994; Levinson 1983). These morphemes, often seen as belonging to the more general category of **honorifics**, might be independent words or **affixes** (a general category that covers prefixes, infixes, and suffixes). Thus, in Korean there are different sets of endings for verbs, depending, among other factors, on the social relationship between the speaker and the addressee as defined in the situation (Lewin 1971; Martin 1964). As shown in table 1, within each set, there are sometimes different forms according to the type of utterance or speech act (see chapter 7):

Table 6.1 *Verbal suffixes indexing social relationship between speaker and addressee (from Lewin 1971: 201)*

	Declarative	Interrogative	Imperative	Optative
informal	-ŏ	-ŏ	-ŏ	-ŏ
	-chi	-chi	-chi	-chi
casual	-(nŭ)nda	-(nŭ)n'ga	-ra	-cha
friendly	-ne	-na	-ke	-se
neutral	-o	-o	-o	-psida
	-chiyo	-chiyo	-chiyo	-psida
	-koyo	-koyo	-koyo	-psida
respectful	-(sŭ)pnida	-(sŭ)pnikka	-(sŭ)psio	-(sŭ)psida

There is also an honorific (Hon) infix (*-si-*) that is inserted in a verb to express deference to the referent of the subject of the utterance:

(9) sunmun-ŭl ilgŭ- si- mnida
newspaper-Acc read-Hon-Respect:Declarative
"(he) reads the newspaper" (Lewin 1971: 198)

Similarly, in Pohnpeian (Micronesia), special verbs are used either by themselves or in combination with locative suffixes of various sorts to form what Keating (1996, 1997) calls **humiliative** and **exaltive** forms, that is, linguistic expressions that carry with them information about the relative status of their referent and the stance taken by the speaker vis-à-vis the situation or (some of) the participants in the event. An example is given in (10) below, where the daughter of a chief first refers to her own action by means of the humiliative form *patoh* and then later uses the exaltive form *ket* in referring to her father's movement. Given the polysemy of these morphemes, they will be glossed interlinearly with the generic label "locative verb" (abbreviated "LocVerb"):

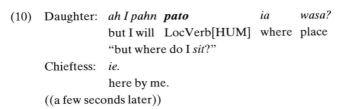

(10) Daughter: *ah I pahn* **pato** *ia* *wasa?*
but I will LocVerb[HUM] where place
"but where do I *sit*?"
Chieftess: *ie.*
here by me.
((a few seconds later))

Daughter: ((to the Chief)) ***ket***   *men ah ...*
               LocVerb[EXAL]   there and
               "*sit*[8] there and..."

The same morphemes, *patoh* and *ket* can be used to form other verbs in combination with suffixes that specify directionality, as shown by the following example taken from the same interaction:

(11)   (The chief's daughter is addressing one of the young men present)
         Daughter: *ice chest en **patoh-sang***   *mwo eri*
                  ice chest to LocVerb[HUM]-from   there so then
                  "*move* the ice chest out of there so then"

                  *Mwohnsapw **ket-la***   *mwo ...*
                  Mwohnsapw LocVerb[EXAL]-there   there ...
                  "Mwohnsapw (=the chief) (can) move there ..."

As shown in table 6.2 (from Keating 1994), the morphological process of adding suffixes to form new verbs is quite productive in Pohnpeian:[9]

Table 6.2. *Humiliative and exaltive verbs in Pohnpeian*

Humiliative form	Exaltive form	English translation
patoh-do	ket-do	come
patoh-la	ket-la	go
patoh-di	ket-di	go down, lie down
patoh-sang	ket-sang	move from
patoh-wei	ket-wei	go there by you
patoh-di-wei	ket-di-wei	go down towards you
pat-pat	ket-ket	staying

The productivity of this kind of morphology is exhibited in the following excerpt, where we find *patoh* used three different times in combination with three different suffixes:

(12)   (The chief and several other titled and untitled people are sitting around before a sakau ceremony)

---

[8] Although *ket* by itself is a stative verb, it acquires here the meaning of a motion verb without having an added suffix (see table 6.2 below). There are at least two possible explanations of this: either *ket-* is short for *ket-la* (see [11] below) or it acquires the motion meaning from the following directive particle *men* (Elizabeth Keating, personal communication).

[9] Keating found examples of all these forms except *ket-sang* and *ket-di-wei*.

CHIEF:	*ahpw*	*ma*	*ke*	*mihmi*	*me*		
	but	if	you	stay	here-by-me		

"what if you stay here"

NALIK.:	*ahpw ma*	*e*	***patoh-long***		*me*
	but	if	she LocVerb[HUM]-inside	here-by-me

"what if she *comes inside* here"

SOU.:	*ah kowe*	***patoh-sang***		*men*
	and you	LocVerb[HUM]-from	there-by-you

"and you *move from* there"

LAMPEIN.:	*soh i pahn* ***patoh-di-wei***		*men*
	no I will LocVerb[HUM]-down-towards-you	there-by-you

"no I will *go down* there"

Given the fundamental role of speech in implying, establishing, and maintaining social relations, it should be apparent that anyone interested in social hierarchy and the processes whereby it is negotiated by real people in real time cannot but be aware of the subtle and yet powerful ways in which language-specific morphologies play a role in such processes.

6.5 From morphology to the framing of events

An informal distinction is often made in linguistics between the ways in which nouns as opposed to verbs change shape depending on the meaning they need to convey. Grammarians thus speak of **nominal morphology** and **verbal morphology**. An important part of both nominal and verbal morphology is the encoding of information about the roles assigned to different participants in an event.

Languages usually allow speakers to encode distinctions between *who* did *what* to *whom*. For example, given a sentence containing a predicate and two nominals representing two different participants in the depicted event, a language may distinguish between the two by means of different suffixes on the nominals or by means of different suffixes on the verb (see section 6.5.2). Nominal morphology is at work when a language uses one ending for the noun describing the participant who acts on something or someone else (the Agent) and another ending for the noun describing the participant who is acted upon (the Object or Patient). Latin is an example of this type of language. In (13) below, we know from the ending of the nouns *lupus* "wolf" and *vulpem* "fox" which one is the one who is doing the action described by the verb *arguebat* "was accusing." The nominative morphology (Nom) is used for identifying the Agent (lupus) and the accusative morphology (Acc) is used for the Patient, *vulpem* "fox."

(13) *Lup-us*   *vulp-em*   *argue-bat*
      wolf -Nom   fox-Acc   accuse-Imperfect
      "The wolf was accusing the fox"

To convey the opposite meaning from (13), we only need to change the endings of the two nouns, leaving the order of words unaltered (notice that the endings for accusative and nominative case vary for *lupus* and *vulpes* because they belong to two different noun classes or "declensions"):

(14) *Lup-um*   *vulp-es*   *argue-bat*
      wolf-Acc   fox-Nom   accuse-imperfect
      "The fox was accusing the wolf"

By using the accusative form *lupum* and the nominative form *vulpes*, speakers communicate that it is the fox who is accusing the wolf. In a language like Latin, the same nominal morphology used for the Agent of a transitive clause like (13) and (14) above is also used for the only nominal of clauses like (15), (16), (17), and (18) below, which are usually called "intransitive":

(15) *Ad*   *rivum*   *lup-us*   *ven-erat*
      to   river   wolf-Nom   come-Pluperfect
      "The wolf had come to the river"

(16) *Ad rivum*   *vulp-es*   *ven-erat*
      to river   fox-Nom   come-Pluperfect
      "The fox had come to the river"

(17) *Lupus*   *malus*   *est*
      wolf   bad   is
      "The wolf is bad"

(18) *Vulpes*   *astuta*   *est*
      fox   clever   is
      "The fox is clever"

In this type of language, the same case, nominative, is used for the Agent of transitive clauses and the participant whose actions or qualities are depicted in an intransitive clause. Whereas a different case, accusative, is used for the Object or Patient of the transitive clause. Taking Latin as a model, this type of case marking has been called **nominative-accusative** and the syntactic role represented by the nominative case has been called "Subject." English is also considered a nominative-accusative language despite the fact that it has very little nominal morphology. In English as well, however, the Agent of transitive clauses and the one nominal of intransitive clauses like the ones in (15)–(18) above are treated or behave similarly. For example, they control verb agreement (zero vs. *-s* in the present tense) and display nominal morphology with personal pronouns (e.g. *he* instead of *him*, *she* instead of *her*). We speak then of the Subject of an English sentence regardless of the nature of the participant role represented in the sentence.

Not all languages work like Latin or English. Some languages choose to group together the Subject of the intransitive verb and the Object of the transitive verb, giving the Subject of the transitive verb a special form – in this way emphasizing the agentive nature of the latter. Linguists working on these languages decided that some new terminology was needed to distinguish this other type of nominal case marking and introduced the term **ergative** and **absolutive** to describe, respectively, the Subject of transitive clauses (which is said to be in the ergative case) and the Subject of the intransitive clause as well as the Object of the transitive clause (both of which are said to be in the absolutive case). Languages of this type have thus been called **ergative-absolutive languages** (usually abbreviated to **ergative languages**). Australian Aboriginal languages are often of this type. Examples of how this pattern works are given in (19)–(22) below from Dyirbal, an Australian language from North Queensland studied by R.M.W. Dixon (1972: 59). In Dyirbal, the ergative marker is a suffix that changes according to the shape of the word to which is attached. In each example nouns are preceded by a special marker that indicate relative proximity and visibility; without such markers or deictic particles (see chapters 4 and 9), the sentences are said to be incomplete:

(19) bayi   yaṛa   baniɲu   (intransitive clause)
       there   man   come
       "the man is coming"

(20) balan   ḍugumbil baniɲu   (intransitive clause)
       there   woman   come
       "the woman is coming"

(21) balan   ḍugumbil bañul   yaṛa-ɲu   balgan   (transitive clause)
       there   woman   there   man-Erg   hit
       "the man is hitting the woman"

(22) bayi   yaṛa   baɲun   ḍugumbi-ṛu   balgan   (transitive clause)
       this   man   this   woman-Erg   hit
       "the woman is hitting the man"

Given that languages like Dyirbal present a different classification of the participant roles expressed in a sentence, some linguists do not see it as appropriate to use the notion of Subject as a universal category, that is, a category valid in the description of all languages. Instead, they think it is better to speak of basic semantic roles that any language starts from but represents in different ways. A universal set of such semantic roles or **cases** were proposed in the mid-1960s and early 1970s by a number of linguists, including the semanticist Charles Fillmore, who presented a theory of grammar he called **Case Grammar**, which comprised six abstract roles or "deep cases":

> The case notions comprise a set of universal, presumably innate, concepts which identify certain types of judgments human beings are capable of making about the events that are going on around them, judgments about such matters as who did it, who it happened to, and what got changed. (Fillmore 1968: 24)

The cases proposed by Fillmore included Agent (or Agentive Case), Instrument (or Instrumental Case), Dative (later replaced by Experiencer), and Object (or Objective Case) – this is the case called "Theme" in Chomsky's model. This theory is an attempt to map the ways in which different languages encode participant roles in a sentence onto a universal list of such roles, called "cases."[10] These cases are called underlying or "deep" because they are relevant at an abstract level of representation and may or may not be encoded at the "surface" level, that is, the level of actual linguistic forms used and interpreted by speakers and hearers of a given language.

6.5.1 Deep cases and hierarchies of features

The attraction of Fillmore's framework was that it seemed easily adaptable to languages with very different morphological and syntactic characteristics. Languages for which the category "Subject" seemed relevant would have rules for "subjectivization" that would select which semantic case should be realized as the Subject. A set of such rules is what Fillmore called "case hierarchies." In English, for instance, there would be the following **case hierarchy**: Agent > Instrument > Object. This would mean that if a sentence contains an Agent, it automatically becomes the Subject of the sentence; if there is no Agent, but an Instrument, the latter becomes the Subject; otherwise, if only the Object case needs to be expressed, it is the Object that becomes the surface Subject of the sentence (Fillmore 1968: 33, see also Fillmore 1977a: 61). This characterizes

---

[10] See also Gruber (1965), Chafe (1970), Jackendoff (1972). For a discussion of Cases as used by generative grammarians, see J. Grimshaw (1990) and Radford (1988: 373). For a more detailed discussion of semantic roles and a longer list of Cases, see Andrews (1985). For a different treatment of cases, called "thematic relations," see Jackendoff (1987, 1990).

English grammar well, given that English has the basic constraint that every sentence needs to have a Subject.[11] For example, for a verb like the English *open*, if present, the Agent would become the surface Subject (as in *the woman opened the door*). If the Instrument and the Object were present, the Instrument would become Subject (*the key opened the door*). If Agent and Instrument were absent, then the Object[12] would become the Subject (*the door opened*).

Fillmore pointed out that languages varied with respect to which underlying Cases they allowed to be expressed as Subjects. On the basis of work by Susumo Kuno (1973), Fillmore (1977a) pointed out that in some languages such as Japanese, one cannot have sentences like (23) and (24) in which the subject is a non-human instrument:

(23) Fifty dollars will buy you a second-hand car.
(24) The smell sickened me.

These constraints, Fillmore argued, can be seen as related to the ways in which grammar is allowed to conceptualize certain **scenes**. In some languages, non-human participants in a scene (Instruments, for instance) are given prominence and can perhaps be seen as having some of the properties that we normally associate with Agents. Thus, in English, in a sentence like (23) above, one assigns a certain level of agency, or ability to make a difference in the world, to the fifty dollars. In other languages, this is not possible and only nouns referring to humans would be possible Subjects of the verb *buy*. Continuing in the same tradition, DeLancey (1981) argued that if we want to understand the ways in which languages organize their morphology and syntax, we need to take the notions of **viewpoint** and **attention flow**.[13] This is an area that has great potential for anyone interested in how grammar represents a particular worldview (see chapter 3).

Any grammatical theory that starts from semantic notions, like Fillmore's Case Grammar, seems better equipped at dealing with ergative languages like Dyirbal, given that for these languages it is not clear which Noun Phrase, the one in the ergative case or the one in the absolutive case, should be considered as the

---

11 That is, English finite clauses always need a subject whether or not such a Subject has an obvious referent in the world. For example, in English one must say *it rains* and *it is important to vote*. In both cases, it is not obvious what the "it" stands for and in many languages (Japanese, Spanish) such sentences would have no overt Subject.

12 It was the confusion between "Object" as a semantic Case and "Object" as a syntactic category opposed to "Subject" that prompted other semanticists to opt for different labels, including "Patient" and "Theme."

13 "ATTENTION FLOW determines the linear order of NPs. The NPs in a sentence are presented in the order in which the speaker wishes the hearer to attend them" (DeLancey 1981: 632). This notion is related to but different from the notion of iconicity introduced by Haiman (1980) (see section 6.8.1).

Subject.[14] Since, as shown by the Dyirbal examples above, the Agent NP typically takes a suffix (i.e. the ergative case) whereas the Absolutive NP is usually left unmarked (e.g. with "zero" suffix or "zero morphology"), some grammarians argued that ergative languages normally treat transitive clauses as **passive** sentences in nominative-accusative languages (Hale 1970). This means that a sentence like (21) above would be translated in English as "the woman was hit by the man" (the English preposition *by* being the translation of the ergative case marker). To many, however, this seemed a rather Euro-centric view of grammar: ergative-absolutive languages are made to conform to the nominative-accusative pattern by being "translated" into syntactic structures (i.e. passives) that make sense to speakers of nominative-accusative languages (Dixon 1972: 136–7; Silverstein 1976a: 114–15). Fillmore offered an appealing solution to this problem. He proposed that ergative languages simply lack the process of subjectivization, that is, they directly express the underlying semantic cases (or roles) instead of deciding each time which nominal phrase should be the Subject (Fillmore 1968: 53–54)

Case Grammar seemed also better at handling the fact that it is possible for languages to subscribe to one system (e.g. ergative-absolutive) in some parts of their grammar and to another system (e.g. nominative-accusative) in other parts. In most known cases of ergative languages, for instance, not all morphological and syntactic phenomena follow the ergative pattern (that is, treating Agents differently from Subjects of intransitive clauses). Pronouns in ergative languages, for instance, often do not have an ergative morphology and seem to act more like pronouns in nominative-accusative languages like English, where distinctions are made between Subject (i.e. nominative) forms (*I, he, she, we, they*) and non-Subject (i.e. accusative) forms (*me, him, her, us, them*). For this reason, grammarians have developed the term **split ergativity** to characterize this situation (see Dixon 1994: ch. 4). Dyirbal is a good example of this mixed system. Whereas sentences with full noun phrases exhibit ergative-absolutive morphology – as shown in (25)–(28) below –, sentences with pronouns exhibit nominative-accusative constructions, as shown below (from Dixon 1972: 60), where the pronouns ŋada "I"

---

[14] This is a controversy that generated a considerable debate in the 1970s, as attested by such collections as Li (1976) and Plank (1979) and lengthy articles such as Comrie (1978) and Dixon (1979). The more recent use of "ergative" by generative grammarians is different from the standard one and somewhat counterintuitive (see Dixon 1994). For generative grammarians, ergative structures are those in which what normally functions as the Object of a transitive verb is instead used as the Subject. Thus, in (1), b would be the ergative structure because *the ball* is the Subject (from Radford 1988: 374):

    (1) a. John rolled *the ball* down the hill
         b. *The ball* rolled down the hill

For an account of ergativity inspired by the logician Richard Montague's work, see Dowty (1982: 110–14).

and ŋinda "you (sing.)" maintain the same form as Subject of both intransitive and transitive clauses, but change when they are made Object of transitive clauses:

(25) ŋada   baniɲu
     I[nom]   come
     "I'm coming"

(26) ŋinda   baniɲu
     you[nom]   come
     "You are coming"

(27) ŋada   ŋinuna   balgan
     I[nom]   you[acc]   hit
     "I'm hitting you"

(28) ŋinda   ŋayguna   balgan
     you[nom]   me[acc]   hit
     "You're hitting me"

To explain this variation of case marking within the same language and capture recurring patterns across languages, Silverstein (1976a) proposed a **hierarchy of features** that was language-independent and hence could be proposed as a universal. The hierarchy of features could account for the fact that, if a language has a split ergative system, certain types of noun phrases are more likely than others to be marked with ergative morphology. Since in many Australian languages, the split in case marking is found within the pronominal systems, with some pronouns following nominative-accusative morphology and other ones following the ergative-absolutive morphology, Silverstein developed a system of classification that could cover the maximum range of semantic distinctions found in the pronominal systems of Australian languages. Some of these distinctions are the contrasts between **inclusive** and **exclusive** "we" and between **dual** and **more-than-two** pronouns. The Guugu Yimidhirr system described by Haviland (1979) provides examples of such distinctions, although contemporary usage tends toward a simplified version of the older system (Haviland 1979: 65).[15] The forms are here in their nominative and accusative forms – the former is used for both Subject of intransitive clauses and Agents of transitive clauses and the latter is used for the Object of transitive clauses:

---

[15] The inclusive-exclusive distinction is here represented only in the dual form (inclusive exclusive "we") but not in the plural (more than two) "we." For a system where the distinction is made in the plural as well, see section 9.3.2.

Nominative (S,A)	Accusative (O)	Translation
ngayu	*nganhi*	"I" (1st singular)
nyundu	*nhina(an(in))*	"you" (2nd singular)
nyulu	*nhinhaan(in)*	"he, she' (3rd singular)
ngali	*ngaliin/ngalinin*	"you and I" (1st dual inclusive)
ngaliinh	*ngalinhun*	"he/she and I" (1st dual exclusive)
yubaal	*yubalin/yubalinh*	"you-two" (2nd dual)
bula	*bulaan(in)/bulangan*	"they-two" (3rd dual)
nganhdhaan	*nganhdhanun*	"we" (1st plural)
yurra	*yurraan/yurrangan*	"you-all" (2nd plural)
dhana	*dhanaan/dhanangan*	"they-all" (3rd plural)

Silverstein's system of classification, inspired by earlier work by Benveniste (1966) and Jakobson (1932, 1936), captures the distinctions between inclusive vs. exclusive and between dual and more-than-two by means of four features: [+/- ego] and [+/- tu], [+/- plural], and [+/- restricted]. An overview of this system is given below (Silverstein 1976a: 117):[16]

		A	B	C	D	E	F	G	H	I	J	K
a.	[+/- ego]	+	+	+	+	+	-	-	-	-	-	-
b.	[+/- tu]	+	+	-	-	-	+	+	+	-	-	-
c.	[+/- plural]	+	+	+	+	-	+	+	-	+	+	-
d.	[+/- restricted]	+	-	-	-	(+)	+	-	(+)	+	-	(+)

A. first person inclusive dual
B. first person inclusive plural
C. first person exclusive dual
D. first person exclusive plural
E. first person singular
F. second person dual
G. second person plural
H. second person singular
I. third person dual

---

[16] Each column represents a cluster of feature categories. However, all the features are not independent and do not combine freely. I have left out a column between B and C, which, while conceivable as a feature cluster, is ruled out by implicational relations between features (Silverstein marks it with an asterisk). This column would represent a noun phrase with positive specification for *ego* and *tu* and negative specification for plural. This is not possible given that by definition any pronoun that includes speaker and addressee is plural. The positive feature of "restricted" is between parentheses (+) when it is redundant, that is, when the form is singular, i.e. [-plural].

    J.   third person dual

    K.   third person singular

In this system, the first person singular (English *I*) is characterized as [+ego, -tu, -plural] and second person singular (German *du*, Spanish *tu*) as [-ego, +tu, -plural], whereas the third person plural (English *they*) is [-ego, -tu, +plural]. The feature [+/- restricted] captures whether or not the individuals indexed by the pronoun are unique and enumerable. It is used to handle the distinction between dual ([+restricted]) and more-than-two ([-restricted]) forms. The feature [+/-plural] handles the distinction between plural and singular. Thus, the first person dual inclusive is [+ego, +tu, +plural, +restricted], in other words, it includes speaker and addressee, is plural, and restricts the number of participants to a specific number (two).[17]

Examining specific language systems, Silverstein found that, although there were subtle differences among languages in terms of which exact sequence of features would be at work (sometimes [+tu] seemed higher than [+ego]), there were clear recurrent patterns. Thus, pronouns that had the features [+ego] and [+tu] tended to be higher in the hierarchy and hence more likely to follow the nominative-accusative system. Pronouns that had negative values for those two features were lower in the hierarchy and more likely to follow the ergative-absolutive system, like nouns in general. By adding a few more features for third person participants such as [+/- human] and [+/- proper], Silverstein was able to cover a wider phenomenology of noun phrase types. His hypothesis was that these features could be organized in a hierarchical sequence such that if a language used ergative morphology at a given point in the hierarchy, it was possible to predict that it would use ergative morphology also for all the noun phrase types below that point. If, on the other hand, a language used accusative morphology at a given point, we could predict that it used accusative morphology at all higher points. The two-way hierarchy is represented in figure 6.1 below, where the vertical lines mark possible divisions of accusative vs. ergative case-marking within the same language. The prediction made is that once the distinction in case-marking system is made between two contiguous sets of categories (e.g. between [+ ego] and [- ego]), then all the sets on the left will behave in the same way and differently from all the sets on the right of the vertical line.[18]

---

[17] A similar system with three features (Speaker, Hearer, and Minimal Membership) had been proposed by Conklin (1962) to account for Hanunóo personal pronouns. Conklin's system, however, does not work for Australian languages like Guugu Yimidhirr, which have ten distinct pronouns. See Bean (1978) for an adaptation of Conklin's system to Kannada pronouns.

[18] A simplified version of the same hierarchy was represented by Dixon (1979: 85) on a horizontal axis.

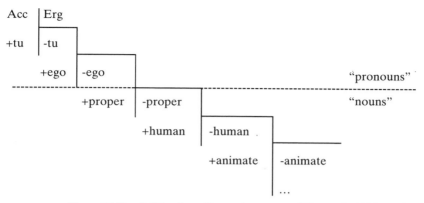

Figure 6.1 Possibilities for split ergative systems (Silverstein 1976a: 122)

The basic idea captured by this hierarchy is that certain types of participants in discourse, the speaker, the addressee and other human participants, are more likely than others to be Agents and that this set of participants is complementary to the set of participants that are more likely to be the Object. Ergative languages would then tend to mark with special morphology (e.g. ergative marker) those participants in discourse that are *less likely* to be Agents, that is, referents on the right side of the scheme in figure 6.1 (e.g. third person lexical nominals, inanimate referents). Conversely, nominative-accusative languages would tend to mark with accusative those nominals referring to participants that are less likely to be Objects, e.g. first and second person pronouns. This means that if a language has ergative morphology, it is more likely to use it for nouns than for pronouns, and even more likely for third person than for first or second person participants. Silverstein's hypothesis makes use of a number of grammatical, semantic, and pragmatic dimensions, including Noun Phrase type (whether a referent is represented by a full noun or a pronoun), person (or type of participant in the speech event), and degree of animacy (Croft 1990: 112–13). The validity of these dimensions has been corroborated in a number of studies in other languages and language families (Dixon 1994) and shows the importance of looking at morphology from a broader perspective, which involves the options a language gives its speakers to take a particular point of view and represent it in discourse (see below). In the last two decades, Silverstein's hierarchy and its implications have been reanalyzed from a number of theoretical perspectives and some authors have proposed alternative explanations (see for instance Jelinek 1993). Its main point, however, continues to be a central working hypothesis of linguistic anthropology: whenever we find that a grammatical system is "mixed" or follows apparently contradicting formal criteria, we should look at the semantic and pragmatic factors involved. What participants talk about seems to play a crucial role in the organization of grammar.

6.5.2 *Framing events through verbal morphology*

Verbal morphology has also been studied a great deal by grammarians, especially in the areas of person, number, tense/aspect marking, and causation. Language typologists know that whereas one language may change verbs for conveying different ways in which a given action is performed or distributed through time, another language may prefer to maintain the same verb root and either add different morphemes to convey different meanings (see examples above from Pohnpeian) or simply rely on the linguistic and/or extralinguistic context for differentiating. Thus, English verbs referring to death typically distinguish between a causative and a non-causative meaning: *kill* (causative)[19] vs. *die* (non-causative). On the other hand, "almost all English verbs expressing the material disruption of an object – e.g. *break, crack, snap, burst, bust, smash, shatter, shred, rip, tear* – apply equally in both non-causative and causative cases (*The balloon burst/I burst the balloon*)" (Talmy 1985: 84). In some languages, the same distinction may be represented either by adding a morpheme to convey the meaning of causation or by adding a morpheme to specify the non-causative use. In Samoan, the first option is common. A causative verb is often derived from a non-causative one by adding the prefix *fa`a-* ([fa?a]), as shown in (29) and (30) below: *pa`ū* "fall" becomes *fa`a-pa`ū* "drop" (or "Cause-fall").[20]

(29)   `*ua*   *pa`ū*   *le*   *tama*
         Pst   fall   Art   boy
         "The boy has fallen (down)"

(30)   `*ua*   **fa`apa`ū**   *e*   *le*   *tama*   *le*   *ipu*
         Pst   Caus-fall   Erg   Art   boy   Art   dish
         "The boy has dropped the dish"

In Spanish, the reverse is done by adding a "reflexive" morpheme, *se*, to the causative verb to make it into a non-causative one, as shown below (from Talmy 1985: 85):

(31)   *Abrió*   *la*   *puerta*
         opened   the   door
         "(he/she) opened the door"

---

[19] Causative verbs are those verbs that describe events involving an agent whose actions bring about a certain change of state in some entity. Typical examples of causative verbs are *kill, open, break, drop, buy.* In generative grammar, causative verbs are analyzed as containing an abstract semantic predicate "CAUSE" (capital letters are used to emphasize the abstract, non-lexical nature of the predicate). Thus, *kill* is represented as involving a semantico-logical structure of the type CAUSE (x, BECOME (NOT (ALIVE (y)))). This type of analysis is meant to capture the inference *y is not alive* from *x killed y*. For a discussion of this and other formal treatments of causative verbs, see Chierchia and McConnell-Ginet (1990: 350–70).

[20] The prefix *fa`a-* does not always carry the meaning of causation in Samoan. It can also be used for producing manner adjectives and adverbs, as in *fa`aSāmoa* "the Samoan way."

(32)   *La*   *puerta*   **se**   *abrió*
        The   door   Refl   opened
        "The door opened"

Native American languages are well known for their rich verb morphology that allows for subtle semantic distinctions, each of which may be traceable to a separated affix. It is such richness and the ways in which the different morphemes are combined in what appears as a single word that prompted in the past the label **polysynthetic** in referring to such languages in the context of language typology (Baker 1996). A good example of this type is represented by Atsugewi, a Hokan language of northern California, which has a vast array of morphemes that convey information about the **path** followed by an object in approaching a particular **ground** (see table 6.3).

Table 6.3 *Subtle semantic distinctions conveyed by verb morphology in Atwugewi (from Talmy 1985: 108–9)*

-ict	"into a liquid"
-cis	"into a fire"
-isp -u· +	"into an aggregate" (e.g. bushes, a crowd, a rib-cage)
-wam	"down into a gravitic container" (e.g. a basket, a cupped hand, a pocket, a lake basin)
-wamm	"into an areal enclosure" (e.g. a corral, a field, the area occupied by a pool of water)
-ipsn^u +	"(horizontally) into a volume enclosure" (e.g. a house, an oven, a crevice, a deer's stomach)
-tip -u· +	"down into a (large) volume enclosure in the ground" (e.g. a cellar, a deer-trapping pit)
-ikn +	"over-the-rim into a volume enclosure" (e.g. a gopher hole, a mouth)
-ikc	"into a passageway so as to cause blockage" (e.g. in choking, shutting, walling off)
-iks̓^{u} +	"into a corner" (e.g. a room corner, the wall–floor edge)
-mik·	"into the face/eye (or onto the head) of someone"
-mic̓	"down into (or onto) the ground"
-cis^u +	"down into (or onto) an object above the ground" (e.g. the top of a tree stump)
-iks̓	"horizontally into (or onto) an object above the ground" (e.g. the side of a tree trunk)

189

Verbal morphology and nominal morphology often interact in a language. For instance, ergativity (see above) is not always exclusively marked in the nominal morphology. There are languages in which it is the verb form, usually through pronominal infixes or agreement markers, that gives out information about which of the nominal arguments is the Agent and which is the Object (Absolutive). In Jacaltec, a Mayan language of Guatemala, the ergative-absolutive distinction is marked in the verb through infixes. The first infix identifies the Absolutive NP and the second infix identifies the Ergative NP. In (33) and (35), there are no independent NPs and therefore the meaning of the sentence must be recovered from the verb morphology alone, which displays information about case (ergative vs. absolutive) and number (first vs. second person) of the arguments of the predicate (hit):

(33) ch-oŋ-ha-maka
ASP-us-you-hit
"you (sing.) hit us" (Craig 1979: 31)

(34) ch-ach-cu-maka
ASP-you-we-hit
"we hit you (sing.)"

In Central Alaskan Yupik Eskimo (Woodbury 1985), both the noun and the verb carry ergative-absolutive morphology, as shown in the following examples (in Eskimo languages, as in some other linguistic families, the ergative marker is the same as the marker for "possession,"[21]):

(35) Nukaq-Ø   ner-'uq-Ø
Nukaq-Abs   eat-Indic-3sg
"Nukaq ate"

(36) Nuka-m   akutaq-Ø   ner-a -a
Nukaq-Erg   mixture-AbsSg   eat-Indic-3sg:3sg
"Nukaq ate the (berry) mixture" (Woodbury 1985: 67)

These examples also suggest that, as argued by Hopper and Thompson (see below), transitivity is not a property of individual verbs, but of clauses. The same verb *ner-* "eat" acquires different morphology depending on whether there is an Object in the clause.

The close connection between nominal and verbal morphology is also shown

---

[21] To avoid confusion, I have replaced Woodbury's gloss "REL" (relative case) with "Erg" (ergative), despite the fact that "relative" is probably a better general category for Eskimo languages. The colons (:) indicate an additional meaning of the same morpheme.

by a verbal grammatical continuum similar to the hierarchy of features discussed by Silverstein and others for nominal morphology. Moravcsik (1974), reviewing agreement phenomena in a number of languages, discovered that certain types of referents were more likely than others to require agreement in the verb. If in a language the verb agreed with only one type of argument, it would be the Subject (this is the case for Latin, see above). If the verb agreed with two types of arguments, it would be the Subject and the definite Object (this is often the case in Bantu languages, where an additional constraint for agreement might be that the Object be human). If the language agreed with three types of arguments, they would be the Subject, the definite Object, and the indefinite Object.

6.5.3 The topicality hierarchy

Givón (1976) proposed to recast these tendencies in terms of what he called a **hierarchy of topicality**, according to which one would predict the types of referents that are more likely to undergo or trigger grammatical rules such as verbal agreement. The term "topicality," derived from "topic," was used because it appeared that the items that are higher in the hierarchy are also the ones that are more likely to be talked about or be "topics."

Figure 6.2 reproduces the topicality hierarchy as a set of distinct but interacting hierarchical relations:

a. HUMAN > NON-HUMAN

b. DEFINITE > INDEFINITE

c. MORE INVOLVED PARTICIPANT > LESS INVOLVED PARTICIPANT

d. 1ST PERSON > 2ND PERSON > 3RD PERSON

Figure 6.2 Hierarchy of topicality (Givón 1976: 152)

Despite some unresolved issues regarding the criteria by which to identify the topic in a sentence, the features in the topicality hierarchy have been found to be relevant to a number of morphological and syntactic processes in a variety of languages and this theory has thus continued to attract the interest of grammarians and fieldworkers committed to a discourse-oriented, functionalist account of why languages behave the way they do, that is, for instance, why they mark morphologically only certain types of categories and only in certain syntactic contexts.

Going back to the discussion of nominative-accusative vs. ergative-absolutive languages, the distinction between the two can be captured by saying that some languages favor a categorization of participants in terms of their semantic role in the depicted event (ergative-absolutive languages), whereas other languages favor a categorization based on the tendency to present events from the point of view of the highest participant in the topicality hierarchy (nominative-accusative languages). Subjects tend to be topics, that is, they tend to present participants that have already been introduced in the discourse and about whom more is being said – they present what Chafe (1976) calls "given information." Languages for which the Subject category is the most relevant tend to treat humans alike, whether they are Agents – as in *the woman opened the door* –, Actors – as in *the woman ran* – or Experiencers – as in *the woman is happy*. On the other hand, languages that favor semantic distinctions over topicality tend to mark humans differently depending on the role they have in the event. Thus, ergative languages tend to separate human participants who are Agents from human participants who are not and to group the latter with the Object of transitive clauses; hence, – *the woman* in *the woman ran* – would be marked in the same way as *the door* in *the woman opened the door*. Other types of languages might make other kinds of distinctions.[22]

6.5.4   Sentence types and the preferred argument structure

John Du Bois (1987) studied how nominative vs. ergative languages present information in narratives and concluded that the ways in which discourse is typically organized can be a motivation for either type of system, depending on which factors a given language chooses to favor. Du Bois pointed that out that in narratives, there is a tendency for only one participant (or, in logical-grammatical terms, one "argument" of the verb) to be expressed by a full noun (this is what he calls the "One Lexical Argument Constraint"). This one participant usually is not the Agent – this finding is summarized in the "Non-lexical A[gent] Constraint"). Instead, it is either the Subject of an intransitive clause or the Object of a transitive clause. Agents, instead, tend to be participants that have already been introduced before in other kinds of roles and are hence referred to via anaphora, that is, by a pronoun or a zero morpheme. This discourse pattern he refers to as the "Preferred Argument Structure" (or PAS).[23] Du Bois sug-

---

[22] By no means do the two types discussed so far exhaust the possible ways in which languages encode participant roles. There are, for instance, so called "active languages" (or "split S languages") that distinguish between Subjects that are active and Subjects that are not (Dixon 1994: ch. 4; Mithun 1991). Durie (1987, 1988) discusses Acehnese, an Austronesian language spoken in the province of Aceh, Indonesia, which has two main grammatical relations, which he calls, following Fowley and Van Valin (1984), Actor and Undergoer – the latter term replaces "Object." Intransitive verbs take either an Actor or an Undergoer, depending on their semantics. For a discussion of "split intransitive" languages, see DeLancey (1981), Garrett (1990), Merlan (1985), Van Valin (1990).

[23] Similar conclusions were independently reached by Elinor Ochs and myself working on Samoan discourse. See Duranti (1981), Duranti and Ochs (1990), and Ochs (1988). See section 6.6 below.

gested that by looking at discourse we can see a number of conflicting motivations for one grammatical system over another. The discourse distinction between Subject and Object on the one hand and the Agent on the other would favor the development of an ergative-absolutive system. But Agents and Subjects are linked in other ways, including the factors that make them high in the topicality hierarchy (see figure 6.2 above). Agents and Subjects tend to be human, topical, and definite. Objects tend to be non-human, non topical, and indefinite.

6.5.5 Transitivity in grammar and discourse

One of the main lessons of discourse-oriented studies of grammar like the one just mentioned has been the realization that what grammarians might analyze as autonomous syntax, discourse analysts might re-analyze as the product of social, psychological, and narrative factors.

Combining language typology with discourse analysis (in this case mostly based on written discourse) Hopper and Thompson (1980) presented a complex argument in favor of the notion of **transitivity** as a universal dimension of grammar. They showed that if we think of transitivity as a property of clauses that share certain types of semantic and pragmatic features, we are able to explain why languages may use the same morphological and syntactic devices for constructions that would otherwise seem quite unrelated and may not use the same morphological and syntactic devices for constructions that would otherwise seem quite similar. Starting from a pre-theoretical understanding of transitivity as "a global property of an entire clause, such that an activity is 'carried-over' or 'transferred' from an agent to a patient," they introduced a number of **parameters**, that is, semantico-pragmatic features of transitive clauses. They included information about whether in the depicted event:

A. there are one or two participants,
B. the sentence represents an action,
C. the action is complete (telic) or not (atelic),
D. it occurs at one particular point,
E. there is volitionality (willingness) in carrying out the action,
F. it is affirmative or negative,
G. it is presented as actually occurring (realis) or as hypothetical (irrealis),
H. there is a high or low degree of potency in the way the action is performed,
I. the Object is totally affected,
J. the Object is individuated, that is, identifiable, specific, or definite.

193

The eight parameters or features are here reproduced schematically in table 6.4.

Table 6.4 *Parameters of transitivity*

	High transitivity	Low transitivity
A. Participants	at least A and O	1 participant
B. Kinesis	action	non-action
C. Aspect	telic	atelic
D. Punctuality	punctual	non-punctual
E. Volitionality	volitional	non-volitional
F. Affirmation	affirmative	negative
G. Mode	realis	irrealis
H. Agency	A high in potency	A low in potency
I. Affectedness of O	O totally affected	O not affected
J. Individuation of O	O highly individuated	O non-individuated

Hopper and Thompson showed that these parameters help explain the extent to which a clause is likely to exhibit morphological and syntactic features associated with transitivity.

> Transitivity, then ... can be broken down into its component parts, each focusing on a different facet of this carrying-over in a different part of the clause. Taken together, they allow clauses to be characterized as MORE or LESS Transitive: the more features a clause has in the "high" column in [the list] A-J, the more Transitive it is – the closer it is to CARDINAL Transitivity.
>
> (Hopper and Thompson 1980: 253)

This list allows us to rank any two sentences in any language along a hierarchy of transitivity. Take for instance the three sentences below. According to the hierarchy presented above, (37) is more transitive than (38) and (39):

(37) The boy ate the fish
(38) The boy ate
(39) The boy likes fish

According to the list of parameters presented above, (37) is the highest in transitivity because it describes an event in which there are two participants (feature A), it is an action (feature B), it is described from the end point (as accomplished), that is, its aspect is telic (feature C), the action is described as punctual (it happens at a precise point) (feature D), the object (the fish) is directly and totally affected (feature I), and is individuated (an animate referent expressed by a singular definite

194

noun) (feature J). On the other hand, (38) describes a situation with only one participant, and (39) depicts a scene in which, although there are two participants, the event depicted is not an action, is not completed, and is not punctual; furthermore, the Object of the sentence is non-individuated (a common noun with a generic meaning) and is not affected by the state of mind attributed to the referent of the Subject. Given the Transitivity Hierarchy, we would expect languages that mark transitivity morphologically and syntactically to treat those sentences differently. This is indeed what happens in Samoan, an ergative language. Only in the first type of sentence – see (40) below – do we find the ergative marker on the Subject (Agent), whereas the Subject of the second sentence is marked as an Absolutive (with no preposition) – see (41). The third type of sentence – in (42) – treats the nominal that is the Direct Object in English as an Oblique Object, with a preposition (*i*), which encodes a different type of participation:

(40)   *na*   `*ai*    *e*    *le*    *tama*    *le*    *i`a*
       Pst   eat   Erg   Art   boy   Art   fish
       "The boy ate the fish"

(41)   *na*   `*ai*   *le*   *tama*
       Pst   eat   Art   boy
       "The boy ate"

(42)   *e*   *fiafia*   *le*   *tama*   *i*   *le*   *i`a*
       Pres   happy   Art   boy   Prep   Art   fish
       "The boy likes (the) fish"

Hopper and Thompson argued that these features of transitivity are discourse related, in the sense that they correlate with the types of sentences that tend to appear in what they call **foreground** and **background**.

> Users of a language are constantly required to design their utterances in accord with their own communicative goals and with their perception of their listeners' needs. Yet, in any speaking situation, some parts of what is said are more relevant than others. That part of a discourse which does not immediately and crucially contribute to the speaker's goal, but which merely assists, amplifies, or comments on it, is referred to as BACKGROUND. By contrast, the material which supplies the main points of the discourse is known as FOREGROUND. (Hopper and Thompson 1980: 280)

This work, in other words, continues in the tradition of looking at language as mainly having a referential and denotational function, but it adds the important dimension of the speaker's (or writer's) **point of view** (or, as Polanyi-Bowditch calls it, **grounding**). Speakers are seen as framing their speech to present particular perspectives on the world and linguistic structures are in turn shown to be sensitive to such discursive and interactional goals.

This kind of work is important to linguistic anthropologists for a number of reasons: (i) it shows that what appear as different morphological systems might in fact be sensitive to the same set of semantic or pragmatic features; (ii) it claims that semantic distinctions are important in the evolution and use of morphosyntactic categories; (iii) it connects morphological, syntactic, and lexical distinctions to discourse features such as foreground and background information; and, finally, (iv) it presents an implicit theory of agency and participation that can be relevant to the work of ethnographers interested in local theories of action, causation, and responsibility.

I pursued some of these questions in my own work on Samoan grammar (Duranti 1994). In 1978–79, while collecting and starting to analyze Samoan adult and child language data, Elinor Ochs, Martha Platt, and I discovered that transitive clauses with fully expressed (that is, lexical) Agents – such as the one in (40) above – were very rare in spontaneous Samoan discourse. As also discovered by Du Bois in analyzing Sacapultec and English narratives (see above), in Samoan discourse Agents are often talked about without being expressed lexically, as shown in (43) below, where the referent of the Agent of the predicate "take your picture" (*pu`e le aka o `oe*) is understood from the context, through what grammarians call "zero anaphora":[24]

> (43) (Pesio, book 16; Mother talks to her daughter about researcher
> Elinor Ochs who has a camera)
> Mother: *kū   i   luga e siva se`i    pu`e le aka   o `oe*
> stand Prep top to dance so-that take the picture of you
> "Stand up to dance so that (she) will take your picture."

Other times, the referent of the Agent is introduced in prior discourse and is not repeated inside of the transitive clause, as in (44), where the sentence *e le`i faia le mea lā i lumāfale* "has not done (i.e. completed) the place there in front of the house" is understood as having Gimei as its Agent:

> (44) ("The inspection"; Orator T. points out to Chief Salanoa that
> the grass in front of Gimei's house has not been properly cleaned)
>
> T: *va'ai iā Gimei e le`i faia le  mea  lā   i  lumāfale,  ali`i Salagoa!*
> look at Gimei Past do the place there in front-house sir Salanoa
> "look at Gimei (she) hasn't done that part in front of the house,
> Mr. Salanoa."

---

[24] For a pragmatic treatment of zero anaphora, see Levinson (1987).

Furthermore, it is not uncommon for propositions that would be expressed by a transitive clause in English to be expressed in Samoan with an intransitive clause in which the participant who performed a particular task appears as a modifier of the Subject of the predicate. Thus, in (45) the Subject nominal, *le lāuga a le kamaloa ʼo Pua* "the (formal) speech of the man (named) Pua" contains a description of a referent that in English can be rendered with an Agent of a transitive clause:

(45)   ("The watch"; three chiefs are discussing the virtues of various
       orators they are familiar with and remembering specific cases
       in which each of them performed)

F: *puʼupuʼu   le   lāuga   a   le   kamaloa   ʼo   Pua.*
   short   the   speech   of   the   man   Pred   Pua
   (literally) "the man Pua's speech (was) short"
   or "The man Pua gave a short speech."

Given these recurrent patterns, I became interested in analyzing the contexts in which lexical Agents do appear. In order to pursue this goal, I examined the speeches of several political meetings or *fono* I had recorded in 1979. I found that speakers tended to express lexical Agents when praising or blaming someone. Thus, it was not unusual for a lexically expressed Agent to be the Christian God (in positive assessments) or a person or group that was being accused of having violated some social norm (in negative assessments). Furthermore, I found that those who were perceived as the most authoritative members of the council used transitive constructions with lexical Agents more often than other members. Less powerful speakers, instead, avoided the use of explicit Agents. This suggests not only that there is a special **moral force** in the use of a transitive clause with a fully expressed Agent, but that there is a correlation between grammatical forms and the political stature of people in the community. Powerful members of the community tend to use a type of discourse that is higher on the transitivity scale than the discourse of less powerful members. In this perspective, Hopper and Thompson's discussion of transitivity acquires a new meaning. It becomes an important tool for sociocultural anthropologists to assess the strategies through which hierarchies are socially constructed. The tools of discourse analysis combined with ethnography allow us to move towards a better understanding of what we might call the culture of grammar.

6.6   The acquisition of grammar in language socialization studies

The integration of grammatical and cultural analysis has been particularly successful in the study of language acquisition done by linguistic anthropologists.

This work was partly stimulated by the growth of psycholinguistics in the 1960s and 1970s inspired by Chomsky's claims about innateness in language acquisition (Chomsky 1959, 1966, 1968).

Although the acquisition of language was often mentioned by cultural and linguistic anthropologists as intimately connected to the acquisition of culture, most of the work in linguistic anthropology up to the mid-1960s was almost exclusively devoted to adult speech. The importance of collecting acquisition data from non-Indo-European languages was first understood by psycholinguists eager to test Chomsky's (1965) notion of "Universal Grammar" and the supposedly innate "Language Acquisition Device" (LAD). It was in this intellectual climate that psychologists like Dan Slobin at the University of California at Berkeley began to collaborate with linguists and anthropologists in search of new methods for obtaining data across societies that could be compared with data from English-speaking children in white middle-class America. The Berkeley group produced a *Field Manual* (Slobin 1967) that was meant to be used as a guide for collecting linguistic data that would be comparable to the considerable English corpus already available. Despite the good intentions, however, the five dissertations written on language acquisition in non-Indo-European languages based on the field manual were disappointing. Their failure reinforced the need for a contextualized, ethnographically based study of language acquisition:

> These disappointing results seem to have come about in part due to the fact that researchers encountered a number of unanticipated difficulties in following the research design in the field situation. Experiments could not be successfully administered and carried out because this type of activity was culturally inappropriate in the societies under study. Researchers found, moreover, that the speech samples they recorded could be collected only in what they admitted were culturally inappropriate situations ...
>
> (Schieffelin 1979: 75)

A new wave of language acquisition research started in the 1970s mostly (but not exclusively) by linguistic anthropologists focused on the situations in which a child would be likely to interact with more mature speakers of the language instead of trying to bring to the field an experimental design that originated in a scientific lab and had little if anything to do with real-life situations (Crago 1988; Demuth 1983; Heath 1983; Kulick 1992; Ochs 1988; Platt 1982; Schieffelin 1990). Once a different, more ethnographically based approach to language acquisition was in place, language appeared not only as the goal of child-adult or younger child-older child verbal interaction but also as an essential instrument of socialization.[25] While learning to speak a language, children become members of their society. In this perspective, language acquisition cannot be separated from **language socialization** – to be interpreted as socialization *to* language as well as socialization *through* language (Ochs and Schieffelin 1984). This new approach to language acquisition has established new theoretical and methodological standards for research. Thus, grammarians (e.g. Chomsky 1965) have typically assumed that the end goal of language acquisition is the production of **competent speakers**, but they have not analyzed the variety of meanings that such a concept might have for the members of a given group. Marjorie Goodwin (1990), for instance, argued that African American boys and girls develop a different kind of competence for verbally dealing with conflict (see chapter 9). Kulick (1992) showed that multilingual adult members of the Gapun community in Papua New Guinea socialize their children to become monolingual (in the local pidgin, Tok Pisin) even though they insist that they would like their children to also acquire the local vernacular (Taiap). In this case, as well as in the Haitian community in New York City studied by Schieffelin (1994), parents' theory of what needs to be done to teach children to speak a given language and parents' socializing practices are intimately related to their ideology of what is valuable and for what purpose. Reviewing these and other studies of language acquisition and socialization, Ochs and Schieffelin (1995: 91) have thus argued that *grammatical development must be seen as an outcome of (1) the socially and culturally organized activities in which children participate regularly, and (2) the language(s) children are implicitly encouraged to acquire.* These two dimensions of language development bring language acquisition studies back where they belong, namely, the context of children's lives. This statement should not be interpreted as a permission to ignore biological and cognitive factors in language acquisition, but as an invitation to document progress in the acqustion of grammar in the context of existing interactional practices and existing ideologies of what it means to be a competent speaker in a given community.

6.7 Metalinguistic awareness: from denotational meaning to pragmatics

Much of the progress that has been made in formal linguistic analysis in the last century is due to what the Russian linguist Roman Jakobson called the **metalinguistic function** of language, namely, the use of language to describe and analyze language ("a 'cat' is a three letter word," "the German word for 'development' is 'Entwicklung,'" etc.) (see chapter 9). This function is an essential part of the ability that native speakers – linguists included – use to isolate certain linguistic

---

[25] For a collection of child language studies in different languages that includes descriptions based on ethnographic work, see Slobin (1985a, 1985b, 1992).

forms and identify their meaning or function in discourse (either in an idealized, imagined context or in a specific one). It is the function of language that allows dictionaries and grammars to be written. The related concept of **metalinguistic awareness** is the knowledge that speakers have of their own language. Such knowledge is typically accessed through introspection and is considered by most linguists today an indispensable resource for linguistic analysis. There is no question that a great deal can be learned about a language by sitting down with native speakers and asking them questions about their language. This is often done with bilingual speakers to whom the linguist asks questions such as "How do you say — in your (native) language?," "What does this (word/phrase/ sentence) mean?," "Does this sound right?" "Does it make sense?" "Could it have a different meaning?", "Is there another way of saying that same thing?" and so on. The same method can be used with monolingual speakers as researchers learn the few basic phrases and questions necessary to elicit a basic vocabulary first and then slowly build up a repertoire of increasingly complex grammatical patterns (e.g. compound words, complex phrases, sentences with embedded clauses). This procedure, based on native speakers' intuitions and fieldworkers' trained ear to transcribe what they hear, is a powerful instrument for gaining access to the grammatical patterns of any language. At the same time, much of the work in sociolinguistics and linguistic anthropology in the last three decades has shown that elicitation techniques alone can be problematic and should always be integrated with other methods, including hypotheses based on when an expression is used or how frequent it is in spontaneous speech. Some of the limits of elicitation techniques have to do with limits inherent in introspection as a guide to speakers' knowledge of their use of language. William Labov's (1966, 1972a) work on phonological variation, for instance, provides evidence of the failure of introspection to capture important regularities in the ways in which the same speaker changes pronunciation from one context to the next or the ways in which a community as a whole treats certain linguistic forms (by moving from one type of pronunciation to another or from a variable rule to a categorical rule). Speakers' metalinguistic awareness does not include their ability to fully predict the type of variation their pronunciation exhibits in different social and cultural contexts.

As suggested by Silverstein (1981), the power of introspection and hence the reliability of metalinguistic awareness native speakers have may vary with the type of linguistic phenomena we are trying to describe. It seems relatively easy, for instance, for speakers to identify the referential meaning of a word when it names a concrete, visible object. In these cases, elicitation can be done by what philosophers call **ostensive definition** ("What is this?" "An apple." "What does 'foot' mean?" "This.").

The same technique can be used for verbs or adjectives that describe activities or ways of being that can be represented by stereotypical movements or gestures. Thus, the meaning of the English verb *walk* can be illustrated by engaging in the act of walking and the adjective *big* can be explained by mimicking with the hands and arms something very large or tall. Things get more complicated, however, when we want to understand the meaning of words like *intelligence*, *implication, responsibility*. In these cases, we need to construct scenarios that can evoke such concepts. As anyone who has tried to teach a foreign language knows, we cannot always assume that a given gesture or even a whole anecdote will trigger the type of understanding we are looking for. When we get into constructing stereotypical scenes and characters, we are entering the realm of culture. How do we represent for instance the meaning of *sad, happy, angry, offended, pleased*? It depends on what conditions a given group of people see as associated with such states of mind. In some cultures, for instance, people might be characterized as sad when they are alone in their house, whereas in other cultures the same situation might be seen as a blessing!

It is even more difficult for native speakers to describe the relationship between linguistic forms and their **pragmatic functions**, that is, the use of speech forms to evoke or establish particular types of contexts, including the speaker's stance or attitude, the social relations or relative status of the participants, and special attributes of particular individuals.

Extending Jakobson's notion of metalinguistic function, Silverstein (1981, 1985b, 1993) introduced the term **metapragmatic function** for the use of language to describe such contextual aspects of speech-as-action (see chapter 7). He posited that the success one might have in getting access to a speaker's **metapragmatic awareness** – that is, their ability to articulate the context for the use of certain linguistic expressions – was not random but tied to certain properties of the linguistic signs in questions. These properties include the referential quality of a linguistic form, that is, its ability to identify a particular referent (e.g. "the pronoun *vous* in this case refers to the speaker's father") and the relative creativity of the pragmatic sign, that is, the extent to which it presupposes the existence of what it refers to or instead helps establish it in the context.

According to Silverstein, when a linguistic sign seems to establish rather than presuppose a particular relationship, stance, or status, it becomes more difficult for native speakers to be aware of such functions. In other words, the more **context-creating** a linguistic sign is, the more difficult it is for native speakers to be conscious of its pragmatic force. I will illustrate this point with an example from my own work on Italian subject pronouns.

6.7.1   The pragmatic meaning of pronouns

In Italian – as in many other languages, but not in English – the subject of a sentence with a finite verb does not need to be expressed for the sentence to be grammatical (a property of Italian syntax that has been called by generative grammarians "pronoun-drop"). Both (46) and (47) are perfectly acceptable Italian sentences and have the same denotational meaning, that is, they are considered true under the same conditions:

(46) *lui è   arrivato alle   sette*
      he   has   arrived   at-the   seven
      "he arrived at seven o'clock"

(47) *è   arrivato alle   sette*
      has   arrived   at-the   seven
      "(he) arrived at seven o'clock"

Grammarians who used native speakers' intuitions (often their own) to study this phenomenon acknowleged that the presence of the subject pronoun in sentences like (46) is somewhat "marked" or special and suggested that it is due to **emphasis** or **contrast**.[26] In other words, since Italian sentences *do not need* a full subject pronoun to be acceptable sentences and in fact most of the time do not have one in discourse, the presence of *lui* in sentences like (46) was interpreted either as an answer to a question about the identity of the subject ("who arrived at seven o'clock?") or as a follow-up to a prior assertion ("nobody arrived at seven o'clock"). When I examined transcripts of Italian conversations, however, I found that the actual use of third person subject pronouns[27] suggested the possibility of a different analysis. I discovered that, rather than indicating contrast or emphasis, pronouns like *lei* "she" and *lui* "he" tended to be used for **main characters**, that is, referents who were recurrently talked about and toward whom the speaker displayed interest and **positive affect**. The same pronouns were not used for **minor characters**, which were instead referred to by demonstratives like *questo* "this one" and *quello* "that one." When a demonstrative was used for a main character, it co-occurred with negative evaluations, that is, it coincided with the speaker describing someone as incompetent or annoying. I concluded then that personal pronouns tended to be used for **positive affect** and demonstratives for **negative affect** (Duranti

---

[26] Summarizing the position of generative grammarians working on Italian, Haegeman (1994: 21) writes: "When no contrast or no special focus on the subject is needed the [subject] pronoun is absent."

[27] I restricted the analysis to pronominal expressions referring to individuals who were not present.

1984b). None of these pragmatic factors had been available to native speakers' consciousness.

In light of Silverstein's suggestions, one might speculate that the unavailability of this analysis to speakers' intuitions is related to the fact that the property of being main character and the property of being presented in a positive light are considerably high on a scale of pragmatic creativity. These properties, in other words, are not independent of pronominal usage. They are, instead, established through such discourse resources as the type of pronominal reference that is used (no subject vs. pronominal subject) (Duranti 1991). Given linguistic anthropologists' interest in the use of language as a resource for establishing particular institutional context and cultural practices, much of their work is likely to center around the more context-creating uses of language.

The more dependent on context a given expression, the more difficult it is to describe its functioning by just using intuitions about isolated sentences or made up stretches of discourse. Knowledge of grammar that includes linguistic structures as well as conditions for their use must thus be obtained by integrating elicitation and introspection with observation and documentation of language use. Recent work on metapragmatic awareness displayed during real-life interaction suggests that what might be difficult to evoke in elicitation contexts might instead be naturally produced during spontaneous interaction. Marco Jacquemet (1994) examined "pronominal violations" during court hearings involving the *pentiti di Camorra*, witnesses who had belonged to the criminal organization known as "Camorra" (the Neapolitan version of the Sicilian Mafia), had "repented" and decided to collaborate with the Justice Department. He showed that speakers involved in public confrontations in front of a judge often produce what he calls "metapragmatic attacks," that is, inpromptu accusations based on the use of address forms by their interlocutor. These attacks typically take the form of complaints about the offence produced by the use of a T-form, that is, a second person singular form in place of a more formal V-form (Brown and Gilman 1960):

(48)　(From Jacquemet 1994: 307, with slightly different transcription
　　　conventions, translation, and the addition of the features [T] and
　　　[V] to signal the address form being used by the speaker. Capitals
　　　for pronouns indicate that a full pronoun is being used instead of
　　　only the subject-verb agreement.)

01 LM: =non deviare i ragionamenti,	01 LM: stick to the point!		
02 Pan: non sto devian-do=	02 Pan: I'm not deviating!		
03 LM: =non girare attorno,=	03 LM: don't circumvent this		
04 Pan: non sto- deviando (? ?)	04 Pan: I am not deviating		
05 LM: mi vuoi portare	05 LM: you [T] want to make me		
06 a dimenticare le cose,	06 forget things,		
07 se tu parli	07 if YOU [T] speak		
08 è giusto?	08 isnt' it right?		
09 di fiancheggiatori-	09 about supporters		
10 Pan: ma scusi- ma lei mi-	10 Pan: excuse me [V], but YOU [V]		
11 mi ha mai conosciuto a me?	11 have you [V] ever met me (before)?		
12 LM: a te? (..) mai,=	12 LM: YOU [T]? never		
13 Pan: e allora pecché dà del tu,=	13 Pan: why then are you [V] using "tu"?		

What is striking about this and the other examples discussed by Jacquemet is that the "metapragmatic attack" takes place right after the prior speaker used the full pronoun *tu*. In the example above, speaker LM is already addressing speaker Pan in the T-form in line 01 (*non deviare* means "(you, sing.) do not deviate," that is, "stick to the point"). The "attack," however, does not take place until LM has used the full pronoun *tu* in line 07. This not only confirms my earlier hypothesis that the optional presence of full subject pronouns in Italian might carry an affective load, but that, as suggested by Silverstein, different linguistic forms evoke different levels of awareness in speakers-hearers.

6.8   From symbols to indexes

The discussion in the last section has highlighted an important feature of linguistic anthropological studies of grammatical forms. They are concerned with what these forms do. In order to find out what they do, researchers need to pay attention to the context in which they are used. A pronoun like the Italian *tu*, for example, may have a pragmatic effect that is not predictable solely on the basis of its grammatical meaning (tu = "second person singular"). It is such a pragmatic effect that makes the use of the pronoun in (48) problematic.

Most grammarians try to avoid discussion of the pragmatic effects of linguistic expressions by focusing on words as **symbols**. They treat linguistic expression as signs whose meaning is strictly defined by convention (Peirce 1940). Symbols are *arbitrary* representations of meanings (Saussure 1959). To say that the English word *go* is a symbol means that it has no iconic or indexical relation with the concept it represents. The lack of iconic relation between a word like *go* and what it stands for is usually demonstrated by pointing out that other languages have totally different sound sequences for the same concept. Italian uses *andare*, Samoan *alu*, English *go*. When philosophers and grammarians work on language and use words like *go, love, red, house, bird*, or sentences like *all men are mortal, birds fly, love is an emotion*, they are relying on words as symbols. In the next sections, I will briefly discuss two other kinds of signs, icons and indexes, which have different properties from symbols. Icons suggest similarity between words and objects or events and indexes, as we already saw in section 1.4.2, have an existential relation with their referent (Burks 1948–49: 674) and therefore they force us to deal with context.

6.8.1 Iconicity in languages

An **icon** is a sign that exhibits or exemplifies its object or referent – this often means that an icon resembles its referent in some respect. Pictures as well as diagrams are typical examples of icons.[28] But words can also have an iconic character. This is the case, for instance, in **onomatopoeic** words, that is, words that, although in a conventional way, do try to reproduce some aspect of the sound they represent or of the sound effects caused by the activity described by the word (English *ding-dong, splash, plop, whack*, Japanese *gacha-gacha* "rattle," *shabu-shabu* "splish-splash," *kasa-kasa* "rustle"). These phenomena are part of a larger class of iconic properties of linguistic sounds, generally included under the more general phenomenon of **phonosymbolism** (or **sound symbolism**). In addition to onomatopoeia, other recognized iconic phenomena include the use of intonation, lengthening, and volume to emphasize particular emotional states or stances and the correspondence between certain types of sounds and certain meanings (Berlin 1992; Cardona 1976: 161–3; Hinton et al 1994; Samarin 1971; Swadesh 1972). Such iconic aspects of linguistic sounds can be language specific or universal. In English, for example, words starting with /sl-/ have been said to be associated with unpleasant experiences (*slime, slither, slug, sloppy*) (Crystal

---

[28] For Peirce even an algebraic formula can be an icon. In this case, the likeness with the "object" it represents is rendered by conventional rules. "... an algebraic formula is an icon, rendered such by the rules of commutation, association, and distribution of the symbols. It may seem at first glance that it is an arbitrary classification to call an algebraic expression an icon; that it might as well, or better, be regarded as a compound conventional sign. But it is not so. For a great distinguishing property of the icon is that by the direct observation of it other truths concerning its object can be discovered than those which suffice to determine its construction. Thus, by means of two photographs a map can be drawn, etc. Given a conventional or other general sign of an object, to deduce any other truth than that which it explicitly signifies, it is necessary, in all cases, to replace that sign by an icon. This capacity of revealing unexpected truth is precisely that wherein the utility of algebraic formulae consists, so that the iconic character is the prevailing one" (Peirce 1940: 105–6).

1987: 174), in Hausa the sounds /kw, gw, 'kw/ – all requiring rounding of the lips – have been said to be associated with round objects (Gouffé 1966), and in Japanese the syllable /ra/ is found in the names of monsters of great size (Beatty 1994). Swadesh (1972: 141) pointed out that in many languages a high front vowel like [i] tends to be used to express nearness whereas non-front or back vowels like [a] and [u] tend to be used for distance. Brent Berlin, who studied the phenomenon of non-arbitrariness of names for plants and animals in many languages, found that in Huambisa Jivaro names for birds tend to have high front vowels much more often than names for fish. Berlin also tested an earlier hypothesis by Yakov Malkiel about the tendency to have the sound [r] in names for "frog" in Indo-European languages and found that [r] and the phonetically closely related [l] are also the most common sounds for names of frogs and toads in thirty-three non-Indo-European languages (Berlin 1992: 250). Hays (1994) reanalyzed the data, adding a wider spectrum of languages and found that there is support for Berlin's hypothesis, but there is even stronger evidence for /g/ and related sounds (e.g. /k/, [x], [ŋ]) in frog names in many languages around the world.

Although there is no general theory about why sound symbolism should occur, a variety of scholars agree that some languages (e.g. Korean, Japanese, Gbeya, Quechua) make abundant iconic use of sounds and that much more attention is due to these phenomena (see Hinton, Nichols, and Ohala 1994). Sound symbolism has been often associated with particular linguistic families. Thus, Bantu languages are well known for their **ideophones** at least since Doke (1935) introduced the term to refer to a vast range of onomatopoeic words that do not fit within other known grammatical categories.[29] More recently, ethno-musicologists like Steven Feld (1982) and sociocultural anthropologists like Ellen Basso (1985) have studied sound symbolism in the context of live verbal and musical performance. By studying sound symbolism in Pastaza Quechua narratives, instead of looking at isolated words, Nuckolls (1992, 1995) has been able to argue that sound symbolic words should not be studied only as iconic signs, given that they also share features of other kinds of signs such as symbols and indexes (see below).

Peirce originally distinguished between different kinds of iconicity, including what Haiman (1980) calls "imagic" and "diagrammatic." The examples mentioned so far are all imagic, given that the sign resembles the referent in some characteristic. Diagrammatic iconicity refers to an arrangement of signs "whose relationships to each other mirror the relationships of their referents" (Haiman 1980: 515). A classic example of this is the sequence of sentences in a narrative.

---

[29] See also Samarin (1967). On the issue of whether ideophones in Bantu and other African languages should be considered adverbs, see Moshi (1993).

In Julius Ceasar's famous *veni, vidi, vici* "I came, I saw, I conquered," the order of mention of different events mirrors the order in which they took place (Hopper and Traugott 1993: 26). Iconicity of this type has been studied by language typologists and other linguists interested in possible motivations for structural similarities across unrelated languages (Croft 1990: 164–92; Haiman 1980, 1985a, 1985b).

From an anthropological perspective, it is important to ask whether the abundance of iconicity in some languages is related to some specific cultural traits or practices. Some linguistic anthropologists have started to work in this direction. For example, Mannheim (1991) linked the abundance of iconic expressions in Peruvian Quechua to a cultural identification between words and objects.

> The Quechua fondness for iconicity corresponds to their orientation toward language in general. For Quechua speakers, language is part and parcel of the natural world. Words are consubstantial with their objects in a deeper sense than in the Western tradition: we have a long standing tradition ... that words stand for their objects and that language is (or at least should be) a mirror of the world. In Quechua culture, words are consubstantial with their objects in the same sense in which the Trinity is consubstantial. Language is both in and of the natural world ... The Quechua identification of word and object helps explain why practical knowledge of the everyday world is identified with knowledge of language and ability to speak and is designated with a single verb stem, yachay, which is usually translated as "to know," but also can be used to mean "to know Quechua" without any modification and without mentioning the language.
>
> (Mannheim 1991: 184)

These observations are not only a description of language ideology (section 3.5). They are also linked to a series of hypotheses about the direction of sound change – especially the development of glottalization and aspiration. As a linguistic anthropologist, Mannheim is interested in integrating previous structuralist and sociolinguistic analyses of language change with an ethnographically informed study of Quechua speakers' aptitude for linguistic imagery.

6.8.2 Indexes, shifters, and deictic terms

An **index** is a sign that identifies an object not because of any similarity or analogy with it, but because of some relationship of contiguity with that object. Such a relationship can best be understood by first considering some of the non-linguistic examples provided by Peirce, namely, a barometer or a weathercock.

The weathercock is an index of the direction of the wind for two reasons: because it assumes the same direction as the wind and because when we see the weathercock pointing in a certain direction, our attention is drawn to that direction.

> A low barometer with a moist air is an index of rain; that is we suppose that the forces of nature establish a probable connection between the low barometer with moist air and coming rain.
> A weathercock is an index of the direction of the wind; because in the first place it really takes the self-same direction as the wind, so that there is a real connection between them, and in the second place we are so constituted that when we see a weathercock pointing in a certain direction it draws our attention to that direction ... (1940: 109)

In other words, indices (or **indexes**, as most scholars prefer today) are signs that have some kind of spatial and/or temporal connection with what they refer to or, more generally, an existential relation with their referent (Burks 1948–49).

Although the importance of the indexical properties of linguistic signs has long been recognized within a number of different theoretical traditions,[30] the meaning of the term *index* varies across some of these traditions. For instance, Charles Bally, a student of the Swiss linguist Ferdinand de Saussure (see chapter 6), used in the 1920s the (French) word *indices* to refer to expressions that give out information about some aspect of the context or situation in which they are used without having been so designed by the speaker. Thus, a particular pronunciation or lexical choice might inform the hearer about the speaker's social class (Bally 1952: 60) – this is close to what Labov and others call *sociolinguistic markers*. For Bally, however, *indices* are different from signs rather than one of their subtypes. Whereas an index (or French *indice*) is the product or effect (*procès*) of a message that was produced for other means, a sign (*signe*) is a means or procedure (*procédé*) purposely used by the speaker to inform about something (Bally 1952: 77).

In the functionally oriented linguistic literature published in English, certain types of indices have been called **shifters** (Jespersen 1923; Jakobson [1957] 1970) and **deictic terms** (Fillmore 1966; Lyons 1977). The term "shifter" calls attention to the property that linguistic signs like *I, you, here, now, yesterday* and tense forms have to "shift" their meaning from one context to the next. The term

---

[30] Husserl ([1913]1970: 682) spoke of "essentially occasional expressions" and wrote:
"'This' is an essentially occasional expression which only becomes fully significant when we have regard to the circumstances of utterance, in this case to an actually performed percept."

"deictic" – from "deixis" (originally a Greek term meaning "pointing" or "indicating") (cf. Lyons 1977: 836) – highlights the spatio-temporal anchoring of linguistic expressions that can only be interpreted vis-à-vis such an anchoring.[31]

> Deixis is the name given to those aspects of language whose interpretation is relative to the occasion of utterance; to the time of utterance, and to times before and after the time of utterance; to the location of the speaker at the time of utterance; and to the identity of the speaker and the intended audience.
>
> (Fillmore 1966: 220)

An extensive analysis of one system of deictic terms that well illustrates the notion of index is Hanks's (1990) study of language and space in Maya (a Mayan language from the Yucatan, in Mexico). Hanks argued that "deixis, both as a linguistic subsystem and as a kind of act, is a *social construction*, central to the organization of communicative practice and intelligible only in relation to a sociocultural system" (Hanks 1990: 5). Hanks's study shows that it is possible to extend structuralist analysis of linguistic forms to complex conceptualizations of the human body as a corporeal field that is routinely used by speakers to make sense of each other's utterances within a culturally defined living space (see also section 9.5).

6.8.2.1   Indexical meaning and the linguistic construction of gender

While telling stories, describing properties of objects or calling someone's attention, speakers also manage to do many other things with language that are less detectable but equally effective. By listening to someone giving directions, for instance, we might be able to gather information on where that person comes from, his social class, his familiarity with the surroundings, his relationship with his interlocutors, and maybe even his political views (Brown and Fraser 1979; Brown and Levinson 1979). This is possible because the language we use carries in it a social history, a series of connections to times and places where the same expressions or the manner in which they are articulated have been used before. To refer to this power of language to evoke realities beyond the literal content of what is being talked about, sociolinguists and linguistic anthropologists in the past used the term **social meaning**. Now the same concept is conveyed in terms of **indexical meanings**. For example, one way of thinking about honorifics is to treat them as indexes of particular social identities or relations (see section 6.4).

The notion of indexical meaning has been particularly fruitful in the study of

---

[31] The Cognitive Anthropology Research Group at the Max Planck Institute for Psycholinguistics in Nijmegen, The Netherlands, has produced a considerable number of empirical studies on the cognitive and cultural aspects of spatial deixis in several languages. For a useful bibliography on this topic, see Peters, van Gool and Messing (1992).

the linguistic constitution of gender. McConnell-Ginet (1988) introduced the notion of *gender deixis* to refer to the phenomenon by which "the particular form of some linguistic unit *expresses* or *means* something about gendered properties of the circumstances of language production, the gendered perspective from which an utterance is produced" (1988: 80). That is, certain linguistic expressions come to be associated with either female or male speakers usually because of the types of activities during which they are used or because of a particular attitude or affective stance associated with one gender over another. For instance, in her study of Tzeltal women's ways of speaking, Brown (1979, 1980) showed that women's tendency to be supportive and avoid disagreement was linguistically realized, in part, by the use of conversational **repeats**, whereby a speaker would repeat part of the prior speaker's utterance, adding an intonation to indicate surprise, interest, or agreement. Sometimes the repeat could also be repeated. Although Tzeltal men also produce repeats, their cycles are not as long and polite as the women's. In this case, the repeat can be seen as an index of gender. Its extended use is associated with a quality, agreement, that is in turn associated with or seen as appropriate to women. Similarly, in Japanese, the particles *zo* and *ze* convey an affective intensity that indicates forcefulness (Uyeno 1971). This is associated in Japanese society with being male. On the other hand, the use of the sentence particle *no* (Cook 1987) indexes that the authority of the utterance lies with a group, of which the speaker is a member.[32] This is a type of stance that indexes, among other values, those associated with being female in Japanese society.

These studies of gender show that we cannot say that certain features (e.g. certain speech acts, lexical terms, morphological markers, intonational patterns, voice quality) *always* presuppose either male or female identity (McConnell-Ginet 1988). For example, Brown (1993) found that Tzeltal women are not as polite as usual when they confront one another in court. In this setting, Tzeltal women may disagree, overlap one another extensively, and overtly express hostility, anger, and contempt. This means that instead of saying that certain expressions or linguistic strategies are used *only by men* and some other expressions *only by women*, "[w]hat we find ... is that the features may be employed more by one than the other sex" (Ochs 1992: 340).[33]

Ochs generalized this and other findings by saying that there is a *non-exclusive relation* between language and gender (Ochs 1992: 340). Typically, the same expressions and strategies associated with gender identity are also associated

[32] "When the speaker uses *no*, he/she authorizes what he/she is saying together with his/her group (i.e. the speaker *and* his/her group hold what he/she is saying to be true)" (Cook 1987: 128).

[33] For some useful methodological considerations on how to gather and use quantitative evidence for research on gender differences, see James and Clarke's (1993) critical review of the use of interruptions by men and women.

with other social features such as stance or social relations. For example, in some dialects of English tag questions (I go straight, *don't I?*) are used more often by female speakers, but they are also associated with a stance of hesitancy. To say that female gender is *indexed* by tag questions is then a simplification. It would be more accurate to say that tag questions index hesitancy and that hesitancy is, in turn, a stance that is associated with femininity (at least in some English-speaking communities). In Japanese, to use the sentence-final *wa* makes one's speech sound more "gentle" (Uyeno 1971). Hence, the particle *wa* indexes female identity because Japanese women are expected to be more "gentle" than men. Among the police officers studied by Bonnie McElhinny (1995), women confessed to using more profanities when they first got on the job because they wanted to sound more "masculine," even though they recognized that they might have overdone it – a case of what Labov (1972c) called "hypercorrection." Interviews revealed that female officers saw swearing as being tough and it was the men's alledged toughness that they wanted to match up to. Swearing becomes then one of the linguistic markers used to construct a particular type of social identity, one that includes such features as "being tough." It is being tough, in turn, that is used to construct "masculinity" in that particular community. In the Tamil village studied by Stephen Levinson, swear words were used more frequently by members of the dominant caste (Brown and Levinson 1979: 306). In that case, swearwords construct "forcefulness," which is in turn a characteristic of higher caste.

In each of these cases, gender identity (or other types of identities) is best seen as constituted by a variety of features, each of which is not necessarily or exclusively associated with either female or male. It is their combination and existential association with particular sets of stances and values that eventually produces one's gender identity. A study of the linguistic constitution of gender identities forces us to understand the cultural attitudes towards particular ways of being in the world. These attitudes often subscribe to hegemonic views of social hierarchies (e.g. men are tough and strong, women are gentle and weak), but other times, they might show some resistance to such views. A review of the ethnographic literature on features usually associated with women's ways of communicating (silence, indirectness, politeness, passivity) reveals that the same feature that in some context expresses submission in other contexts might index resistance, rejection, protest (Gal 1991). Similarly, in her discussion of how power and solidarity are expressed in discourse, Deborah Tannen warned us against the identification of certain linguistic forms with intentions to dominate. Silence, for example, does not always index feeling powerless. It can also be an instrument of power (Tannen 1993b: 177).

6.8.2.2 *Contextualization cues*
The more we learn about indexicality, the more we realize that speaking is a con-

tinuous process of contextualization. If talk helps establish what is going on, what one particular interaction is about, who the speakers are or who they would like to be, indexes are the basic tools that help participants negotiate such issues. They are used to clarify implicit questions such as: Where is this talk leading to? How is it relevant to what we were just talking about? Who should be talking next? What is an appropriate answer? Are we agreeing or disagreeing?

By studying multicultural settings in which people from different ethnic backgrounds come together using the "same" language, John Gumperz has identified a set of indexes, which he calls *contextualization cues*, that help "speakers signal and listeners interpret what the activity is, how semantic content is to be understood and *how* each sentence relates to what precedes or follows ... These features are ... habitually used and perceived but rarely consciously noted and almost never talked about directly. Therefore they must be studied in context rather than in the abstract" (Gumperz 1982a: 131). When a speaker's contextualization cues are misinterpreted or missed altogether, communication is in trouble and participants can end up speaking across purposes. This kind of situation is what Gumperz called **crosstalk**.

Gumperz (1992) showed that contextualization cues can operate at various levels of speech production, including the aspects of grammar introduced in this chapter (phonology, morphology, lexicon, syntax) as well as (i) prosody – i.e. intonation, stress or accenting and pitch –, (ii) paralinguistic signs – e.g. whispery, breathy, husky or creaky voice –, (iii) markers of tempo, including pauses and hesitations; (iv) overlaps (see chapter 8); (v), laughter, and (vi) formulaic expressions. Given the emphasis on syntax and phonology in theoretical linguistics and the difficulty of representing paralinguistic prosodic information with traditional orthography, most of these features of talk are often left out of linguistic analysis. Gumperz's study of interethnic communication and miscommunication has helped focus on these neglected characteristics of speech in interaction (see Couper-Kuhlen and Selting 1996).

Gumperz's work connects research on linguistic structures to cultural variation. He argues that immigrants' ability to apply for a job or get access to other economical resources is based on their ability to interpret and use the appropriate contextualization cues. This research links grammar to culture because contextualization is a universal process that produces and implies culture-specific knowledge. It is universal because it is based on the division of labor, "which in one form or another is characteristic of all human collectivities" (Gumperz 1996: 403), and it is culture-specific because division of labor implies differentiated exposure to particular communicative practices; hence, some sectors of the population are not exposed to the communicative resources necessary for gaining access to higher paid jobs. The economic separation between social groups is both the cause and the outcome of the cultural differences embedded in language use (see section 1.3).

6.9 Conclusions

If we try to understand how phrases and sentences can tell us something about relationships among people, objects, and events in the world, we must get down to analyze their constitutive parts, that is, words, morphemes, and even phonemes. As native speakers of a language, we do this most of the time intuitively, but as researchers, we need to be systematic, which means that we need sophisticated analytical tools; we need procedures that can be shown to yield the same results under the same conditions. The distinction between relations of oppositions and relations of contiguity illustrated at the beginning of this chapter is a first important step toward systematicity. In the discussion of some of the basic aspects of grammar as described by linguists in the last few decades, I have been mostly concerned with giving readers a sense of the logic of argumentation and representation followed by those who have been studying linguistic forms and their relationships. By no means have I done justice to the wealth of empirical data and theoretical discussion that characterizes the field of grammatical analysis. Those pursuing these topics further can choose among a number of useful introductions to linguistics and to its many subfields including discourse analysis, pragmatics, semantics, language typology, syntax, morphology, phonology, phonetics.

I have spent more pages on morphology than on any of the other aspects of linguistic structure. I believe that an understanding of morphology (especially in those languages that have a rich morphology!) is crucial for developing a systematic approach to the formulaic as well as creative aspects of language use, a theme that is an important part of many linguistic anthropological studies.

Although a large part of grammar is made out of components and principles that are quite frozen and not easily traced to functional contextual explanations, many grammatical phenomena have their motivation or explanation in domains that are larger than or of a different nature from grammar per se. I have tried to illustrate this point by discussing the marking of agency, transitivity, and the use of personal pronouns in conversation. In other words, although grammars have partly a logic of their own, it is important to uncover how much of that logic is intrinsic in the grammatical phenomena and how much of it is a product of other kinds of factors. This is particularly evident in the study of language acquisition and language socialization. It is only with a mind open to the interface between structure and use on the one hand and grammatical versus social and cultural units on the other that linguistic anthropologists can hope to establish language as a rich object of inquiry within the larger field of anthropology while contributing to the field of both descriptive and theoretical linguistics.

7

Speaking as social action

> It is written: "In the beginning was the Word!"
> Even now I balk. Can no one help?
> I truly cannot rate the word so high.
> I must translate otherwise.
> I believe the Spirit has inspired me
> and must write: "In the beginning there was Mind."
> Think thoroughly on this first line,
> hold back your pen from undue haste!
> Is it mind that stirs and makes all things?
> The text should state: "In the beginning there was Power!"
> Yet while I am about to write this down,
> something warns me I will not adhere to this.
> The Spirit's on my side! The answer is at hand:
> I write, assured, "In the beginning was the Deed."
>
> Johann Wolfgang von Goethe, *Faust*[1]

As in Faust's reinterpretation of John's Gospel, in this chapter, we will learn that words themselves can be seen as actions and that actions and activities should then be the units of analysis for the anthropological study of language use. In chapter six, we started to see that when we use language, we help constitute the reality we are trying to represent. This was made apparent in the discussion of indexical relations between linguistic expressions and features of the context in which they are used. Not only do certain expressions require an understanding of the surrounding world for their interpretation, they also actively shape such a surrounding world, especially in terms of social identities. The use of certain expressions provide more than the information necessary to identify the referent in discourse. They reveal the stance a speaker is taking vis-à-vis a given character in a story (see the discussion of Italian pronouns in section 6.7). The use of honorific morphemes and words entails a particular relation between speaker and hearer or between speaker and whom and what is talked about. All of these cases show that words can be not only symbols but also deeds.

[1] Translation by Peter Salm, *Faust, Part I*, New York: Bantam Books, 1985, p. 77.

In this chapter I will first discuss anthropologists' discovery of the pragmatic force of words and Malinowski's conceptual apparatus for dealing with this discovery. Then, I will introduce the basic concepts of speech act theory as developed by John Austin and John Searle. Some of those concepts will be critically assessed from an ethnographic and crosscultural perspective. Finally, I will introduce Wittgenstein's notion of "language game" and suggest ways in which it can be a useful notion for linguistic anthropological research.

7.1 Malinowski: language as action

The Polish-born British anthropologist Bronislaw Malinowski (1884–1942) was the first fieldworker who, in addition to combining all the methods previously used by other anthropologists (Sanjek 1990a: 210), learned the language of the people he was studying sufficiently well not only to ask questions but also to listen to everyday conversation and participate in it.[2] Knowledge of the language became essential to accomplish what was for him the major goal of ethnography, namely, "to grasp the native's point of view, his relations to life, to realize *his* vision of *his* world" (Malinowski 1922: 25). The two major concepts of Malinowski's ethnographic theory of language are: (i) the notion of **context of situation** and (ii) the view of **language as a mode of action**.

Malinowski was very intrigued by problems of translation. He soon realized that traditional grammatical analysis was only of limited help in capturing the meaning of native utterances.[3] He concluded that in several cases a word-by-

---

[2] British social anthropology placed a strong emphasis on the use of the native language for data collection. The sixth edition of *Notes and Queries on Anthropology*, for instance, contains a short but informative chapter (chapter IX, pp. 208–18) on language and a note on the importance of native texts: "The writing of texts, so valuable for obtaining linguistic material, gives important data, and cultural facts as well. Complete texts may be taken down from dictation by an informant who has been asked to relate some incident in his own daily life, some process in which he is interested, a story, myth, or event in family or tribal history. Such texts should be amplified by direct questioning; they then become valuable anthropological data. Further, texts should be made of everyday speech, of children's talk, of talk between kinsfolk, fellow workers, etc. Unless the investigator has a very good knowledge of the language he should try to have every text translated at once" (pp. 49–5).

[3] Malinowski was not alien to some of the pitfalls of earlier anthropologists so harshly criticized by Boas. In particular, in addition to the repeated use of such words as "primitive" and "savage," Malinowski occasionally slipped into the same type of preconception about "exotic" languages that had characterized earlier travelers who had no training in anthropological and linguistic analysis: "In a primitive tongue, the whole grammatical structure lacks the precision and definiteness of our own, though it is extremely telling in certain specific ways" (1923: 300).

Boas and others after him repeatedly demonstrated that what had often been called "primitive" in non-European languages was due not to any fault in their grammatical systems but to the descriptive and analytical limitations of the observers (cf. Boas 1911; Hill 1964).

word gloss or literal translation of a linguistic expression did not reveal the way in which a native speaker would understand it. A listener would also need "to be informed about the situation in which [certain] words were spoken. He would need to have them placed in their proper setting of native culture" (1923: 301).

To deal with these cases, he devised the concept of *context of situation* "which indicates on the one hand that the conception of *context* has to be broadened and on the other that the *situation* in which words are uttered can never be passed over as irrelevant to the linguistic expression" (Malinowski 1923: 306). This concept was just a corollary of a more general principle "namely, that the study of any language, spoken by a people who live under conditions different from our own and possess a different culture, must be carried out in conjunction with the study of their culture and of their environment" (ibid.). This meant that one cannot use the methods devised for the study of dead languages (e.g. Ancient Greek, Latin) to approach living languages. One needs instead an **ethnographic theory of language**. To the development of such a theory, he dedicated the second volume of his *Coral Gardens and Their Magic* (1935), an ethnographic study of the rituals associated with the cultivation of yams, taro, palms, and bananas in the Trobriand Islands.[4]

By the time he wrote this book, Malinowski had reached the conclusion that "the main function of language is not to express thought, not to duplicate mental processes, but rather to play an active pragmatic part in human behaviour" ([1935] 1978, vol. 2: 7). This is a major change with respect to his earlier writings and especially with respect to what he had stated in "The Problem of Meaning in Primitive Languages" (1923), where he introduced the notion of context of situation. There, he had drawn a sharp difference between "civilized" and "primitive" languages, with the former characterized as primarily devoted to communicating thoughts and the latter to getting things done.[5] Instead, in *Coral Gardens and Their Magic* ([1935] 1978) the **pragmatic** use of utterances was recognized as typical of any language.[6]

---

[4] The second volume is entitled *The Language of Magic and Gardening*. It starts with "Part four": "An ethnographic theory of language and some practical corollaries."

[5] "... language in its primitive function and original form has an essential pragmatic character; ... it is a mode of behaviour, and indispensable element of concerted human action" (Malinowski 1923: 316).

"... in one of my previous writings, I opposed civilized and scientific to primitive speech, and argued as if the theoretical uses of words in modern philosophic and scientific writing were completely detached from their pragmatic sources. This was an error, and a serious error at that" ([1935] 1978: 58).

[6] We find here also an early criticism of the "conduit metaphor" (cf. Reddy 1979): "The false conception of language as a means of transfusing ideas from the head of the speaker to that of the listener has, in my opinion, largely vitiated the philological approach to language" ([1935] 1978: 9). For a similar type of attack on the philological approach based on different theoretical premises, see Vološinov (1973).

Malinowski's writings on an ethnographic approach to language anticipate many of the ideas that later became the founding blocks of pragmatics as an interdisciplinary enterprise (Levinson 1983). Such ideas were in fact common in European intellectual circles of the time. Malinowski's notion of "verbal act" ([1935] 1978, vol. 2: 9) is akin to Austin's notion of "speech act," which was developed around the same time; the emphasis on translation as involving "whole contexts' is reminiscent of Wittgenstein's rethinking language in the 1930s and his emphasis on the interpretive method of embedding individual words within larger "language games" (see section 7.4). Even Malinowski's strongly behavioristic tone,[7] which seemed so anachronistic during the "cognitive revolution" of the 1960s – when it became fashionable to speak of minds as if they were computers –, could now be recast in a new light. It could be seen as anticipating recent concerns with the place and function of the body in the constitution of linguistic practices (Johnson 1987; Goodwin 1981; Hanks 1990). If speaking is a mode of action and words must be understood in their context, the bodies of the speakers can be important semiotic resources for understanding how language is produced and processed in face-to-face communication (Kendon 1990; 1992). In the second volume of his *Coral Gardens and Their Magic*, Malinowski offered an example of the kind of work that an ethnographic theory of language should produce by analyzing Trobianders' magic spells.

Malinowski's actual practice of translation of magic spells and his theory of the magical power of words has been criticized by a number of authors, most prominently by Tambaiah (1968, 1973, 1985), who argued that Malinowski's extensive word-by-word translations of the Trobianders' magic spells contradicted his contextual theory of language. Tambaiah also noted that Malinowski's view of the language of magic as consisting of untrue statements that are in direct opposition to reality (Malinowski [1935]1978, vol. 2: 239) missed the difference between statements that can be evaluated in terms of truth conditions and statements that must be evaluated in terms of their effects on the world. For Tambaiah, when Malinowski tries to assess how Trobianders could believe that what is said in magic will be realized, he is looking at the wrong types of effects. The issue is not whether a magic spell can make objects appear, transform plants, animals, and humans. Rather, magic formulas allow for the comparison of elements belonging to different realms (for instance, the natural world and the human body) and provide a guide for what the people themselves should expect or do under present circumstances. Thus, a magic formula that compares men (who have painted red designs on their body) to red fish does not mean that

---

[7] "Between the savage [sic] use of words and the most abstract and theoretical one there is only a difference of degree. Ultimately all the meaning of all words is derived from bodily experience" ([1935] 1978, vol. 2: 58).

people believe that men become red fish. Rather, the comparison is metaphorical and invokes a taboo to be followed by the people and not a transformation from the human to animal world (Tambaiah [1968] 1985: 47):

> It is a truer tribute to the savage mind to say that, rather than being confused by verbal fallacies or acting in defiance of known physical laws, it ingeniously conjoins the expressive and metaphorical properties of language with the operational and empirical properties of technical activity. (Tambaiah [1968] 1985: 53)

Tambaiah's criticism points to one of Malinowski's main problems. Despite his grasp of the pragmatic dimensions of language use and the realization that magic spells were both special and yet related to ordinary language, Malinowski did not develop a conceptual framework for analyzing different functions of speech or different types of relations between utterances and social acts.

7.2 Philosophical approaches to language as action

For an analytically more sophisticated theory of words as deeds, we must turn to two philosophers who were working in England at roughly the same time Malinowski was proposing his "speech in action" approach (see above): J. L. Austin and Ludwig Wittgenstein. Despite their common commitment to what we might call now a **pragmatic view** of language (language is used for doing things), these two remarkable thinkers had quite diverse positions on a number of key points, including the nature and goals of philosophy and its relation to other sciences. Between the two, Austin is certainly the more popular among linguists, although not necessarily among linguistic anthropologists (see section 7.3). Austin's popularity is partly due to the work of the American philosopher John Searle, who through his **Speech Act Theory** made Austin's ideas accessible to a wider audience including literary critics and psychologists, and partly due to the content and style of Wittgenstein's writings, which defy systematization and modeling.[8] As I will show below, however, it is precisely Searle's accentuation of certain features of Austin's theory, such as sincerity and intentionality, that have prompted the harshest criticism of speech act theory by linguistic anthropologists. Wittgenstein's ideas, on the other hand, are much closer in content and

---

[8] This characteristic of Wittgenstein's philosophical writings did not escape some of his interpreters, including the American philosopher Saul Kripke, who wrote: "I suspect ... that to attempt to present Wittgenstein's argument precisely is to some extent to falsify it" (1982: 5). And again: "[Wittgenstein's] own stylistic preference obviously contributes to the difficulty of his work as well as to its beauty" (ibid., fn. 4). Similarly, Bloor (1983: 138) wrote: "... the present chapter will have a distinctly un-Wittgensteinean tone. Exposition is going to give way to development. Analysis will give way to synthesis and theoretical construction."

spirit to an anthropological program for the study of language as social action and for this reason I will return to them later in this chapter.

7.2.1   *From Austin to Searle: speech acts as units of action*

In the 1940s Austin argued that philosophers' obsession with truth and truth values was due to the limited set of linguistic expressions used as data for the analysis of meaning. Sentences (1)–(3) are good examples of such expressions. They are all instances of what philosophers call *assertions* (and grammarians call *declarative sentences*[9]).

(1)   All men are mortal
(2)   The snow is white
(3)   The king of France is bald

Austin pointed out that there are many other uses of language besides assertions.[10] Like Malinowski, he argued that language is not just used to describe particular states of affairs (e.g. *the snow is white*) but to do things, that is, to perform some action:

> Suppose, for example, that in the course of a marriage ceremony I say, as people will, "I do" – (sc. take this woman to be my lawful wedded wife). Or again, suppose that I tread on your toe and say "I apologize." Or again, suppose that I have the bottle of champagne in my hand and say "I name this ship the *Queen Elizabeth*." Or suppose I say "I bet you sixpence it will rain tomorrow." In all these cases it would be absurd to regard the thing that I say as a report of the performance of the action which is undoubtedly done – the action of betting, or christening, or apologizing. We should say rather that, in saying what I do, I actually perform that action. When I say "I name this ship the *Queen Elizabeth*" I do not describe the christening ceremony, I actually perform the christening; and when I say "I do" (sc. take this woman to be my lawful wedded wife), I am not reporting on a marriage, I am indulging in it. (Austin [1956] 1970: 235)

---

[9] See footnote 15 on the meaning of "declarative" for grammarians.

[10] The idea of different "uses" or "functions" of linguistic expressions was quite popular in European circles in the 1930s and 1940s. As discussed in chapter 9, Jakobson's model of speech event with his six functions of language, for instance, draws heavily from Karl Bühler's theoretical work, which starts from assumptions such as the following: "Though we do not dispute the dominance of the representational [read 'referential-denotative'] function of language, what now follows is suited and intended to delimit it. The concept 'things' or the more adequate conceptual pair 'objects and states of affairs' does not capture everything for which the sound is a mediating phenomenon, a mediator between the speaker and the hearer" (Bühler [1934] 1990: 37).

Austin presented an analytical apparatus to talk about how utterances become social acts. His units of analysis reflected an interest in moving beyond grammatical and logical levels of analysis without completely losing track of them.

He distinguished three types of acts that we simultaneously perform when we speak:

1. *A locutionary act:* the act *of* saying something, that is, the act of uttering sequences of sounds that can be interpreted according to grammatical conventions and (sometimes) assigned truth values, e.g. *you're fired, I'll pay you back next week, what time is it?*

2. *An illocutionary act:* the act the speaker can accomplish *in* saying something by means of the conventional *force* of the locutionary act. Thus, *you're fired* may be used in our society to change someone's status from "employed" to "unemployed" (when uttered under the appropriate circumstances); the locution *I'll pay you back next week* may be used to commit oneself to a future action; the locution, in the form of a question, *what time is it?* can be used as a request for information (tell the time).

3. *A perlocutionary act:* the act produced by the uttering of a particular locution, that is, the consequences or effects of such locution regardless of its conventional force. These acts may or may not coincide with the goal of the illocutionary act. For instance, *you're fired*, pronounced by the right person (e.g. an employer) to the right person (e.g. an employee) under the appropriate circumstances (e.g. they are not both drunk) should produce the effect that the addressee loses his job. But it may also have the effect that the addressee becomes depressed and suicidal or conversely feels liberated (e.g. he no longer needs to resign from the job he hates). In either case, these consequences are not part of the conventional force of the illocutionary act expressed by the locution *you're fired*.

Austin restricted the use of the term **meaning** to the locutionary act and introduced the term **force** for the illocutionary act and the term **effect** for the perlocutionary act. The locutionary act is the level at which the propositional content of an utterance is established through the conventions of grammar and lexicon. These conventions are studied by linguists in terms of grammatical units and by logicians in terms of truth values (Allwood et al. 1977). The illocutionary act is realized on the basis of the conventional goals of an utterance (what a given utterance is supposed to get done) and the contextual conditions under which it is produced. The perlocutionary act consists of actions that might be beyond the conventional interpretation of an utterance and/or outside the control of the speaker.

Austin's distinction between *meaning* and *force* is what makes his approach new and at the same time connects it to previous traditions of linguistic study.

This distinction sanctions the notion of language as action and captures the fact that the same sequence of words can perform quite different kinds of acts (in each case, having a different force) and also recognizes that there is something constant ("meaning") across different uses of the same utterance and that therefore linguistic and logical studies of language still have something important to contribute.

Consider as an example the sentence in (4)

(4)   Tom is drinking coffee

This is a grammatical English sentence that describes a situation in which someone named "Tom" is engaged in the activity of drinking coffee. The type of grammatical structure (a transitive clause in the present progressive) or the truth value of this proposition (whether or not it matches a particular state of affairs) remain the same regardless of the context of the use of this utterance by the speaker. For instance, it can be used to inform someone of what Tom is doing (the recipient of this utterance might have asked what the other people in the house are up to) or to warn someone (the recipient might have assumed that Tom was getting ready to go out). Austin would say that in these two cases the meaning of (4) stays constant, but its force changes.

As example (4) makes clear, the illocutionary act performed by an utterance is not always obvious from the surface form of an utterance – especially if we rely exclusively on lexical and syntactic information and ignore intonation and paralinguistic features (quality of voice, volume, etc.). To clarify the force of an utterance, it is useful to think of declarative sentences like (4) above as embedded in a higher clause with a verb that defines the force of the utterance. Thus, the two mentioned interpretations of (4) can be paraphrased as:

(4i)   I inform you that Tom is drinking coffee
(4ii)   I warn you that Tom is drinking coffee

Austin called verbs such as *inform* and *warn* **performative verbs** because they make explicit the action performed by the embedded (typically following) sentence. There are many other verbs of this sort in English as well as in all other known languages. When we say *I apologize, I assume, I promise*, or *I am ordering you to do this* the verb we are using in the first person singular and with the present tense expresses the very act we are performing. Other examples of such verbs in English include: *state, argue, conclude, admit, salute, greet, approve, criticize, assert, deny, assume, suppose, demand, approve*. When we use one of these verbs in the first person singular and in the present tense, assuming that various contextual conditions hold (see below), we are performing the very action that the verb is supposed to describe (see also Searle 1969: 23).

However, doing something through words (the performance of an illocutionary act) is not restricted to the use of these verbs. We do not need to hear performative verbs to realize that what is being said counts as action. Instead, every time we perform a locutionary act we also perform an illocutionary act (Austin 1961: 98). In speaking we do not just establish meaningful sequences of sounds to be judged only in terms of grammaticalness and truth values. Rather, *in saying something, we are always doing something.* This is true not only of such obvious cases as commands, warnings, promises, and threats, but assertions as well. Even the simple act of stating something about ourselves or others is a social act, it is the act of informing (this means that assertions are in principle no different from other kinds of speech acts[11]). To understand this point, we must realize that any act of speaking (and more generally of communicating) takes place within a particular *context* and is evaluated with respect to such a context. Austin's concern with context goes beyond the idea that context is important for assessing the truth of a statement (Austin 1961: 144). He also wants us to recognize that in using speech, people do not just try to match the world with appropriate descriptions, they also use words to make the world conform to their wishes or needs. Searle (1976) expanded on this point by making a distinction between cases in which language must "fit the world" (i.e. provide an adequate description of an independent state of affairs, e.g. *the tank is full*) and cases in which the world must "fit the language" (i.e. match the state of affairs described by language, e.g. *fill up the tank*).

Once we realize that describing the world is only one of the many things we do with language, a question naturally comes to mind: is there a limit to the kinds of things we do with language? The answer is not obvious. Wittgenstein, for instance, believed that one could not determine once and for all the number of uses of language:

> But how many kinds of sentence are there? Say assertion, question,
> and command? – There are *countless* kinds: countless different
> kinds of use of what we call "symbols," "words," "sentences." And
> this multiplicity is not something fixed, given once for all; but new
> types of language, new language-games, as we may say, come into
> existence, and others become obsolete and get forgotten.
> (Wittgenstein 1958: 11)

Austin, on the other hand, was inclined to think the opposite, namely, that the number of illocutionary acts is finite. His presupposition is very much tied to his view that a science of language as social action should follow the rules and methods of other sciences:

---

[11] Austin (1962) starts out by setting up a false dichotomy between constative and performative utterances. By the end of the book he has shown that all utterances are performative.

Certainly there are a great many uses of language. It's rather a pity that people are apt to invoke a new use of language whenever they feel so inclined, to help them out of this, that, or the other well-known philosophical tangle; we need more of a framework in which to discuss these uses of language; and also I think we should not despair too easily and talk, as people are apt to do, about the *infinite* uses of language. Philosophers will do this when they have listed as many, let us say, as seventeen; but even if there were something like ten thousand uses of language, surely we could list them all in time. This, after all, is no larger than the number of species of beetle that entomologists have taken the pains to list.

(Austin 1970: 234)

As is typical in science, the first step in creating order out of the potential chaos of complex lists is the establishment of a typology. A potentially infinite set of phenomena is reorganized into a limited set of types. Austin (1962) presents five basic types of illocutionary acts, which have since been redefined by Searle (1976) and Searle and Vanderveken (1985).

According to Searle, in using language, we can do five things: (i) tell people how things are (*assertives*[12]), (ii) try to get them to do things (*directives*), (iii) express our feelings and attitudes *expressives*), (iv) bring about changes through our utterances (*declaratives*); (v) commit ourselves to some future actions (*commissives*). It is also possible to do more than one of these things at the same time. Although these speech acts are abstract notions and do not necessarily or uniquely correspond to particular English verbs, Searle (like Austin before him) lists a number of English verbs as examples of the different types of speech acts (adapted from Searle and Vanderveken 1985):

(i) Assertives: *assert, claim, affirm, state, deny, disclaim, assure, argue, rebut inform, notify, remind, object, predict, report, retrodict, suggest, insist, conjecture, hypothesize, guess, swear, accuse, blame, criticize, praise, complain, boast, lament.*

(ii) Directives: *direct, request, ask, urge, tell, require, demand, command, order, forbid, prohibit, enjoin, permit, suggest, insist, warn, advise, recommend, beg, supplicate, entreat, beseech, implore, pray.*

(iii) Expressives: *apologize, thank, condole, congratulate, complain, lament, protest, deplore, boast, compliment, praise, welcome, greet.*

(iv) Declaratives: *declare, resign, adjourn, appoint, nominate, approve, confirm, disapprove, endorse, renounce, disclaim, denounce, repudiate, bless, curse, excommunicate, consecrate, christen, abbreviate, name, call.*

---

[12] Searle (1976) had used the term "representatives" as the general category, but Searle and Vanderveken (1985) opted for "assertives."

(v) Commissives: *commit, promise, threaten, vow, pledge, swear, accept, consent, refuse, offer, bid, assure, guarantee, warrant, contract, covenant, bet.*

We must remember that all of these verbs work as performative verbs only when used in the present tense and in the first person singular. Thus, the verb *resign* works as a *declarative* only if the speaker says *I resign*, but not if he says *John resigned* or *resign!* Of course, most of the time illocutionary acts are not expressed or introduced by performative verbs. Speakers usually do not go around saying things like *I warn you, I threaten you, I command you*, or *I greet you*. Nevertheless, hearers take (most of the time appropriately) certain utterances to be warnings, other ones as threats, or commands, or greetings.[13] How does this happen? In other words, how do speakers manage to get their words to do what they want done and how do listeners manage to interpret those words in appropriate ways? As soon as we start thinking about these questions we realize that the answer required is nothing but a theory of interpretation and that these are the same kinds of questions routinely asked by ethnographers while they engage in participant-observation (see chapter 2). Can the answers given by speech act theorists be adopted by ethnographers? In what follows I will argue that although speech act theory offers some important insights into a theory of interpretation of speech as action, it does not satisfy the goals of linguistic anthropology as defined in chapter 1.

To account for how illocutionary acts do their work, Austin introduced a number of criteria, which he called **felicity conditions** to differentiate them from truth conditions, given that speech acts are not true or false, but, in Austin's terms, **felicitous** or **infelicitous** (Searle later introduced the term "successful"). Thus, for a speech act to be "happily" (or successfully) performed, there are certain conditions that must be respected (from Austin 1962: 14–15):

A1. *Conventionality of procedure*. There must be an accepted conventional procedure having a certain conventional effect, including the uttering of certain words by certain persons in certain circumstances.

A2. *Appropriate number and types of participants and circumstances*.

These first two conditions mean, for instance, that a husband saying to his wife *I divorce you* in many countries would not count as a declarative speech act whereby the two of them would be from that point on considered divorced. There is usually a need for a special procedure, including the pronouncement of the speech act by a person (e.g. a judge) who has the institutional authority, in the appropriate place, to give the words the power to be effective.

B1. *Complete execution of procedure*.

B2. *Complete participation*.

---

[13] Thus, Searle (1969: 30) wrote: "Often, in actual speech situations, the context will make clear what the illocutionary force of the utterance is, without its being necessary to invoke the appropriate explicit illocutionary force indicator."

The two B conditions mean that for a speech act to be successful all required participants must correctly complete whatever task they have been assigned as part of the conventional procedure. As made clear by Austin's own examples, these conditions introduce the important element of **uptake**, that is, the role of the interlocutor in making a given illocutionary act successful:

> For example: my attempt to make a bet by saying "I bet sixpence" is abortive unless you say "I take you on" or words to that effect; my attempt to marry by saying "I will" is abortive if the woman says "I will not"; my attempt to challenge you is abortive if I say "I challenge you" but I fail to send round my seconds; my attempt ceremonially to open a library is abortive if I say "I open this library" but the key snaps in the lock; ... (Austin 1962: 37)

These examples also show that to assign an interpretation to a speech act, we often need to consider interactional units that go beyond the individual utterance and the individual speaker. This is the route pursued by Levinson (1983: ch. 6) who proposes to look at speech acts as part of larger sequences (see also chapter 8).

C1. *Sincerity conditions*. Participants must have certain thoughts, feelings, and intentions. Thus, when performing a bet speakers are expected to sincerely think that they will be willing to pay if proven wrong or when expressing condolences speakers are expected to sympathize with their addressees (Austin 1962: 40). These conditions are meant to capture the commitments and expectations produced by a speech act and hence be a measure of the responsibility implicit in the uttering of certain words under certain conditions. Austin was well aware that these conditions are difficult to evaluate in absolute terms and spent several pages discussing different situations and degrees to which one might be insincere. In Searle's work, however, these reservations seem to vanish and sincerity and intentionality acquire a much more central role.[14] As we'll see in the next section, it is the sincerity conditions and the reliance on intentionality implicit in such conditions that have been the focus of most of the criticism of speech act theory by linguistic anthropologists.

C2. *Consequent behavior*. Participants must carry out whatever actions are specified or implied by the force of the speech act.

---

[14] This is not the case, however, with all speech act theorists. Bach and Harnish (1979), for instance, have revoked sincerity conditions for those acts such as apologizing, expressing condolence, greeting, and thanking, which they call *acknowledgments*. These are part of the category called *expressives* by Searle (see above): "Because acknowledgments are expected on particular occasions, they are often issued not so much to express a genuine feeling as to satisfy the social expectation that such a feeling be expressed" (Bach and Harnish 1979: 51).

Austin's criteria give us insights into the kinds of factors that are involved in making a given speech act successful (both in terms of its production and its comprehension). At the same time, they leave us with several questions unanswered, including the range of ways in which illocutionary force is encoded in an utterance and the extent to which the interpretation of illocutionary force could follow universal principles. These issues have been behind the attention given since the 1970s to **indirect speech acts**, that is, utterances that, without having the grammatical form of imperatives or commands, conventionally have the force of a directive (see the articles in Cole and Morgan 1975).

7.2.1.1 Indirect speech acts

Indirect speech acts might have the shape of questions and hence be classifiable as requests for information – see examples (5) and (6) – or the shape of declarative sentences (in the grammatical sense of "declarative"[15]) and hence be classifiable as assertions – see (7) and (8) –, but in most contexts they seem to work as requests for action (from Searle 1975):

(5)   Can you reach the salt?
(6)   Could you be a little more quiet?
(7)   I can't see the movie screen while you have that hat on.
(8)   I would like you to go now.

Several competing proposals were made to account for these phenomena (see Levinson 1983 for an insightful review of several theories). These proposals had to face the issues of generalizability and universality. Where does the knowledge that speakers of English have in interpreting these sentences come from? Could generalizable, perhaps universal principles be found that would account for how indirect speech acts were produced and understood? Different principles were proposed, including the principle of conversational cooperation (Grice 1975; Levinson 1983), conversational postulates (Gordon and Lakoff 1975), and generalizations based on the notion of preparatory (read "felicity") conditions like the following (from Searle 1975: 72):

---

[15] The term "declarative sentence" here must be distinguished from "declarative speech act" used by Searle (see above). "Declarative sentence" (which is in this case closer to what Searle calls "assertion") is used by grammarians to refer to sentences in the form of statements, that is, utterances that are "subject to judgments of truth and falsehood" (Sadock and Zwicky 1985: 160). The terminological confusion is not helped by those grammarians who have used illocutionary force as one of the criteria for defining "declarative sentences." For instance, Sadock and Zwicky (1985: 165) attempted a match between form and function by defining declarative as a sentence type that conveys "assertions, expressions of belief, reports, conclusions, narratives, assessment of likelihood, expressions of doubt, and the like."

(9)   A speaker can make an indirect request (or other directive) by either asking whether or stating that a preparatory condition concerning the hearer's ability to do a certain action obtains.

This principle says that one can make a request for action by asking *can you reach the salt?* by virtue of the fact that the ability to reach the salt would be a necessary condition for the hearer to be able to satisfy the request for action.

7.3   Speech act theory and linguistic anthropology

From the perspective of linguistic anthropology, these discussions about how and where to locate the knowledge that speakers and hearers have in producing and interpreting utterances are important and yet problematic for at least two reasons. First, they are done without apparent awareness that the phenomena and principles invoked by the analyst might be culture-specific. Whether or not they relied on English examples, the scholars involved in speech act analysis usually automatically assume that their intuitions and findings have a universal relevance. Second, speech act analysts – like most philosophers – believe that reasonable generalizations can be made by introspection, that is, by thinking out relevant examples and imagining possible situations, without having to actually observe and systematically collect data from real-life interactions. These assumptions about universality prompted strong criticism from ethnographers and linguistic anthropologists working in societies outside of Europe and the United States.

To do ethnography (chapter 4), we need to know whether a question counts as a greeting, a statement about the future as a promise, or a statement about the past as an accusation. Austin's distinction between saying and doing (locutionary and illocutionary acts) and his discussion of felicity conditions becomes then a first step toward a discussion of **contextualization**, that is, the activity whereby acts (whether verbal or otherwise) are understood as connected to or embedded in other acts and, in the process, made sense of in culturally meaningful terms. It should not be surprising then that ethnographers interested in rituals were among the most eager to adopt or draw from speech act theory (Rappoport 1974; Tambaiah 1968, 1973), but, as pointed out by Du Bois (1993: 49), these early enthusiasts "either left the ... standard Searlean speech-act theory implicit in their application of it, or perfunctorily repeated those elements which they saw no reason not to endorse" (Du Bois 1993: 49).

In particular, cultural anthropologists did not immediately realize that whereas most of the examples discussed by Austin had to do with highly ritualistic and institutionally defined speech acts such as naming a ship or marrying people,

Searle's extension of Austin's theory to a much wider range of acts constituted a more general theory of human communication and human psychology (Searle 1969, 1983). As pointed out by a number of linguistic and cultural anthropologists, such a theory seems at odds with an anthropological understanding of human action and its interpretation in context .[16]

I will hereafter concentrate on Michelle Rosaldo's (1982) critique based on her fieldwork among the Ilongots, a group of about 3,500 hunters and horticulturalists living in the province of Nueva Vizcaya, Northern Luzon, in the Philippines (Rosaldo 1980).

In a posthumously published article,[17] Rosaldo argued that people display through language use an understanding of their own peculiar ways of being in the world and that speakers' use of language reproduces a particular social system – one for instance, in which men tend to make requests and women tend to be those who satisfy them. This means that any classification of speech acts in a society must see those acts as part of cultural practices through which a particular type of social order is at once represented and reproduced. In other words, any analysis of speech acts must rely on and, in turn, inform analysis of people's thoughts, feelings, and beliefs about how the world is organized.

In an approach that is quite close to poststructuralist theories of social action (Ortner 1984), Rosaldo's confrontation with speech act theory represented a confrontation between two radically different notions of meaning and hence two radically different notions of the goals of linguistic interpretation. For Searle and other speech act theorists, the goal is to produce a method for arriving at the necessary and sufficient conditions of human communication. This is what felicity and sincerity conditions are supposed to do, together with a number of inferential principles such as conversational postulates or Grice's conversational implicatures (see below and Levinson 1983: chapter 3). For Rosaldo and other linguistic anthropologists, the goal is to understand how particular uses of language might sustain, reproduce, or challenge particular versions of the social order and the notion of person (or self) that is part of that order.[18] Starting from this premise and relying on her fieldwork among the Ilongots, Rosaldo criticized the following features of speech act theory:

---

[16] For earlier criticism of the cultural assumptions found in speech act theory and related paradigms, see Keenan [Ochs] (1974), Silverstein (1977).

[17] Michelle Rosaldo fell off a cliff and died on October 11, 1981 while conducting fieldwork in the Philippines (R. Rosaldo 1989: 9).

[18] It should be pointed out that Rosaldo represents a fairly extreme relativist position on these issues, which is not necessarily shared by all sociocultural or linguistic anthropologists. See Hollan 1992 for a review of different theories.

(i) its emphasis on truth and verification as exemplified by the sincerity conditions in both Austin's and Searle's model;

(ii) the centrality of intentions in its theory of interpretation;

(iii) its implicit theory of person (or "self").

Let us examine each of these features a bit more closely.

7.3.1 Truth

Austin (1962: 40) talks about the need to have the "requisite feelings" for certain kinds of acts such as congratulating or condoling; Searle (1969) also includes sincerity as one of the conditions for most of the speech acts he discusses. One of his **preparatory conditions** for an assertion, for instance, is that the speaker has evidence for the truth of the proposition that is being asserted and the sincerity condition is that the speaker believes the proposition asserted to be true. For a promise to be non-defective, the speaker must *sincerely* intend to do the act promised (Searle 1969: 60).

Rosaldo argued that such a concern for sincerity is not shared by Ilongots and therefore cannot be considered a universal strategy in verbal interaction.[19] Thus, if we look at when assertive verbs corresponding to the English *saying, speaking, giving news* are used by Ilongots, we find them in oratorical formulas, especially at the beginning of encounters or during an oratorical debate. They seem to be more about "formulations of relationship and claims" (p. 213) than about reporting some experienced truth. Speakers' concern in making assertions seems to be more with who can claim what than with the details of what is actually said.

> ... Ilongots use denial and assertion in discourse as a device for the establishment of interactional roles.
>
> Thus, for example, I have known Ilongots to deny that they had taken heads of kin of interlocutors who in fact *had* been their victims in the past, and then, when challenged, to pronounce a readiness to undergo dangerous ordeals and oaths in order to test the mettle of accusers who appeared less certain, or more fearful, than they thought themselves. As always, what they claimed was "true" depended less on "what took place" than on the quality of

[19] Austin and Searle recognize that it is possible for an act to be successful even though the speaker is insincere. However, sincerity remains for both of them an essential quality of speaking. This feature of the theory is maintained in more recent developments: "An insincere speech act is defective but not necessarily unsuccessful. A lie, for ex., can be a successful assertion. Nevertheless, successful performances of illocutionary acts necessarily involve the expression of the psychological state specified by the sincerity conditions of that type of act" (Searle and Vanderveken 1985: 18).

> an interaction where what mattered most was who spoke out and claimed the privilege to reveal or hide a public secret hitherto clothed in silence. (Rosaldo 1982: 214)

Rosaldo also argues that Ilongots do not have in their conceptual repertoire the act of promising as discussed by Searle (1965, 1969). Promising in the western (read "English") sense implies sincerity by the speaker. This, in turn, implies the notion of "meaning as a thing derived from inner life" (Rosaldo 1982: 211; see Du Bois 1993; Duranti 1988b; 1993a, 1993b). The criticism of the sincerity question is thus closely linked with the criticism of the centrality of intentions in interpreting social action (see section 7.3.2) and with the notion of person implicit in such centrality (see section 7.3.3).

More generally, even when recognized by members of the society, the act of promising, or whatever one might call a certain display of commitment to some future action, might be separated from the fulfillment of that act. This is a point made by Rappoport (1974) in discussing rituals. The Mareng dance together in a ritual called *kaiko* that is supposed to commit dancers to be fighting partners in the future, but there is no assurance that such commitment will be fulfilled. We might have to recognize that for a promise to correspond to some future action, there may have to be other acts, in the future, that need to be fulfilled. Some of these acts might be known in advance and hence can be listed as a set of felicity conditions, but other ones might not be foreseeable. Bourdieu's (1977) discussion of exchange emphasizes the role of this element of the unknown in future action as the basis of what gives meaning to social interaction. Saying that an exchange means that if A gives to B, then B gives to A misses the temporal dimension in between the two acts, with its emotional and ethical aspects. Whether or not something counts as a promise – or a challenge, a gift, a retribution – is partly determined by what happens *after* the act. It depends on what others do to consolidate or undermine its force. The sincerity of a party's feelings toward the other party might be (or be made) quite irrelevant.

As Moerman (1988: 108) wrote,

> "Truth," "accuracy," and other mappings between what is said and what is referred to are locally occasioned. Even if we restrict our attention to talk about the world out there, truth and accuracy are not always the relevant or appropriate standards. Being amusing, touching, or polite sometimes counts too.

From an anthropological perspective, truth is sometimes an achievement as much as a precondition for a satisfactory transaction, communication included (Duranti 1993a).

7.3.2 Intentions

Although for Austin, as we have seen, having certain intentions is part of the felicity conditions necessary for an utterance to count as action, it is in Searle's version of speech act theory that intentions assume a central place in the definition of communication:

> In speaking I attempt to communicate certain things to my hearer by getting him to recognize my intention to communicate just those things. I achieve the intended effect on the hearer by getting him to recognize my intention to achieve that effect, and as soon as the hearer recognizes what it is my intention to achieve, it is in general achieved. (Searle 1969: 43)

This definition is inspired by Grice's earlier definition of "non-natural (i.e. conventional) meaning":

> Perhaps we may sum up what is necessary for *A* to mean something by *x* as follows. *A* must intend to induce by *x* a belief in an audience, and he must also intend his utterance to be recognized as so intended. (Grice [1957] 1971: 441)

To illustrate how this definition works, Grice draws a distinction between a situation in which we try to get a very avaricious man out of a room by throwing some money out of the window and a situation in which we try to get him out by pointing to the door or giving him a little push. Only in the latter case, can we be said to mean (non-naturally) that the avaricious man leave the room. The difference is that in the first case, we can get him to leave without him recognizing our intentions, whereas in the second case we need him to recognize our intentions in order for him to leave.

Rosaldo sees a number of interconnected problems with this view of communication. First, she argues, the emphasis on intentions and their recognition by the addressee places too much emphasis on individual actions and individual achievement. It implies that any form of action is mostly (or simply) "the achievement of autonomous selves, whose deeds are not significantly constrained by the relationships and expectations that define their local world" (1982: 204). This view of social action is a prerequisite to accepting Grice's and Searle's logic of argumentation. Without realizing it, when we read about speakers' intentions in the speech act literature, we forget to ask questions that would enlarge the context of the interaction and force us to find out more about dimensions that are not introduced into the discussion. As Elizabeth Povinelli (1995) points out in her discussion of the role of narratives about the Dreaming in Australian courts, the Aborigines' view of rocks and other objects as intentional beings that can feel, hear, and smell, is incomprehensible to the land commissioner representing the non-Aboriginal community. The only thing he can do is to classify the Dreaming narratives as native "beliefs" which provide evidence for the authenticity of the land claims. But, Povinelli argues, such statements are much more than religious beliefs. They index a set of relations to nature and a set of practices *with* and *in* natural environments that are in contrast with the western (capitalist) notion of "labor." The Belyuen women Povinelli lived with assume that

> humans are simply one node in a field of possible intentionality and appropriation. The Dreaming epitomizes the transformation and appropriation of landscapes', humans', and animals' bodies and personalities for reasons individuals and social groups can only try to interpret. [...] Belyuen women compare hunting activities and capitalist wage-labor, saying that the one produces a lightening and lifting of the body while the other produces anxiety and despair.
>
> (Povinelli 1995: 513)

Only if we understand land and humans as interlocutory subjects, can we understand the Aborigines' notion of leisure as a labor with social and economic value (Povinelli 1995: 514).

This example points to the fact that to engage in interpretation, an activity which includes the assignment of intentionality, involves understanding the relationship between individuals (e.g. speakers and addressees) and the social and natural world within which they operate.

Going back to Grice's example of how to get rid of an avaricious man, we must realize that there is much cultural content left out in Grice's description of the situation. As ethnographers, if faced with a situation similar to the one described by Grice, we would want to ask many questions. How was the evaluation of the man being "very avaricious" established? To what extent does this category depend on the specific encounter and/or relationship between people? What notion of social responsibility is implied by the fact that a person would leave the room to get money he sees being dropped from a window? Why are we assuming that the person would not connect the money he finds with our presence and not assume that we are responsible for it? How would responsibility be assigned if the avaricious man were run over by a car while trying to get the money thrown from the window? And so on.

These questions are partly motivated by another claim made by Rosaldo, namely, that for Ilongots attention to **social relations** seems to be a more central part of communication than interest in individual intentions. In other words,

Ilongots seemed to Rosaldo more concerned with figuring out how to maintain social relationships than with reconstructing motives and psychological states (see also Duranti 1993a, 1993b; Kuipers 1990: 42–3; Ochs 1982; Schieffelin 1986, 1990; Shore 1982: ch. 10). When Rosaldo was outraged by people not showing up to work with her, they would not give excuses or regrets but present gifts and other things that might help control and soften her anger. Ilongots did not seem interested in evaluating the intentions of the parties involved, but in controlling the potential consequences or effects of the situation as defined by Rosaldo's reaction. What actually happened earlier seemed to matter less. The apparent lack of interest in factual details and reconstruction of past psychological states is intimately related to what Rosaldo describes as a different theory of person among the Ilongots.

This type of cultural practice can be better accounted for by assuming an institutional view of intentions, as proposed by Wittgenstein, who was wary of psychological explanation for linguistic behavior:

> An intention is embedded in its situation, in human customs and its institutions. If the technique of the game of chess did not exist, I could not intend to play a game of chess. In so far as I do intend the construction of a sentence in advance, that is made possible by the fact that I can speak the language in question.
>
> (Wittgenstein 1958: 108, §337)

This perspective is an implicit call for the kind of work that ethnographers do, namely, the documentation of particular practices and their relationships to larger societal institutions and concerns.

> One cannot guess how a word functions. One has to *look at* its use and learn from that. (Wittgenstein 1958: 109, § 340)

Unfortunately, this statement has often been trivialized and reduced to the slogan "meaning is use." This characterization of his theory misses the complexity of Wittgenstein's argument about language forms as activities or cultural practices that must be understood within the context of a community of users.

7.3.3   Local theory of person

One of Rosaldo's goals was to "bracket" (in the phenomenological sense of "suspending judgment about") the notion of speaker as social actor assumed by speech act theorists and thus suggest that it was not a universal notion but a culture-specific one.

> I want to argue here that ways of thinking about language and
> about human agency and personhood are intimately linked: our
> theoretical attempts to understand how language works are like the
> far less explicated linguistic thoughts of people elsewhere in the
> world, in that both inevitably tend to reflect locally prevalent views
> about the given nature of those human persons by whom language
> is used. (Rosaldo 1982: 203)

Rosaldo's statement means that Searle's preoccupation with sincerity and
intentionality reflects and at the same time reproduces western ideas about
human agency. These ideas favor attention to the speaker's psychological state
and pay little attention to the social sphere in which such a putative psychological state is investigated. Speech act theorists do not reflect upon the type of
thinking and acting subject that is being implied by their work. This lack of
reflexive thinking is a major difference between the analytical philosophical
tradition represented by speech act theory and the ethnographically based
interpretive work done by Rosaldo, whose critique of speech act theory is
reminiscent of Whorf's critique of commonly held assumptions about human
mind and human action based on western European languages:

> One significant contribution to science from the linguistic point of
> view may be the greater development of our sense of perspective.
> We shall no longer be able to see a few recent dialects of the
> Indo-European family, and the rationalizing techniques elaborated
> from their patterns, as the apex of the evolution of the human
> mind, nor their present wide spread as due to any survival from
> fitness or to anything but a few events of history – events that
> could be called fortunate only from the parochial point of view of
> the favored parties. They, and our own thought processes with
> them, can no longer be envisioned as spanning the gamut of
> reason and knowledge but only as one constellation in a galactic
> expanse.

> (Whorf [1940] 1956e: 218)

With the analytical tools of linguistic and interpretive anthropology, Rosaldo
recast Austin's and Searle's theory of how speakers do things with words as an
interesting but rather poor ethnography of western personhood and action. One
of the characteristics of the western subject as understood by speech act theorists
is that of "an inner self continuous through time" (Rosaldo 1982: 218). It is only
on the basis of such an assumption that certain kinds of judgments can be made
about sincerity, responsibility, and intentionality. But such an assumption is not

necessarily shared by all cultures and, in fact, much of contemporary cultural anthropology is dedicated to studying the different ways in which cultures represent the relationship between individuals and their public personae. Whereas Austin and Searle's perspective privileges the individual's thoughts and intentions in interpretations, cultural anthropologists like Geertz and, before him, the founders of the "culture and personality" school (see Langness 1987) have tended to emphasize the separation found in many cultures between the private and the public self or the individual and the collective. Although Hollan (1992) is right that some cultural anthropologists have exaggerated the contrast between "western" and "non-western" selves, different ethnographic studies reveal a variety of ways in which context plays a role in the construction of the person. For example, Adjun Appadurai's (1990) discussion of begging and praise in Hindu India cautions us that the self is not just contained "inside" the individual. It also lives in embodied practices that rely on ritualized, interactive public behavior.

> ... praise is *not* a matter of *direct* communication between the "inner" states of the relevant persons, but involves the public negotiation of certain gestures and responses. When such negotiation is successful, it creates a *"community of sentiment"* involving the emotional participation of the praiser, the one who is praised, and the audience of the act of praise. Praise is therefore that set of regulated, improvisatory practices that is one route to the creation of communities of sentiment in Hindu India.
> (Appadurai 1990: 93–4)

To say that there are ritual, aesthetic, hyperbolic, and emotional aspects of begging that are embedded in a "community of sentiment" means that the meaning of one's words or actions cannot be restricted to what the individual speaker/ actor intends. Culture is more than a shared set of beliefs. It includes practices and predispositions that can only live within a community (see section 2.5).

These ethnographically informed discussions of speech act theory epitomize some fundamental differences between analytical philosophers and contemporary cultural and linguistic anthropologists. Given the variability assumed by ethnographers in the notion of person across cultures (and contexts), any ethnographic discussion of the use of words in social interaction could not just be a factual reconstruction of events but also (or rather) an attempt to describe the participants' interpretive strategies in deciding which reconstruction is contextually acceptable or more appropriate. This different focus does not necessarily mean that all ethnographers subscribe to a hyper-pragmatistic view of meaning ("truth is whatever works in this context") but that they do have different priorities and goals in interpreting human behavior. Speech act theorists start from the assumption that "language is action" but do not question their own notion of "action." They assume that "action" itself is a universal dimension of human existence that does not need further analysis. Thus, in analyzing directives, the issue is "what are the rules we need to assume to explain how a person can get another to do something?" The question of who is doing what for whom and why is not entertained. Such an issue would be seen as outside the domain of the theory.

Ethnographers, on the other hand, believe it is important to extend the philosophical characterization of "action" to include the notion of person implicit in such a characterization and the relationship between language use and local theories of truth, authority, and responsibility. This means that for ethnographers interpretive analysis of words as deeds is different partly because the notion of *context* is different. For a linguistic anthropologist, as suggested by Lindstrom (1992: 104)

> ... contextual analysis begins ... by asking what kinds of talk can be heard and understood, and what kinds of talk cannot. Are all participants qualified to speak and to speak the truth? Can talk carry all meanings?

These are far more complex and far-reaching questions than those usually addressed by speech act theorists. Should we then conclude that any kind of interface between philosophers and anthropologists is destined to be ill-fated? Not necessarily. There have been attempts within western philosophy to sketch a theory of language as action that is closer in spirit to that practiced by most linguistic anthropologists. One such theory is the one developed by Wittgenstein in the 1930s and 1940s after his return to Cambridge.

7.4 Language games as units of analysis

In his later writings, Wittgenstein often invoked the metaphor of games for talking about how people use and understand language.

> The use of a word in the language is its meaning.
> Grammar describes the use of words in the language.
> So it has somewhat the same relation to the language description of a game, the rules of a game, have to the game.
>
> (Wittgenstein [1933 ca.] 1974: 60)

Wittgenstein's analogy between language and games has often been taken too literally. Searle (1969: 43), for example, contends that the analogy does not work because when one makes a move in a game like chess one is not said to *mean* anything by that move.[20] Phrased in this way the parallelism does not work precisely because playing a game of chess and speaking are two different activities – Wittgenstein might have been the first one to admit this. We must look for what the metaphor points to rather than for what is obviously different between the two activities.[21] What Wittgenstein is proposing with the chess metaphor is that understanding a word in a sentence is like understanding a move in a game. Part of this knowledge is what psychologists call *procedural knowledge* (the knowing-how) (see chapter 2) but it goes beyond that. We get an understanding of how a word is used by matching it with other words and other contexts and by projecting its impact on future words and utterances just as we project a move of chess against past and future moves. The game metaphor also implies a differentiated understanding among users. An expert chess player understands a move differently from a novice or someone who has never played the game.[22] Similarly, not everyone understands a word or an utterance in the same way. There are many different domains or contexts (read "games") for language use. Not everyone is the same in terms of the ability to act within a certain domain. Whereas Austin's and Searle's goals of finding a finite set of conventions and conditions give the impression of a universally shared linguistic knowledge, in reality different speakers, even neighbors or close friends, can have quite different understanding of the same linguistic expressions. I remember telling an artist friend that I had bought a Fender electric guitar. "What color?" he asked. "White," I said. When I later took it out of the case, he looked at it and, with a disappointed look on his face, complained "You said white! This is ivory!" The difference between our linguistic characterization of the color of the guitar implied, as Wittgenstein

---

[20] "Characteristically, when one speaks one means something by what one says; and what one says, the string of sounds that one emits, is characteristically said to have a meaning. Here, incidentally, is another point at which our analogy between performing speech acts and playing games breaks down. The pieces in a game like chess are not characteristically said to have a meaning, and, furthermore, when one makes a move one is not characteristically said to mean anything by that move" (Searle 1969: 42–43).

[21] Searle's reading of Wittgenstein seems vulnerable to the same kind of criticism presented by Tambaiah regarding Malinowski's misunderstanding of magical spells (see section 7.1).

[22] "When a man who knows the game watches a game of chess, the experience he has when a move is made usually differs from that of someone else watching without understanding the game. (It differs too from that of a man who doesn't even know that it's a game.) We can also say that it's the knowledge of the rules of chess which makes the difference between the two spectators, and so too that it's the knowledge of the rules which makes the first spectator have the particular experience he has. But this experience is not the knowledge of the rules. Yet we are inclined to call them both 'understanding' " (Wittgenstein 1974: 49–50). On the difference between experts and others, see also Putnam (1975), who proposes a theory of meaning based on the idea of a "division of labor" among speakers, with experts knowing what common people do not need to bother with.

would have said, a different "form of life" ("... And to imagine a language means to imagine a form of life" [Wittgenstein 1958: 8]). Colors and color differentiations mean something different to a painter. They are part of different forms of life.

Wittgenstein's point is not only that to know how to use a word (or any kind of linguistic expression) means to know the kinds of things we can do with it – a piece of chess can move only in limited ways but there are countless new situations in which we can use it and in each case there is a new "meaning" – but also that there is a particular kind of existence that a use implies.[23] That is why he wrote, "If a lion could talk, we could not understand him" (Wittgenstein 1958: 223).

This view of language has important consequences for how one should write a grammar of a language. To write a grammar of a language means to describe what people do with certain expressions (see section 7.2.2). As we shall see in chapter 8, an analysis of sentence structures as parts of interactional sequences comes close to the kind of analysis envisioned but never fully realized by Wittgenstein.

Given his recurrent use of the game metaphor, it should not be surprising that the closest thing Wittgenstein ever came to what we might call a unit of analysis is his notion of **language game**,[24] which he first introduced in *The Blue Book* and is amply used in his subsequent manuscripts:

> I shall in future again and again draw your attention to what I shall call language-games. These are ways of using signs simpler than those in which we use the signs of our highly complicated everyday language. Language-games are the forms of language with which a child begins to make use of words. The study of language-games is the study of primitive forms of language or primitive languages. If we want to study the problems of truth and falsehood, of the agreement and disagreement of propositions with reality, of the nature of assertion, assumption and question, we shall with great advantage look at primitive forms of language in which these forms of thinking appear without the confusing background of highly complicated processes of thought. When we look at such simple forms of language the mental mist which seems to enshroud our

---

23 The theory of gender differences by Maltz and Borker (1982) follows a similar logic: men and women use language differently because boys and girls learn to use language in different contexts, in other words they have been socialized differently, or, in Wittgenstein's terms, they use the same words but experienced different "forms of life." A similar view is held by Tannen (1990).

24 For a discussion of the development of the notion of language game in Wittgenstein's writings, see Baker and Hacker (1985: 47–56).

ordinary use of language disappears. We see activities, reactions, which are clear-cut and transparent. On the other hand we recognize in these simple processes forms of language not separated by a break from our more complicated ones. We see that we can build up the complicated forms from the primitive ones by gradually adding new forms. (Wittgenstein 1960: 17)

The notion of "language game" is thus a *working* notion, it is not a category like "speech act" or "illocutionary act" and is not something that is out there in the phenomenological world of speaking. It is only an instrument for analysis, a heuristic device, which is used to first isolate "primitive" cases ("primitive" here means "simple" and does not have an evolutionary connotation). Only once we become expert at analyzing these simpler cases, we can graduate to looking at more complex ones. Simplicity is the only concession that Wittgenstein seems to make to traditional scientific methods. Otherwise, the emphasis here as elsewhere in Wittgenstein's teaching is on the importance of observation and description. We must resist the scientistic drive to make quick generalizations. This drive leads us to confusion because it is based on the wrong assumption that things that have the same name will necessarily share a common set of characteristics. We must instead cultivate and enjoy the practice of description of particular cases. It is an investigation of particular cases that will clear the confusion brought about by wrong ways of thinking about language such as the tendency to conceive of meaning as a mental image shared by everyone. The metaphor of the "game" is used to stress that different uses of language are like different games, namely, that they *may* share some features but they need not. Just like we might call "games" a number of activities that do not share the same basic features or rules, upon inspection we might find that language activities might not always share the same set of properties.

It should be clear by now that Wittgenstein uses the notion of language game to argue some of the main points of his view of meaning and interpretation. These points include the idea that connecting words with objects cannot be the basic method for acquiring a language and the observation that the same word or sentence can acquire different meanings depending on the activity within which it is used. But Wittgenstein also uses language games to argue against the idea that the meaning of a linguistic expression is just in someone's head. Through the concept of language game, he invites us to look at the context of what speakers do with words and for this reason constitutes an insight into what linguistic anthropologists are interested in. At the beginning of *Philosophical Investigations*, for instance, Wittgenstein gives the example of a situation in which a builder is working with an assistant. The assistant has to pass the proper stone to the builder in the order in which the latter requests them. In this context, the builder's use of simple nouns like *block, pillar, slab, beam* must be understood as an order, that is, an instruction for the assistant. Linguists have often suggested that to account for how a single word can, in certain contexts, be understood as a command, we must assume that the word, e.g. *slab!*, stands for an entire sentence, e.g. something like *give me a slab!* This is a process of "deletion" that grammarians call **ellipsis** (the same process that accounts for how expressions such as *I do* or *me too* can be interpreted as some related but different version of what has just been said). Wittgenstein argues that the analysis of single-word sentences as **elliptical** – i.e. as missing something – is unnecessary and leads to absurdities. The force of *slab!* as an order is not only in the linguistic form – which may or may not be pronounced with a particular type of intonation – but also *in the activity* that is being performed.

> The sentence is "elliptical," not because it leaves out something that we think when we utter it, but because it is shortened – in comparison with a particular paradigm of our grammar.
>
> (Wittgenstein 1958: 10)

In other words, even the explanation of the meaning of a single word as a shortened version of a longer expression is a language game, the language game played by grammarians! There is nothing wrong with such a language game, of course, but it is only *one* of the many possible ones in providing an interpretation of *slab!* in the context described above. The same type of analysis can be applied to the use of ostensive definitions (*"chair" means "this"* – while pointing to a chair). Ostensive definitions too can be used to explain the meaning of words and sentences but they must be understood as part of specific language games such as the routines used in foreign language classrooms. The teacher points to the blackboard and says *blackboard* (if he is teaching English) or *lavagna* (if he is teaching Italian). This is a perfectly legitimate way of teaching words and meanings, but it has a restricted range of uses and, according to Wittgenstein, is by no means more basic than other uses of language. Think for instance of the familiar routine when the teacher points to himself and says *My name is John* and then goes around the room asking each student *what is your name?* The successful accomplishment of this speech act depends on the students' success at conforming to the rules and expectations implicit in the teacher's actions. Beyond the fact that the teacher's question must be understood as a request for information and hence as requiring a linguistic performance on the part of each student, there are a number of culture- and context-specific assumptions that are implicitly at work, a crucial one being the criteria for what constitutes an appropriate answer. The students, for instance, must come up with something that satisfies the requirements of the English word *name* in the particular context of the class-room. The teacher's answer to his own question provides a model to be followed (*My name is John*), but such a model is not an instruction that can be universally followed; it does not contain all the possible ways in which the rule could be sat-isfied (and hence all the ways in which it could *not* be satisfied). Students, for instance, must decide which of their several names or nicknames should be pro-vided in the allowed slot. In my case, for instance, I would have to decide whether to give *Alessandro* or *Sandro* as an answer. But in fact even a decision of this sort does not exhaust the possible alternatives available in the context. Some students might interpret the model offered by *my name is John* as suggesting that they should provide an *English* name. This is how *Yosef* becomes *Joseph* and *Gianni* becomes *Johnny*. In my case, I would then have a much larger set of pos-sibilities including Alexander, Alex, Sandy.[25] Choices of this sort provide resources for locating one's teacher and classmates within different networks of acquaintances and may implicitly constitute a particular stance with respect to one's identity in a foreign country – not a simple task for the students and cer-tainly something of a magnitude that most English-as-a-Second-Language teachers might not be prepared to deal with. Finally, the activity of exchanging names in a classroom does not easily transfer to other situations, when goals or participants differ. Thus, if a student is stopped by the police and has no identifi-cation with him, the model *my name is John* will not do. To get a first sense of the different meanings this utterance might acquire it is sufficient to start imagining it said by different people: a student, a teacher, a waiter, a doctor, a prostitute. In each case, we could build a simple language game within which *my name is John* constitutes a different move and hence affords different following moves. More generally, speaking is an activity that involves particular forms of cooperation among participants in an interaction.

> Here the term "language-*game*" is meant to bring into prominence the fact that *speaking* of language is part of an activity, or of a form of life. (*Philosophical Investigations*, § 23)

The notion of language game is appealing to ethnographers, who must make sense of linguistic interpretations that do not follow the western grammarian's model of providing glosses of words. For instance, Rumsey (1990) uses the notion of language game to explain the unexpected answer he received from a Ngarinyin man (in northwestern Australia) when he asked him for the meaning

---

[25] As we go deeper into this analysis we realize that the issue of what constitutes an appro-priate or acceptable answer to the question *what is your name?* is nothing but the condi-tion for generating all the names that could constitute a natural class with "John." See Sacks (1972).

of *baba*. This is a term that Rumsey believed to be an address term and in fact later identified as a vocative kin term for *mamingi* "my mother's father," "my mother's brother's son," and so on. The man, however, did not provide the kind of paraphrase expected by the anthropologist. He said, instead, that *baba* meant something "like a *jannjuli* ['give me'], give me tobacco, or thing like that."

> What he was giving me was obviously not what we would think of as the sense, or possible reference term, but rather, a locution that makes explicit the pragmatic function of this term of address within a typical context of use – *mamingi* being someone from whom I am entitled to demand things. Of course it was possible in time for this man to learn *my* language game of glossing on the basis of *referential* function as distinct from other pragmatic ones, just as it was possible in time for me to come to a better understanding of his. But in order to do so, both of us had to put aside our everyday, commonsense way of talking about language. (Rumsey 1990: 353)

If speaking a language is part of an activity, to provide metalinguistic statements is also part of an activity and one that follows local theories (or "ideologies") about the relationship between words and the world (Schieffelin, Woolard, and Kroskrity 1997; Silverstein 1979; Woolard and Schieffelin 1994). The notion of language game allows fieldworkers to deal with different interpretive strategies without giving up on the idea that there is order (or a logic) behind the apparently strange answers they receive. As units of analysis, language games assume that language is a set of unbounded and yet manageable (and learnable) set of cultural practices. There are however two sorts of criticisms that are leveled at the notion of language game as a unit of analysis:

(i) Language game is such a general category that it is difficult to see where it would *not* apply. It would include very simple as well as very complex uses of language. How do we distinguish between them? How do we know where a language game starts and where it ends?

(ii) The notion of language game, with its implicit rejection of a "core" meaning of linguistic expressions, makes it impossible to make generalizations about language structure and language use.

The first criticism could be answered by saying that, as discussed earlier, Wittgenstein thought of language games as rather simple kinds of speech activities. The study of such simple activities is a prerequisite for the study of the more complex real-life situations. What Wittgenstein's theory needs is a better way of defining the boundaries of such situations. As long as we continue to create our own examples and imaginary situations, we are never going to know whether simplicity is in the situation or in the eyes of the observer. Wittgenstein's method of inquiry needs to be complemented with the ethnographic methods and transcription techniques described in chapters 4 and 5.

With respect to the second objection, it should be pointed out that Wittgenstein was not really interested in presenting a systematic theory of language as action of the type presented by Austin. He was more interested in the **practice** of doing philosophical-linguistic analysis than in its results, meant as a bounded body of knowledge. The whole idea of his later philosophy was to abolish boundaries or rather show that they were artificial or temporary. Philosophical argumentation is itself a type of activity that we engage in, not necessarily the most rational or the most adept at explaining all other activities, language use included. The gist of his line of argumentation was that there is no such a thing as *the* theory of what something means because a description that might fit one particular context might not work for another context. Philosophy consists of engaging in interpretations that show us different sides of things, different possibilities of being in the world and being meaningful. This is not to renounce the description of linguistic phenomena, but, on the contrary, to think of linguistic description as an on-going, open-ended enterprise that, because it can help us clarify our goals and assumptions, is an invaluable tool for human understanding.

7.5   Conclusions

Austin stated that "The total speech act in the total speech situation is the *only actual* phenomenon which, in the last resort, we are engaged in elucidating" (Austin 1962: 147). This statement amounts to a program for a theory of language as action. In this chapter, I have presented three different proposals for such a program: speech act theory, an ethnographically oriented approach to speech as action, and Wittgenstein's program for an activity-oriented philosophy of language. These different paradigms have some points in common and other points of contrast. I reviewed and compared some of their similarities and differences, not just in search of historical ties and intellectual debts, but also with the hope of establishing a fruitful dialogue based on ideas drawn from empirical research.

To accept the complexity of an issue is not the same thing as giving up hopes of making sense of it. Similarly, the acceptance of the historicity of our own methods and theories is not the same thing as accepting the view that any theory is valid or any interpretation is acceptable. Any interpretation is certainly possible, even the one that argues that this chapter was completely written by a computer program. But we as humans have the ability to engage in dialogues where alternatives points of view can be compared and evaluated. What a discipline needs to provide for its practitioners is a set of criteria to engage in such evaluations and, when necessary, revise them. One of the evaluation measures for linguistic anthropology is the extent to which a paradigm for the study of language as action can help us understand linguistic activities as cultural practices. As we saw in this chapter, speech act theory is an important starting point for such an enterprise, but remains confined to a practice of analysis that privileges individual speakers, individual utterances, and individual intentions. Such a perspective is vulnerable to criticism based on purely theoretical grounds (Wittgenstein) and on empirical investigation based on crosscultural comparison (Rosaldo). Wittgenstein addresses aspects of linguistic meaning and the process of interpretation in ways that are closer to an ethnographic study of linguistic practices, but does not discuss how such a study would fare when confronted with data taken from the real world. Wittgenstein's repeated invitation that we need to look at how language is used if we want to understand what linguistic expressions mean was never fully realized within philosophy where argumentation still proceeds by comparing imagined contexts. Some of his ideas have however been incorporated in subsequent attempts to study language activities systematically by starting from real-life situations. We will examine some such attempts in the next two chapter, where I will examine units of interaction and units of participation.

8
Conversational exchanges

Wittgenstein's notion of *language game* discussed in the last chapter points to something that is usually neglected in those studies that look at individual speech acts: talk is *exchanged*, it involves the alternation between different speakers. People do not just produce questions, answers, commands, promises, apologies. They jointly construct and participate in exchanges which comprise different parts and each part acquires its meaning from its location in a sequence of acts.

Take greetings, for example. We can provide a list of expressions people use in greetings. For instance, in English, people use expressions like *hello, hi, how are you, see you later, have a nice day, good-bye*. But to really understand how these words work, they need to be seen as part of larger units, often a sequence of two turns produced by two different speakers. In other words, they are organized in pairs. A person says something and someone else says something back. What the first party says both conditions and creates an expectation for what the second party will say. More generally, the most common type of speech in everyday life does not consist of individual words, or sentences, or long monologues, but of *sequences* of relatively short utterances produced by different speakers who are particularly attuned to when to speak and particularly careful at fitting what they have to say with what has just been said.

For a long time both anthropologists and linguists alike neglected the study of conversation. Linguists felt that conversation is too messy, full of false starts and ungrammaticalities, and would not provide a coherent set of data for analyzing grammar in a systematic way. Even sociolinguists like Labov who have always been interested in actual language use, still favor interviews, which are conversation-like but certainly peculiar in their organization (given that one of the party is controlling the direction of talk).

Although anthropologists had long been interested in exchanges and hence in sequences of acts between individuals and groups, up to recently, when they turned to language, they tended to avoid conversations as an object of study. Ethnographers either looked at individual words and phrases (to get the local taxonomy about kinship, illness, etc.) or collected stories or myths told by one individual usually to another individual (often the fieldworker). Even those researchers working within the tradition of the ethnography of communication (see sections 1.3.1 and 9.2), for a long time concentrated on monologic genres like oratory, poetry, and personal narratives produced for the ethnographer. Despite the fact that conversational exchanges had always been important sources of information for anyone interested in cultural practices and social organization, it was not until the early 1970s that conversation per se became a proper subject for study. This was mainly due to a small group of sociologists – most prominently Harvey Sacks and Emanuel Schegloff – who concentrated on conversational exchanges as the battle ground on which to challenge commonly held assumptions about social order and the units of analysis needed for its study. They called their program "conversation analysis" to stress the point that conversation could be a legitimate topic for sociological inquiry[1] and embarked on a research project that has continued to flourish, despite Harvey Sacks's tragic death in a car accident in 1975. Although their work is still viewed with some suspicion by mainstream sociologists – especially those who consider everyday verbal interaction as a dependent variable and hence conditioned by supposedly more important societal contexts and forces (e.g. economic structures, political and legal institutions) –, conversation analysts' research has had a considerable impact among those interested in how language is used in social interaction, linguistic anthropologists included. Conversation analysts' terms like *turn taking, floor, adjacency pair, repair, preference*, have become part of the tools of the trade of researchers interested in units of analysis larger than individual sentences or individual speech acts. In this chapter I will review some of the basic units introduced by conversation analysts and discuss their epistemological assumptions vis-à-vis grammarians and ethnographers. As with other approaches and paradigms discussed in this book, in this case as well I will not be able to do justice to the wealth of contributions that have been made in the last twenty years by a small but very productive group of scholars who are regarded as the "hard core" conversation analysts.[2] I will instead limit myself to two topics: (i) "units of analysis" introduced by conversation analysts and (ii) the critical

---

[1] "[In Sacks's 1964–5 lectures] there is the distinctive and utterly critical recognition ... that the talk can be examined as an object in its own right, and not merely as a screen on which are projected other processes, whether Baleasian system problems or Schutzian interpretive strategies, or Garfinkelian commonsense methods. The talk itself was the action, and previously unsuspected details were critical resources in what was getting done in and by the talk; and all this in naturally occurring events, in no way manipulated to allow the study of them" (Schegloff 1992a: xviii).

[2] A detailed introduction to conversation analysis can be found in Levinson (1983: ch. 6). See also Coulthard (1977: ch.4) and Schiffrin (1994: ch. 7). For a review of the main features of conversation analysis written by two practitioners, see Goodwin and Heritage (1990).

appraisal of conversation analysis by anthropologists and other social scientists who have objected to what they see as a "narrow" focus of interest and a lack of proper deployment of ethnographic methods.

8.1   The sequential nature of conversational units

From the beginning, conversation analysts shared with Malinowski, Austin, Searle, and Wittgenstein the view that talk itself is social action. The way conversation analysts went about studying language as a form of social action, however, was quite innovative and introduced methods and concepts that have changed forever the way many scholars think about language. The first innovation consisted of the simple methodological requirement that one should use as objects of study recordings of "naturally occurring" conversations, that is, conversations that occurred during an occasion that had not been planned or controlled by the investigators (as would be the case in an ethnographic interview or in an experimental setting where people are asked to role play). Conversation analysts treat members' opinions on their own behavior as just another type of data in further need of an account (this partly explains why conversation analysts usually do not rely on interviews for finding out what participants are doing with words). The method is rather a systematic analysis of what people do with language across situations.

Second, rather than starting from a number of predefined notions such as *status*, *social relationship*, *role*, *situation*, conversation analysts began by isolating what appeared as recurring types of utterances and asking questions such as "what are they doing?" This means that utterances are treated as **social objects**, that is, structures or moves around which people organize their interaction.

The first type of conversational exchanges Sacks became interested in were telephone calls to a Suicide Prevention Center in Los Angeles.[3] From the transcripts of the tapes of these calls, Sacks started to pull out portions that displayed phenomena that caught his attention. Here are some excerpts he used in his lectures:

(1)   A: Hello
      B: Hello

(2)   A: This is Mr Smith may I help you
      B: Yes, this is Mr. Brown

---

[3] "In 1963, Garfinkel arranged for Sacks to move to Los Angeles. He was to have an appointment as Acting Assistant Professor of Sociology at UCLA, with the first year off. During that year, 1963–4, Garfinkel and Sacks were to serve as Fellows at the Center for the Scientific Study of Suicide in Los Angeles, under the sponsorship of its director, Edwin Schneidemann" (Schegloff 1992a: xv).

(3)   A: This is Mr. Smith may I help you
      B: I can't hear you.
      A: This is Mr. *Smith*
      B: Sm*i*th

Sacks argued that the way these exchanges are organized shows an important property of verbal interaction, namely, the fact that communication is organized **sequentially**. This idea includes but goes beyond Saussure's concept of syntagmatic relations (see section 6.1). Saussure was interested in the *spoken chain*, meant as a succession of elements that complement each other and are used to build higher-level units of meaning. Saussure and those who later developed his main ideas about linguistic structures were interested in how relations of contiguity are used at different levels of grammar. For instance, sequences of phonemes build words and sequences of words build clauses. Eventually, some linguists became interested in how clauses can build paragraphs and other larger units (see Brown and Yule 1983; Schiffrin 1994). The study of conversational exchanges introduced another aspect of sequentiality, namely, **succession of speakers**. What Sacks and his colleagues did was to show that such a succession was just as systematic and orderly as sequences of phonemes studied by phonologists and sequences of words studied by syntacticians. They refer to such an organization as the **turn-taking system** (Sacks, Schegloff, and Jefferson 1974). Its study developed into a central concern of conversation analysts, who became fascinated by the principles whereby participants in a conversation are able to alternate their speech in an orderly way so as to avoid simultaneous talk ("overlaps") and silences ("gaps"). The general (much simplified) principle of conversational exchanges became known as *no gaps no overlaps*. How can such a system work? How can participants be so good at coordinating with one another's actions as to know when to start and when to stop talking? One way would be to decide ahead of time on a particular order. Participants (or someone else for them) could decide that people speak according to an independently assigned rank system or, according to categories of persons, for instance, seniority or gender could be the determining factor. In other cases, political affiliation might be the relevant category. Although such systems of **pre-allocation** (that is, systems of turn-taking in which order is decided in advance) exist – in court, in political meetings and debates, in interviews, etc. –, in most conversations, the order of speakers and the length of each party's contribution is negotiated during the interaction.

Starting from the empirical observation that during a conversation speakers alternate and they do so usually with no gaps or slight ones and with no overlaps or short ones, Sacks and his colleagues proposed a set of rules that account for such smooth transitions. Such rules have two components: (i) the **turn-constructional component** and (ii) the **turn-allocation component**.

The turn-constructional component defines the types of **units** a speaker can use in participating in a conversation. These units usually correspond to what linguists call utterances and range from one word – like *hello* in (1) above – to fully expressed sentences like *I can't hear you* in (3) above, which has a Subject (*I*), a complex Verb (*can't hear*), and an Object (*you*). A speaker is entitled to have a "turn" to such a unit. An important feature of a unit is that once it is started, it allows a hearer to **project**, that is, to make a prediction about, where it will end. The point at which it ends is called by conversation analysts **transition-relevant point** because it is the moment at which change of speaker may (but does not have to) take place. This component of the system not only explains how speakers manage to know when the floor is available, but also explains why overlaps occur. In some cases the next speaker overlaps because the point of possible completion, as predictable from the speaker's talk, is, for some reason, delayed. An example is shown in (4) below, where the last word of the turn is unpredictably stretched and thus ends up overlapping with the beginning of the next speaker's turn (see "transcription conventions" section 5.5).

(4) B: Well it wasn't me ::

             [

    A: No, but you know who it was.

                               (Sacks et al. 1978: 17)

The turn-allocation component specifies how a next speaker is chosen. There are two techniques: (i) the current speaker selects the next speaker (this is called **other-selection**), and (ii) next speaker selects himself (**self-selection**). To account for how speaker selection takes place, conversation analysts proposed the following ordered rules:

(i) a current speaker can select the next speaker, in which case the selected party has the right and is obliged to speak next (at the transition-relevant place);

(ii) if the current speaker does not select a next speaker, once a transition-relevant place is reached, there are two possibilities: (a) someone else might self-select to speak next; or (b) if no one else self-selects, then the current speaker may continue to talk (or the last speaker may resume talk).

These rules account for smooth transitions from one speaker to the next as well as for cases of simultaneous talk. Thus, in (5), the fact that both Vic and James start at the same time can be explained by rule (iia). Since Mike's turn does not select the next speaker (rule [i]), then other speakers are allowed to self-select and they do so right after the transition-relevant point, namely, after Mike's utterance *I know who d'guy is*:

(5) Mike: I know who d'guy is.=
     Vic: He's ba::d.
              =[
     James: You know the gu:y?   (Sacks et al. 1978: 16)

This is a very powerful system that not only accounts for how conversational interactions can run smoothly, but also for how they are similar or different from other kinds of **speech exchange systems**, that is, interviews, debates, press conferences, classes, trials, religious ceremonies, and so on (Sacks, Schegloff, and Jefferson 1978: 45). In many events that we call "formal," for instance, the order of speakers is pre-allocated or partly pre-allocated (Atkinson and Drew 1979; Drew and Heritage 1992; Duranti 1981, 1994a; Irvine 1979). Even in such cases, however, some of the rules proposed for conversation might still work given that participants need ways of knowing when to begin and when to end their talk and might need to avoid long silences and overlaps.

Conversation analysts treat the turn taking system as a form of social organization.[4] What they find interesting about studying such a system is that it can be described without relying on predetermined notions of what constitutes social structure. The concepts and rules proposed by conversation analysts are said to emerge from the data themselves, that is, from what participants actually do, from what participants themselves show that they are *oriented to*.

An important consequence of looking at conversations and their sequential organization was the realization that conversation is often organized in units that are larger than an individual utterance, turn, or speech act. Sacks (lecture 1, Fall 1964) noted, for instance, that certain utterances by one speaker would call for a particular type of response by another speaker. If a person says *hello*, the other can also say *hello* – in (1) above –, if a person gives his name – in (2) above –, the other also tends to provide his name in the next turn, and if a speaker said *I can't hear you* – in (3) –, the other usually repeats some version of what he said earlier. To talk about such two-turn sequences, Sacks and his colleagues introduced two important concepts: the notion of **adjacency pair** and the notion of **preference**.

8.1.1 Adjacency pairs

An adjacency pair is a sequence of two utterances, next (i.e. adjacent) to one another, and produced by two different speakers (Schegloff and Sacks [1973] 1984: 74). Adjacency pairs can be classified in terms of (i) the types of utterances that constitute its two parts (first pair part and second pair part), and (ii) the type

[4] Schegloff (1991: 46), for instance, wrote: "The work which is focused on the organization of talk-in-interaction in its own right ... is itself dealing with social organization and social structures, albeit of a different sort than in the received uses of those terms [in traditional sociology], and is no less sociological in impulse and relevance ...".

of pair that the two parts constitute together. Thus example (1) above – repeated below as (6) – provides an example of an adjacency pair in which both the first pair part and the second pair part are a greeting (*hello*), with the entire pair being a greeting exchange (see more on this later in this section).

(6)   A: Hello   (first pair part)
       B: Hello   (second pair part)

A similar type of greeting/greeting adjacency pair is the English closing greeting *(good)bye/(good)bye* and the Italian *ciao/ciao*, as shown from the following exchange at the end of a telephone conversation:[5]

(7)   Ro: *salutami: //le figlie.*
             say hi (to) (your) daughters
                          [
       Ri: *grazie. pure a voi. tutti.*
                        thanks. also to you all.
                                      [
       Ro: *grazie.*
                                    thanks.

→   *ciao.*
             bye.
               [
→   Ri: *ciao.*[6]
             bye.   ("Rita 1")

Not all greetings nor adjacency pairs, however, exhibit two identical words or types of utterances. In many societies, for instance, greetings are exchanged in the form of question/answer pairs. Here is an example from Kasigau, a Bantu language of southern Kenya (Milton 1982):[7]

(8)   A: *wawuka?*   (first pair part: question-greeting)
            have you woken (well)?
       B: *nawuka.*   (second pair part: answer-greeting)
            I have woken (well).

[5] This and the following examples from Italian telephone conversations are taken from a set of audio recordings made by the author in Italy in 1987 and 1988.
[6] This overlap of the last greeting can be explained with the turn-taking system discussed earlier. In this case, since Ro's *grazie* is a one-word turn-unit, Ri's *ciao* would have occurred after an appropriate transition-relevant place, had not Ro decided to continue with her own *ciao*.
[7] For a general discussion of types of greetings and relevant bibliographical information, see Duranti (1992).

When we look for adjacency pairs in conversations, we find a vast range of types. Here are some examples:

> *Question/Answer:*
> (9) A: What's the name of that color?
>   B: Blue. (Merritt 1982: 235)

> (10) A: phõ: raw   ch ŷ: araj?
>   father   Pro   name   what
>   "What is your father's name?"
>   B: naːj   inta: sɛŋjaj khap
>   Title PN   FN   Particle (PN = personal name; FN = family name)
>   "Nai Intaa Saengjaj." (Moerman 1988: 157)

> *Offer/Acceptance:*
> (11) A: How about carrots?
>   B: Yeah. (Merritt 1982: 234)

> *Offer/Rejection:*
> (12) A: You wanna sandwich?
>   B: No thanks, (Pomerantz 1978: 87)

> *Compliment/Acceptance:*
> (13) A: It's very pretty.
>   B: Thank you. (Pomerantz 1978: 84)

> *Assessment/Agreement:*
> (14) A: That's fantastic
>   B: Isn't that good (Pomerantz 1978: 94)

> *Assessment/Disagreement:*
> (15) A: Good shot
>   B: Not very solid though (Pomerantz 1978: 99)

> *Initiation/Reply:*
> (16) A: I called the tractor a "mmm ..."
>   B: Machine. (Mehan 1979: 42)

The notion of adjacency pair constitutes an important innovation with respect to the notion of speech act proposed by Austin and Searle for a number of reasons. Some of the differences between speech acts and adjacency pairs stem from the fact that the latter are more complex units than a single utterance or a single speech act. Although this idea was foreshadowed in Austin's notion of uptake and his intuition that certain types of speech acts like a bet need a response or acceptance in order to be felicitous (see section 7.1.1), in general, speech act theory takes individual speech acts produced by individuals as its unit of analysis.[8] Both the force of an illocutionary act and the conditions for its satisfaction are typically assigned and evaluated independently of other, especially following, speech acts. But the analysis of units larger than a single utterance/speech act such as adjacency pairs provides us with important insights precisely into those aspects of language such as action that speech act theory was meant to study. If we are really interested in what speech *does*, it would seem crucial to look at hearers' reactions to what is said to them. This is not done by speech act theorists.

In speech act theory, the force of an utterance must be described in terms of certain conditions that describe a context that is typically prior to or contemporary with the utterance, but not in terms of its consequences or effects. This is something that pertains to the perlocutionary act (see section 7.1.1), the most underdeveloped of the three acts introduced by Austin. Thus, in speech act theory, an assessment about someone would be judged to be a compliment, given certain pre-existing conditions.

> To compliment is to express approval of the hearer for something. Complimenting presupposes that the thing the hearer is complimented for is good, though it need not necessarily be good for him. One might, for example, compliment him on his heroic and self-sacrificing behavior. (Searle and Vanderveken 1985: 215)

The conditions found in Searle and Vanderveken's definition are important for distinguishing between compliments and other kinds of related speech acts, e.g. praising, but they frame compliments almost exclusively in terms of (i) an evaluation of the positive value of the "thing" being praised, and (ii) the pre-existing relationship between the "thing" and the hearer. The examination of compliments as parts of adjacency pairs, on the other hand, allows for a new way of examining what compliments *do*. As shown by Anita Pomerantz (1978), who studied compliments in conversation, compliments do not just "express approval," they also create a "problem" for hearers, who are faced with a conflict between two general principles of interaction identified by conversation analysts, namely, the preference for agreement and the avoidance of self-praise (on the concept of "preference," see section 8.2). To accept a compliment means to follow the general preference for agreeing with our interlocutor, but violates the dispreference for praising oneself. To reject a compliment creates the opposite situation, that is, it follows the preference for avoiding self-praise but violates the preference

---

[8] Recently, in his discussion of "collective intentionality" Searle (1990) has introduced the idea of more complex and collective types of "acts" but these are seen as special cases, distinct from such things as questions, answers, offers, etc.

for agreement. In looking at how speakers deal with this conflict in conversation, Pomerantz identifies two strategies: **praise downgrades** (see examples [14] and [15] above) and **referent shifts**. "Referent shift" means that the recipient of the compliment responds by reassigning the praise:

(17) {A praises B}   (first pair part)
      {B praises other-than-self}   (second pair part)

This is a "solution" to the conflict between agreement and self-praise avoidance because speaker B shifts the praise without disagreeing with the positive assessment made by A. An example is provided in (24) (from Pomerantz 1978: 102):

(18) A: You're a good rower, Honey.
      B: These are very easy to row. Very light.

The method of looking at the type of responses compliments receive recognizes an important aspect of language as social action, namely, that, if we want to find out what words *do*, we must look beyond individual utterances, given that in spontaneous social interaction, speakers use and interpret speech acts as parts of larger sequential units. The adjacency pair is an example of such a larger sequential unit, in which one can easily see that the meaning of each of the two pair parts is constrained, explained, and amplified by the other.

Empirically, since utterances do not usually appear with tags on them clarifying what their illocutionary force (or "point") is, the method of looking at adjacency pairs rather than isolated utterances offers a better sense of what speakers are accomplishing. Thus, in (18) above, the utterance *These are very easy to row* is not simply an assertion (to be judged in terms of truth values and beliefs), but a response to the utterance produced by A and a "solution" to the problem created by it. If we just say that *These are very easy to row* is an assertion, we still have not said anything really interesting about what that utterance is *doing*. Conversely, the assertion, by trying to "deal with" the "problem" created by A's utterance, convalidates A's utterance as a compliment and gives us a hint about what compliments do once uttered.

More generally, then, we can say that an adjacency pair provides a **frame for interpretation**.[9] This is important not only for ethnographers as observer-participants interested in making sense of the actions constituted by their subjects' talk. It is also a fundamental tool that the participants themselves use for interpreting each other's actions.

In the identification of the mechanism of the adjacency pair as a resource for social interaction, conversation analysis shares an important insight with

---

[9] On the notion of "frame," see Bateson (1972), Goffman (1974), Kendon (1992).

ethnomethodology (see section 1.2.4), namely, the idea that what we need to do as analysts is first of all look at what social actors themselves do, what *methods* they use for solving practical everyday problems. Such problems include not only (or not necessarily) the ones explicitly recognized as problems, but also much more mundane and often unrecognized issues such as how to respond to a compliment (see above) or, more generally, the problem of letting others know that we understand what is going on and we have a particular stance with respect to it:

> Adjacency pairs organization is thus an elementary framework
> through which conversational participants will inevitably display
> some analysis of one another's action. Within this framework of
> reciprocal conduct, action and interpretation are inextricably
> intertwined. Each participant must analyze the developing course
> of others' actions in order to produce appropriate reciprocal action.
> (Goodwin and Heritage 1990: 288)

When speakers produce the first pair part of an adjacency pair, they create an interpretive frame within which what happens next is bound to be not only an "answer" or "second move" but also a display of how the recipient has interpreted the first pair part. Adjacency pairs are thus important mechanisms for establishing **intersubjectivity**, that is, mutual understanding and coordination around a common activity.[10] Schegloff and Sacks (1984), for instance, have shown that both openings and closings of telephone conversations are typically done in an adjacency pair format. Why should it be so? Because by producing a second utterance, speakers can display their understanding of what the prior utterance is doing and their willingness to go along with whatever plan is implied by it (e.g. starting a conversation, closing, providing further information, changing topic) (Schegloff and Sacks 1984: 75). The adjacency pair mechanism can be very handy, especially in those cases in which a decision has to be made about continuing or terminating an interaction. In closing a conversation, participants must agree that there is nothing else to be talked about, otherwise one of the parties would feel 'cut off' or abruptly dismissed. For this reason, although greetings can be used to do the job of closing (one person says "good-bye" and the other person answers with another "good-bye" or some other type of closing salutation), it is important to arrive at closing salutations in a smooth and agreeable way. We cannot say "good-bye" in a conversation without preparing our conversational partners, even when we feel that everything has been said. Children's first telephone conversations ("Hello. How are you? Fine. Goodbye.") often sound humorous to adult listeners precisely because they violate such adult

[10] The theme of intersubjectivity has been explicitly approached by Schegloff (1991) in the context of a discussion of what he calls "third position repair."

expectations (Garvey 1984: 35–6). Usually, we prepare our conversational partners for the possibility of a closing coming up soon. On the telephone, this is
done with utterances that are taken to be **possible pre-closings** (Schegloff and
Sacks 1984: 80). One way of doing this work is to provide an item whose only
business is to show that the speaker, for now, has nothing else to say. This is done
in English by such expressions as *we-ell, okay, so-oo* (with downward intonation
contours). At this point the other speaker has the option of introducing a new
topic or accepting that there is nothing more to say, hence agreeing that the conversation can come to an end. Such adjacency pairs as "okay/okay" or
"alright/okay" are often found in these contexts. The following examples are
from Schegloff and Sacks's article:

(19)	Dorinne:	Uh-you know, it's just like bringin the- blood up.	
	Theresa:	Yeah well. THINGS UH ALWAYS WORK OUT FOR THE BEST	
		[	
	Dorinne:	Oh certainly.	
→		Alright Tess.	**(pre-closing: first pair part)**
		[	
	Theresa:	Uh huh,	
→	Theresa:	Okay.	**(pre-closing: second pair part)**
	Dorinne:	G'bye.	**(closing: first pair part)**
	Theresa:	Goodnight,	**(closing: second pair part)**
(20)	Johnson:	... and uh, uh we're gonna see if we can't uh tie in our plans a little better.	
	Baldwin:	Okay fine	
		[	
	Johnson:	ALRIGHT?	
	Baldwin:	RIGHT.	
→	Johnson:	Okay boy.	**(pre-closing: first pair part)**
→	Baldwin:	Okay.	**(pre-closing: second pair part)**
	Johnson:	Bye bye.	**(closing: first pair part)**
		[	
	Baldwin:	G'night.	**(closing: second pair part)**

It should be clear by now that conversation analysis not only introduces a new
methodology for studying language as action, but also provides new concepts for
identifying what individual utterances and words *do* in interaction. These new
concepts constitute a new way of looking at speech as action, although they are
also reminiscent of Wittgenstein's later philosophy of language. Conversation

analysis provides a method for following Wittgenstein's suggestion that we should look at words as always embedded in larger activities – adjacency pairs being examples of "language games." Since the same word can appear in very different points in a conversation, we cannot speculate about what it does until we look at the larger sequence within which it occurs. For instance, the first *okay* by the speaker named Baldwin in (20) is different from the *okay* subsequently produced by the speaker named Johnson. The first *okay* is part of an agreement (*okay fine*) to a proposal and hence closes a topic. The second *okay* (in *okay boy*) is the first pair part of an adjacency pair that sets the tone for the forthcoming closing salutations.

The lack of attention to conversational sequences in Searle's theoretical apparatus produces analyses that are often at odds with those proposed by conversation analysts. An obvious case is provided by greetings. Searle and Vanderveken (1985: 215–16) state that "[w]hen one greets someone, for example, by saying 'Hello,' one indicates recognition in a courteous fashion." This description, which does not take into consideration the larger contexts in which greetings may appear, does not capture the use of *hello* or other kinds of greetings in telephone conversations. We know, for instance, that the first "hello" on the telephone, rather than indicating recognition, answers the summons constituted by the rings (Schegloff 1972b) and provides a resource for the caller, who can use it to "do" or "attempt" (but not "indicate" *yet*) recognition. Callers use the first *hello* to try to identify who answered the phone (Schegloff 1979a, 1986). As shown in example (21) below, it is after the first *hello* that the caller is in a position to display a claim to recognition. Recognition is then done through the use of a proper name (*Connie* in [21]):

(21) C: Hello.   **(answer to summons – resource for recognition)**
      J: Connie?   **(claim to recognition by caller)**
                                            (Schegloff 1979a: 51)

At this point, the answerer can display that she has, in turn, recognized the caller. This is done through the reciprocal use of NAME by C in the third turn (*Yeah Joanie*).

(22) C: Hello.   **(answer to summons – resource for recognition)**
      J: Connie?   **(claim to recognition by caller)**
      C: Yeah Joanie   **(claim to recognition by answerer)**

When the answerer on the telephone does not reciprocate the use of name and only uses a greeting (e.g. *hi*), as in (23) below, callers may speculate that complete recognition has not taken place and might then proceed to self-identify, as in the last turn below (*It's Barbie*) (Schegloff 1979a: 53–4).

(23) B: 'hhh Hello,
     Ba: Hi Bonnie,   **(other-identification)**
     B: Hi.=
→   Ba: =It's Barbie.=   **(self-identification)**

                             (Schegloff 1979a: 53)

This last example shows that greeting by itself (*hi* by B in [23]) is not necessarily interpreted as evidence of recognition. Hence, even for greetings such as "hi" Searle and Vandervaken's description is inadequate.

Sequential order is important not only within each adjacency pair but also in the relation between an adjacency pair and other (preceding or following) units. Just as *hello* or *hi* do different things depending on whether they are in the first or second part, an entire adjacency pair may have a different force depending on where it appears within a larger sequence (e.g. an entire conversation). This is the case, for instance, for the Italian greeting pair *ciao/ciao*, which, differently from its use in English- and Spanish-speaking communities, can be used in Italy as either an opening or closing greeting. In (7) above, we saw an example of the pair *ciao/ciao* used in closing a telephone conversation. In (24), we see it used as an opening greeting at the beginning of a telephone conversation:

(24) G: *pronto,*
        hello,
     S: *Giorgio?*
        Giorgio?
→   G: *ah ciao.*[11]   **(opening greeting: first pair part)**
        oh hi.
→   S: *ciao.*   **(opening greeting: second pair part)**
        hi.
        [...]

                          (from "Giorgio 3")

In this case, consideration of the sequential aspects of the interaction provides us with a perspective on greetings and other verbal exchanges that is not immediately available within the framework of speech act theory. We can certainly acknowledge that the second *ciao* in example (24) is doing something, but we cannot easily agree with Searle and Vandervaken that it is doing "recognition" given that speaker S had already done recognition with the earlier turn (*Giorgio?*).

---

[11] As often happens during greeting exchanges, the greeting co-occurs with other linguistic material such as the *ah* in this example, which seems similar to the English *oh* used as an indication of success at recognition (see Schegloff 1979a). For more discussion of this example, see below.

The difference between conversation analysis and speech act theory is not only due to a different methodology (although methodology is claimed to be an important discovery procedure by conversation analysts). Nor is it simply a matter of different units of analysis. The analysis of what comes before and after an utterance is only part of what conversation analysts bring to the study of language as action. More importantly, for them, conversations become the places where one can study the mundane activity of being a social actor in the ethnomethodological sense of someone who is **accountable** for his actions (Garfinkel 1967; Sacks 1992a, 1992b). By looking at sequences like adjacency pairs we can see how talk establishes frames which evoke, suggest, and even impose certain expectations on participants. This important aspect of conversational systems is partly captured by the notion of preference.

8.2 The notion of preference

Early on in his lectures Sacks became interested in the fact that we hear certain utterances as "idioms" (he also used the word "composites" [1992a: 8]), that is, as chunks that we associate with certain routine activities. He gave as an example *may I help you* (or its variant *can I help you*). This utterance in most contexts is not thought of as a real question, but rather as an offer of help by a person who is qualified to do so. It might be said by a clerk in a department store or by an operator who will direct your call. In the calls to the suicide prevention center studied by Sacks, this phrase was used by a professional who listened to callers' problems. In speech act theory, an utterance like *may I help you* would be analyzed as an indirect speech act (see section 7.2.1.1). As in the cases of indirect requests, a question would be said to function as an offer by virtue of a series of inferences (e.g. a question has the force of an offer if the speaker uses it to ask whether a preparatory condition concerning the speaker's ability to do a certain action obtains). But Sacks was not just interested in how we understand a question as an offer. He was drawn to the sequential contexts of such questions, namely, to what usually follows. He noticed that there is a tendency to answer "yes" to a question like *may* (or *can*) *I help you*? This caused him to reflect on what happens when a different type of answer, e.g. *I don't know* occurs:

(25) A: Can I help you?
      B: I don't know hheh   I hope you can
      A: Uh hah   Tell me about your problems
      B: I uh   Now that you're here I'm embarasssed to talk about it. I
         don't want you telling me I'm emotionally immature 'cause I
         know I am

(Sacks 1992a: 10)

259

In this example, by taking a different course of action than expected, the caller seems to reject the "routine" nature of the question. Sacks speculated that this might be a way of rejecting the "routine" nature of the treatment; the caller in this case seemed to have previous (probably negative) experience with routine treatment, as shown by the following comment *I don't want you telling me I'm emotionally immature 'cause I know I am*.

Since these preliminary observations, conversation analysts have shown that in all kinds of situations there are **preferred courses of action** and that the study of both *preferred* and *dispreferred* replies to questions and other first pair parts can give us a sense not only of what social actors are after, but also of what is considered to be normal or expected in any given situation. Looking at preference structure is a way of getting to the heart of what makes language such a powerful instrument of culture.

Similarly to those who think of culture as a public phenomenon – whether in the form of rules or in the forms of embodied practices (see chapter 2) –, Sacks and other conversation analysts did not think of preferences as psychological properties, residing in an individual's consciousness. Rather, they saw preferences as tendencies provided in the system and by the system. Thus, when conversation analysts examine the tendency for the recipient of an accusation in a British court to deny it (Atkinson and Drew 1979), they are not invoking or looking for individual motivations. They are simply describing a cultural preference (Bilmes 1988). Preferences are interpretive frameworks within which members must operate at the very moment of engaging in the mediating activity of talk:

> The concept of "preference" has developed in conversation analytic research to characterize conversational events in which alternative, but nonequivalent, courses of action are available to the participants ... The term "preference" refers to a range of phenomena associated with the fact that choices among nonequivalent courses of action are routinely implemented in ways that reflect an institutionalized ranking of alternatives. Despite its connotations, the term is *not* intended to reference personal, subjective, or "psychological" desires or dispositions.
>
> (Atkinson and Heritage 1984: 53)

This conceptualization of preferences has a number of theoretical and methodological implications. Theoretically, by pointing to what is more likely to be said on any given occasion, the notion of preference uncovers the subtle and yet powerful ways in which individuals are subjected to the pressures of culture, where choice is possible but alternatives are by no means equal. The discussion of preferences is thus a potentially powerful tool for discussing the role played by language in shaping human behavior that was so central to early linguistic anthropologists like Edward Sapir:

> It is strange how frequently one has the illusion of free knowledge, in the light of which one may manipulate conduct at will, only to discover in the test that one is being impelled by strict loyalty to forms of behavior that one can feel with the utmost nicety and can state only in the vaguest and most approximate fashion.
>
> (Sapir [1927] 1963: 549)

Preferences are not strictly controlling mechanisms. It is always possible to resist or violate a preference in favor of a dispreferred move (see example [25] above). Such alternative moves, however, need some extra work and are not without consequences. Dispreferred activities (e.g. saying "no" to an offer, disagreeing on an assessment, etc.) "are usually performed with delay between turns, are commonly delayed within turns, and are variously softened and made indirect" (Atkinson and Heritage 1984: 53). Thus, it is not by accident that when, in example (25) above, we do not find "yes" after *can I help you?*, there is laughter and then in the next turn some hesitation by the person who offered assistance. The preferred course of action has not been followed and some extra work (in the form of justification, explanation) is necessary to go on and deal with the problem created or implied by the unusual move.

8.2.1 Repairs and corrections

A set of phenomena where one can see the notion of preference at work is what conversation analysts call **repair**. The term "repair" has a wider scope than the term "correction," given that "[t]he term 'correction' is commonly understood to refer to the replacement of an 'error' or 'mistake' by what is 'correct'" (Schegloff, Jefferson, and Sacks 1977: 363). The phenomena called "repairs" by conversation analysts, however, are not contingent upon error in the traditional sense, they are attempts at resolving what is being perceived and/or defined as a "problem" or "trouble" in the course of an interaction. The notion of repair is closely connected to the sequential nature of conversational interaction. People who talk to one another need a mechanism that allows them to maintain continuity in the interaction while taking care of whatever problem arises in the course of their conversation.[12] For instance, sometimes a person might have difficulty finding the right word or making sense of what someone else said. Other times, a participant might simply feel that what has been said is not accurate or needs to be rephrased, corrected, or augmented. There are times, in other words,

---

[12] Such continuity need not be thematic. It might be about maintaining the attention of an interlocutor, as shown by Goodwin (1979, 1981).

when a person feels the need to "fix" what is being said or done. This "fixing" can be done by the same speaker, as in (26) below, where the speaker rectifies his earlier description making it more specific (*my son* becomes *my oldest son*):

(26) Ralph: Somebody said looking at my:, son my oldest son,

(Goodwin 1981: 130)

Other times the repair may be initiated by another speaker and then corrected by the person who originated the "trouble." This **other-initiated repair** is typically done by what conversation analysts call **repair initiators**, that is, by one-word questions such as *huh? What? Who?* or by an echo question, that is, a question that repeats part of the structure that is defined as "trouble" adding a wh-word, e.g. *the who?* and *the what?* may be used for repairing a noun and the *do what?* or *go where*? may be used for repairing a predicate. Here are two examples of repairs done with echo questions:

(27) A: Well who'r you workin for.
     B: 'hhh Well I'm working through the Amfat Corporation.
→   A: The *who*?
     B: Amfah Corporation. T's a holding company.
                          [
     A: Oh

(Schegloff et al. 1977: 368)

(28) (Members of a rock band are discussing how to organize their performance)
     Will: That might be kinda weird to do *tha*:t.
           (0.8)
→   Russ: Do what?
           [
     Joy: For*get* the mikes: step o:ut step out in front
                    [
     Will: Tryin ta do ((gestures with guitar))

(Keating 1993: 418)

Repair can also be both initiated and fixed by another speaker, as in (29):

(29) Ben: Lissena *pi*geons.
           (0.7)
     Ellen: Coo-coo::: coo:::
            [
→   Bill: Quail, I think.

(Schegloff et al. 1977: 378)

Schegloff, Jefferson, and Sacks found that repairs are organized in predictable, that is, common, recurrent ways. Thus, when another party initiates the repair – as in (27) and (28) above –, he or she does so in the next turn. This means that participants other than the current speaker withhold repair initiations until the next transition-relevant place (see above). In fact, usually other-initiated repairs are delayed a bit after the turn in which they occur, suggesting that the speaker is providing some extra time for the person who produced the "trouble" to correct on his or her own – this is the case in (28) and (29). In some cases, the other party might wait so long that no repair occurs at all. This organization is connected to a preference in conversation to let speakers fix their own "troubles." In other words, English conversational data suggests that there is a **preference for self-repair** and a **dispreference for other-repair**. Further evidence of this preference is shown by the tendency to modulate or downgrade other-corrections, e.g. by the addition of hedges or uncertainty markers, e.g. the use of *I think* in (29) or the common use of the form *you mean X?* or the framing of the correction as a joke.

8.2.2 The avoidance of psychological explanation

One of the features of conversation analysis is that it examines such phenomena as repairs without entering the issue of the individual motivations for such behaviors. Researchers simply look at what speakers *do*. From such observations, they inductively arrive at the organization of public behavior. This means that the notion of preference is not individually but collectively defined. It represents a type of organization, a set of rules or tendencies that anyone who participates in conversational interaction must reckon with. The meaning of a speaker's actions is given by the expectations routinely associated with a particular type of exchange. Speakers have choices, but those choices are constrained by the system within which they must operate in order to be members of a society.

The view of language as a public phenomenon and the need to understand individual moves as part of larger social institutions is reminiscent of Wittgenstein's later philosophy (see section 7.2.1). This perspective is difficult for many students in western academic environments to grasp because people in the west commonly explain behavior in terms of individual motivations. Sacks was quite aware of this problem, as shown by these concluding remarks in his opening lecture in the Fall of 1964:

> One final note. When people start to analyze social phenomena, if
> it looks like things occur with the sort of immediacy we find in some
> of these exchanges, then, if you have to make an elaborate analysis
> of it [i.e. the way Sacks does it] ... then you figure that they couldn't

have thought that fast. I want to suggest that you have to forget that completely. Don't worry about how fast they're thinking. First of all, don't worry about whether they're "thinking." Just try to come to terms with how it is that the thing comes off. Because you'll find that they can do these things. Just take any other area of natural science and see, for example, how fast molecules do things. And they don't have very good brains. So just let the materials fall as they may. Look to see how it is that persons go about producing what they do produce. (Sacks 1992a: 11)

In this passage, Sacks is trying to free students from their prejudice about what constitutes an explanation of human behavior. But he is also hinting at a method of investigation that is reminiscent of the structuralist paradigm within linguistics, anthropology, and other social sciences (see chapters 2 and 6). In both cases, analysts look at the actions and try to leave out (or "bracket") what they think the participants might be thinking. In both cases, there is an attempt to break the nineteenth-century division between the human sciences (*Geisteswissenschaften*) and the hard or natural sciences (*Naturwissenschaften*). In both cases, as we shall see more clearly below, there is a tendency to emphasize the context-independence of certain structures over their context-dependence and thus build a repertoire of mechanisms that can repeatedly do the same job regardless of the circumstances in which they are used. For a linguistic anthropologist the question always is: how do we know that it is the "same job" that is being done? This is an epistemological question that is related to the emic perspective on human interaction that characterizes the anthropological perspective (see chapter 6). It points to the different conceptualization of context that often divides formal approaches, conversation analysis included, from interpretive ones. More specifically, if we are not talking about individual preferences, what is the sociological status of the system that seems to guide such preferences? Are they to be conceived as included in the notion of culture? But if so, why is such a notion avoided in conversation analytical writings? I will return to this question at the end of the chapter.

8.3   Conversation analysis and the "context" issue

Conversation analysts have uncovered a wealth of social behaviors that are potentially relevant for crosscultural comparison. Conversation analysts have repeatedly demonstrated that conversations are cooperative achievements, where one can see members working hard at coordinating their actions with those of their interlocutors. In isolating short sequences of talk, Sacks, Schegloff, Jefferson, and their colleagues have revealed new ways of studying what words do in interaction. The notion of preference is a powerful instrument for thinking about cultural expectations, values, and their reproduction. For these reasons and the centrality of talk in conversation analysts' data and findings, one might expect an enthusiastic embracing of conversation analytical notions and methods by linguistic anthropologists. However, while sociolinguists, pragmaticians, and discourse analysts who are not trained or interested in ethnographic methods have often borrowed conversation-analytical terminology and methods for their work, with a few exceptions, linguistic anthropologists have been reluctant to employ conversation-analytical methods or take advantage of their findings. Some have even expressed open criticism of conversation analysis. An understanding of such criticism can help us better clarify the goals and methods of linguistic anthropology while making suggestions for a better integration across fields.

At the heart of the intellectual tension between conversation analysts and some linguistic anthropologists are what appear to be fundamental disagreements in analytical procedures and data collection. Most disagreements center around the issue of methods. Conversation analysts are accused of ignoring the cultural or historical "context" in which the interactions they analyze take place. An early attack along these lines can be found in the following passage, where, after a brief critique of a paper by T. Turner on performatives, Dell Hymes launches into a full-scale criticism of the entire school of conversation analysis (obliquely identified as "some sociologists"):

> Some sociologists become so absorbed in words as to fail to renew their relation to actual contexts. Admittedly, it is fascinating to discover the richness of speech, coming from a disciplinary background that has neglected it; but it is a bit absurd to treat transcribed tapes of interaction as if they were the Dead Sea Scrolls. When a society is gone, we must glean all we can from texts that remain, and contrary to some opinion, such work is arduous, disciplined, and often revealing. But again, it is a bit absurd to invent an amateur philology to deal with the life outside one's door. I have read elaborate analysis of verbal interaction that failed to consider the other aspects of verbal interaction to each other, attributing to complexities of words what may have depended on eye-contact; and imputations of intention and construal that neglected intonation (like many grammarians to be sure) and that failed to consult or consider the interpretations of the participants themselves.
>
> (Hymes 1974a: 81)

This passage is instructive because it contains the foundations of the three main problems many linguistic anthropologists and ethnographers see in the conversation analysis paradigm:

(i) a repeated disinterest in the "larger context," for instance, where and when the exchanges being analyzed took place, and a disregard for non-verbal or gestural aspects of face-to-face communication;[13]

(ii) a rudimentary notion of what constitutes speech (as demonstrated by a transcription system that does not take full account of the prosodic features of spoken language);

(iii) a disregard for the interpretations that the participants themselves might provide of their own behavior.

Since I have already mentioned some of the reasons for (iii) above (e.g. speakers are often not aware of their own speech behavior) and have already discussed some of the limitations of the transcription conventions used by conversation analysts in chapter 5, I will here concentrate on (i) and some of its ramifications. Hymes's first criticism is akin to what Goffman ([1976]1981: 32) later characterized as the "sins of noncontextuality," that is, "the assumption that bits of conversation can be analyzed in their own right in some independence of what was occurring at the time and place."[14] It would presumably be "sinful" for Goffman and Hymes to discuss an adjacency pair like (9) above, here repeated as (30), without saying that A is a teacher and B is a student:

> (30) Teacher: What's the name of that color?
>   Student: Blue.   (Merritt 1982: 235)

Without providing the contextual information that the questioner is a teacher, how would we account for the fact that a person is asking a question about something that she already knows? Similarly problematic would be a discussion of the other adjacency pairs. The exchange in (10), for example, is taken from a trial in the northern province of Nan in Thailand. A lawyer asks his client a question

---

[13] But see Goodwin (1979, 1981) on the fine interaction between eye gaze movements and turn construction (see section 8.3.2).

[14] Goffman had been Sacks's teacher at Berkeley and undoubtedly had an influence on him in the early graduate years (Schegloff 1989: 194, 1992a: xxiii-xxiv), but he later became critical of Sacks's approach to the study of conversation and refused to sign Sacks's dissertation, which was eventually approved by a committee chaired by Aaron Cicourel (Schegloff 1992a: xxiii fn 18). Goffman's relationship to conversation analysis is certainly made more complex by the apparent contradiction between his advocacy of the study of everyday behavior and his protracted disinterest in, if not aversion to, electronic recording of verbal interaction, as demonstrated, for instance, by his initial opposition to Marjorie Goodwin's audio recording of children's conversations (M.H. Goodwin, personal communication).

which is meant to be for the judge who needs to record the information in a particular format: Title + Personal Name + Family Name (Moerman 1988: 58). This format, hence, is designed for a third party. Without knowing who the third party is or what the conventions are, we would not be able to make sense of the answer to the question.

The examples of greetings – in (7) and (8) – must be understood within the context of a range of possible greetings in the community. Since not everyone greets in the same way in either Italy or Kenya – and in fact Milton (1982) argues that greetings in Kenya are important strategies for defining one's affiliation with a particular group within the same speech community–, how can we discuss greetings without reference to the relationship between the parties involved? The line of reasoning should be obvious by now: adjacency pairs (or any other unit proposed by conversation analysts) do not happen in a vacuum. Hence, their study must include the "context" in which they occur.

How have conversation analysts answered such criticism? Primarily in two ways. I will refer to them as (i) the autonomous claim and (ii) the relevance issue.

8.3.1 The autonomous claim

The first type of rebuttal is a claim that turns the criticism about "noncontextuality" on its own head. Conversation analysts claim that what appears to be a problem to anthropologists and sociologists like Hymes and Goffman is in fact a strength of conversation analysis. This position is clearly articulated in the following programmatic statement made by Sacks in one of his lectures:

> Now, what I'm going to be doing is taking small parts of a thing and building out from them, because small parts can be identified and worked on without regard to the larger thing they're part of. And they can work in a variety of larger parts than the one they happen to be working in. I don't do that just as a matter of simplicity, but ... the image I have is of this machinery, where you would have some standardized gadget that you can stick in here and there and that can work in a variety of different machines. And you go through the warehouse picking them up to build some given thing you want to build. So these smaller components are first to be identified because they are components perhaps for lots of other tasks than the one they're used in. (Sacks [1965] 1992a: 159)

This quote exposes what I have elsewhere called the "autonomous" quality of conversation analysis (Duranti 1988a: 223). Paradoxically, the stress on the autonomy of conversational mechanisms aligns conversation analysts with generative grammarians and other structuralist linguists who focus on grammar and ignore use (see chapter 6).[15] As we saw earlier, however, the fact that a question will call for an answer, an assessment (preferably) for an agreement, and a greeting for another greeting is just a starting point. What researchers do with these observations depends on their creativity and the kinds of questions they are interested in. If the same interactional mechanisms can be used to do many different things, there are many different questions and issues that can (and should) be pursued – and Sacks's brilliant lectures provide a wealth of such questions, albeit not always compelling solutions. The "autonomous" stand can thus be seen as a strategy for unveiling recurring conversational structures that can be later connected to "larger" or simply "different" contexts (Schegloff 1987 and 1992a). A few extensions of conversation analysts' findings to communities outside of the United States have followed this assumption. This is the case with Michael Moermon's (1977, 1988) research on Thai conversations, Niko Besnier's (1989) account of self-initiated repair in Tuvaluan conversation, and Elinor Ochs's discussion of the practice of "clarification" by Samoan caregivers (Ochs 1984, 1988: 130–43). All three studies, among others, are in fact mentioned by Schegloff (1987) as successful examples of conversation analytical concepts applied to crosscultural research.

When we look at these studies in some detail, we realize that the claims made in them crucially rely on extended ethnographic work among the people whose talk is being analyzed. In each case, ethnography provides important insights into the analysis of the repair mechanism, and shapes the kinds of questions asked by the researchers. Linguistic anthropologists analyzing repair mechanisms tend to be interested not only in how repairs are sequentially organized but also in what they accomplish for the participants as members of a particular community of speakers. Besnier (1989), for instance, analyzes how Tuvaluan speakers in Nukulaelae (Polynesia) "commonly *withhold* an essential piece of information or proffer an ambiguous or problematic reference at certain strategic locations in gossip interactions, thereby eliciting repair-initiation by the audience" (Besnier 1989: 325). An example is provided in (31) below, where speaker K's utterance is framed by F as not providing sufficient information on whom K is talking about. This type of ambiguity is made possible by the grammatical structure of the language which, through so-called zero anaphora (see chapter 6), allows for a sentence to occur without a Subject.[16]

---

[15] This is a *paradoxical* similarity because of the contrast between conversation analysts' insistence on looking only at actual conversation to build hypotheses about rule-governed behavior and Chomsky's skepticism toward such a methodology (see, for instance, Chomsky 1965, 1986). For a discussion of the differences between generative grammar and conversation analysis, see Bilmes (1988b).

[16] For a similar phenomenon in Italian conversations, see Testa (1991).

(31) (Long pause)

K: *A   koo vau   o   fakatootoo mo tena tautai   i aso nei.*=
    and Inc come Comp Caus+fall with his   fishing-lore in day this
    "An' (he) comes along an' starts to pontificate about his
    knowledge of fishing"

→ F: *= A ai?*=
    Foc who
    "Who?"

K: *= Manono.*
    "Manono."

(Besnier 1989: 325)

In similar situations analyzed by Goodwin (1987) in American English conversations, the interlocutors are expected to make explicit proposals about the identity of the missing or problematic material.

> In contrast, Nukulaelae interlocutors refrain from providing
> possible identifications for the problematic material and instead
> initiate repair sequences that encourage the principal speaker to
> supply the problematic material. (Besnier 1989: 332)

This information-withholding routine is interesting to Besnier not only because
of its sequential structure, but also because (i) it displays a tendency not to guess
what the other speaker is thinking, and (ii) it tells us something about how the
people in Nukulaelae organize the dissemination of information that might be
problematic. The avoidance of guessing what another is saying seems related to
a pan-Polynesian or perhaps Pan-Pacific resistance toward reading the mind of
another person (Duranti 1988b, 1993b; Ochs 1984, 1988; Schieffelin 1986). The
way in which information is disseminated shows a preference for sharing the
responsibility for what is being revealed. This strategy is seen by Besnier as part
of spontaneous gossip sessions between two people of the same gender who
become the primary participants among a larger group of people. One of the
effects of withholding information is that the teller of the story shares responsibility with the story's primary recipient. Besnier suggests that revealing who said
or did what is constructed by the participants as initiated by the primary recipient's question. The audience becomes co-author (Duranti and Brenneis 1986).
On the other hand, one might also speculate that the use of repair-initiators such
as "who?" or "what?" forces the person who is gossiping to be more explicit and
foreground information that otherwise might have been left as ambiguous or
vague. This research links the discussion of repair to the issue of **responsibility**, a
dimension of human interaction that used to be the preoccupation of legal

anthropologists (Gluckman 1965, 1972; Nader 1969) and has recently become a rich area of investigation for linguistic anthropologists, given that evidence is so often produced by means of narrative accounts and reported speech (Hill and Irvine 1993).

What this example shows is that, although the structures analyzed by Besnier and other linguistic anthropologists are based upon and benefit from conversation analysts' work, the goals of their research and the kinds of questions they ask about such structures are different. Such questions can only be asked when researchers have access to the wealth of information provided by ethnographic methods. One cannot speculate about what is known by the participants or the consequences of what is said without having lived in a community and having gained an understanding of local norms for sharing information and making claims about what is important and valuable.

The fact that conversation analysts (or other discourse analysts) often work in their own community or on linguistic material in their native language is often given as a justification for the lack of ethnographic methods. Prolonged participant-observation is cast as a need only for those who want to analyze an "exotic"or different culture. But it is a myth that one needs ethnography only to study other cultures or people who speak a different language. The entire history of anthropology is based on the idea that there is important value, however limited, in becoming "professional strangers" (Agar 1980), that is, in placing ourselves in a world that we do not take for granted and try to understand from someone else's point of view, engaging in the task of bracketing our prejudice and any previous knowledge. The fact that such a task is difficult and perhaps never fully realizable is not a reason to avoid it altogether. Although conversation analysts would agree on the need to suspend our judgment and our preconceived ideas about how speakers behave and why they do what they do, some of them also implicitly support the view that less work needs to be done when the subjects of our investigations are our neighbors or people who speak our dialect. However, an argument could be made that it is precisely in the study of our own culture that we, as members, are more likely to take things for granted and thus assume what should not be assumed. Finally, to the extent to which we recognize the need of ethnography in *some* cases,[17] we cannot in principle rule it out in *any* case, given that we cannot know in advance *when* we will need the information that would be made available only through ethnographic research.

---

[17] Thus, in writing about Cicourel's (1992) plea for the need of ethnography in making sense of how certain terms are used in a medical context, Schegloff admits that "[e]thnographic research may, of course, have been necessary to enable the analyst to recognize the sense and import of such terms as display the relevance of some aspect of context, or to recognize that seemingly ordinary words have such an import" (Schegloff 1992b: 223).

8.3.2   The issue of relevance

A different strategy used by conversation analysts for dealing with the accusation of "noncontextuality" has been to directly address the issue of what context
is. This has been done, for instance, by Schegloff in his discussion of what he calls
"the problem of relevance"(Schegloff 1991: 49–52).

One of Schegloff's recurrent replies to those who criticize him and his colleagues for not taking "context" (or "enough context") into consideration has
been to reframe the issue from "who's got *more* context?" to "how do we decide
which context matters?" To say whether or not an analysis has taken into consideration "enough" (or "the proper") context would then mean for Schegloff to
say whether or not the *relevant context* and not *any* kind of contextual information potentially available to an observer has been taken into consideration
(Schegloff 1992b: 195). Since each individual is characterizable in many different
ways, how do we know which way counts in *this* case?

> Once we recognize that whoever can be characterized as "male" or
> as "protestant," or as "president" or whatever, can be characterized
> or categorized in other ways as well, our scholarly/professional/
> scientific account cannot "naively" rely on such characterization,
> that is, cannot rely on them with no justification or warrant of their
> relevance. (Schegloff 1991: 50)

The same argument can be extended to features of the environment and definitions of the situation. For example, how can we say ahead of time which contextual conditions are relevant to what I will talk about while having dinner
tonight? Will it be relevant that I have been spending several hours by myself
writing at a portable computer, that I have not been wearing shoes, and that I
have been hearing people speaking Spanish downstairs?

Since, in most cases, we cannot say *a priori* which aspects of context are going
to be relevant, conversation analysts like Schegloff have been arguing that the
only empirically appropriate way to evoke context is to attend to what the participants themselves make relevant, through their linguistic actions, the idea being
that **"the search for context properly begins with the talk or other conduct being
analyzed"** (Schegloff 1992b: 197, emphasis in the original). Thus, we cannot *a
priori* decide whether a person's social identity as a "cousin" or "doctor" or
"friend" counts, simply on the basis of the information that is available to us
about such a person and his interlocutor. It is indeed possible that even in her
own office a doctor might relate to a patient as a "doctor" at one point and as a
"friend" at another. For this reason, any kind of analysis of interactional material should make reference to a sound justification of the reason for choosing

a particular type of characterization or description of the situation over other possible ones.

There is, however, a potential weakness not in the problem of relevance itself but in the methods whereby relevance is established. In particular, if relevance means that out of a number of possible contexts or features of context, some are chosen (mentioned, discussed) while others are left out (because assumed known or claimed irrelevant), the issue remains of the *access* to or *discovery* of relevant contextual features. We need ways, in other words, of retrieving contextual information that may not be available in the talk itself. For instance, in order to think about whether a participant is being (or "doing") "doctor" we need to know that she is indeed a doctor or that the conversation is taking place in a medical facility. Although we can expect doctors to speak in a way that would easily identify them as medical experts, there are situations where we might need to be more specific and know whether someone is an expert on infectious diseases or the head of a laboratory (Cicourel 1992). The participants may or may not refer to each other's specific medical qualifications. For this reason, to render a contextual analysis possible we need to use ethnographic methods that could give us the richest documentation of the on-going situation and its temporal and spatial surroundings (see chapter 4).

Some conversation analysts have argued that we cannot in principle rule out an analysis of something simply because some aspect of the context has not been mentioned or properly recorded. However, unless we have ways of enlarging the context of a particular verbal exchange, it is difficult to know what else is relevant. Thus, although one should not ignore an analysis of something said in a face-to-face interaction simply because there is not enough information available on eye gaze or on where the participants were located with respect to one another, we will never be able to know whether such features were relevant unless we do have the opportunity to have access to participants' eye gaze and positions. The issue, as always, is one of scope. Just like an audio recording of a spontaneous interaction allows us to see regularities that we could not have imagined before (see section 8.1), visual recordings also widen the range of phenomena that can be examined. Goodwin (1981), for instance, showed that at least some self-repairs can be connected to the attempt to secure a recipient. Example (26) above, for instance, is analyzed by Goodwin as part of an interaction in which the speaker loses the gaze of his recipient in midutterance. "When it has been regained, the speaker repeats the noun phrase that was spoken while his recipient was disattending him, this time adding a new adjective to it" (Goodwin 1981: 130). Example (26) is here repeated as (32), with the additional information about eye gaze (a straight line indicates that the party so marked is gazing toward the other, a comma marks withdrawing of gaze, a period marks the movement that brings gaze to another, and a capital X shows the exact place where gaze reaches the other participant):

(32)   Ralph: Somebody said looking at my:, son my oldest son,
       Chil: _____ ,   . X_____

(Goodwin 1981: 130)

Thanks to the visual record, Goodwin established that repair phenomena are (at least in some cases) related to the construction of precise eye gaze coordination between participants. This does not discredit earlier analyses of repair (e.g. Schegloff, Jefferson, and Sacks 1977), but it adds a new and, in some respects, richer analytical dimension. Similarly, recordings of the same speakers over an extended period of time – what psychologists call **longitudinal studies** – provide an opportunity to ask questions about individual variation that would not be otherwise possible. Susan Philips (1992), for instance, has argued that the lack of longitudinal methods in conversation analysis does not allow researchers to find out the extent to which certain linguistic phenomena are truly spontaneous or the result of personal style (or even planned strategy). In examining the speech of judges to defendants in four Arizona state courts, for instance, Philips found that some judges corrected themselves at the same point and in the same manner in talking to different defendants. Here are examples of the same judge introducing a *uh* always after the complementizer *that* on four different occasions:

(33)   You have the right to have the Court tell the jury – instruct the jury
       that, uh, you are to be presumed innocent.
(34)   And the Court would instruct the jury **that, uh**, you are to be
       presumed innocent. ...
(35)   I'll order **that, uh**, a pre-sentence investigation and report be made
       by the Adult Probation Officer in this Court.
(36)   Alright. It's ordered **that, uh** a pre-sentence investigation and
       report be made by the Adult Probation Office of the Court.

(Philips 1992: 316)

The question in this case as in others that could be presented is whether the different ways of defining the boundaries of the relevant context forces earlier analyses to be revised or be simply augmented or enriched (Schegloff 1992b is dedicated to this question). This I believe to be an important question because it sets the agenda for any kind of collaboration between conversation-analytical methods and ethnographically oriented research of the type usually carried out by linguistic anthropologists (see chapter 4).

In (24) above, for instance, I gave an example of the beginning of a telephone conversation in Italian that I will now recontextualize. The exchange is here repeated as (37):

(37)   G: *pronto,*
           hello,
       S: *Giorgio?*
           Giorgio?
→   G: *ah ciao.*
           oh hi.
       S: *ciao.*
           hi.
       [...]   ("Giorgio 3")

In the third turn, Giorgio produces what I earlier characterized as the first pair part of the opening greeting (*ciao*). He does so, however, by prefacing the *ciao* with an *ah* which I had left unanalyzed. There is evidence in my data that this Italian *ah* is similar to the *oh* sometimes found in the same position (third turn) in American telephone conversations:

(38)   C: Hello.
       M: Hello, Charlie?
→   C: Oh, hi.   (Schegloff 1979a: 52)

Schegloff (1979) informally characterized this English *oh* as a marker of "success just now" at recognizing the caller. That the *oh* is indeed such a marker is shown by the fact that it sometimes appears after the answerer had tried to "fake" recognition by returning a greeting without using the name of the caller:

(39)   A: Hello
       B; Hi:
       A: Hi: (0.3) Oh *H*i Robin (Schegloff 1979a: 43)

Similar examples are found in my Italian data, as shown in (40), where the *ah* appears after a significant one-second pause and is followed by a series of "upgrades" whereby the answerer seems to make up for the delayed recognition of the caller:

(40)   MLuisa: *pronto,*
                hello,
       Franco: *pronto Marialuisa?*
                hello Marialuisa?
                (1.0)
       MLuisa: *ah Franco ciao bello come va?*
                oh Franco hi handsome how is it going? ("MLuisa")

When we enlarge the context of (37) above, however, the *ah* gets tinted with a new meaning. Because of the way the data were collected (all from the same telephone over a number of days), we have access to a previous call by Giorgio to Sandro's house, when Sandro was not at home and Giorgio had asked Sandro's father to tell Sandro to call him back. Therefore, Sandro's call to Giorgio in (37) is not just *any* call or any call by Sandro to Giorgio, but a "returned call." In the context provided by this new piece of information, the *ah* does not just sound as a "oh, I see now who you are" but "oh, I see that you did call me back." Does this change the preliminary analysis of *ah* in Italian? Does it give us possible hints about reexamining the *oh*'s in Schegloff's data? The answers to these questions are best answered empirically, that is, on the basis of actual investigations over diverse materials. It is likely that in some cases, as argued by Schegloff (1992b), the widening of the context of the interaction – e.g. adding prior or subsequent talk, visual documentation, background information about participants – may not challenge the validity of an earlier analysis. It is also possible, however, that in some other cases, additional information on the situation and its participants may affect our analysis. For these reasons, the issue of relevance is one that must be dealt with empirically and not on *a priori* principles. Such an empirical testing, however, is not as easy as it seems due to fundamental differences in methods and theories between most conversation analysts and linguistic anthropologists.

8.4 The meaning of talk

One of the problems with the empirical validation of conversation analysts' findings and claims and the extension of their work to a wider range of speech communities has been the relatively small number of studies of conversational interaction carried out by linguistic anthropologists outside the US (or the UK). This is partly due to the fact that many linguistic anthropologists tend to concentrate on ritual and political speech and they rarely record casual conversational exchanges.[18] This has made it difficult to have comparable data for crosscultural analysis. Unfortunately, some of the earlier refutations of the universality of the English turn-taking system were not based on actual recordings (Godard 1977; Reisman 1974).

But there are other factors that make the utilization of conversation-analytical findings and methods somewhat problematic for some linguistic and cultural

---

[18] This criticism was made by Bloch (1976) and was reiterated by Moerman (1988: 11). Things have changed considerably in the last decade, as students of conversations and other genres have started to interact more within linguistic anthropology. However, many social and cultural anthropologists continue to record only ritual or political speech and miss the opportunity to carefully examine how language is used in the most common everyday interactions.

anthropologists. Conversation analysts look at conversation as a series of structures which include recurring patterns of certain types of "acts" or "moves." What drives most conversation analysts is an interest in the logic (or "syntax") of such moves and the extent to which they display systemic orientations or preferences, e.g. to agree, to avoid simultaneous talk, to allow speakers to correct themselves. The analysis usually begins with conversational data and ends with some generalizations about how conversation is organized. Conversation constitutes both a means and an end of analysis.

Many anthropologists, on the other hand, are interested in conversation as a means to understand other types of structures. For example, they are interested in how what is being said in one particular context by a group of people relates to what the same people say in another setting. This means that it is important to record interaction of the same individuals in different situations. This implies not only a longitudinal study, but also an extended commitment to a group of people (a family, an organization, a political unit) as a community of speakers who share verbal as well as economic resources. Their movements, meetings, life choices become important for the researcher who wants to continue to keep track of where they are and what they are up to. Rather than conversational sequences per se, it is social actors that matter. This partly explains why ritual exchanges and the language that accompanies them are more important to linguistic anthropologists than to conversation analysts. Rituals mark important moments in the life of a community. They also require units of analysis, like activity or event, which are different from conversational sequences (see chapter 9).

Linguistic and cultural anthropologists use linguistic units and methods to unveil the role played by linguistic resources in constituting an interpretive frame like the establishment of an institutional context or the expression of a given ideology of self and other. Ultimately, linguistic anthropologists believe that if we want to understand what people mean with, through, and sometimes despite their words, one must look beyond linguistic means. The mechanisms of talk do not by themselves carry the burden of intentionality, accountability, and truth. Utterances, words, morphemes, prosodic and paralinguistic means are powerful tools to carry on an idea, to point to a certain connection. Language may very well be the House of Being (Heidegger 1971, 1977) but it is not Being itself. From looking at how language is used in people's lives, we learn that meaning lives through the connections that talk helps create within as well as beyond itself, across contexts. This means that anthropologists who study marriage ceremonies consider the role played by speech in such contexts, but within the overall structure of the event, where objects and not only words are exchanged (Keane 1994). Researchers working on the use of deictic particles study conversational interactions to understand how a particular morphological system that indexes the speaker's spatial orientation and visual access to the immediate surrounding context can also be seen as presupposing a particular conceptualization of the wider living space of the community (Hanks 1990). Ethnomusicologists who study myths or musical performance try to connect the stories told in the narratives and songs they record to what a given group of people care about, emphasize, or see as part of their place and destiny (Basso 1985; Feld 1982). Those who study chanted ceremonial exchanges try to establish correlations between the social organization of such exchanges and the local ideology of social relations with the outside (Urban 1988).

In her study of Xavante men's councils, Graham (1993, 1995) saw the Xavante tendency to routinely overlap one another's speech by repeating or paraphrasing what the current "principal speaker" is saying as a practice that obscures individuality and constructs a collectively produced discourse – in which speakers echo each other's talk and sometimes incorporate or reformulate what has just been said by others. Graham hypothesizes that this type of polyphonic discourse represents and indexes a more egalitarian type of ideology than the monologic discourse characteristic of those genres controlled by one particular speaker.

The comparison of these studies with studies carried out by conversation analysts suggests that the questions asked by linguistic anthropologists and conversation analysts may differ because the notion of meaning implied in the two traditions is not the same.[19] In anthropology, meanings are seen as located not only in language, but in social values, beliefs, social relationships, and larger exchange and support systems, including family structure and the social organization of the community. Most ethnographers believe that such meanings certainly need and make use of language – to be articulated, tested, negotiated, recreated –, but they do not just reside in talk. It is the issue of the supremacy and autonomy of talk itself in social and cultural analysis that is at the core of the issues discussed in this chapter. Those fieldworkers who emphasize the power of words and the interactional structures supported by talk tend to take conversation analysis more seriously than those who emphasize the role of social institutions and see them as overpowering and controlling the meaning of talk. Only by raising our standards for theoretical clarity and empirical validity can we hope to resolve such issues.

8.5 Conclusions

In this chapter I have shown that conversation analysis provides us with useful units of analysis and concepts that make conversational exchanges into microcosms of

---

[19] This dichotomy between linguistic anthropologists and conversation analysts is overcome by many researchers who try to combine the two approaches.

the social order and enlighten the culture that makes such an order not only possible but meaningful. By studying in great details the sequential nature of conversational interaction, conversation analysts have significantly improved our ability to think about speech as the product of an interaction, thereby expanding the context of individual speech acts studied by Austin and Searle and coming closer to the type of language games discussed by Wittgenstein. I have also argued that the notion of preference can be a powerful tool for the study of the constraints under which human actors must communicate and make sense of their own as well as of others' action, a classic concern of linguistic anthropology at least since the formulation of the Sapir-Whorf hypothesis (see section 3.2). If, as suggested by Wittgenstein and others, individual motives and intentions must be understood in the context created by public institutions, the study of turn-taking systems and the expectations generated by continuous participation in them is an excellent example of how to relate individual behavior to larger institutional structures.

I have also examined some of the criticism of conversation analysts by anthropologists and other social scientists and concluded that whereas the hypotheses made by conversation analysts cannot be dismissed *a priori* on the basis of their methods of collecting data and defining context, ethnographic and longitudinal methods allow us to enter new areas of inquiry and in some cases question earlier analyses based on data collected without using ethnographic methods.

More generally, an interest in conversational interactions cannot be, from an anthropological perspective, exclusively an interest in the forms or mechanisms through which such interactions are made possible. Just as it is important for anyone working on everyday speech to recognize the type of recurrent patterns and preferences unveiled by conversation analysts, it is equally important for anyone working on conversation to realize that such mundane exchanges acquire their meaning from inside as well as from the outside of the exchanges themselves. The fact that such an analysis is difficult is not a reason to avoid it altogether. Successful conversation is not made possible only by turn-taking mechanisms just like proper pronunciation of certain sounds is not just made possible by the shape and position of the larynx in humans (as opposed to other species). An ontology of conversation – a detailed study of what makes conversation what it is – must rely on an understanding of the implications and consequences of a system of communication with a number of interesting and yet still largely unexplained features such as the overall reluctance to correct others and the difficulty of excluding the participation of specific individuals without resorting to a violation of the very system that makes conversation possible. Are these preferences and features due to universals of human politeness or are they necessary features for the survival of the species? Or both? Is the nature of conversational interaction inherently democratic and pluralistic? Why? The reluctance to face these questions by conversation analysts is partly a by-product of the formal nature of their work. It resembles Chomsky's reluctance to face either a psychological or a sociological level of explanation for the linguistic phenomena he studies. It makes conversation analysis suggestive of a wide range of issues and yet impermeable to the criticism that the formulation of those other issues might evoke. Such wisdom, however, comes with a price. As new generations of students are exposed to the subtleties of conversational practices revealed by conversation analysts, they will have to choose whether to stay within the boundaries of the discipline as defined by its founders or adventure into the dangerous waters of cultural analysis where formalism must often be left behind in order to grasp the uniqueness of the human experience.

In the next chapter we will venture into units of analysis that further expand our analytical horizon to include not only more complex exchanges but also situations where talk merges with other communicative resources.

9

Units of participation

A common thread across the human sciences in the nineteenth and twentieth century has been the conceptualization of human behavior as a series of interacting and yet autonomous systems, each of which can be further divided into smaller and smaller components. As we saw in chapters 5 and 6, in linguistics this trend has meant the decomposition of human discourse into sentences, phrases, words, morphemes, phonemes, and distinctive features. This work has given us a more sophisticated understanding of the complexity of human speech, its different layers, and some of the ways in which the different layers feed into each other, but it has not answered the question of how speakers manage to connect the smaller units of language to the larger entities such units participate in. The approaches discussed in the last two chapters are attempts to come to grips with this problem by connecting linguistic forms with either individual acts or sequences of acts. In this chapter, I will expand the discussion presented in those chapters by exploring other units of analysis. The running theme this time will be "participation."

Participation – to be discussed here as both a dimension of human interaction and a perspective of analysis – is a concept that draws from a variety of schools within linguistics, anthropology, sociology, and psychology. Sociolinguists have tended to focus on participation as an issue between the individual and larger reference groups or aggregates such as networks (Milroy 1980; Milroy and Milroy 1985) and speech communities (Hudson 1980; Labov 1966; Romaine 1982; Walters 1988). Linguistic anthropologists, on the other hand, have tended to study language as used in face-to-face interactions such as ceremonial exchanges, oratorical performances, narrative activities, jokes, and arguments. This difference in the object of inquiry is partly due to the different field conditions in which sociolinguists and linguistic anthropologists participate, with the former usually working in large urban communities and the latter in smaller, typically rural communities. Although the concept of participation discussed in this chapter is an outcome of the latter type of research, its extension to other field conditions and research endeavors is a challenge that new generations of linguistic anthropologists working in urban settings should feel encouraged to take on.

As I have done in prior chapters, here I will briefly review the intellectual roots of the concepts introduced. I will also give some examples of the kinds of analyses that are possible within the framework established by the notion of "participation." I will argue that to think in terms of units of participation helps us reconnect those aspects of language discussed in previous chapters with other, often forgotten, dimensions of the human experience, including the role played by the speakers' bodies, the material resources that surround and are used by speakers, and the social institutions constituted by linguistic practices. To think about speakers as participants means then to move beyond speech and even beyond speech as action to include the fuller experience of what it means to be a member of a speech community. At the same time, participation is a dimension of speaking that has grammatical roots as well, as shown by the work on deixis and metalinguistic or metapragmatic frames. This chapter brings together these different dimensions of participation, which have so far been studied within separate research traditions. I will start with the notion of "activity" as used in Vygotskian psychology (section 9.1), and the notion of speech event (section 9.2), first in Jakobson's and then in Hymes's formulation. I will then discuss three related but different units of analysis that claim to take participation as the starting point for the study of face-to-face interaction (section 9.3). The deconstruction of the notions of "speaker" and "hearer" done by Goffman and other authors will allow us to enter the discussion of authorship, intentionality, and the joint construction of interpretation (section 9.4). I will then conclude the chapter by extending the context of analysis to the built environment and the use of the human body and vision in interaction (section 9.5). A study of face-to-face greetings will provide an example of the kind of integrated analysis that is possible by combining the focus on participation with the use of audio-visual documentation proposed in chapters 4 and 5.

9.1 The notion of activity in Vygotskian psychology

Wittgenstein's notion of language games (chapter 7) takes the notion of activity as central for the study of meaning. This is a major shift in the study of language as action because while it attempts to integrate language with action it also provides a way of thinking about larger frames within which language operates. Rather than starting from utterances, as speech act theorists do, Wittgenstein suggested starting from what people were actually doing together – remember the example of the use of nouns like *block, pillar, slab, beam* between a builder and his assistant at the beginning of *Philosophical Investigations* (see section 7.4).

Wittgenstein was not alone in thinking in terms of activities. A similar approach was developed within Soviet psychology roughly around the same time.[1] It began with Lev Vygotsky's theory of cognitive development as crucially implying **mediated activity** between a novice (e.g. a child) and an expert (an adult) (see section 2.1.4). After Vygotsky's death, his ideas were elaborated by some of his disciples, A. N. Leontyev in particular, into what became known as **activity theory**. As discussed by Wertsch (1981), one of the basic issues that activity theory tries to address is the relationship between consciousness and the material world. For Soviet psychologists like Vygotsky, Leontyev, and Rubinshtein this question arises out of a theoretical position that was influenced by Marx and Engels's discussion of ideology and Marx's criticism of previous materialistic theories (see articles in Wertsch 1985a). In his *Theses on Feuerbach*, Marx emphasizes the importance of maintaining a relationship between consciousness and humans' sensual, practical activity in the world:

> The chief defect of all hitherto existing materialism ... is that the thing, reality, sensuousness, is conceived only in the form of the object of *contemplation*, but not as *human sensuous activity, practice*, not subjectively. Hence it happened that the *active* side, in contradistinction to materialism, was developed by idealism – but only abstractly, since, of course, idealism does not know real, sensuous activity as such.
>
> (Marx [1845] 1978: 143) (Emphasis in the original)

This position was transformed by Vygotsky and his colleagues into the question of how to develop a theory of the human mind that would take seriously the fact that thinking subjects do not just think, but they also move, build, touch, feel, and, above all, interact with other beings and material objects through both physical and semiotic activity. This perspective, which is often absent in North American cognitive psychology,[2] is close to (and in some cases supported by) recent anthropological theories that treat culture as practices rather than simply patterns of thought (see chapter 2). In both cases, the issue is how to reconcile what appear to be individually controlled cognitive processes with interactionally achieved public performances where individuals are involved in producing a

---

[1] Although there seems to be no evidence of a direct link between Wittgenstein and the Soviet psychologists I am about to discuss, some indirect or mediated links exist. For one thing, Vygotsky read Bühler, who was in Austria at roughly the same time while Wittgenstein was meditating his "turn" (see chapter 7). Other connections are also possible. It would be safe to say that the idea of "activity" as a unit of analysis of mental and linguistic faculties was "around" in European intellectual and academic circles in the 1920s and 1930s.

[2] But see Newman, Griffin, and Cole (1989), Rogoff (1990), Rogoff and Lave (1984), Wertsch (1985a, 1985b).

joint activity that seems more than the mere sum of its parts. Vygotsky's solution to this problem was to reverse the usual relationship between the individual and society. Rather than starting from the individual and thinking of joint activity as the sum of individual cognitive processes and actions, Vygotsky proposed a theory of development in which individual (or *intra*psychological) faculties arise out of interactional (or *inter*psychological) processes. An example he gives is the development of **pointing**, which starts with the child's unsuccessful attempt to reach for an object (see also Cassirer 1955: 181). The movement of the child's arm becomes a communicative act (a sign) when the mother interprets it as a manifestation of the child's attempt to do something.

> Consequently, the primary meaning of that unsuccessful grasping movement is established by others. Only later, when the child can link his unsuccessful grasping movement to the objective situation as a whole, does he begin to understand this movement as pointing. At this juncture there occurs a change in that movement's function: from an object-oriented movement it becomes a movement aimed at another person, a means of establishing relations. *The grasping movement changes to the act of pointing.* As a result of this change, the movement itself is then physically simplified, and what results is the form of pointing that we may call a true gesture.
>
> (Vygotsky 1978: 56) (Emphasis in original)

Starting from this perspective, Leontyev extended Vygotsky's work mainly in two ways. First, by taking an evolutionary perspective, Leontyev ([1959] 1981) proposes to think of consciousness as a human faculty that arose from human labor. Humans learned to coordinate their actions around a common goal that superseded and in some cases went against their individual needs. For example, in an organized hunt, the beater, instead of satisfying the immediate need to feed himself, must chase the prey away. This is a truly intellectual move.[3] Leontyev believes that it is in the context of such complex activities that humans developed consciousness. Second, Leontyev expanded Vygotsky's intuition about the importance of social interaction for cognitive development into a theory that took activity as the basic unit of analysis. Activity for Leontyev is a "unit of life for the material, corporeal subject" ([1975] 1979: 46). The function of activity is "to orient the subject in the world of objects" (ibid.).

This perspective includes dimensions of interaction that are crucial for the

---

[3] It should be pointed, however, that this move alone could not be the determining factor in the development of consciousness given that there are other animals who hunt in a group (e.g. wolves) and are thus capable of subordinating their individual goals to those of the group.

connection of cognitive processes and linguistic structures with the material world around them (see below).

9.2 Speech events: from functions of speech to social units

Grammarians' first serious step toward studying speech as embedded in social units was the introduction of a model in which both speaker and hearer play a crucial role. At the Conference on Style organized at Indiana University in 1958, the Russian linguist Roman Jakobson, by expanding earlier work by the Austrian psychologist Karl Bühler,[4] proposed a **speech event model** composed of six "constitutive factors," each of which "determines a different function of language" (Jakobson 1960: 353). Figure 9.1 reproduces the six factors and figure 9.2 the six functions, as schematically represented by Jakobson.

CONTEXT

MESSAGE

ADDRESSER .... ADDRESSEE

CONTACT

CODE

Figure 9.1 Jakobson's six constitutive factors of a speech event

REFERENTIAL

POETIC

EMOTIVE   PHATIC   CONATIVE

METALINGUAL

Figure 9.2 Jakobson's six functions of language

As shown by the fact that Jakobson's examples consist of single utterances, in this model, "speech event" must be interpreted as equivalent to Austin's and Searle's notion of speech act. The idea of looking at utterances as "events" allows us to examine how the different factors play a role in the shaping of the message and in its interpretation.

---

[4] Karl Bühler was an Austrian psychologist who became very interested in language and wrote a major treatise, *Sprachtheorie*, published in 1934, which was very influential in European linguistic circles, including the Prague School of Linguistics, of which Jakobson was a member. Bühler's model of language (an earlier version of which can be found in a 1918 article of his) included three factors: (a) representation (*Darstellung*), (b) expression (*Ausdruck*), and (c) appeal (*Appel*) (Bühler [1934]1990). To each of these three factors corresponds a function. Jakobson's functions referential, emotive, and conative are based on Bühler's model (Jakobson 1960: 355). For an insightful review of Bühler's intellectual and social life, see Eschbach (1990).

For Jakobson, to concentrate on one aspect of the speech event means to privilege the corresponding function of language. Thus, a verbal message in which context is primary for Jakobson means a message in which the speaker privileges the **referential** function of language.[5] A message predominantly aimed at describing a situation, object, or mental state is an example of this function of language. This function includes descriptive statements with definite descriptions (e.g. *the snow is white, kids like to believe in Santa Claus*) as well as utterances with deictic terms such as *I, you, here, there, now* (e.g. *Alice lives here, I was sleeping*). This model recast the referential (which also includes what we earlier defined as "denotative") function as the predominant one in most messages but not in all: "... even though ... an orientation toward the CONTEXT ... is the leading task of numerous messages, the accessory participation of the other functions in such messages must be taken into account by the observant linguist" (Jakobson 1960: 353). The model also allows for the relevance of more than one factor and hence for more than one function at the same time in the same speech event.

A focus on the addresser brings instead into prominence the **emotive** (also called "expressive" and, more recently "affective") function. The classic example here is interjections (English *oh, ah, ugh, phew*)[6] and certain modifications of linguistic sounds that do not change the denotative meaning of an expression but add information about a particular attitude or stance that the speaker is taking (see Gumperz 1992; Ochs 1996).

Orientation toward the addressee means an exploitation of the **conative** function, the classic example being the vocative, which in some languages is marked morphologically (like in the Latin *Brute!* "oh Brutus!" where the final vowel *e* tells us that this is not said *about* Brutus but *to* Brutus) and in others by intonation alone (English calling intonation in *John! come here!*). The difference between the referential function on the one side and the conative and emotive on the other is that only when the first is used can one assess the truth value of what is being said. In the other two cases, such a judgment is not appropriate. Thus, as pointed out by Jakobson, we cannot challenge someone who says *drink!* (conative function expressed in the imperative form) by saying "is it true or not?" (see also Austin's position on the same point in section 7.2). To these three

---

[5] "Context" here is used in the limited sense of a world outside of language and does not have the implications associated with the concept of context in contemporary discussions (see Goodwin and Duranti 1992).

[6] Interjections form an interesting and much understudied area of spoken language. Among other features, they allow for the adoption of sounds that are not otherwise part of the linguistic systems. An example is the voiceless velar fricative or "achlaut" /x/ of the English *ugh* pronounced [ʌx] or [əx] (Quirk, Greenbaum, Leech, and Svartvik 1985: 74) and the glottal stop found in the negation *uh-uh* pronounced [ʔəʔə] (see Ferguson 1982).

functions, which he took from Bühler, Jakobson added three more functions: poetic, phatic, and metalingual.

The study of the sequential aspects of talk (see chapter 8) has taught us that both the emotive and conative functions are usually at play, although they might be more or less dominant. For instance, even when people express imprecations after an adverse happening (e.g. stumbling, slipping, missing a bus, dropping an icecream on the floor) and produce expletives such as the English *fuck!*, the French *merde!,* the Italian *cazzo!*, or the Samoan *oka!*, a certain level of recipient design is at work. This is made evident by speakers' ability to monitor the quality and manner of articulations of such imprecations, which can range from whispers to loud cries (Goffman 1981: 97-8).

The **poetic** function is at work when there is a focus "on the message for its own sake" (Jakobson 1960: 356). This function, which is part of but not identical with the language of poetry, is what allows for verbal play, phonosymbolism (see section 6.8.1), and any other linguistic device that manipulates or concentrates on the shape or sound of the message. The poetic function may let the form of the message control the content. For example, when song writers or poets look for a word that rhymes with a word in a preceding line, they are favoring the poetic function over the referential function. In fact, in some cases, if they find a word or phrase that "sounds good," they might even rephrase something written earlier to fit the acoustic frame established by the new expression. The poetic function is not prominent only in poems, but also in genres such as political slogans and commercials.

The predominance of contact over other factors gives us what Jakobson, following Malinowski's (1923) notion of "phatic communion," calls the **phatic** function, which characterizes what is said just (or mainly) for establishing, prolonging, or discontinuing communication, like when speakers check whether the channel works, as in *Hello, can you hear me?* For Jakobson, greetings are seen as serving the phatic function, given that they often do not have a "content" (they are not "about something") or when they do, their content does not to seem their main purpose. The same is true of expressions about the weather said in elevators and other closed spaces where spatial proximity makes people feel (in many societies) that they should say "something."

The **metalingual** (now usually called **metalinguistic** or **reflexive**) function is the use of language to talk about language (Lucy 1993). The term is taken from logic where a distinction is made between the "object language" (for instance mathematical symbols) and the "metalanguage," that is, the language we use to talk about the object language (e.g. English) (Tarski 1956). Jakobson extended the metalingual function to all cases in which we talk about talk, including the discussion of the meaning of words in our own language (*when people say "I hate* *you" it means they don't know how to relate to you*) and the explanation of a word in a foreign language (*"hon" means "book" in Japanese*) (see section 6.7 on metalinguistic awareness). In writing, we typically use quotes to separate the expression in the object language from what said in the metalanguage. In speaking, often the cues to quoted speech are in the form of subtle changes in voice quality and prosody or other suprasegmental features such as volume and tempo (Cruttenden 1986; Crystal and Davy 1969). In some cases, these and other linguistic features are used to signal that what is being said is a quotation not necessarily from a different speaker but from a different dialect or way of being. This use of the metalinguistic function is what Morgan (1996) calls **reading dialect** in the African American community, a practice whereby members, often in a humorous or ironic way, contrast or highlight ("read") commonly known features of African American English and American English to make a point.

> For example, to stress a point members might say "It's not simply that I am cool. I be cool. In fact, I been cool (a very long time)." In the African American community, not only the two dialects of A[frican] A[merican] E[nglish] and A[merican] E[nglish] are consistently read but also varieties within those dialects are consistently read by interlocutors. (Morgan 1996: 410)

In these cases, then, certain grammatical features like the uninflected verb *be* in a main clause (in *I be cool*) or the absence of the auxiliary *have* (in *I been*) become indexes of the contexts of use of these forms, which become then, in turn, almost like quotations.

Jakobson's model owes a great deal not only, as I mentioned earlier, to Bühler, but also to the linguistic theory of the Prague School of linguistics.[7] The members of the Prague School established an approach to the study of language that paid equal attention to structure and to function. This meant that language was seen as embedded in and at the same time an instrument of human activity:[8]

> Produit de l'activité humaine, la langue partage avec cette activité le caractère de finalité. Lorsqu'on analyse le langage comme expression ou comme communication, l'intention du sujet parlant est l'explication qui se présente le plus aisément et qui est la plus naturelle. (*Thèses présentées au Premier Congrès des philologues slaves*, 1929, in Vachek 1964: 33)

---

[7] On the relationship between Bühler and the members of the Prague School, see Vachek (1966).

[8] The similarity with activity theory is not too accidental given that Vygotsky knew Bühler's work and frequently cited it in his writings.

The emphasis on language as a goal-oriented activity was important because it forced researchers to connect the study of linguistic forms with the study of social functions. This premise, which had inspired Jakobson's model, became even more central in Dell Hymes's call for an *ethnography of communication*. In this case, the influence of anthropological concerns and methods was apparent in the three building blocks of Hymes's (1964b) approach: (i) ethnographic methods, (ii) a study of the communicative events that constitute the social life of a community, (iii) a model of the different components of the events.

> The starting point is the ethnographic analysis of the communicative habits of a community in their totality, determining what count as communicative events, and as their components, and conceiving no communicative behavior as independent of the set framed by some setting or implicit question. The communicative event thus is central. (In terms of language proper, the statement means that the linguistic code is displaced by the speech act as focus of attention.) (Hymes 1964b: 13)

As shown by this quote, the task that Hymes set up for himself and his students (many of whom became major figures in linguistic anthropology) was to connect the specifics of language use to the community within which such uses took place, were interpreted, and reproduced. The link with the community was established through the **communicative event** as a unit of analysis. He wrote: "In one sense, the focus of the present approach is on communities organized as systems of communicative events" (1964b: 18).

Hymes explicitly built on Jakobson's speech event model by refining and expanding Jakobson's six "factors" into a list that grew from seven (Hymes 1964b) to sixteen (Hymes 1972a).[9] To make his long list easier to remember, Hymes regrouped the sixteen components under the letters of the term "S-P-E-A-K-I-N-G": **S**ituation, **P**articipants, **E**nds, **A**ct sequences, **K**ey, **I**nstrumentalities, **N**orms, **G**enre.[10]

These factors were components of speech or components of speech acts

---

[9] Hymes (1972a: 51) recognized a number of other influences, including Kenneth Burke, who, in the 1940s, constructed a theory of *motives* that relied on such concepts as agency, act, purpose, and scene (Burke 1945).

[10] Each of these eight components, with the exception of "key" and "genre" was further divided into two or more components: Situation (1. Setting , 2. Scene); Participants (3. Speaker or sender, 4. Addressor, 5. Hearer, or receiver, or audience, 6. Addressee); Ends (7. Purposes – outcomes, 8. Purposes – goals); Act sequences (9. Message form, 10. Message content); Key (11. Key); Instrumentalities (12. Channel, 13. Forms of speech); Norms (14. Norms of interaction; 15. Norms of interpretation); Genre (16. Genres). See Hymes (1972a, 1974) and Duranti (1985).

(Hymes 1972a: 58). The earlier term "communicative event" (Hymes 1964b) was later abandoned and "**speech event**" was introduced. Speech events were to be understood in the restricted sense of those "activities, or aspects of activities, that are directly governed by rules or norms for the use of speech" (Hymes 1972a: 56). Examples of speech events include a lecture, a phone conversation, a prayer, an interview, the telling of a joke. In such activities speech plays a crucial role in the definition of what is going on – that is, if we eliminate speech, the activity cannot take place. **Speech situations**, on the other hand, are activities in which speech plays a minor or subordinate role. Examples of speech situations are a game of soccer, a walk with a friend, a ride on a bus, a visit to an art gallery. This analytical distinction between speech events and speech situations is intuitively appealing but can be problematic, especially if, as analysts, we expect clearcut distinctions between speech events and speech situations. In the real world what we find are situations or parts of situations in which speech is used in a **constitutive** way, that is, as an instrument for sustaining or defining that particular type of situation. Such a use is what characterizes a conversation, but it can also characterize a game or a walk with a friend. The absence of speech in these cases might be just as important as its presence in those situations that we would define as speech events (see Duranti 1985).

Hymes emphasized the heuristic nature of his S P E A K I N G model, which was to serve as a guide (or etic grid) for fieldwork and crosscultural analysis (ethnographers of speaking were supposed to go to different communities around the world and study language use in terms of the components described by Hymes) (see Sherzer and Darnell 1972). The idea seemed not so much to invite a series of ethnographic descriptions of speech events or speech acts that illustrated each of the sixteen components with examples – these descriptions tend to be particularly dull to read –, but to offer a sense of the factors involved in the study of language as part of social life (hence the title of Hymes's 1972 article "Models of the Interaction of Language and Social Life"). The real innovation in Hymes's expansion of Jakobson's model was thus not so much in the number and types of components, but in the nature of the unit of analysis.

For Jakobson the notion of speech event was a way of unifying his six components and their corresponding functions of language. With the linguistic code as still the central concern of his model, Jakobson offered important suggestions on how to link different forms of participation with grammatical patterns. Jakobson, however, was not interested in the sociocultural organization of speech events or their role within a community. For Hymes, on the other hand, the community is the starting point. Speech events are where communities are formed and held together. With Hymes, the unit of analysis is no longer a linguistic unit as such, but a **social unit** which includes or is based on speech. Hymes is thus less concerned with the functions of speech as defined by Jakobson and more concerned instead with how different aspects of the interaction help define what is said and how it is said. Speech acts and speech events are thus units of participation for Hymes in at least two ways: (i) they are ways for people to belong to a community; (ii) they are ways of constituting a community. Community, in turn, can be understood at different levels. At the micro-interactional level, "community" refers to the small or large group of people organized around a common activity – this set includes a two-party conversation on the phone, a ceremony of initiation involving a few dozen participants, and a political rally with thousands of people. At the macro-interactional level, I understand "community" as meaning a typically larger, real or imaginary (cf. Anderson 1983), reference group, whose constituency exceeds the boundaries of the here-and-now of any given situation and is established on the basis of one or more of a number of criteria, including geo-political, kin, ethnic, professional, and linguistic affiliation.

9.2.1 Ethnographic studies of speech events

Although Hymes's SPEAKING model has been rarely used in its extended version,[11] it has inspired a considerable number of ethnographic studies of linguistic communities from the point of view of speech events. Central to the organization of these studies is the relationship among components of the speech events, especially setting, participants, and genres.

Sherzer (1974, 1983), for instance, discusses much of social life among the Kuna of Panama from the point of view of the speech events taking place inside the "gathering house" (*onmakket neka*), where people chat, argue, plan about the future, and talk about the past. Sherzer shows that the different speech events inside the "gathering house" are largely defined by the genre used and by the type of participation required by the audience. Thus, whether or not a chief will "chant" (*namakke*) or "speak" (*sunmakke*) in part depends on the presence of another chief in the house who can respond (*apinsue*) using "chief language" (*sakla kaya*) (Sherzer 1983: 98). Furthermore, although all chanting is performed in "chief language," participation formats are quite different from one type of event to another. During the *konkreso* "congress," a type of event that occurs every other evening and includes both men and women, after some public discussion of community issues which might include economic matters and recent

---

[11] Given Hymes's insistance on events as units of analysis, several authors, myself included, have in the past interpreted the components of the SPEAKING model as referring to features of events rather than speech acts (Duranti 1985; Saville-Troike 1989). Given the dynamic nature of any speech event, however, it makes more sense to think of those components as constitutive parts of speech acts, in the sense of speech act theory (see chapter 7).

arguments between people, the chant will start in the form of a ritualized dialogue in which each of the chanting chief's verses (*ikar*) is followed by the comment *teki* "indeed, it's true" by the responding chief.

(1) (CC=chanting chief, RC=responding chief)
    CC: *we yalase papal anparmialimarye sokl ittole*
        "God sent us to this mountain say hear."
        eka masmul akkwekarye oparwe.
        "In order to care for banana roots for him utter."
    RC: *teki.*
        "Indeed."
    CC: *ekal inso tarkawamul akkwekaryey sokel ittolete*
        "In order thus to care for taro roots for him say hear."
        sunna ipiti oparwe.
        "In truth utter."
    RC: *teki.*
        "Indeed."
        (...)   (Sherzer 1983: 50)

While the performance is taking place, local "policemen" patrol the house calling out *kapita marye* "don't sleep!" and *nue ittomarye!* "listen well!" Audience involvement is further reinforced by the work of the *arkar* or chief's interpreter, who must "translate" in more ordinary language what the chief has just chanted in the esoteric *sakla kaya*. This type of event is different from other kinds of exchanges with different kinds of audience participation. In the exchange of formal greetings (*arkan kae*, literally "handshake") between a visiting chief and a host chief, for instance, there is no official audience. Some people might come inside the "gathering house," sit down, and listen, but they might also talk to each other or with the entourage of the visiting chief, sometimes rather loudly. No "policeman" walks around ensuring proper attention and participation. When the exchange of greetings is over, there is no official translation. What accounts for the different forms of participation in the two events? In the chants performed during a *konkreso* the main goal of the performance seems to be the teaching of moral values. Thus, the popularity and success of a Kuna chief, according to Sherzer (1983: 90) "reside in his ability to develop moral positions, argue for modes of behavior, and espouse particular points of view through creative, innovative, and often indirect language." This is also the time when novices are exposed to the esoteric language of the chants and have a chance to hear their interpretation by the official translator. The chanting in this case is thus framed and organized as an opportunity for the transmission of knowledge and the reproduction of collective memory (Severi 1989). The formal greetings instead are intended for the chiefs only and are framed as almost accidentally witnessed by the rest of the community. In yet another kind of speech event, the curing ritual, the larger audience is usually excluded. In this case, in addition to the "shaman" (Severi 1989) or, as Sherzer calls him, the "*ikar* knower," the only other participants are the sick person and the "stick dolls" (*suar nuchukana*), which represent "the spirits of good, whose role it is to counter the evil spirits causing the disease" (Sherzer 1983: 111). What the typology of Kuna chants shows is that the higher the level of participation by the audience, the more creative is the performance. In the curing events, the performer is concerned with convincing the spirits of his knowledge of tradition; there is thus less room for individual creativity. In the chants performed at the *konkreso*, instead, the chiefs are trying to impress the audience with their ability to establish particular connections between the past and the present.

> The most striking aspect of "gathering house" chanting as well as speaking is their focus on creative adaptation, on the ability of individuals – "chiefs" and followers, women and men, young and old – to perform verbally for long periods of time, on the spot, with no preparation, taking a theme, an idea, or a metaphor and developing it to make it fit the particular issue at hand. In curing and magical *ikarkana*, on the other hand, the texts appropriate for particular diseases or other purposes are putatively fixed, and the "*ikar* knowers" make changes, really choices, in these fixed texts only according to the origin of the disease or the particular goal of the *ikar*. (Sherzer 1983: 134–5)

It is the ability to move in and out of the same event and from one part of the event to another that has made ethnographers of speaking particularly aware of the dimension of **performance** to be understood as a dimension of linguistic production in which aesthetic canons provide both resources for and constraints on the use of language as a tool for public speaking (see section 1.4.1). Within the same community, speech events are often classified along a continuum, from ritualized or formalized to casual or informal speech (Bloch 1975; Irvine 1979; Keenan 1975; Kuipers 1990). Much of the discussion of speech events has thus tended to concentrate on the linguistic features of the speech genre used. Bloch (1975), for instance, argued that formalized language – a type of speech in which there are special restrictions of both form and content – coerces speakers and hearers into accepting the status quo. The predictability of much of traditional oratory is seen by Bloch as an instrument of power whereby both speakers and hearers are forced to follow a path that has been already decided. Another important dimension of speech genres is the extent to which they make reference to or index the context of the performance as opposed to an apparently timeless voice that is detached from the here-and-now and carries the power of tradition (Bauman 1992a; Bauman and Briggs 1990; Duranti 1994a; Kuipers 1990). This is what Bakhtin (1981a: 13) characterized as the "world of epic":

> The world of epic is the national heroic past: it is a world of
> "beginnings" and "peak times" in the national history, a world of
> fathers and founders of families, a world of "firsts" and "bests," ...
> The epic ... has been from the beginning a poem about the past, and
> the authorial position immanent in the epic and constitutive for it ...
> is the environment of a man speaking about a past that is to him
> inaccessible, the reverent point of view of a descendent.

One of the consequences of speaking with the voice of the past is that what is being said is less vulnerable to the contingencies of the present. When the language that is being used is presented as the words of the ancestors, to challenge the content of someone's speech means to challenge the foundations of the social order. For this reason, Bloch (1975: 26) argues, we often find that in political arenas speakers rely on two different genres or two different styles within the same genre (Comaroff 1975; Duranti 1984; Salmond 1975). One genre is used for speaking about the past and the other for the contingencies of the present. One is dedicated to the celebration of an eternal, immutable structure and the other for the discussion of temporary matters, including the actions of mortals.

In my own work (Duranti 1994), I have argued that, in fact, rather than two separate styles or genres, in Samoan political arenas we are more likely to find a mixing of forms and contents that illustrates what Bakhtin called "heteroglossia," that is, the combination of features that represent "the co-existence of socio-ideological contradictions between the present and the past, between differing epochs of the past, between different socio-ideological groups in the present, between tendencies, schools, circles and so forth" (Bakhtin 1981a: 291). Such a coexistence of socio-ideological contradictions is found in the discussion part of the Samoan *fono* I studied, where I found the following heteroglot features:

    (a)   mixing of different speech registers or codes
    (b)   more pronounced display of affect
    (c)   invocation of personal identities
    (d)   use of quoted direct speech
    (e)   some dialogical, almost conversational exchanges
    (f)   logical argumentation (especially "if-then" propositions)
    (g)   complaints and accusations.

In contrast with the speeches delivered in ceremonial exchanges, in the discussion part of the *fono*, different norms for speaking and for interpreting speech are applied, and genres are blatantly mixed or "corrupted," while participants struggle to define which context is relevant for their talk to make sense and achieve what they expect it to achieve, including the definition of truth (Lindstrom 1992).

The focus on the context-creating aspects of verbal performance is a natural consequence of the interest in studying communities through speech events. To further understand these performative dimensions of speech, we need to examine a number of models that build upon or reframe the notion of "participant" found in Hymes's SPEAKING model.

9.3 Participation

Although participation is an important dimension for Hymes's (1972a) approach to the study of speech communities, it is not the central aspect of his model. We have to look at other authors, some of whom were his students or colleagues at the University of Pennsylvania, to find analytical notions that take participation as the starting point of the study of speaking. In the next three sections, I will discuss three related and yet different units of participation, namely, Philips's **participant structure** (section 9.3.1), Goffman's **participation framework** (section 9.3.2), and M. H. Goodwin's **participant framework** (section 9.3.3).

9.3.1 *Participant structure*

In her work on American Indian children's school performance, Philips (1972, 1983) introduced the notion of participant structure, to be understood as a particular type of encounter or structural arrangement of the interaction.

> Teachers use different participant structures, or ways of arranging verbal interactions with students, for communicating different types of educational material, and for providing variation in the presentation of the same material to hold children's interest.
>
> (Philips 1972: 377)

According to Philips, there are four basic participant structures in a classroom, each of which differs from the others in the number of the students in interaction with the teacher, the non-verbal structuring of attention, and the principles used in regulating student turns at talk (Philips 1983: 78). The first type of participant structure involves the entire class in interaction with the teacher and therefore excludes any other type of interaction. In this case, the teacher either selects a particular student to speak or the entire class. A variant of this model is the structure in which a student takes over some of the teacher's prerogatives and addresses the whole class, e.g. in a "Show and Tell" event or in the presentation of an individual report. Students, however, in this variant continue to address the teacher instead of the whole class, as shown by the fact that teachers must remind students to address the rest of the class. The second type of participant structure is the small group. In this case, "the teacher engages in focused interaction with a portion of the class, usually five to ten students" (1983: 80). The students who are not engaged in interaction with the teacher are instructed to carry on individual work at their desk. The third type of participant structure is the one-to-one involvement between the teacher and a single student. "These encounters usually occur during periods when all of the children are focusing their attention on desk work. A student with questions about such work either raises a hand, or approaches the teacher at the teacher's desk" (1983: 81). The fourth type of participant structure is quite different from the other three. It is "desk work," that is, the situation in which a child is working on some written material at the child's desk and is not interacting with anyone else in the classroom. The advantage of thinking about types of participant structures is that they provide us with a way of evaluating the different consequences of each format. Which type requires more active participation by the students? Which type is more likely to attract the attention of individual students? For instance, Philips found that Indian students tend to ask more questions than their peers in response to the teacher's instructions. They ask both the teacher and one another. These questions are often asked in a type of participant structure where the teacher is pressed for time or wants to maintain the attention of the whole class and may see conversation between students as disruptive. Philips argues that American Indian children are socialized to participate in interactions with adults and with other children in ways that are in sharp contrast to the participant structures organized by non-Indian teachers in the classroom. She hypothesizes that these differences are partly responsible for the poor performance of American Indian children.[12]

In her work, Philips makes reference to and often relies on concepts such as "social encounter" and "ratified participant" introduced by one of her teachers, Erving Goffman. In the next section, I discuss Goffman's own attempt to develop a model of participation.

9.3.2 *Participation frameworks*
The distinction made by Hymes among different types of participants (speaker, sender, addressor on the one side and hearer, receiver, audience, and addressee, on the other) was echoed (and expanded) in Goffman's discussion of **footing**

[12] For the extension and elaboration of this approach to other educational settings, see Tharp and Gallimore (1988), Au (1980), Au and Mason (1981).

(Goffman 1979, 1981).[13] By "footing," Goffman refers to the position or align-ment an individual takes in uttering a given linguistic expression. This includes a particular key (one of Hymes's components) with which to interpret speech or the participant role played by either speaker or hearer (Levinson 1988: 163).

> Now consider footing and its changes. Differently put, consider the multiple senses in which the self of the speaker can appear, that is, the multiple self-implicatory projections discoverable in what is said and done at the podium. (Goffman 1981: 173)

Goffman gives the example of a competent lecturer who alternates between moments in which he takes some distance from his own previously written text and moments in which he allows "his voice to resonate with feeling, conviction, and even passion" (ibid. 175). Footing, in other words, is another way of talking about indexing (see section 6.8.2), the process whereby we link utterances to particular moments, places, or personae, including our own self at a different time or with a different spirit (e.g. emotional vs. distant, convinced vs. skeptical, literal vs. ironic). Footing is a form of metapragmatic discourse (see chapter 6). We let the hearer know how an utterance should be taken, the illocutionary force we mean to give it, the scene in which it should be placed, the character it is being said by, to, or on behalf of. The theme of "life as a stage" is always present in Goffman's work on social interaction, as illustrated by this passage from *Frame Analysis* (Goffman 1974):

> All in all, then, I am suggesting that often what talkers undertake to do is not to provide information to a recipient but to present dramas to an audience. Indeed, it seems that we spend most of our time not engaged in giving information but in giving shows. And observe, this theatricality is not based on mere displays of feelings or faked exhibitions of spontaneity or anything else by way of the huffing and puffing we might derogate by calling theatrical. The parallel between stage and conversation is much, much deeper than that. (Goffman 1974: 508)

In applying the **dramaturgic metaphor** to human interaction or, in our case, to speech, Goffman identifies speakers with actors on the stage. This perspective forces us to think about the fact that just as actors take on different personalities and behave differently when they assume the role of a particular character in a

---

13 In the present context I am assuming that it is not too interesting to find out who thought about the need for a deconstruction of speaker and hearer first. Goffman and Hymes had many occasions to benefit from each other's work while remaining faithful to their own unique visions of communicative practices.

play, speakers in real life continuously enter different roles or *personae* (from the Latin word used for the "masks" worn by actors on the stage) in recounting experience.[14] This model, which was first explicitly enunciated in Marcel Mauss's (1938) classic essay on the notion of "person," should not be interpreted as the recognition of a social illusion. Speakers do not just *pretend* to be different characters, they *become* and are treated *as if* they were those characters; humans exist as social beings precisely as entities that can assume different social personae and represent different points of view. The constitution of our own being, our peculiar and yet similar-to-others' way of acting in the world is accomplished through talk by the subtle ways whereby we assume different types of statuses and stances with respect to our own as well as others' words. Goffman uses the term **participation status** for the particular relation any one person in a situation has with what is being said and **participation framework** for the total configuration of such statuses at any given time (Goffman 1981: 127 and passim).

For instance, it would be quite misleading to assume a model of linguistic interaction in which first person singular pronouns (*I* in English) would be identified with the category "speaker" (or "writer"). Instead, Goffman (1981) argues, the pronoun "I" can refer to (at least) three distinct roles, namely, **animator**, **author**, and **principal**. The animator, sometimes referred to as the "sounding box," is the one who produces or gives a voice to the message that is being conveyed. The author is the one who is responsible for the selection of words and sentiments that are being expressed. The principal (a term Goffman borrows from legal discourse) is the person or institution whose position or beliefs are being represented. The principal is also the one who is held responsible for whatever position is being presented. Although speakers often assume all three roles at the same time, the roles need to be distinguished in more cases than we might think. Everyone knows that the Press Secretary typically acts as the animator of words that may have been authored by someone else (one or more of the White House writers) and that are said on behalf of the President (the principal). But even in more casual encounters involving a few people, speakers move in and out of these different roles when they quote what someone else said, as in (2) below:

(2)   CHOPPER: *L*emme-tell-ya.=**Gu**ess what. (0.8) We
                    was comin' home from **pr**actice, (0.4)
                    and, three boys came up there (.) and
                    asked~us~money~and~Tony~did~like~this.
                    (0.6) *hh ((raising hands up))

---

[14] For a criticism of Goffman's apparent dismissal of morality as a true force in human motivation, see Abu-Lughod (1986: 237).

> **"*I AINT* GOT n(h)(hh)₁o °m(h)oney"**

PETE: Ah-hih-ha,

> (M. H. Goodwin 1990: 245)

Other times speakers switch to an institutional voice whereby they mark what they say not so much as their own personal opinion but as what they happen to think or want as representative of a certain group (an office, a firm, a school, a team, a family, a political group) – these are also contexts in which speakers often switch to the first person plural "we" (a different "we" from the royal one, Goffman reminds us). Analyzing an audio taped three-day conference on health, industry and the environment held near the US-Mexico border, Donna Johnson (1994) discusses different meanings of *we* in the speeches of one speaker and shows how the pronoun is used to set up distinctions that have important political assumptions about community involvement in state and federal policies. At one moment *we* refers to the conference participants, at another moment it is broadened to include the people in the US-Mexico border region, and yet at another moment *we* becomes part of a contrast with a *they* referring to the federal governments of the US and Mexico. In shifting from one meaning of "we" to another, the speaker has a chance to establish opposition, distinctions, differentiations. Participation in shared views, needs, and goals is partly constituted by the use of a pronominal form that suggests identification with the speaker and yet over time establishes a hierarchy among different kinds of "we."

For Goffman, animator, author, and principal constituted what he called the **production format** of an utterance (1981: 226). To this format, there corresponds a set of statuses that distinguish among different kinds of recipients.[15] Given the politics of inclusion and exclusion in pronominal usage and address forms, it is not surprising that Goffman proposed to substitute the term "hearer" with a number of more subtle distinctions. Goffman pointed out that in any given situation there might be all kinds of people who "hear" what is being said, but only a few (sometimes only one) who are entitled and expected to be part of the communicative event (see also Goffman 1964). These he called **ratified participants** and the rest he called **unratified participants**. Among ratified participants, further distinctions are possible, especially when one person in the audience is selected as the primary recipient, the one to whom a speech act is addressed or a story is told. Ratified recipients need to mark their participation in distinctive ways. As mentioned earlier, among the Kuna (Sherzer 1983), for instance, in the

---

[15] Goffman (1981) seems at times to contrast the notions of production format and participation framework, with one referring to the different roles usually subsumed under the label "speaker" and the other referring to the roles usually subsumed under the label "hearer." At other times, however, participation framework seems a more general term that covers both production and reception.

chants by chiefs in the gathering house, there is always a respondent chief who must participate with a set of conventional responses at predictable moments. The rest of the people in the house are also ratified participants but they are expected to be quiet, albeit attentive, listeners. This type of participation framework is similar but not identical to the one found in Samoan *fono* (meeting of the village council), where someone delivering a speech does not have an official respondent but brief responses are provided at predictable moments in the form of conventional appreciation markers such as *mālie*! "well said!" and (more rarely) *mo ʾi* "true" (Duranti 1984a: 231). Such responses, however, only come from those members of the village council sitting in the inner circle of titled individuals. The comparison of the Kuna chanting and the Samoan speechmaking suggests that responding in certain ways or responding at all projects future types of participation. In other words, to respond might be a way of accepting or anticipating future contributions. The respondent is implying "I am listening to you now, you will have to listen to me later." In political contexts this implicit message has of course a range of important connotations.

The identity of the ratified *primary recipient* is important because it often provides a speaker with the point of view from which to tell a story. One of the contributions of conversation analysis (see chapter 8) has been the discussion of the ways in which speakers design their speech according to whom their recipient is. Schegloff (1972b) pointed out that the study of how people define places tells us not only about what speakers know and want but also how they conceptualize the knowledge, wants, or social persona of their recipient. It is in this context that the notion of **recipient design** comes into play. Speakers are said to "design" their speech, among other things, according to who their recipient is. More precisely, *speakers design their speech according to their on-going evaluation of their recipient as a member of a particular group or class*. This is an important observation because it supports the idea that the study of talk is a central aspect of the analysis of society. By looking at how speakers formulate questions or identify people, objects, and places we learn about the participants' own sociological analysis of the situation. To ask someone about "Econ 1" minimally means to identify that person as a member of an English-speaking, probably North American college community. People outside of such a community are not likely to know that "Econ 1" means "the course labeled number 1 in the Economics Department on campus." In Los Angeles, to speak of "the Industry" carries a number of assumptions about the addressee's (and the speaker's) line of work or at least the addressee's knowledge of the *film and television* industry.

Recipient design plays an important role not only in the definition of referents, but also in the content of interaction. Charles Goodwin (1979, 1981) showed that in ordinary conversation *speakers change the content of what they say depending on whom they identify as their primary recipient.* If we use eye gaze as an index of the primary recipient of the speaker's utterance, a visual record of an interaction can give us the exact moment at which a person selects a new recipient. Using this type of analysis Goodwin shows that the illocutionary force or nature of one's communicative act can change within the same utterance as the speaker moves from an unknowing recipient to a knowing one. For instance, what might have been at first framed as "news" must be recast if directed at someone who already knows about it. In the course of the utterance *I gave up smoking cigarettes one week ago today actually*, the speaker changes the nature of what is being communicated three times as his eye gaze moves each time to a new recipient. For instance, what started as an announcement of news (the speaker's successful attempt to stop smoking) to a friend is reframed as the announcement of an anniversary (it has been a week) once the speaker ends up addressing his wife, who already knew about it. Similarly, in another example, the offer of information on how to count points in a game of cards to an **unknowing recipient** is reframed as a request for verification of the instruction from **knowing recipients** (Goodwin 1981: 149–53).[16]

Goffman's (1964) earlier emphasis on the **situation** as the starting point of the sociological analysis of talk is reflected in his concern for types of recipients who might not be the official addressees. What is interesting about unratified participants is that (i) they can *become* ratified, (ii) their presence might still be taken into consideration by speakers. **By-standers** are those unratified participants who have some kind of (aural and/or visual) access to the encounter. As Goffman (1981: 132) warns us, "[t]heir presence should be considered the rule, not the exception." By-standers can be **overhearers** or **eavesdroppers**. Contexts and cultures vary, of course, with respect to what by-standers are expected to do. In some contexts, by-standers might have to act as if they were not present (Goffman 1981: 132), but in others, they might make both their presence and their understanding of the on-going interaction quite obvious and thus force themselves on the exchange. This is the case in the following example quoted by Levinson (1988: 166), where Karen is not directly addressed but her participation is evoked by the content of Mark's talk:

(3) SHARON: You didn' come tuh talk tuh Karen?
     MARK: No, Karen- Karen' I 're having a fight,
             (0.4)
     MARK: after she went out with Keith an' not with (me).

---

[16] "for convenience, a recipient who is proposed to lack relevant information that the speaker possesses will be referred to as an unknowing recipient; a recipient who is supposed to possess information that the speaker lacks will be referred to as a knowing recipient" (Goodwin 1981: 150).

RUTHIE: hah hah hah hah

KAREN: Wul Mark, you never asked me out.

(Sacks et al. 1978: 29)

In some cases, speakers seem to routinely, if not purposely, make unratified participants into overhearers as a way of inviting their participation without assuming the responsibility of having done so. This is the case, for instance, when people who have dropped or lost something speak to their dog or small infants in the presence of other adults, who might then feel entitled to offer their service and help. Other times, speakers might purposely design an utterance to be overheard by someone. This is one of the uses of what in African American communities is called **signifying**, to be understood as "a way of encoding messages or meanings in natural conversations which involves, in most cases, an element of indirection"[17] (Mitchell-Kernan 1972: 165). In distinguishing among different types of signifying, Morgan (1996) introduces the term **pointed indirectness** for the use in which "a speaker ostensibly says something to someone (mock receiver) that is intended for – and to be heard by – someone else and is so recognized." In these cases, like in the practice called "reading dialect" (see section 9.2), it is important to pay attention to the features used to index the intended **target** – the notion of "target" in this case is necessary to distinguish between the apparent recipient of the message ("mock receiver") and the person toward whom a remark is directed. In the following exchange, for instance, after Morgan introduces the topic of "teenage days," Judy's remark about her own look is followed by a series of turns by other participants (Baby Ruth in particular) who assess Judy's self-description as gorgeous without directly addressing Judy. The ambiguity about the extent to which Baby Ruth and Ruby are convincingly questioning Judy's earlier remark is typical of signifying.

(4)   1   "Teenage Days"   (...)

    2   M.Morgan: what was teena- being a teenager like I mean what
                  was::

    3   Judy: O:h I was: gor[geous
                          [

    4   Baby Ruth: [Oh well by that time HO:NEY? her
               hea:d was SO: big
                          [

    5   Ruth: [O:H my GO:D O:H my GO:D
    6   (pause)

---

[17] Another commonly mentioned use of signifying is in verbal dueling where it takes on a life of its own over an extended sequence of turns by two speakers who try to outdo each other (see Kochman 1972, 1981; Labov 1972b: ch. 8).

7	M.Morgan:	This is the Coca Cola pha:se?
8	Baby Ruth:	O::H BABY The whole works
9		(pause)
10		She was the only one
11		(pause)
12		She ran in the Miss black WHAT ((high pitch)) EV?:ER thing they
13		was RUNNING in those da:ys=
14	Ruth:	=Sure di:d (Morgan 1996: 418)

Signifying is done here by introducing words and prosodic features that have negative connotations in African American English, including the use of "honey" followed by the description of Judy's head as "so big" (line 4) and the vocative term "baby" (line 8), and the negative quantifier "whatever" (line 10) (see Morgan's article for more discussion of these terms).

In cases in which speakers use different linguistic varieties for talking to different participants, the use of a variety that is not usually used with one recipient may index that the target is someone else. This is the case, for instance, in an interaction examined in Duranti (1990), where a wife who is angry with her husband for being drunk speaks to the researcher in a phonological variety ("bad speech") she normally uses with her husband but not with the researcher.

Traditional oratory, especially in societies where people of high rank have an official spokesperson, is a good test case for Goffman's participation framework. A good example is provided by Yankah's (1995) study of the *òkyeame* (plural *akyeame*), the Akan orator, who is the only one, in a public meeting, to have direct communicative access to the chief or king. In formal settings, the chief acts as the Principal. He gives his message to his *òkyeame*, who, acting as the Animator, presents the chief's wishes and opinions to the *òkyeame* of the addressee, who, in turn, performs a similar function by conveying the message to his chief. Goffman's scheme allows us to make a number of inferences: a) the first *òkyeame*, to the extent to which he embellishes what the chief (Principal) has told him, participates in authoring the message (we might say then that in these cases there are two distinguishable Authors, with some interesting differences between the two); b) the receiving chief, on the other hand, is made into an Overhearer of two messages: the addressing chief's message and the message as relayed by that chief's *òkyeame*; finally, c) the presence of a second *òkyeame* affects the output of the first, who becomes more committed to aesthetic canons of verbal performance (Yankah 1995: 110).

By widening the range of phenomena made relevant to face-to-face communication, Goffman also drew attention to what he called **subordinate communica-**

tion, that is "talk that is manned, timed, and pitched to constitute a perceivedly limited interference to what might be called the dominating communication in its vicinity" (Goffman 1981: 133). It is ordinarily possible for participants to speak without having the floor or without trying to get it (Goffman 1981: 29). This is often done by quick remarks, expansions, or clarifications that do the job of adding to the on-going conversation without officially stopping it or deviating from its projected course of action. Goffman distinguished among three types of subordinate communication: (i) **byplay**, communication among a subset of the ratified participants, (ii) **crossplay**, communication between ratified participants, and (iii) **sideplay**, communication among bystanders. M. H. Goodwin (in press) studied byplay and argued that it should be seen as a negotiated feature of inter-action, which can have consequences for the talk by the primary speaker or for its interpretation. By engaging in byplay, participants may force the teller of a story to modify what she is saying or even abort the telling without officially competing for the floor. For instance, in the conversation going on at the dinner table shown in figure 9.3, Fran is describing a table in a mansion belonging to the Christian Coalition group of which she is a member.

Figure 9.3 Participants in conversation analyzed by M. H. Goodwin (in press)

As shown in (5), Fran's choice of an embedded question "I~don't~know *how*~many~people" – a form characteristic of a *word search* – triggers Bob's play-ful insertion of "*Hun*dreds" in line 4, accompanied by looks toward Ed. This, in turn, initiates a sequence of other playful byplays (line 8 "°King *Ar*thus:'s *ta*ble" and line 10 "*Wa*s it *rou:nd*?") that end up competing with Fran's main story line.

(5)   1   Fran: *They* have a hu:ge *lon::g* table in the *m*iddle
          that would seat h I~don't~know
          *h*ow~many~people.=[*h And *then they* have- a
      4   Bob: [*Hun*dreds.
      5   Fran: *little* [dining room *t*able at the *e*:nd.
      6   Al: [(°*Hun*dreds~at~*least*.)
      7   Fran: Which [is the~size~of~*ours*.
      8   Ed: [°King *A*rthus:'s *t*able.
      9   Fran: *h *BY* [their ba:y *w*indow.
      10 Bob: [Was it *rou:nd*?
      11 Fran: Y'know? *plus* they have- *h in *a*ll their
          *b*edrooms they have: *w*hat~are they
          called.=Window seats?   (Goodwin, in press)

Byplay is produced so as not to intrude upon the ongoing talk by the main
speaker. For example, Ed uses lower volume and tilts his head backwards while
looking at Bob (see figure 9.4). On the other hand, despite the fact that Fran
does not officially recognize the byplay, during the talk in line 5 she adjusts to it.
She "leans her body towards Dianne, her addressed recipient, and increases her
volume and the expansiveness of her gestures over "*BY* their ba:y *w*indow" (see
figure 9.4). As shown by the arrows in figure 9.4, two parallel interactions take
place within the conversational space of the same narrative.

Figure 9.4 Parallel interactions within the same narrative sequence

What is powerful about this type of analysis is that it gives us some tools for understanding how what might appear at a particular point as the dominant discourse is in fact challenged in subtle but effective ways by talk that is not officially in competition with the ongoing dominant communication. Thus, in (5) both Al and Ed speak in a low voice (as marked by the symbol ° before their utterance), overlap with Fran's talk instead of waiting for the transition-relevant point (see chapter 8), and produce utterances with a rhythm that parallels Al's first utterance in line 6, that is, all three byplays have a two-beat syllabic stress. An extension of this type of analysis to institutional settings such as political arenas, courtrooms, or classrooms can give us a powerful measure of solidarity versus resistance to the dominant discourse. The analysis of byplay offers a way of measuring audience involvement, a crucial dimension across all kinds of speech events.

In discussing Goffman's notion of footing, Levinson (1988) appropriately raises the issue of the **grammaticalization** of participant roles discussed by Goffman, that is, whether his distinctions are in fact encoded by languages. We know that all languages make a lexical and/or morphological distinction between first, second, and third person – with the third often considered as a non-person or "residual" category.[18] Some languages also make subtler distinctions within each category in terms of number, gender, and social status or rank (Anderson and Keenan 1985). Samoan, for instance, distinguishes among singular, dual, and plural pronouns. The non-singular first-person pronouns can be further distinguished in terms of inclusive and exclusive[19] (see table 9.1).

Table 9.1 *Samoan personal pronouns*

	1st	2nd	3rd
Singular	*a`u*	*`oe*	*(`o)ia*
Dual (inclusive)	*tā`ua*		
(exclusive)	*mā`ua*	*`oulua*	*lā`ua*
Plural (inclusive)	*tātou*		
(exclusive)	*mātou*	*`outou*	*lātou*

There are languages that have even more complex systems. Fijian dialects, for instance, have the three number distinctions found in Samoan plus the trial (or

---

[18] Thus, in some languages, there are no third-person pronouns (Dixon 1980; Levinson 1988: 183). The idea of the third person as a 'non-person' is found in Benveniste (1956).
[19] For a componential analysis of a similar pronominal system, that of Hanunóo (Philippines), see Conklin (1962). For a discussion of some of the implications of Conklin's analysis, see Bean (1978).

paucal)[20] form. Other languages have special pronouns for the expression of respect or politeness (Agha 1994; Brown and Levinson 1978, 1987). We do not, however, find languages with lexical or morphological distinctions that can be immediately related to categories like animator, author, or principal, or that univocally represent the distinction between ratified and unratified participants. These are categories that are lexically or morphologically hypocognized, that is, underplayed, backgrounded in terms of overt grammatical categories. What we do find, instead, is that languages display their speakers' concern for the inclusion or exclusion of participants in events and qualities that are being talked about. Thus, in addition to the universal distinction between speaker (*I*) and addressee (*you*), many languages have the more subtle distinctions illustrated in table 9.1 above for Samoan. Languages, in other words, offer their speakers tools to constitute groups and mark divisions. However, by no means do personal pronouns and personal adjectives reflect a predefined objective world. They constitute, bring about, and foreground particular groups and types of relationships. When a husband says to his wife *your son* speaking about their child, he is highlighting her relationship and backgrounding his. When employees use *we* in talking about their company, they show identification with their work place. When a Samoan asks *tā ô?* "two-of-us (inclusive) go?" he means "can I go with you?" If one says *mā ô* "two-of-us (exclusive) go," it means that the addressee is not invited. The choice of a pronoun can thus have implications for the ways in which actual and potential participants are defined, and authority or moral stance established. But these dimensions of human interaction and conceptualization of participation are typically constructed or inferred from a multitude of indirect and often subtle semiotic means (see section 5.4.1), some of them of a kinetic or gestural nature.

One of the targets of Goffman's criticism of the terms speaker and hearer is the emphasis on sound that these terms imply. "[I]t is obvious that sight is organizationally very significant too, sometimes even touch" (1981: 129). I mentioned the importance of visual documentation in chapter 5 while discussing transcription. What the notion of participation does for us is to give us a theoretical framework within which to use the information on visual access made possible by new technologies. Researchers who have worked on visual records of interactions[21] have shown that body posture and eye gaze are important for establishing who is the ratified recipient in an interaction. As mentioned earlier, Goodwin (1981) discussed how "by combining shifts in gaze with modifications of her talk,

---

[20] Writing on Boumaa Fijian, Dixon (1988: 53) argues that the forms that have been labeled "trial" can in fact refer to more than three people.

[21] See, for instance, Goodwin (1979, 1981, 1984), Goodwin and Goodwin (1992a), Heath (1982, 1984), Kendon (1967, 1990).

speaker has the ability to change focal addressee and thus to reorder her recipients within a single utterance" (1981: 152). Kendon (1992) started from Goffman's (1974) notion of different **attentional tracks** in interactions to stress the importance of the **spatial-orientational organization** of focused encounters.

> Participants in focused encounters typically enter into and maintain a distinct spatial and orientational arrangement. By doing so, it seems, participants can provide one another with evidence that they are prepared to sustain a common orientational perspective.
>
> (Kendon 1992: 329)

This "common orientational perspective" is crucially achieved, according to Kendon, by the coordinated use of body postures and body movements. Such features of interaction produce specific types of participation frameworks, including culture-specific patterns of authorship and recipientship (see section 9.4 and 9.5).

9.3.3 Participant frameworks

In her study of boys' and girls' talk in a Philadelphia neighborhood, Marjorie H. Goodwin (1990) introduces the notion of *participant* (as opposed to *participation*) *framework*. Although related to Goffman's, this notion also builds on the relevance of the sequential organization of talk in the constitution of a speech activity:[22]

> I use [participant framework] to encompass two slightly different types of phenomena. First, activities align participants toward each other in specific ways (for example, the activity of constructing a turn at talk differentiates participants into speaker and hearer[s]), and this process is central to the way in which activities provide resources for constituting social organization within face-to-face interaction. ... Second, in addition to being positioned vis-à-vis each other by the activity, relevant parties are frequently characterized or depicted in some fashion, for example, animated (Goffman 1974, 1981) as figures or characters within talk.

Goodwin's work starts from the assumption made within conversation analysis that the way in which conversation is structured is itself a type of social organization (see chapter 8). She uses this assumption to study the consequences that certain types of conversational organization, including participants' voices and alignments, have for the participants themselves. By focusing on the differences

---

[22] To maintain the analytical difference between Goffman's and Goodwin's notions, when I felt it appropriate, I substituted Goodwin's (1990) occasional uses of *participation* framework with *participant* framework.

between boys' and girls' verbal strategies, Goodwin shows that taking participation as a unit of analysis gives us new and empirically more sound ways of studying a wide range of phenomena, including how the organization of a **story** can be used to structure the relationship among people and the social organization of an emerging argument (Goodwin 1990: ch. 10).

One of the participant frameworks for a dispute discussed by Goodwin is what she calls *paired counters*. These are two turn sequences in which something that the first speaker said is countered, opposed by another speaker. Here are some examples:

(6)   (Chopper moves up the steps to where Tony is seated)
    TONY: Get off my steps.
    CHOPPER: No. You get on **my** steps. I get on yours.
                    (Goodwin 1990: 104)

(7)   MALCOM: Get **out** of here Tony.
    TONY: I'm not gettin' out of **no**where.
                    (Goodwin 1990: 105)

(8)   TONY: **Gimme the things**.
    CHOPPER: You sh:ut up you **big** lips. (Y'all been
              hangin' around with thieves.)
    TONY: (**Shut** up.)
    CHOP: Don't gimme that.=I'm not *t*alking to you.
              (1.4)
    TONY: I'm talking to **y**:ou!
    CHOPPER: Ah you better sh:up **up** with your little- **di**:ngy sneaks.
              (1.4)
    TONY: I'm a **d**ingy your hea:d.=How would you like **that**.
                  (Goodwin 1990: 295)

As shown by the last example where Tony and Chopper keep responding to the last turn with a new turn, one of the consequences of reciprocal counters is that they *restrict participation in the sequence to a small set of parties*, typically two speakers (Goodwin 1990: 241). The organization of reciprocal counters (ABAB...) also raises the question (for the participants themselves) of how to end such a sequence. In contrast, the telling of a story presents a participant framework where more than two people can be involved and the party that was the *exclusive* ratified participant of the reciprocal counters becomes just *one* of the ratified participants. This last feature is indexically realized by the switching of pronominal usage: the same party who used to be a *you* becomes a *he*. While telling a story, a speaker can expand the participant framework of a dispute by getting parties not

initially involved in the argument to align themselves with particular positions presented in the story. Here is an example of the beginning of a story that started at
the end of the last example. Chopper stops in the middle of a counter (*No you
won't you little-*) to tell a story about Tony's cowardly behavior:

(9) TONY: I'm a **d**ingy your hea:d.=How would you like **that**.
                (0.4)
→ CHOPPER: No you won't you little- *h **guess** what.
                                  [
     JACK: (°foul) foul thing.
                (0.4)
     CHOPPER: **Lemme~tell~ya.**=**Gu**ess what. (0.8)
                We was comin' home from **pr**actice, (0.4)
                and, three boys came up there (.) and
                asked~us~for~money~and~Tony~did~like~this.
                (0.6) *hh ((raising hands up))
                "*I AINT* GOT n(h)(hh)₁o °m(h)oney"
     PETE: Ah~hih~ha,
                *hh Hah~hah!   (Goodwin 1990: 243)

In this sequence, Chopper starts his story with a typical **story preface** (*Guess
what?*) which announces to everyone present that he is about to tell a story and
therefore will be occupying the floor for more than one turn. Without waiting for
his recipient(s) to provide a **warrant** for the telling, Chopper launches into his
story about Tony. This move has several consequences, one of which is that "since
the utterance containing Chopper's counter is not brought to completion, Tony is
not given the opportunity to respond to it. The return and exchange sequence has
in effect ended" (Goodwin 1990: 244). Everyone present and not just Tony is the
ratified recipient of the story. Furthermore, once a story is told, different kinds of
actions are possible, including the public evaluation of the events in the story.
This will give Chopper the opportunity to elicit support from other parties present and hence restructure the social organization of the argument.

Another domain of study for which the participant framework approach is
particularly powerful is **gender**. In comparing boys' and girls' verbally enacted
disputes, Goodwin shows that although the boys' and girls' verbal disputes share
several features – including (1) the principal topic is offences of another, and (2)
one of the characters in the story is a present participant –, they differ in that
"[a]mong girls, ... offenses concern *reported deeds of absent parties*" (p. 278).
Here is an example of a "He-said-she-said" sequence in which a speaker (Bea)
tells how another girl (Kerry) willfully excluded the primary recipient of the
story (Julia) from a particular group:

(10)   BEA: **She** said, **She** said that um, (0.6)
            that (0.8) if that **girl** wasn't there=
            You know that girl that always makes those funny jokes,
            *h Sh'aid if that **girl** wasn't there **you** wouldn't be **actin'**,
            (0.4) a:ll **stu**pid like that.

            ((several lines skipped))
            (p. 265)
     BEA: I s'd- I s'd "**How**: co:me you ain't put Julia name down here."
            *h So she said, she said ((whiny, defensive tone))
            "That other girl called 'er so,
            she no:t **wi**:th **u**:s, so,"
            That's what she said too. (0.2)
            So **I** said, s- so I snatched the paper wi'her.
            I said wh- when we were playin' wi'that paper?

            ((a few lines skipped))
     BEA: But she ain't even put your **na**me down there.
            I just put it **down** there.
            Me and Martha put it down.=An' I said,
            and she said "**Gi**mme-that-paper.=I don't
            wannt have her **na**me **d**own here."
            I s- I s- I s- I said "She woulda allowed **you** name."
                                              (Goodwin 1990: 263)

The absence of the reportedly offending party has consequences. Whereas boys who are the offended parties can directly confront the storyteller-offender, the girls who are offended must direct their counterattacks to absent parties. At the same time, "the talk of the moment creates a field of relevance that implicates those present to it in a variety of different ways" (Goodwin 1990: 270). This means that those in the audience who are not defined as the offended party and are not part of the story must design their contributions accordingly. One way is to provide general comments on the offender's character. This is what Barbara does in the following examples:

(11)   BARBARA: Kerry~always~mad~at somebody.
                  °I'on' care.

                                    (from Goodwin 1990: 270)

(12)   BARBARA: Kerry **al**ways say somp'm.=
                  When you **jump** in her **face** she gonna de**ny** it.

                                              (Ibid.)

These contributions create a context for the offended party to test the amount of support she has from her peers and receive expressions of solidarity or suggestions about future actions. The organization of talk as defined by the particular type of participant framework established in interaction is thus shown to be a powerful instrument in the construction of social units, relationships, and identities.

More recent work on gender differences in verbal interaction has continued in this tradition of examining the specific contributions of male and female speakers within particular types of participant frameworks. Ochs and Taylor (1992), for instance, discuss how family narrative practices recreate what they call the "Father-knows-best" dynamic through a particular configuration of introducers of a story, protagonist(s), and primary recipient:

> Within this dynamic, the father is typically set up – through his own
> and others' recurrent narrative practices – as primary audience,
> judge, and critic of family members' actions, thoughts, feelings,
> and conditions either as a narrative protagonist (acting in the past)
> or as a co-narrator (acting in the present).
>
> (Ochs and Taylor 1992: 447)

Ochs and Taylor show that, contrary to current beliefs about the impact of the feminist movement, this patriarchical ideology is still in place in the narratives of mainstream Anglo-American families. In examining a vast corpus of dinnertime narratives collected from seven Anglo-American families in the Los Angeles area, Ochs and Taylor found that (i) children are more likely to be protagonist in dinner narratives; (ii) parents are more likely to introduce such narratives; (iii) parents are also the privileged primary recipients of narratives; and (iv) fathers outrank mothers as primary recipients. These data show that there is a "fundamental asymmetry in family narrative activity whereby children's lives are told to parents but by and large parents do not address their lives to their children" (1992: 453). Furthermore, analysis of the participant frameworks established during the narrative activities shows that fathers are primary recipients not just because they take on such a role but because mothers, at least in some families, regularly select their husbands as primary recipients through a number of rhetorical strategies, including the famous "You wanna tell Daddy what happened to you today?" and the tendency to initiate a story by orienting their own telling toward their husbands. The organization of participation in the activity of telling stories at the dinner table has a number of important consequences, including the setting up of the father as the judge[23] and problematizer.

---

[23] Citing Foucault (1979), Ochs and Taylor evoke here Bentham's *panopticon* as a metaphor that well illustrates the "all-seeing eye" or monitoring gaze of the father in dinner-table narrative activity. See also Foucault (1980a: ch. 8 "The eye of power").

Although mothers and children also problematize, fathers assume this role 50 percent as often as mothers and 3.5 times as often as children. Problematization is carried out by treating something that has just been said as untrue, incredible, or doubtful, as in (13):

(13)   MOTHER: ((to Jodie))=oh:: you know what? You wanna tell
                        Daddy what happened to you today?=
       FATHER: ((looking up and off))=Tell me everything that
                        happened from the moment you went in – until:
                                                  [
       JODIE: I got a sho:t=
       FATHER: EH ((gasping)) what? ((frowning))
       JODIE: I got a sho::t
                        [
       FATHER: *no*
                        (0.4) ((father begins shaking head no))
       FATHER: couldn't be
       JODIE: (yeah) ((with upward nod toward Dan))
                        [
       OREN: (a) TV test? – TV test? Mommy?
       MOTHER: ((nods yes)) -mhm
       JODIE: and a sho:t
       FATHER: ((to Jodie)) (what did you go to the ih::) ((to Mother))
                        Did you
                        go to the ?animal hospital?
       MOTHER: .hh – *no:?*
       FATHER: (where/what)
       JODIE: I just went to the doctor and I got a shot
       FATHER: ((shaking head no)) I don't believe it
       JODIE: *ri:lly::*

                                                  (Ochs and Taylor 1992: 449)

Other times problematization is done by emphasizing negative ramifications or implications of an event, as in (14), where the father reacts to his wife's story about a broken chair by pointing out that it might just be a sign of the fact that she needs to lose weight:

(14)   (The mother has just scooted Ronnie's [4;11] chair in to the table)
       MOTHER: (Oh) this *chair?* broke - today
       FATHER: I? know
                        ((mother heads back toward kitchen, stops by Josh's

chair, Josh [7;10] begins looking at mother's chair and
under table))

MOTHER: *No::* I mean it *rea:?lly* broke today
                 [

FATHER: *I?* know
I know?

MOTHER: Oh you knew that it was split?

FATHER: yeah?,

MOTHER: The whole wood('s) split?

FATHER: yeah,

MOTHER: Oh did *you* do it?
          (0.4)

FATHER: I don't know if I *did?* it but I saw that it *wa:?s*=
                               [

MOTHER: (oh)
((Josh goes under table to inspect chair))

RONNIE?:   (   )
=[

MOTHER: yeah I sat *down?* in it and the whole *thing* split so I –
((bending over as if to indicate where on chair)) I tie:d
                                          [

FATHER: ((somewhat bratty intonation))   That's
(a) *rea:l si:gn?* that you need to go on a *di:?*et.

MOTHER: hh ((grinning as she rises from stooped position next to
Josh's chair))

                                      (Ochs and Taylor 1992: 450)

This research shows that the notion of participation is an important tool for the
empirical investigation of how family and gender roles are constituted through
speech. It also shows that to speak of participation means to speak of *differentiation*. It is through the different ways in which different individuals (in families,
workplaces, service encounters) are allowed to be part of certain kinds of activities that social identities (including gender identities) are created and reproduced.
It is through specific and reproduceable participant frameworks that authority,
hierarchy, and subordination are constituted. Whether or not someone's voice
will be expressed, someone's accusation accepted or rejected, someone's point
of view recognized depends in part on the interactional arrangements that are
possible and the choices that are favored by such arrangements – see for instance
the above discussion of byplay. The deconstruction of the pair speaker-hearer
and its substitution with different kinds of participant statuses and frameworks

allow us to see patterns we couldn't see before. Participation as an analytical dimension becomes a powerful instrument for the study of the constitution of society, with its pre-established roles and statuses and its routine negotiation of such roles and statuses through communication. The recognition of participation as a contested ground where differentiation is not only possible but systematically achieved can also help us reconceptualize previously neutral terms like *linguistic repertoire* (see section 3.4):

> What sociolinguists call the *linguistic repertoire* is a set of resources for the articulation of multiple memberships and forms of participation. And an individual's ways of speaking in a particular community of practice are not simply a function of membership or participation in that community. A way of speaking in a community does not simply constitute a turning on of a community-specific linguistic switch, or the symbolic laying of claim to membership in that community, but a complex articulation of the individual forms of participation in that community with participation in other communities that are salient at the time. In turn, the linguistic practices of any given community of practice will be continually changing as a result of the many saliencies that come into play through its multiple members.
>
> (Eckert and McConnell-Ginet 1992: 97)

The challenge, then, for linguistic anthropologists and other students of language as an instrument, carrier, and product of social relations is to test different units of analysis to find the one that allows us to make previously unseen or undocumented connections between the micro-level of face-to-face verbal interaction and the macro-level of institutional statuses, roles, and identities.

9.4 Authorship, intentionality, and the joint construction of interpretation

The subtle distinctions and the examples discussed above not only imply that the categories "speaker" and "hearer" are too crude for linguistic analysis but also that the notion of **authorship** must be reconceptualized. If our starting point in analyzing speech is participation instead of individual speakers, we must reconsider what it means to encode and decode meaning. Individuals are of course involved in meaning-making, but the responsibility for the shape and content of messages shifts from individual speakers to particular types of participant frameworks. Once we enlarge the domain of investigation to include the social organization of how messages are collaboratively constructed and interpreted, we also need to move beyond traditional notions of language-mind relations. Empirical

314

investigations show that many (if not all) of the acts that in the idealized world of intuitions and imagined interactions might be seen as the product of one individual, namely, the speaker, are in fact the **collaborative work** of several participants.[24] This collaborative and collective nature of encoding and decoding messages is true not only of ritual encounters where a person speaks on behalf of another or on behalf of a group, but also of more ordinary speech events, where individuals seem to be speaking and acting for themselves.

Earlier accounts of narrative activities within conversation analysis (e.g. Sacks 1992b: 222ff; Jefferson 1978) identified fairly strict roles in the telling of stories in conversation. In particular, a distinction was typically made between **teller** and **recipient** of the story. The teller is the one who must introduce the story and get permission by the recipient(s) to go on. More recently, Jennifer Mandelbaum (1987) has drawn some more subtle distinctions in the participant frameworks found during storytelling. She distinguishes between **teller-driven** and **recipient-driven stories**. The former is a series of extended turns by one speaker interrupted by demonstrations of attentiveness by the recipients through various kinds of back channel signals (e.g. *mhmh, really?*). The latter is an activity in which "teller and recipient together work out what a storytelling is 'about' and how it is to be understood" (Mandelbaum 1987: 238). This distinction may not always work. In particular, the work on family narratives mentioned above shows that

> The assignment of the roles of teller and audience, or teller and
> recipient, to whole narratives ultimately breaks down in
> conversational storytelling in which many participants construct the
> story. Particularly where storytelling includes close friends and
> family members, the telling can be widely distributed. Particularly
> in these cases it makes better sense to assign the roles of teller and
> audience/recipient turn-by-turn as the storytelling evolves. At one
> moment a participant may be teller and the next a recipient.
>
> (Ochs 1997: 200)

In the study of family storytelling all family members present are considered **co-tellers**. A distinction is made, however, between an **initial teller**, the person who introduces the story, and other tellers, who contribute to the telling as the story proceeds. Ochs, Taylor, Rudolph, and Smith (1992) show that co-narrators often re-script narratives and in so doing provide alternative explanations or framings of the narrated events – hence their argument that stories should be seen as "theories" and storytelling as "theory building." Co-narrators might

---

[24] The term "collaborative" in this case should not be interpreted as implying an equal sharing of interpretive resources and interpretive rights (see, for instance, the discussion of byplay and "father-knows-best" above).

bring in new information that implicitly challenges an initial version of a story or explicitly challenges an initial interpretation of events (Ochs et al. 1992: 59). For example in (15) below, although it was Lucy who introduced the story about a schoolmate who gets only one day of detention, it is her mother who continues the story illustrating Lucy's psychological response to the offensive actions:

(15) Lucy: When we were back at school um – this girl? – she pulled
                um – Vicky's *dress* ((puts hand to knee)) up t'here
                ((gestures with hand high on chest)) in front of the boys
      Mother: mhm?
      Lucy: She only – all se did was get a *day* of de*ten*tion
      Mother: mhm? – *you* think she should have gotten suspended?
                (0.6)
      Lucy: at *LEAST* - That's

                [a few lines left out]

      Mother: (cuz Lucy) was *really* embarassed ((nodding yes, talking
                while eating))
                (1.6)
      Mother: (I mean you/Lucy really) would have like to kill the – the
                girl – huh?
      Lucy: ((nods yes slowly, as she chews, fork in mouth))
                [
      Mother: (cuz) you were upset with her – ((speaking very fast)) But
                you were held back because you (thought) your school was
                goin' to do it and the school didn't do it and you feel up*set*
                                    (Ochs et al. 1992: 47)

These data show that in actual conversation stories are co-authored by a number of speakers. Co-authorship might in fact be a much more widespread phenomenon (Duranti and Brenneis 1986). When we look at utterances from the point of view of the participant framework within which they occur, even speech acts that seem produced solely by one individual (e.g. making an offer, accusing, greeting, expressing an opinion, making a request) are in fact the cooperative effort by a number of participants, only some of whom (the ratified ones) see their behavior recognized as relevant. This means that at any given moment in social interaction, there are a number of potential and actual co-authors. Whether or not someone's verbal or kinetic acts are recognized as contributing to what is being said and done depends on a number of factors, including local theories of authorship, intentionality, responsibility (Duranti 1993a, b; Heritage 1990/91;

Hill and Irvine 1993; Mandelbaum 1993; Rosen 1995), and context-specific uses of the available perceptual resources. The question "whose voice is heard?" often translates into the question "whose voice counts?" (Lindstrom 1992). Ideology plays a bigger role than is usually realized in the organization of perception. This is true of the researcher's theory of communication as well as of the the participants'. In traditional quantitative sociolinguistics, for instance, the interview is used as the main and often only speech event from which to gather data on speech patterns. When we look at the transcripts of data collected in this fashion we are often given the wrong impression that the speaker is engaged in a lengthy monologue whereas in fact the interviewer is constantly providing feedback and the interpretive frame for the answer to make sense. When these tapes are played, we may also hear that the voice of the interviewer is in the background (e.g. it is less loud and less clear). An important theoretical choice has been made to favor one individual speaker as the producer/author. Similarly, when we hear reports about what participants say went on in a particular setting – e.g. in ethnographic interviews –, we must remember that within each situation there are locally accepted and locally acceptable theories of who speaks, on what topic, on behalf of whom, and to whom. Participants in a public meeting, for instance, might remember or be willing to remember or mention only portions of what the official speaker(s) said and may leave out the side comments, gasps, or silences of the audience which might be just as important.

The focus on units of participation contrasts with speech act theory's traditional interest in individual speakers and their intentions (see section 7.1.2). Searle's theory of communication not only privileges the speaker over other participants in the interpretive process, it also uses the notion of intentions in an unproblematic way. Intentions are discussed as something readily available to anyone's reflections on the basis of introspection. This is true even of the notion of collective intentionality recently introduced by Searle (1990).

There is no question that, as semioticians have long been arguing (e.g. Morris 1938), for something to be a "sign" (see section 5.3), it needs to be a "sign for someone." Puffs of air produced through someone's mouth acquire a meaning, that is, can be the representation of some message, if there are people who can assign an interpretation to them. The question is where does such an interpretation come from? How is it assigned? Who or what is responsible for it? Searle believes that the source of representation, what makes it possible for something to be a sign and gives it content, is the human mind. Utterances can mean something because we have mental states. Such mental states are intentions (to do something) which can be externalized through speech (or other forms of human action). For Searle, this does not mean that we must consciously think before speaking "I am going to say X in order to achieve Y," but that even when we speak spontaneously and apparently without premeditation, we are acting out intentions – Searle's distinction between *prior intentions* and *intentions in action* is supposed to capture the difference between conscious and unconscious intentional action (Searle 1983: 84ff).

The problem with this theory is not the reliance on the human mind. Of course the mind is involved in anything we do, including and especially thinking and speaking. Nor is a problem the fact that intentions enter the discussion. Intentionality, as the property of human consciousness to focus on something, to be *about* something, is central to understanding human action. This was Franz Brentano's original definition of intentionality, as Husserl reminds us:

> We understand under Intentionality the unique peculiarity of experiences "to be the consciousness *of* something." ... perceiving is the perceiving of something, maybe a thing; judging, the judging of a certain matter; valuation, the valuing of a value; wish, the wish for the content wished, and so on. (Husserl [1913]1931: 223)

When people engage in conversation or any other form of social intercourse, their interactions are definitely about something, in that sense there is intentionality in them. However, the use of intentions for explaining people's behavior, speech included, runs into several problems when used as the paramount interpretive tool. There are two sorts of problems with the emphasis on intentions that characterize speech act theory: (i) participants do not always display orientation toward (or interest in) what others are intending; (ii) any reconstruction of participants' intentions (included the reconstruction made by the analyst) must rely on information that is available in the context of the interaction.

As admitted by speech act theorists, intentions in order to be realized must rely on particular contextual (or felicity) conditions (see chapter 7), which are not a predefined set of features. The range of factors or dimensions that constitute context change in the course of the interaction and hence for the interpreters themselves, who routinely restrict or enlarge the relevant context (Goodwin and Duranti 1992). Time and space are part of any act of interpretation. This means that participants in a joint activity must on any given occasion rely on a number of features that they see as relevant to interpreting what is going on, what is likely to happen, and what to do next. Since no one can really read other people's mind, guessing what others are up to or "mean" must crucially involve the interpretation of information that is outside the speaker's mind. Thus, in the real world the locus of meaning and by implication the locus of interpretation is typically external, in publicly available behaviors, in already made symbols, and in the built environment we inhabit, use, and modify (see section 9.5). In other words, meaning is not only in people's mind, it is also in routine actions –

e.g. types of participant frameworks (see above) – and ready-to-use artifacts (e.g. houses, rooms, furniture, pencils, notebooks, computers, telephones, etc.) that allow us to interface with one another in particular ways. The idea that the meaning of the use of such routine courses of action and artifacts can be described as due to intentional states in the mind of the participants misses a crucial dimension of human action, namely, what Heidegger called the **unobstrusiveness** of the beings we encounter in everyday life.

> We do not always and continually have explicit perception of the things surrounding us in a familiar environment, certainly not in such a way that we would be aware of them expressly as handy. It is precisely because an explicit awareness and assurance of their being at hand does not occur that we have them around us in a peculiar way, just as they are in themselves. In the indifferent imperturbability of our customary commerce with them, they become accessible precisely with regard to their unobtrusive presence. The presupposition for the possible equanimity of our dealing with things is, among others, the *uninterrupted quality* of that commerce. At the basis of this undisturbed imperturbability of our commerce with things, there lies a peculiar temporality which makes it possible to take a handy equipmental contexture in such a way that we lose ourselves in it. (Heidegger 1988: 309)

For social interaction to work, most of the time we must "lose ourselves in it." When we stop to think about what is happening or what went wrong, we enter a particular type of monitoring of social action during which we can invoke a set of norms that explain what went wrong or what should have happened (Garfinkel 1967; Heritage 1984). This type of monitoring or reflexive activity is also what produces the kinds of interpretations of speakers' intentions proposed by speech act theorists. The discourse of intentionality is thus intimately connected to a discourse of responsibility. This is true not only because intentions are typically reconstructed to assign responsibility for something that has been done, but also because in many contexts responsibility is one of the main criteria whereby an act is interpreted. Participants often do not ask themselves and each other "what did he mean?" but "what does this mean?" That is, once performed, an act is evaluated on the basis of its social consequences.[25]

---

[25] The issue of the role of intentionality in interpreting language has received much attention in the last two decades. In addition to the references already cited, see Apel (1991), Bogen (1987), De Mulder (1993), Dennett (1987), Derrida (1977[see Hoy 1986]), Du Bois (1993), Duranti (1988b, 1993a, b), Grice (1971), Hoy (1986), Leilich (1993), Lepore and Van Gulick (1991), Nuyts (1991, 1993, 1994), Searle (1983, 1986, 1990).

In fact, in many societies, people do not believe that it is possible to get into "someone else's mind" (Ortner 1979; Schieffelin 1986; Shore 1982). Discussing the issue of interpretation from a crosscultural perspective, Rosen (1995a: 1) writes:

> ... what might at first seem a wholly ideational issue [namely, interpretation] is, in fact, deeply entwined with the nature and distribution of power, the portrayal of events and the assessment of personhood, the relation of trust and deception, and the social assigning of moral and legal responsibility.

An anthropologically minded theory of interpretation must incorporate these intuitions about language and power or language and personhood, in the analysis of specific communicative acts. As we saw in chapter 7, Rosaldo and others argued that speech act theorists' ideas about interpretation are influenced by western theories and practices, including existing beliefs about what a person is and how we can know about reality or influence other people's thoughts and actions. Linguistic anthropologists see the reliance on mental states to explain what we mean by language as influenced by these beliefs. But there is more to it. I believe – and in this I am very much in agreement with conversation analysts (see chapter 8) – that such an exclusive interest in speakers' intentions is also due to methodological and analytical limitations. Searle, like many other philosophers, argues about language or social action starting from made-up situations based on his own intuitions on individually conceived acts. He typically discusses what an act or expression might mean in a generalized, that is, idealized context. It is only in such an idealized world that speakers produce utterances completely on their own, without having to reckon with their audience and without seeing their speech acquire meaning as part of a joint activity in which others help shape what is being said and what is being meant. When we examine the ways in which different participants enter the production of even the smallest utterance, we find that the responsibility for its interpretation is typically distributed across participants as well as material resources. Interpretation is social not simply because there must be publicly shared conventions, a point that Searle has no problems recognizing, but because the more we look at how people engage in interpretation, the more we realize that it is an activity that involves a range of publicly shared resources and products. Participants' intentions are one of such resources and not always the most important one. The intentions of a speaker may or may not be what the recipient takes to be the relevant context for interpreting speech. I have argued this position in the past on the basis of linguistic and ethnographic material collected during my field work in Western Samoa. In Duranti (1988b, 1993b), I show that participants in political arenas such as the *fono* seem to be more interested in issues of responsibility and hence the social consequences of someone's words rather than in issues of intentionality or speakers' state of mind. Since then, I have become convinced that the focus on the speaker's intentions is problematic not only because it uncritically assumes a shared understanding of the speaker's state of mind, but because it leaves out of the communicative process the work done by other participants as well as by the full range of semiotic resources that enter any interpretive act. The focus on the speaker's mental representation does not take into account the continuous interpenetration of codes and modes of speaking and acting that are at work during any speech event.

9. 5   Participation in time and space: human bodies in the built environment

> Before instrumental techniques there is the ensemble of techniques of the body. (Mauss [1935] 1979: 104)

Given the emphasis on the symbolic nature of linguistic systems, it is not surprising that most discussions of language structure and language use make no reference to the *built environment*, that is, the products of human building activity that surround and support human interaction (Lawrence and Low 1990).[26] Words, morphemes, or even sentences are usually seen as representing ideas and as such inherently detached from the physical objects produced by human labor. Even the advent of speech act theory, with its emphasis on utterances as deeds (see chapter 7), has not increased the attention paid to the material world in which and through which social interaction, communication included, takes place. The only major exception in this domain is the study of deixis, that is, the property of those linguistic expressions, called indexes (see sections 1.4.2 and 6.8.2), that cannot be interpreted without reference to the nonlinguistic (or extralinguistic) context of their use (Anderson and Keenan 1985: 259; Levinson 1983: ch. 2; Lyons 1977).

An analysis of speech that starts from units of participation allows us to rethink deixis in new ways. As pointed out by Hanks (1990), given that the participation framework shifts continuously throughout an interaction or speech

---

[26] For Lawrence and Low (1990: 454), building environment refers "in the broadest sense to any physical alteration of the natural environment, from hearths to cities, through construction by humans ... it includes *built forms* ... spaces that are defined and bounded, but not necessarily enclosed, such as the uncovered areas in a compound, a plaza, or a street ... they might include landmarks or *sites*, such as shrines, which do not necessarily shelter or enclose activity ... specific elements of buildings (such as doors, windows, roofs, walls, floors, and chimneys) or to spatial subdivisions of buildings ... often referred to in terms of their *plans*."

event, participants need ways to signal to each other whose voice is speaking now and whose attention or point of view is being assumed or required. Hanks (1990) shows that Maya deictic terms can only be understood by taking into consideration the human bodies of the participants as well as the material world where they interact (see section 6.8.2). The work on deixis by Hanks highlights the need to understand the process whereby meaning is encoded and decoded as always embedded in a *phenomenal field*, that is, a field of acting and thinking that becomes relevant as participants move through it with their body and their senses. Hanks is the first linguist to attempt an integration of structuralist methods of analysis (see chapter 6) with phenomenological characterizations of the human body as a crucial mediator of our relation to the world of objects around us (Merleau-Ponty 1962; Schutz 1967). Deictic expressions enter this process by orienting utterances, glances, and movements in space and time, by relying on a set of already established conventions, and by setting up a conceptual world which is not detached from but based on our corporeal understanding of the phenomenal world. To say "I" or "you" or to use one type of locative expression over another means to evoke, establish, reassess *corporeal fields*, that is, units of participation that rely on sociocultural models and modes of corporeality (Hanks 1990: 262).

The human body and the built environment are crucial elements in the analysis of any interaction that involves movement through space and time. We often forget that the human body is the first instrument we experience. Our mouth, hands, eyes, feet, and other body parts are the first mediating elements in our interaction with the people and objects around us. But our body does not operate in an empty space. We move in a space that has been shaped by others before us, a space that has history, meaning, that is, a range of possibilities. As pointed out by Frake (1975: 37) in his analysis of how to enter a Yakan house,

> ... a house, even a one-roomed Yakan house, is not just a space. It is
> a structured sequence of settings where social events are
> differentiated not only by the position in which they occur but also
> by the positions the actors have moved through to get there and the
> manner in which they have made those moves.

Once we start taking seriously the importance of the spatio-temporal coordinates of human encounters, we realize that we need to enlarge the context of verbal exchanges beyond the study – no matter how careful and sophisticated – of what is said. We need a microhistory of human interaction that does not fall prey to ideological reconstructions and does not suffer from the usual limitations of mere observation. As stressed in chapter 3, what people do while talking is not something that can be just imagined or remembered. It must be seen, above all because sight is a fundamental domain of human experience and sighting is a fundamental dimension of any encounter. What participants see and when they see it is more than a background against which to make sense of what is said. Sight as an activity that occurs in a material world is itself social action, it is the instrument and product of an interpretive journey that can only be understood spatio-temporally. This is why, as human ethologists have argued for years, visual documentation of human encounters is so crucial for an analysis of what people do with, to, and through one another (Eibl-Eibesfeldt 1968, 1974; Kendon 1967, 1977, 1990, 1992; Kendon and Ferber 1973). However, despite the availability of technologies that allow for the mechanical or electronic reproduction of an encounter and the preservation of some of its spatio-temporal features, much of the study of language use is exclusively based on audio recordings. Such studies do not necessarily produce inadequate analyses – there is certainly value in the careful examination of how talk itself is organized (see chapter 8) –, but they do tend to reproduce a skewed view of what matters to participants in an interaction. If we are serious about our commitment to the study of language as resource for and product of cultural practices, we cannot systematically isolate speech from the movement of the participants' bodies through a symbolically and materially rich space.

Starting from these assumptions, in Duranti (1992) I provided an analysis of Samoan ceremonial greetings that emphasized how the performance and the interpretation of the words used in the greetings are contingent upon the temporal unfolding of the participants' movements in the house during and after their arrival. The audio-visual data – Sound Super 8 film clips and video recordings collected over a period of several years in the same village – demonstrate that words used in the greetings are part of a sequence of acts which include bodily movements and cannot be fully understood without reference to such movements. An analysis focusing exclusively on the linguistic execution of the greetings would represent the exchange as a complex adjacency pair (see section 8.1.1), where a group of participants who are already in the house welcome a newcomer who, in turn, responds by addressing the welcoming party either as a group or as a number of individuals, typically identified through their titles or contextually made-relevant positional roles.

(16) Schematic representation of a Samoan ceremonial greeting
  Party A: {WELCOMING}
  Party B: {RESPONSE}

As typical of adjacency pairs, once the first pair part is produced (by Party A), the second pair part is expected. However, what party A says counts as a first pair part only after Party B has positioned himself inside the house in a place that warrants the welcoming. This means that to understand this kind of interaction we must first of all take into consideration *the local conceptualization of the space inside a house as a symbolic representation of the social organization relevant to the on-going or soon-to-be-started event.* The distinction between "front" (*luma*) and "back" (*tua*) or between *tala* and the other two sides, for instance, establishes some general coordinates in terms of status and rank in any Samoan house: orators (and important guests) are expected to be seated in the "front," high chiefs in either one of the two *tala*, and lower-ranking orators in the "back." However, which person will choose to or be invited to occupy such positions is partly due to the specific type of event that is taking place inside the house – figure 9.5 shows how the different parts of the house are determined on the basis of an external coordinate such as a road (or sometimes the *malae* or ceremonial ground).

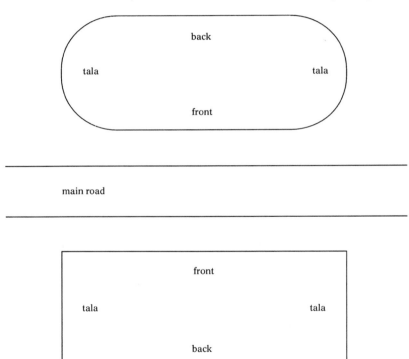

Figure 9.5 Local conceptualization of spaces in two Samoan houses facing the road (Duranti 1992)

If we take into consideration what participants do, that is, how they move with their body through this space, what is described above as the first pair part of the greeting can be reanalyzed as the second pair part of an exchange which starts with a non-verbal act, namely, the occupation of a place in what I renamed as the "front region" – an area that comprises the two *tala*, the "front," and the "back." This interaction is schematically represented in figure 9.6.

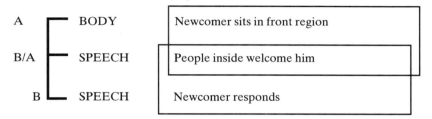

Figure 9.6 Two interlocking interpretations of sequences of adjacency pairs in ceremonial greetings

This recognition of the role of the body of the newcomer in the interaction shifts the responsibility of the initiation of the greeting to the new arrivals who are in fact much more in control of whether or not they will be greeted than it might appear at first. But even this interpretation must be revised in some cases in light of other possible or actual moves by the people who are already seated in the house. The people in the house are not completely passive while the new party enters the common space. Whereas there are cases in which no doubts are displayed by either the newcomer or the parties already seated about where the former should sit, there are also times when a certain amount of negotiation takes place. It is not uncommon for the already seated participants to try to lead or invite the arriving party to a particular spot. Equally common is for the new-comer to resist the "offer" of a high status position. This is the case, for instance, in the following interaction, where chief Agaiataua is invited to sit in the *tala*, but manages to sit at the edge of it and with the highest-ranking orator in the house (and in the subvillage where the meeting was taking place), Leuta, on his left.

(17) (Fono in the subvillage of Sanonu; Chief Agaiataua arrives
      when the meeting has already started)

      ((Shot of chief Agaiataua walking by outside, past
      the front entrance towards back))
      ((Filming is interrupted for a few seconds and resumes
      with the chief already in the house walking with a
      kava root in his right hand and trying to get a spot
      in the back row, among the orators))

1	?:	(*afio fo`i `i ō!*)
		do go over there!
2	??:	*`o ikū lā!*
		that side!
3	Chief A.:	*ia` `o `i lā!*
		okay over there!
4	Orator O.:	*ia` afio ifo `i ō*
		okay go down over there

[

5	Chief A.:	*`o `i lā*
		over there
6	?:	(*uh uh*)
7	?:	*uh::::*
8	??:	*ia` (`ua makua ā)* ((Chief A. starts sitting down))
		well (it's really very)
9		((Chief A. puts down kava root in front of him, to the right))
10	?:	(? ? ?)
11	??:	*hehe*
		hehe
12	Chief A.:	((Sighs)) *hahh!*
13	?:	(*ia` afio maia*)
		well welcome

[

14	`Auga:	*ia` afio maia!*
		well, welcome!
15	Chief A.:	*ia`,*
		well
16	?:	*afio maia*
		welcome

[

| 17 | ?Leuta: | *afio maia- lau afioga Aga(ia)taua!* |
| | | welcome- your highness Agaiataua! |

[...]

Figure 9.7, based on the film of the interaction, traces chief Agaiataua's route and his attempts to sit in the "back" region, with lower-ranking orators.

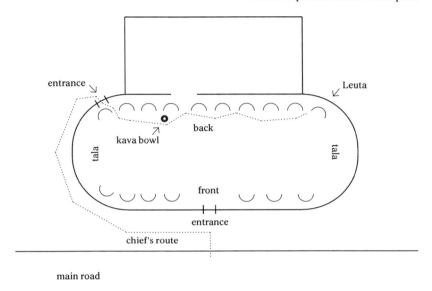

Figure 9.7 Route followed by chief Agaiataua when arriving at house full
of orators from his subvillage (Duranti 1992)

The protracted resistance to accept a high-status position in this instance is not
simply due to "politeness" (e.g. one party offers a higher position and the other
takes a lower one) but to the fact that a higher-status location always carries
political and economic implications (see Goody 1972; Irvine 1974, 1989). Because
of the association between the seating position and the status and rank implied
by it, chiefs who are not fully confident of their place in the local hierarchy and
the associated socioeconomic system may try to resist what appears as a generous "offer" but can turn out to be a mixed blessing from a financial point of view
(viz. those in higher-ranking places are expected to give more than those in
lower-ranking spots). Ethnographic information reveals that Chief Agaiataua's
status in the community is rendered structurally ambiguous by a number of factors including the origin of his title which comes from another village – in most
encounters he is in fact addressed with a local title which is not as high –, his living situation (he lives on the land of his father-in-law, an old and well-respected
orator), and his occupation (schoolmaster), which gives him at least a partial
identification with western values. Such ambiguity of status identity is further

sustained by his actions: he has walked into the house carrying a dry kava root, a traditional offer for the assembly, but when he first speaks he does so in the "good speech" (*tautala lelei*), a phonological variety of Samoan that is common in church, school, and other western-inspired institutional settings but not in meetings of village-level kinship-based political units.[27]

The Samoan ceremonial greetings also speak to the question of differentiation and the constitution of hierarchy. Whether or not someone will be greeted depends on a number of factors that establish his entrance as worthy of public recognition. Participation in the exchange of greetings, a highly negotiated and negotiable activity, is also an important aspect of the reproduction of the social order. Its organization, with multiple speakers jointly and yet not simultaneously greeting the newcomer, allows for individual voices and specific epithets to be heard and be played against one another. What someone is called and how he or she reciprocates the greeting are important indexes of the social stature of the individuals and groups involved in the encounter. The extension of the same ritual from events based on kinship-based hierarchies such as the *fono* to events involving representatives of the local church or the government encourages a reading of such modern institutions in terms of traditional values and perpetrates the ideological fiction of a world that is made to appear the same while in fact changing.

9.6   Conclusions

I started this chapter with the notion of activity and its importance in the study of philogenetic and ontogenetic development and I ended with an example of an analysis of greetings that relied on audio-visual documentation and ethnographic methods. How are these two domains of inquiry connected? The answer I propose is that they are connected through the notion of participation, that is, the idea that to study human behavior, including speech, means to engage in the detailed and systematic study of the semiotic and material resources that go into the constitution of usually multi-party joint activities. To make sense of what people do as members of particular groups – and *to be* members of such groups – means to understand not only what one person says to another, but how speaking and non-speaking participants coordinate their actions, including verbal acts, to constitute themselves and each other in particular spatio-temporally fluid but bounded units. Linguists, anthropologists, and sociologists have provided us over the last half a century with a number of units of analysis that try to capture the dynamic functional systems speech is part of. Jakobson's speech event model

---

[27] For a discussion of the contextual distribution of the two phonological registers, "good speech" and "bad speech," see Duranti (1981, 1990, 1994a), Duranti and Ochs (1986), Shore (1982)

owes a great deal to the European tradition of functional linguistics based on instrumental models of language (Bühler, the Prague School). His model reframes the referential function of language – the ability to talk about the world – as only one among a number of functions performed by speech in speaker-hearer interactions. Hymes's SPEAKING model further extends Jakobson's scheme adding a sensitivity to dimensions of speech and participation in speech events that makes the study of communicative events the starting point for the study of entire communities. The revolutionary idea in this case is the call for a social unit of analysis, the event, that is in turn defined by the speech that goes on in it. Hymes invited researchers to simultaneously take into account and study in some detail several dimensions of language use, including the setting, the genre, and the goals of the event.[28] Out of the rich list of components of speech events proposed by Hymes, I decided to focus on "participants" for a number of reasons. First, by deconstructing the categories "speaker" and "hearer," two cornerstones of contemporary work in linguistics, we can reframe the act of speaking as a joint and yet differentiated and differentiating activity where what appears as a message produced by one individual is in fact the achievement of a socially organized unit. Second, the subtle distinctions made by Goffman within each category allow us to think about the different ways in which one's speech can simultaneously represent the voices and social personae of different individuals or institutional roles. This adds an analytical richness that is essential for the recognition of speaking as an activity with sociohistorical depth, where to establish, negotiate, and challenge who we are and what we are up to vis-à-vis a real or imaginary group. Third, by shifting away from individual utterances to participant frameworks, we are able to use some of the insights of the study of conversational interaction to investigate the consequences of different kinds of sequential organizations for the constitution of social roles and categories within specific social systems. Finally, the emphasis on participation reframes speech as only one of the semiotic resources used by social actors and leads us to take more seriously into consideration the material resources and the visual information available in any social encounter. The analysis of Samoan ceremonial greetings presented above was meant to provide an example of such a study, where information gathered through traditional ethnographic methods (e.g. participant-observation, interviews) is integrated with detailed, in some cases frame-by-frame analysis of audio-visual records of interactional exchanges. The interplay of verbal, corporeal, and visual resources found in the Samoan greetings should not be seen as unique, but as quite ordinary in any social encounters where participants have

---

[28] His model was put into operation by Sherzer and Darnell (1972) in a set of research questions for fieldworkers that covered such topics as linguistic varieties, attitudes, language acquisition, and typology.

access to both aural and visual information. It also shows that speech activities that we might otherwise analyze as bounded do in fact interact with other (prior or ensuing) activities in interesting ways. The result of these complex inter-lacing of semiotic layers and communicative channels is a kind of "multi-channel architecture" that greetings share with many other human social activities. The possibility of sequentially and sometimes simultaneously communicating through different resources (speech, body movements, interaction with and use of the material environment) can keep alive multiple versions of the on-going social scene as well as multiple identities of the participants. The ability to capture such qualities of an interaction is an important instrument for the study of the formation of social identity. By looking at greetings in the way I suggested, we can show that multiple channels and modes of interaction (voice, body, body/space) are used not only because they are available, but because they each offer different solutions to the problem of establishing and sustaining a particular version of the social world – with its assumptions about knowledge and power, access and denial, continuity and change – without denying the possibility of other versions, with their orders and power relations. In this way, the detailed micro-level analysis of speech in interaction proposed in the last few chapters can be shown to enter a realm of investigation that is much larger than the specific situation that is being studied and links the details of everyday encounters to the larger social organizations and institutional settings that give direction and meaning to the social life of any community.

10

Conclusions

One of the challenges in writing any textbook – and this one is certainly no exception – is the need to build a continuous narrative out of what are often only fragments of stories, originally told to different audiences and for different purposes. Like any other search for thematic or theoretical continuity, the writing of a book on any field of inquiry entails an attempt to construct both an object of study and a method out of usually quite diverse traditions. If the work is done properly, readers should be able to see a synthesis or at least a common thread that ties together the different traditions and projects an image whose outline can be easily recognized, critically appraised, and remembered. If the work is done poorly, readers might see bits and pieces but be unable to make them into a whole. In this concluding chapter, I will take up the challenge of facing the question of the whole. I will do this by foregrounding some of the questions raised and some of the ones just implied throughout the previous chapters. I will not engage, however, in an attempt to summarize what I wrote in previous chapters. While looking back, I will try to give a sense of the future, a future that hopefully some of my readers will be involved in constructing.

10.1 Language as the human condition

The central question of any anthropological inquiry has always been: what makes us human? The answers to this question have been as varied as the many brands of anthropology proposed since the beginning of the discipline, which is usually traced back to Edward B. Taylor's *Primitive culture* (1871). One way of answering this question has been to look at the evolution of the human species; this is what biological anthropologists and paleoanthropologists do. Another way has been to look at the different ways in which humans change the environment, organize their lives, and represent them symbolically. This is what archaeologists and sociocultural anthropologists do. A third way has been to examine what it means to be a species that has developed such a sophisticated system of communication, usually referred to as "language." This is what linguistic anthropologists do. Or perhaps, I should say, this is what linguistic anthropologists are *expected* to do.

Our colleagues in the other subfields often expect linguistic anthropologists to provide them with answers about the origins of language and the role of language in human evolution. To those colleagues, this book might have been a disappointment. For instance, very little can be found in this book on language evolution. This is not due to a bias against any discourse of origins. Nor is this part of a rejection of the question "what makes us human?" Rather, it is part of a concerted effort to rethink an object of study, language, that has often been uncritically adopted by most of those so far engaged in the study of language evolution or in the study of cultural phenomena where language *must* have had a role. My aim has been to offer more than a deconstruction of the notion of "language." It represents an interdisciplinary effort to improve on the notions of linguistic communication currently used or implied in the social sciences and the humanities. The examination of different approaches and different "units of analysis" has two goals. One is an evaluation of the work done by the analysts themselves in producing objects of inquiry, including the cultural aspects of such a production. In this spirit, the emphasis on individual speech acts was presented as part of existing ideologies of person, human cognition, and society (chapter 7), whereas the work on conversation and participation was seen as originating from and inviting more dynamic and constructivist notions of authorship in communication (chapter 8). The other goal is to suggest how different perspectives of analysis can help us identify different aspects of that multifarious phenomenon we ordinarily call "language." In other words, the recognition of the fact that units of analysis – just like transcripts (see chapter 5) – are artifacts, should by no means be interpreted as implying that they are "invented" or that they have no predictable relationships with "the real world." They do have such relationships. In the following sections, I will try to direct the readers toward such relationships.

10.2 To have a language

To have a culture means to have communication and to have communication means to have access to a language. But does it mean "to have a language"? Perhaps we can start answering this question by thinking about some of the contradictions involved in the arguments over whether some individuals have a language.

When a child who enters a new school system is judged "not to have language" or "not to have *enough* language," a heavy ball is chained to his feet. A discipline like linguistic anthropology gives us some important tools for empirically assessing the foundations of such evaluations. We can actually empirically test such an assessment by asking such specific questions as: Is the child able to produce meaningful sequences of sounds? Does he recognize differences in meaning? Can he use language while engaged in different activities (e.g. playing, arguing, working with tools, telling a joke)? Does he know how to participate in conversation? What is the language variety that he is the most comfortable in? Once we engage in these evaluations with an open mind and a sound background in the study of linguistic practices as cultural phenomena, we might realize that children who are judged "not to have language," may have plenty of *it*. The question then comes down to an issue that has important practical, political, and moral consequences, namely, "what is language?" I cannot think of a better example than the issue of the language of deaf children. We know now that when deaf children are raised with sign language, they definitely "have a language" and, in fact, a very complex and rich one, although manifestly different from the language used by their hearing peers. But in the high days of "oralism," this was not a common assumption and deaf children were assumed to be "without a language" simply because they didn't have the language of the hearing majority. In most cases, in fact, they were forbidden from using the language that was the most natural for them – sign language – and forced to conform to a language that was unnatural for people who cannot easily hear sound distinctions – spoken language – (Lane 1984; Monaghan 1996; Padden and Humphries 1988; Sacks 1989).

Despite Labov's (1970) brilliant demonstration of the perfectly logical structure of non-standard English, similar conclusions are sometimes reached today by teachers and other school administrators who come in contact with children who speak a different linguistic variety or non-standard dialect and are used to different ways of speaking and behaving around adults.

It is in the context of such discussions that we realize how important it is to think of language broadly and to have a discipline that can speak to a variety of people who think of themselves as "language experts." We must be able to help these experts to assess the implications of different ways of speaking and different ways of being together, with or without words. This is not the same as saying that school authorities should leave their job to linguistic anthropologists or that differences should be ignored and all children should be seen as linguistically equal. Such conclusions would be as misleading and damaging as the theories that see middle-class patterns of interaction as the "right" or "rational" ones and everyone else's as deficient. Just like any form of universalism forgets the details out of which human life is built and ends up constructing a model of human existence that is, in the best cases, formally elegant but lifeless, any form of particularism, including extreme cultural relativism, risks denying the possibility of communion across races, ages, and genders. The contributions discussed in the previous chapters should be a good antidote for either one of such extreme positions. They should minimally force us to consider carefully certain generalizations while reminding us that the differences cannot be ignored, but must be compared, analyzed, reconsidered. If it is true, as structuralism taught us, that without differences there would be no meaning, it is also true that what counts as different today might be the norm tomorrow. If chaos and order are two parts of the same whole or two phases of the same cycle, as argued by eastern religions and modern physics, it should not matter too much whether we start from an assumption of diversity or one of universality. What counts is that we keep the other perspective in focus. Unfortunately, however, grammarians too often forget to remind themselves and others of the reasons for the study of language. The rules of language as a game of chess too often overshadow the rules of language as a game of life. The conventionality of linguistic systems and their arbitrary nature have often obfuscated their historicity, the experience that lives in them and through them. Even proper names, which used to be characterized as the most arbitrary type of linguistic sign, have been shown to have indexical relations to places, people, events, to be mini-narratives about the past or the future (Basso 1984; Rymes 1996). Having a language is like having access to a very large canvas and to hundreds or even thousands of colors. But the canvas and the colors come from the past. They are hand-me-downs. As we learn to use them, we find out that those around us have strong ideas about what can be drawn, in which proportions, in what combinations, and for what purposes. As any artist knows, there is an ethics of drawing and coloring as well as a market that will react some-times capriciously, but many times quite predictably to any individual attempts to place a mark in the history of representation or simply readjust the propor-tions of certain spaces at the margins. This is the way I understand Rossi-Landi's idea that language should be thought of as a market (see chapter 3). Just like art-works, our linguistic products are constantly evaluated, recycled or discarded. We as speakers are also approved, praised, followed or disapproved, scolded, avoided. Our professional fame might come in the number of speeches we give or the number of books we get to publish, but more commonly our standing in a community is measured through our everyday language use, in making a point, gaining a new friend, handling a criticism, comforting a lost soul. To have a lan-guage then means to be part of a community of people who engage in joint, com-mon activities through the use of a largely, but never completely, shared range of communicative resources. In this sense, having a language also means being part of a tradition, sharing a history, and hence access to a collective memory, full of stories, innuendoes, opinions, recipes, and other things that make us human. Not having a language or having only a very limited set of its resources means to be denied such access.

10.3 Public and private language

The communal, public, shared properties of language define another sense in which language can be seen as the human condition. Language as a shared prac-tice is one of the great dilemmas of social life. If, in order to express ourselves and communicate our thoughts to others, we need to have access to such a public resource as we know language to be, how can we ensure that we can still control it, bend it to our needs, that we as individuals are not crushed under the weight of the socially shared code? How can words born and used in other times, by other people, in different contexts, still be relevant, appropriate, and meaningful for us? To what extent are our words ever *really* ours?

This is of course a topic that has fascinated and puzzled generations of scholars. It is, after all, at the heart of the problem of linguistic relativity (see chapter 3). Recent work within cultural and linguistic anthropology suggests, however, that these questions may assume a concept of person that does not correspond to what social actors experience. On the plane of concrete, sociohistorically constituted social life, the choice between being yourself and joining in with the group is only theoretically, but not practically available. One can be oneself only over against the background of identities, expectations, and practices sustained by the presence and by the actions of others, linguistic activities included. This tension is part of what Myers (1986) characterizes as the contrast between distinctiveness and relatedness and Urban (1991) sees as the tension between difference and sameness, a tension often acted out in the South American ritual encounters he analyzes (see also Graham 1993, 1995). The issue of linguistic autonomy or creativity is then part of a more general set of questions: how can individuals struggle to maintain autonomy while being part of a group? (Duranti 1994b, 1997) How can we be individuals while paying homage to tradition? How can we be free in our choices while being moral? These dilemmas are clearly evident in societies like the Australian Aboriginal ones where individuals are working hard at exhibiting their political independence from the group. But they also play a role in so-called 'hierarchical' societies, where people are expected to renounce their individual prerogatives and wants in order to be identified as part of larger political bodies or as subjects of powerful leaders. Self and other are thus two sides of the same coin and language clearly plays an important part in the constitution and reproduction of this necessary and still little understood dichotomy.

The variation found in linguistic performance and linguistic knowledge is but an effect of the tension between private and public, inner and outer, same and different. Such tension is constantly reproduced in our private thoughts. Linguistic practices help to sustain it. But such a tension is possible above all because of the basic indeterminacy of any linguistic characterization and categorization. Although words and sentences do a good job at describing reality for most purposes, they can never exhaust it. Any description is a categorization and any categorization is too large and too narrow. While giving generality to a unique experience, any linguistic expression leaves out details and nuances which might have been crucial for someone else. These issues used to be confined to the work of semanticists and ethnoscientists. We are now placing them in the empirical realm of face-to-face encounters. By so doing, we are learning that categorizations are not only done by minimal lexical oppositions (big vs. small, consanguineal vs. affine, people vs. animals). They are also done through indexical relations (see chapter 6), the sequential organization of speaking (see chapter 8), and participation frameworks (see section 9.3). We have learned that there are infinite interactional sources of categorization. In one society a sibling might be someone who can finish up a sentence and a friend someone who knows who you are talking about before you mention any names; in another society a distinction might need to be made between a brother's brother and a brother's sister. Ways of speaking or ways of avoiding speech enter in such distinctions. Linguistic anthropologists have shown that categorizations and generalizations are not only found in academic writing or scientific discussions, they are present during the telling of stories by all kinds of people. This is the sense in which narrative accounts are not too different from detective stories, whether at the dinner table (Ochs, Smith, and Taylor 1989) or in a judiciary or political arena (Duranti 1994a: 175). Through the temporality of speaking, details are slowly revealed one at the time, giving different participants a chance – although by no means assuming the same authority or linguistic ability – to affect the construction of a story and the moral identities of its characters (Jacquemet 1994). As we saw in chapter 9, the organization of the telling favors certain types of sequences and certain types of solutions (e.g. in conflict situations). Furthermore, as we saw in chapter 6, grammatical framing is not only a typological feature that gives us the range of case markings possible in a given language; it is also a constitutive feature of a point of view, of presenting events and participants in particular ways. Transitivity in discourse is part of the construction of agency. An anthropological theory of language cannot but be attentive to the details of morphological markings and other grammatical devices because it is also through such devices that intentionality and responsibility are defined and assessed.

10.4 Language in culture

But any theory that presents language as an image-producing instrument risks assuming a separation between language and reality that linguistic anthropologists have long seen as problematic. To have a language is more than having at our disposal an infinite repository of metaphors through which we make sense of our experience. Language also entertains metonymic relations with our society and culture. As Harry Hoijer (1953) insisted, one should think of language *in* culture and not just of language *and* culture. The linguistic system interpenetrates all other systems within the culture. To expand this idea, we could say that language is in us as much as we are in language. By connecting people to their past, present and future, language *becomes* their past, present, and future. Language is not just a representation of an independently established world. Language is also that world. Not in the simplistic sense that all we have of our past is language but in the sense that our memories are inscribed in linguistic accounts, stories, anecdotes, and names just as much as they are contained in smells, sounds, and ways of holding our body. If language is action, as proposed by Malinowski, and the ways we speak provide us with ways of being in the world, as suggested by Sapir, Whorf, and many others, linguistic communication is part of the reality it is supposed to represent, interpret, and evoke. If a language is, in Wittgenstein's words, "a form of life," then to have a language not only means to have an instrument to represent events in particular ways, it also means to have the ability to interact with such events, affect them or be affected by them. Hence, for linguistic anthropologists the question of the nature of language cannot be separated from the question of the use of language by particular individuals at particular times. The study of language is inherently historical, that is, located in time and with time as one of its fundamental dimensions.

10.5 Language in society

"To say language is to say society," Lévi-Strauss once wrote. But what does this really mean? It means that it is through repetitive, recursively linked and yet not necessarily identical communicative acts that society is reconstituted. It means that government, workplaces, families and other institutions that make up societies rely on language to reproduce such institutions over time, across different territories, and despite the differences among the people who comprise them. It is inconceivable to think of any modern bureaucratic system without the specific ways of speaking, writing, and printing that guide people through its often forbidding principles and justify its existence. How could a bureaucracy exist without its language specialists, without its written forms or spoken questions through which individuals are catalogued and separated in groups, according to wealth, descent, race, and even dialect? Similarly, could we imagine a chiefdom (in Oceania, America, Africa, or any other part of the world) without the language that distinguishes a chief from the rest of the population, without honorific systems, without the mediation of those whose job is to represent the thoughts and wishes of the powerful? So much of social hierarchy is both represented by and instantiated through speech that the study of any social system would not be possible without an understanding of the language that supports and represents such a system. Even in those societies, misleadingly called "egalitarian," where individuals are said to only represent themselves and where no (male) adult can really force another to do, think, or say what the other does not want to do, think or say, language is what ultimately keeps the balance, reasserts the individual rights, and sanctions anyone who thinks and acts differently (Brenneis and Myers 1984). Even before a physical fight is started, there are usually words to be said, heard, interpreted or misinterpreted. Afterwards, of course, there is room for even more linguistic activity, with the narrative celebration or condemnation of the physical confrontation, where points of view can be compared and understanding negotiated (Brenneis 1988; A. Grimshaw 1990; Watson-Gegeo and White 1990).

Having a language does not only allow us to make sense of what we see and hear out there. It also allows us to look inside of our mind and soul to ask such questions as: Who are we? Where do we come from? Where are we going? Why are we here? Language is there for questions to be formulated and for answers to be proposed. To be engaged in the analysis of the language of everyday interaction means to believe, first of all, that these questions are not just restricted to the great rituals of our religious or political life and that their possible answers are not just reserved for the skilled language professionals, that is, the great poets, novelists, and orators. As Edmund Leach and other sociocultural anthropologists of the old school have taught us, a great deal of what humans do is concerned with the issue of continuity, that is, with the finitude of our lives, with the material and symbolic reproduction of our own individuality as well as our own sociability. Such a concern, sometimes turned into a ritual obsession, is pervasive of all kinds of everyday interactions just as the language of every person – as Paul Friedrich's (1986: 26) discussion of poetic indeterminacy reminds us – has moments of poetic salience, when the words used, the pace of their production, and the sound of their temporal unfolding have the richness and authoritative power of the poet's, the novelist's, or the great orator's. This is not to say that every speaker is by definition an artist, but he or she is certainly an author and authors have good days and bad days.

10.6 What kind of language?
In this book, I have tried to show that the concept of language emerging from the work of linguistic anthropologists over the last century has changed. From the view of language as a system of classification, a window on mental reality and hence an instrument for the study of culture as a system of knowledge, linguistic anthropologists have been moving toward a notion of language as an aggregate of features, tendencies, and acts that are sometimes the background and other times the foreground for the constitution of the social world in which we live. There is no question that such a theoretical turn has had its price. What used to be thought of as *outside of* language is now more and more often seen as *part of* language, constitutive of its organization and, hence, of its meaning. For some,

this has meant that we have amplified the phenomenon "language" to such an extent that it seems increasingly difficult to identify what is *not* language. If language becomes synonymous with social interaction, as I have often stated in the previous chapters, how can we still distinguish between words and actions and, ultimately, between words and objects? How can we specify the boundaries of our observations?

The answer is that it is not up to a discipline or its practitioners to set the limits of their inquiry. It is up to others to show linguistic anthropologists that they have left too much behind or that they have stepped into a territory they have no resources to explore. Language as the human condition is too interesting to let it slip away. Linguistic anthropologists must thus face the risk of an object of inquiry that keeps expanding – just like the universe languages and speakers struggle to control.

Appendix: Practical tips on recording interaction

A full-scale discussion of the many practical issues one encounters when recording human interaction would require an entire book. In this appendix, I will limit myself to a few practical tips that should allow students to avoid some commonly made mistakes and hopefully guarantee a minimum quality of recording. Students and fieldworkers who intend to become more knowledgeable in this area should consult other existing sources, especially Jackson (1987) and Goodwin (1993). I will start with a few tips on how to get ready for recording sessions, followed by tips on how to use a microphone, record on audio tapes, and record on video tapes.

1. Preparation for recording

Getting ready

The use of any type of recording equipment other than pencil and paper requires special attention to the preparatory conditions for recording. Machines need special care and must be routinely checked to ensure their best performance during recording. In addition, it is important to develop a set of steps to follow before, during, and after the recording session.

1. The day before recording, check all the equipment to make sure it works properly and make sure that the batteries are fully charged.
2. Develop a check list of all the things you must remember, including a list of the different pieces of equipment you need to take with you. After the recording session is over, you can use the same list to make sure that you take back the same pieces you brought to the site.
3. Whenever possible, bring with you extra tapes, batteries, and various pieces of equipment. If you arrive at the site and discover that, for some reason, your microphone needs a new battery or your camera is jammed, you want to be able to rely on back-up equipment.
4. If possible, check the site ahead of time and try to get some information on what the activity is going to be like.
5. Explain what you will be doing to the people who will be there and get permission to record. Find out how you can be present without being in people's way.
6. If you are working in a team, divide up the tasks ahead of time (for example,

one person could be in charge of sound recording and ethnographic notes, while another could be totally occupied with the video recording). If you work by yourself, try to understand from earlier experiences what you can handle at any given time and prepare accordingly (for instance, it might be the case that you cannot attend a tape recorder and a video camera at the same time and trying to do too much might affect the quality of your work).

Microphone tips
1. Whenever possible, use an external, unidirectional microphone, placed as close as possible to the participants – if you are forced to make a choice, as might be the case with a large group of people, place the mike close to (or directed toward) those participants whose speech and other audible actions (e.g. singing) are of particular interest to you.
2. If the participants are stationary (e.g. sitting around a table or on the floor of a room), duct tape the wire of the mike on the table, on the floor or dangle a mike from the ceiling. If participants are moving, sling the tape recorder over your shoulder and point the microphone in the direction of the people who are moving.
3. If the participants move around a lot, you might consider a wireless mike attached to the person whose talk is the most important for research purposes.
4. Always make sure that the microphone has a fresh or active battery before you start recording.
5. Always carry with you extra batteries and extra tapes.
6. Always bring with you earphones to listen while you are recording. This is the best way to ensure quality and to find out whether the microphone is still working!

Recording tips for audio equipment
1. Place fresh batteries in the recorder or make sure the extra ones are charged (if rechargeable).
2. After putting a tape into the tape recorder, plug the microphone into the "mic" jack input and plug a pair of earphones into the "phones" input, turn the tape recorder on and press "pause" and then "record" to test the quality of the sound.
3. Once you release the "pause" button and start recording, make sure that the tape is actually running.[1]
4. If possible, keep earphones on at all times to monitor the quality of recording.
5. Remember to take out batteries after finishing recording.
6. If possible, use stereo equipment.

---

[1] An alternative to steps 2 and 3 is to do a test run before starting to record.

Tapes (for audio and video recording)

1. Use good quality audio tapes, 60 or 90 minutes long (longer tapes tend to stick and can break more easily). For video equipment, if you can afford it, use the best quality video tapes available on the current market.
2. Label tapes before session with date, names of participants, place.
3. Sequentially number each tape to keep track of chronology and maintain a sense of how much you have been recording.
4. After you have finished recording, make copies of originals for listening and transcribing. If you used Hi-8 video equipment, you may want to use regular 8 mm tapes for work copies (they are cheaper) or even VHS format. If you have access to an editing deck with a keyboard for titles, create titles on the copies with information that will be useful later on to match the tape with fieldnotes (e.g. about the place and time of the recording, name of the camera person).
5. If working in a humid place or in a rainy climate, do your best to keep tapes in a dry and cool location. (Use silica gel or hot locker if necessary.)
6. Keep a record of the contents of each tape. The best way to do this is to create your own labels (see figure A1) and have a content log in a separate place (e.g. in a file in your computer) (see figure A2).

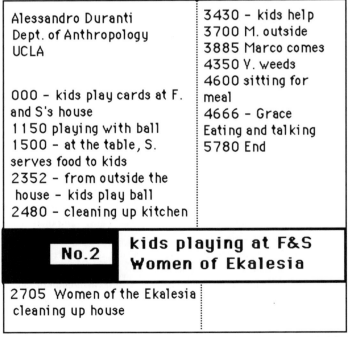

Figure A1 Video label produced with Hypercard (originally an audio label modified by Charles Goodwin)

342

Tapes can be coded by the number on the counter or by time. The former method, which is the only one available on certain recording machines becomes problematic when you change machine. Coding by time is the best method. On video tapes that have time code on them, the time on the screen is a constant (i.e. remains the same every time one plays the tape). If one uses the counter, however, there could be discrepancies across different viewings. The best method is to first transcribe and then go through the transcript adding time notation at regular intervals (e.g. every minute or every five minutes).

Time	CAM/Place	Action/talk
00	**parking lot**	woman pushing woman in wheel chair
00:15	**Pan to hall**	360 pan on empty tables and tables with chairs
00:50	**CUT**	
	Church	Sunday school classes are sent to their teachers
1:35	**inside hall**	students and teachers arriving
		Three teachers, K., J., and F., arrive
2:30		S. is asked by Teacher J. to say the prayer
	Zoom on S. praying	
	table with students	Teacher J. is talking
3:20		S. is asked to move up
3:50		What day is today?
		Teacher K. comes to the table and sits down while Teacher J. is talking
4:20		Everybody turns to page ... 51 ...
4:50		two other students come in (M., P.)
	CUT	
	other class in other corner	E's class (younger kids)
5:28	**Pan back to J. & K.**	girl is asked to read, while boy sitting in back seat gives money to Teacher F. for collection
6:36		"Next one ..." (each student is asked to read a passage)
		Teacher K. takes sheet from girl and reads it
7:20		Teacher J. threatens to hit student while saying "listen!"
		Teacher J. is reading.
		Teacher J. asks question and students raise hands
8:00	**PAN to younger group of students**	reading the *pi tautau* (alphabet table) Teacher T. holds up the poster with letters and pictures – N. is in the group
		Teacher T. reads alphabet (she reads "re" instead of "ro" and child corrects her),
		etc.

Figure A2 Log of video tape of a Sunday school lesson in the Samoan community in Los Angeles

When analyzing their data, researchers need to be able to retrieve as much information as possible, including overlapped talk, eye gaze movements, and other details of the interaction that might be relevant to what was said and done but are difficult to capture without excellent recording tools. For these reasons, when applying for financial support for research, fieldworkers need to stress the importance of obtaining the best equipment available. As is made apparent in the rest of this book, some of the most important points made about human interaction are based on the detailed transcription of face-to-face encounters where everything participants do is potentially relevant to the analysis. It is also important to clarify in any grant proposal the need for a specific type of equipment. Members of review panels might not be up to the latest technological innovations or might not share the same assumptions about the advantages of a particular type of equipment over another. Finally, in asking for funds, one should take into consideration and make clear whether or not some of the equipment needed is already available at one's institution.

2. Where and when to record

One should record as much as possible. After the initial purchase of the equipment, the cost of video tapes is relatively low (cost is a major factor for choosing video taping over filming). Don't save recording for special events. Start recording as soon as possible. Don't wait for the event to start. Especially during the first few weeks, a fieldworker has no idea of what is going to happen next. It is better to get extra footage of uninteresting interaction than to miss part of the beginning of an event. Beginnings – as many students of human interaction remind us – are always analytically interesting. By recording extensively at first, participants also get used to you recording. It becomes something that is part of your social persona. It is not something special for which a special demeanor is needed. At the same time, remember that, depending on the situation, a recording device, especially a camera, might be seen as intrusive. Be sensitive to people's reactions and expectations. Always explain what you are doing, why you are recording, and ask permission.

Once you have a better sense of what happens in the community you are studying, you should develop a recording schedule, which will take into consideration the best times of day for recording. In making such decisions, you will take into consideration the particular activity and the types of participants you are interested in. For those who study child language and socialization, for instance, it is important to find out when toddlers are awake and have an opportunity to interact with their parents or their older siblings (Schieffelin 1990: 25). Those who study ceremonial or oratorical language must keep up with village social life to be able to know in advance when public events will take place. One can never stress enough how important it is to get to the site of a performance ahead of time, to set up the equipment and be ready for the action (see Jordan 1993: 104–11).

3. Where to place the camera

The placement of the video camera is one of the most difficult decisions a fieldworker must make. If participants are stationary, for instance, at a table having dinner, one can use a tripod and leave the room. This will allow the participants to be a bit more natural and less concerned with how to deal with the researcher's presence. The only problem with this method is that if, for some reason, the participants move or something happens to the equipment (e.g. it gets knocked over or the batteries run out), the researcher will not be able to adjust the camera or fix the problem. For this reason it is advisable to stay close or come back regularly to check the camera and the situation. In some cases, the researcher might manage to be sitting or standing near the camera, scribbling down notes or reading and thus be less intrusive than he would be by standing behind the camera and constantly looking through the lens. In terms of choice of focal lens, one should always try to record using the widest possible angle (on a commercial 8mm video camera the smallest focal length is usually 12 or 11mm, but there are wide conversion lenses that can be added to shorten this length and thus increase the angle of view). Telephoto lenses are usually more difficult to use, create problems with focus, and leave out contextual information one will want to have while watching the tape later. Unless you really know what you are doing, *use the zoom only in a limited, calculated fashion*. The zoom should be used whenever you cannot get any closer and still need detailed information. For instance, you might want to occasionally zoom on people's faces if you want to make sure that they be identified later or if you are particularly interested in their facial expressions or reactions (e.g. to see what or whom they are looking at). You might also want to try to capture the shape of a tool, a tattoo on someone's body, or the writing on a piece of paper or a picture that is being talked about. In general, try to have as many participants as possible inside your frame without being too far away and move as little as possible. If participants move around a lot (this is the case with children inside a house or participants in certain kinds of outdoor public events), you might consider using two cameras, one on a tripod in one locale and one hand held. Hand-held camera requires training and lots of practice and students who feel the need or propensity for this type of recording should look for courses or workshops that will give them basic skills in documentary techniques. It is very important for students to learn to feel comfortable with the camera and have confidence in the quality of one's recording. The more one feels comfortable using a camera, the easier it is to fit into a situation and make others feel at ease. After more than twenty years of experimentation with different types of filming and recording techniques, I have found that most people quickly get used to having me around with a camera. I usually follow participants around using a wide-angle lens and staying very close to the action. In some of my video tapes participants seem so "natural" that many viewers think the event was set up and people are acting. Contrary to common belief, the trick is not to hide oneself or the camera or pretend that one is not there, but instead to be quite upfront about filming without being in people's way. Eventually, participants find a way of naturalizing the presence of the camera and concentrating on their own actions rather than on the researcher's (see figure A3).

Whenever possible, it is a good idea to view the first video recordings with colleagues to discuss the use of the camera and ways in which it could be improved or adapted to the specific goals of the project.

Figure A3 Children reciting the Samoan alphabet in a Sunday school class in Los Angeles (1993)

There is always a lot of talk about how the participants in a situation feel about being recorded. This is an appropriate preoccupation; at the same time, one must also consider how the researcher feels about being there and recording. It is important for the researcher to feel that what he is doing is legitimate and is not damaging or too intrusive. If there are reasons not to record, one should be willing to turn the camera off. One must always remember that the camera adds another eye, a potentially very public one, to the scene and that therefore its presence, like any other participant's presence, must be negotiated. In a sense, no one, including the researcher, can really know how a video recording might be used in the future. For this reason, a few basic principles should be kept in mind.

1. Consent forms should be signed by the participants ahead of time (usually universities have a special office or committee that provides assistance for writing consent forms and might need to approve them).

2. Situations might arise that were not foreseen in writing the grant proposal or preparing the consent form. Commonsense and respect for the privacy of others should guide researchers at all time. For instance, researchers should be ready to turn off the

camera when they feel that they have or they are about to overstep the boundaries of what might be appropriate to show to people outside of the situation at hand.

3. Fieldworkers should be aware of whether their recorded data will be made available for others to study. In principle, fieldworkers should try to maintain as much as possible control of the original tapes and their copies, but this might not be always possible. When data are going to be shared with other researchers, it is important to do everything possible to make sure that data will not be misinterpreted or used in inappropriate ways given the original conditions for recording (see 1 above). One must be particularly wary of proposals by colleagues or foundations to participate in the creation of large data banks. Although often well meaning and defined as central to the scientific nature of research on human interaction, these types of enterprises can become dangerous in the case of data that do not allow researchers to fully protect the identity of the participants in the interaction (when this was defined as one of the conditions for recording). Despite their rich texture, visual recordings are not immune from interpretations that might appear inappropriate to participants or the researchers who collected them. Unless detailed ethnographic notes and interpretive framings are provided, misinterpretation of visual material is just as likely as with any other kind of data of human behavior. Ultimately, one should not forget that the type of video recording or filming discussed here is part of the whole ethnographic process, with its experiential and moral aspects. Linguistic anthropologists are *not* hired film makers for foundations, corporations, or well-meaning but uninformed colleagues in other disciplines. They are first of all ethnographers who use visual documentation as an important part of *their* research agenda.

4. When researchers decide to show publicly footage of people engaged in their daily affairs, either inside someone's home or in more public arenas such as schools, hospitals, courts, theaters, and street corners, they must be aware of the responsibility that such a choice implies. One must think ahead about possible consequences of a public showing of the data.

REFERENCES

Abu-Lughod, Lila. 1986. *Veiled Sentiments*. Berkeley: University of California Press.

　1991. Writing Against Culture. In R. G. Fox (ed.), *Recapturing Anthropology* (pp. 137–62). Santa Fe, NM: School of American Research Press.

Agar, Michael H. 1980. *The Professional Stranger: An Informal Introduction to Ethnography*. New York: Academic Press.

Agha, Asif. 1994. Honorification. *Annual Review of Anthropology*, 23: 277–302.

Albó, Xavier. 1979. The Future of the Oppressed Languages in the Andes. In W. C. McCormack and S. A. Wurm (eds.), *Language and Society* (pp. 309–30). The Hague: Mouton.

Allwood, Jens, Lars-Gunnar Andersson and Östen Dahl. 1977. *Logic in Linguistics*. Cambridge University Press.

Andersen, Elaine S. 1990. *Speaking with Style: The Sociolinguistic Stem of Children*. London and New York: Routledge.

Anderson, Benedict. 1983. *Imagined Communities: Reflections on the Origin and Spread of Nationalism*. New York: Schocken.

　1991. *Imagined Communities: Reflections on the Origin and Spread of Nationalism. Revised Edition*. London and New York: Verso.

Anderson, Stephen R. 1985a. Inflectional Morphology. In T. Shopen (ed.), *Language Typology and Syntactic Description*, vol. 3: *Grammatical Categories and the Lexicon* (pp. 150–201). Cambridge University Press.

　1985b. *Phonology in the Twentieth Century: Theories of Rules and Theories of Representation*. University of Chicago Press.

Anderson, Stephen R. and Edward L. Keenan. 1985. Deixis. In T. Shopen (ed.), *Language Typology and Syntactic Description*, vol. 3: *Grammatical Categories and the Lexicon* (pp. 259–308). Cambridge University Press.

Andrews, Avery. 1985. The Major Functions of the Noun Phrase. In T. Shopen (ed.), *Language Typology and Syntactic Description*, vol. 1: *Clause Structure* (pp. 62–154). Cambridge University Press.

Apel, Karl-Otto. 1991. Is Intentionality More Basic than Linguistic Meaning? In E. Lepore and R. Van Gulick (eds.), *John Searle and His Critics* (pp. 31–55). Oxford: Blackwell.

Appadurai, Arjun. 1990. Topographies of the Self: Praise and Emotion in Hindu India.

In C. A. Lutz and L. Abu-Lughod (eds.), *Language and the Politics of Emotion* (pp. 92–112). Cambridge University Press.

1991. Global Ethnoscapes: Notes and Queries for a Transnational Anthropology. In R. G. Fox (ed.), *Recapturing Anthropology* (pp. 191–210). Santa Fe, NM: School of American Research Press.

Argyle, Michael. 1969. *Social Interaction*. London: Methuen.

Argyle, Michael and Mark Cook. 1976. *Gaze and Mutual Gaze*. Cambridge University Press.

Armstrong, David F., William C. Stokoe and Sherman E. Wilcox. 1994. Signs of the Origins of Syntax. *Current Anthropology*, 35(4), 349–68.

Aronoff, Mark. 1985. Orthography and Linguistic Theory. *Language*, 61: 28–72.

Atkinson, J. Maxwell and Paul Drew. 1979. *Order in Court: The Organisation of Verbal Interaction in Judicial Settings*. London: Macmillan.

Atkinson, J. Maxwell and John Heritage. 1984. *Structures of Social Action*. Cambridge University Press.

Atran, Scott. 1987. Origin of the Species and Genus Concepts: An Anthropological Perspective. *Journal of the History of Biology*, 20: 195–279.

1990. *Cognitive Foundations of Natural History: Towards an Anthropology of Science*. Cambridge University Press.

Atran, Scott and Dan Sperber. 1991. Learning Without Teaching: Its Place in Culture. In L. Landsman (ed.), *Culture, Schooling and Psychological Development*. Norwood, NJ: Ablex.

Au, K. H. 1980. Participation Structures in a Reading Lesson with Hawaiian Children: Analysis of a Culturally Appropriate Instruction Event. *Anthropology and Education Quarterly*, 11(2): 91–115.

Au, K. and J. Mason. 1981. Social Organizational Factors in Learning to Read: The Balance of Rights Hypothesis. *Reading Research Quarterly*, 17: 115–52.

Austin, J. L. 1961. *Philosophical Papers*. London: Oxford University Press.

1962. *How to Do Things with Words*. Oxford University Press.

1970. *Philosophical Papers*. 2nd edn. Oxford University Press.

Bach, Kent and Robert M. Harnish. 1979. *Linguistic Communication and Speech Acts*. Cambridge, MA: MIT Press.

Baker, Mark. 1996. *The Polysynthesis Parameter*. Oxford University Press.

Baker, Gordon P. and Peter M. S. Hacker. 1985. *Wittgenstein: Meaning and Understanding*. University of Chicago Press.

Bakhtin, Mikhail M. 1968. *Rabelais and His World*, trans. Hélène Iswolsky. Cambridge, MA: MIT Press.

1973. *Problems of Dostoevsky's Poetics*. Ann Arbor: Ardis.

1981a. *The Dialogic Imagination: Four Essays*, ed. M. Holquist, trans. C. Emerson and M. Holquist. Austin: University of Texas Press.

1981b. Discourse in the Novel. In M. Holquist (ed.), *The Dialogic Imagination: Four Essays* (pp. 259–422). Austin: University of Texas Press.

Bally, Ch. 1952. *Le Langage et la vie*, 3rd edn. Geneva: Droz.

References

Barthes, Roland. 1968. *Elements of Semiology*, trans. Annette, Lavers and Smith. New York: Hill & Wang.

Basso, Ellen B. 1985. *A Musical View of the Universe*. Philadelphia: University of Pennsylvania Press.

Basso, Keith. 1972. "To Give up on Words": Silence in Western Apache Culture. In P. P. Giglioli (ed.), *Language and Social Context* (pp. 67–86). Harmondsworth, Penguin Books.

    1984. "Stalking with Stories": Names, Places, and Moral Narratives among the Western Apache. In E. Bruner (ed.), *Text, Play and Story: The Construction and Reconstruction of Self and Society* (pp. 99–137). Washington, DC: American Anthropological Association.

Bateson, Gregory. 1958. *Naven*. 2nd edn. Stanford University Press.

    1972. *Steps To An Ecology Of Mind*. New York: Ballantine Books.

Bateson, Gregory and Margaret Mead. 1942. *Balinese Character: A Photographic Analysis* (Vol. II Special Publication). New York: New York Academy of Sciences.

Baudillard, Jean. 1975. *The Mirror of Production*. St. Louis: Telos.

Bauman, Richard. 1975. Verbal Art as Performance. *American Anthropologist*, 77: 290–311.

    1977. *Verbal Art as Performance*. Rowley, MA: Newbury House.

    1983. *Let Your Words Be Few: Symbolism of Speaking and Silence Among Seventeenth-Century Quakers*. Cambridge University Press.

    1986. *Story, Performance, and Event*. Cambridge University Press.

    1992a. Contextualization, Tradition and the Dialogue of Genres: Icelandic Legends of the *Kraftaskáld*. In A. Duranti and C. Goodwin (eds.), *Rethinking Context: Language as an Interactive Phenomenon* (pp. 125–45). Cambridge University Press.

    (ed.). 1992b. *Folklore, Cultural Performances, and Popular Entertainments*. New York: Oxford University Press.

Bauman, Richard and Charles L. Briggs. 1990. Poetics and Performance as Critical Perspectives on Language and Social Life. *Annual Review of Anthropology*, 19: 59–88.

    1992. Genre, Intertextuality, and Social Power. *Journal of Linguistic Anthropology*, 2(2): 131–172.

Bean, Susan S. 1978. *Symbolic and Pragmatic Semantics*. University of Chicago Press.

Beatty, John. 1994. Sound Symbolism and Japanese Monsters. *Journal of Linguistic Anthropology*, 4: 72–73.

Benveniste, Emile. 1956. La nature des pronoms. In M. Halle et al. (eds.), *For Roman Jakobson* (pp. 34–37). The Hague: Mouton. Reprinted in Benveniste 1971.

    1966. *Problèmes de linguistique générale*. Paris: Gallimard.

    1971. *Problems of General Linguistics*. University of Miami Press.

Berlin, Brent. 1975. Speculations on the Growth of Ethnobotanical Nomenclature. In B. G. Blount and M. Sanchez (eds.), *Sociocultural Dimensions of Language Change* (pp. 63–101). New York: Academic Press.

1992. *Ethnobiological Classification: Principles of Categorization of Plants and Animals in Traditional Societies*. Princeton University Press.

Berlin, Brent and Paul Kay. 1969. *Basic Color Terms: Their Universality and Evolution*. Berkeley: University of California Press.

Berliner, Paul F. 1994. *Thinking in Jazz: The Infinite Art of Improvisation*. Chicago University Press.

Besnier, Niko. 1989. Information Withholding as a Manipulative and Collusive Strategy in Nukulaelae Gossip. *Language in Society*, 18: 315–41.

1994. The Truth and Other Irrelevant Aspects of Nukulaelae Gossip. *Pacific Studies*, 17(3): 1–39.

Bhabha, Homi, K. 1994. *The Location of Culture*. London: Routledge.

Biber, Douglas and Edward Finegan (eds.). 1994. *Sociolinguistic Perspectives on Register*. New York: Oxford University Press.

Bilmes, Jack. 1988a. The Concept of Preference in Conversation Analysis. *Language in Society*, 17(2): 161–81.

1988b. Category and Rule in Conversation Analysis. *International Pragmatics Association Papers in Pragmatics*, 2: 25–59.

Birdwhistell, Ray L. 1970. *Kinesics and Context: Essays on Body Motion Communication*. Philadelphia: University of Philadelphia Press.

Bloch, Maurice. 1975. Introduction. In M. Bloch (ed.), *Political Language and Oratory in Traditional Society* (pp. 1–28). London: Academic Press.

1976. Review of R. Bauman and J. Sherzer (eds.), Explorations in the Ethnography of speaking. *Language in Society*, 5: 229–34.

1993. Domain-Specificity, Living Kinds and Symbolism. In P. Boyer (ed.), *Sign to Symbol, Symbol as Sign: Cognitive Aspects of a Social Process* (pp. 111–20). Cambridge University Press.

Bloomfield, Leonard. 1935. *Language*. London: Allen & Unwin.

Bloor, David. 1983. *Wittgenstein: A Social Theory of Knowledge*. New York: Columbia University Press.

Boas, Franz. 1911. Introduction. In F. Boas (ed.), *Handbook of American Indian Languages* (vol. BAE-B 40, part I,). Washington, DC: Smithsonian Institution.

1966. *Kwakiutl Ethnography*. ed. Helen Codere. University of Chicago Press.

n.d. *Introduction to the Handbook of American Indian Languages*. Washington, DC: Georgetown University Press.

Bogen, James. 1987. Finding an Audience. *Papers in Pragmatics*, 1(2): 35–65.

Bolinger, Dwight. 1950. Rime, Assonance, and Morpheme Analysis. *Word*, 6: 117–36.

Bourdieu, Pierre. 1977. *Outline of a Theory of Practice*, trans. Richard Nice. Cambridge University Press.

1982. *Ce que parler veut dire*. Paris: Fayard.

1985. *Distinction: A Social Critique of the Judgement of Taste*. Cambridge, MA: Harvard University Press.

1988. *The Political Ontology of Martin Heidegger*. Stanford University Press.

1990. *The Logic of Practice*, trans. Richard Nice. Stanford University Press.

351

References

Bourdieu, Pierre, Jean-Claude Passeron and Monique de Saint Martin. 1994. *Academic Discourse*. Stanford University Press.

Bourdieu, Pierre and Loïc J. D. Wacquant. 1992. *An Invitation to Reflexive Sociology*. University of Chicago Press.

Boyer, Pascal. 1990. *Tradition as Truth and Communication: A Cognitive Description of Traditional Discourse*. Cambridge University Press.

    1993a. Pseudo-Natural Kinds. In P. Boyer (ed.), *Sign to Symbol, Symbol as Sign: Cognitive Aspects of a Social Process* (pp. 121–41). Cambridge University Press.

    (ed.). 1993b. *Sign to Symbol, Symbol as Sign: Cognitive Aspects of a Social Process*. Cambridge University Press.

Bremmer, Jan and Herman Roodenburg (eds.). 1992. *A Cultural History of Gesture*. Ithaca, NY: Cornell University Press.

Brenneis, Donald. 1988. Language and Disputing. *Annual Review of Anthropology*, 17: 221–37.

Brenneis, Donald Lawrence and Fred R. Myers. 1984. *Dangerous Words: Language and Politics in the Pacific*. New York University Press.

Briggs, Charles L. 1986. *Learning How to Ask: A Sociolinguistic Appraisal of the Role of the Interview in Social Science Research*. Cambridge University Press.

    1988. *Competence in Performance: The Creativity of Tradition in Mexicano Verbal Art*. Philadelphia: University of Pennsylvania Press.

Brown, Gillian and George Yule. 1983. *Discourse Analysis*. Cambridge University Press.

Brown, Penelope. 1979. Language, Interaction, and Sex Roles in a Mayan Community: A Study of Politeness and the Position of Women. Unpublished Ph.D. dissertation, University of California at Berkeley.

    1980. How and Why Are Women More Polite: Some Evidence from a Mayan Community. In S. McConnell-Ginet, R. Borker and N. Furman (eds.), *Women and Language in Literature and Society* (pp. 111–49). New York: Praeger.

    1993. Gender, Politeness, and Confrontation in Tenejapa. In D. Tannen (ed.), *Gender and Conversational Interaction* (pp. 144–62). New York: Oxford University Press.

Brown, Penelope and Colin Fraser. 1979. Speech as a Marker of Situation. In K. Scherer and H. Giles (eds.), *Social Markers in Speech* (pp. 33–62). Cambridge University Press.

Brown, Penelope and Stephen Levinson. 1979. Social Structure, Groups, and Interaction. In K. Scherer and H. Giles (eds.), *Social Markers in Speech* (pp. 291–341). Cambridge University Press.

    1978. Universals of Language Usage: Politeness Phenomena. In E. N. Goody (ed.), *Questions and Politeness Strategies in Social Interaction* (pp. 56–3ll). Cambridge University Press.

    1987. *Politeness: Some Universals in Language Usage*. Cambridge: Cambridge University Press.

Brown, Roger and Albert Gilman. 1960. The Pronouns of Power and Solidarity. In T. A. Sebeok (ed.), *Style in Language* (pp. 253–76). Cambridge, MA: MIT Press.

Bühler, Karl. 1934. *Sprachtheorie. Die Darstellungsfunktion der Sprache*. Jena: Gustav Fischer.

1990. *Theory of Language: The Representational Function of Language*, trans. Donald Fraser Goodwin. Amsterdam/Philadelphia: John Benjamins.

Burke, Kenneth. 1945. *A Grammar of Motives*. Englewood Cliffs, NJ: Prentice-Hall.

Burks, Arthur W. 1948–49. Icon, Index and Symbol. *Philosophy and Phenomenological Research*, 9: 673–89.

Bynon, Theodora. 1977. *Historical Linguistics*. Cambridge University Press.

Calame-Griaule, Genevieve. 1965. *Ethnologie et langage: La parole chez les Dogon*. Paris: Gallimard.

Cardona, Giorgio Raimondo. 1973. La linguistica antropologica. *Parole e Metodi* (6): 255–80.

1976. *Introduzione all'etnolinguistica*. Bologna: Il Mulino.

1985. *La foresta di piume. Manuale di etnoscienza*. Rome–Bari: Laterza.

1990. *I linguaggi del sapere*. Rome–Bari: Laterza.

Carnap, Rudolf. 1942. *Introduction to Semantics*. Cambridge, MA: Harvard University Press.

Carroll, John B. 1956. Introduction. In J. B. Carroll (ed.), *Language, Thought, and Reality: Selected Writings of Benjamin Lee Whorf* (pp. 1–34). Cambridge, MA: MIT Press.

Cassirer, Ernst. 1955. *The Philosophy of Symbolic Forms*, vol. 1: *Language*. New Haven: Yale University Press.

1979. Language and Art II. In D. P. Verene (ed.), *Symbol, Myth, and Culture* (pp. 166–95). New Haven: Yale University Press.

Caton, Steven C. 1990. *"Peaks of Yemen I summon": Poetry as Cultural Practice in a North Yemeni Tribe*. Berkeley: University of California Press.

Chafe, Wallace. 1970. *Meaning and the Structure of Language*. University of Chicago Press.

1976. Givenness, Contrastiveness, Definiteness, Subjects, Topics, and Points of View. In C. N. Li (ed.), *Subject and Topic* (pp. 25–56). New York: Academic Press.

(ed.). 1980. *The Pear Stories: Cognitive, Cultural, and Linguistic Aspects of Narrative Production*, vol. 3. Norwood, NJ: Ablex.

1987. Cognitive Constraints on Information Flow. In R. S. Tomlin (ed.), *Coherence and Grounding in Discourse*. Amsterdam: Benjamins.

Chierchia, Gennaro and Sally McConnell-Ginet. 1990. *Meaning and Grammar: An Introduction to Semantics*. Cambridge, MA: MIT Press.

Chomsky, Noam. 1957. *Syntactic Structures*. The Hague: Mouton.

1959. Review of Verbal Behavior by B.F. Skinner. *Language*, 35: 26–58.

1965. *Aspects of the Theory of Syntax*. Cambridge, MA: MIT Press.

1966. *Cartesian Linguistics*. New York: Harper & Row.

1968. *Language and Mind*. New York: Harcourt Brace Jovanovich.

1986. *Knowledge of Language: Its Nature, Origin and Use*. New York: Praeger.

Chomsky, Noam, Morris Halle and Fred Lukoff. 1956. On Accent and Juncture in

English. In M. Halle, H. Lunt and H. MacLean (eds.), *For Roman Jakobson*. The Hague: Mouton.

Cicourel, Aaron. 1972. Basic and Nonbasic Rules in the Negotiation of Status and Role. In H. P. Dreitzel (ed.), *Recent Sociology, no. 2: Patterns of Communicative Behavior* (pp. 4–45). New York: Macmillan.

1973. *Cognitive Sociology*. Harmondsworth: Penguin.

1992. The Interpenetration of Communicative Contexts: Examples from Medical Encounters. In A. Duranti and C. Goodwin (eds.), *Rethinking Context: Language as an Interactive Phenomenon* (pp. 291–310). Cambridge University Press.

Clark, Katerina and Michael Holquist. 1984. *Mikhail Bakhtin*. Cambridge, MA: Harvard University Press.

Clifford, James. 1986. Introduction: Partial Truths. In J. Clifford and G. F. Marcus (eds.), *Writing Culture: The Poetics and Politics of Ethnography* (pp. 1–26). Berkeley: University of California Press.

Clifford, James and George E. Marcus. 1986. *Writing Culture: The Poetics and Politics of Ethnography*. Berkeley: University of California Press.

Cole, Michael and Peg Griffin. 1986. A Sociohistorical Approach to Remediation. In S. De Castell, A. Luke and K. Egan (eds.), *Literacy, Society, and Schooling* (pp. 110–31). Cambridge University Press.

Cole, Peter and Jerry L. Morgan (eds.). 1975. *Syntax and Semantics*, vol. 3: *Speech Acts*. New York: Academic Press.

Comaroff, John. 1975. Talking Politics: Oratory and Authority in a Tswana Chiefdom. In M. Bloch (ed.), *Political Language and Oratory in Traditional Society* (pp. 141–83). London: Academic Press.

Comrie, Bernard. 1978. Ergativity. In W. P. Lehmann (ed.), *Syntactic Typology*. Austin: University of Texas Press.

Conklin, Harold C. 1962. Lexicographical Treatment of Folk Taxonomies. In F. W. Household and S. Saporta (eds.), *Problems in Lexicography*. Bloomington: Indiana University Research Center in Anthropology, Folklore, and Linguistics.

1969. Lexicographical Treatment of Folk Taxonomies. In S. A. Tyler (ed.), *Cognitive Anthropology* (pp. 41–59). New York: Holt, Rinehart, & Winston.

Connor, Linda, Patsy Asch and Timothy Asch. 1986. *Jero Tapakan: Balinese Healer. An Ethnographic Film Monograph*. Cambridge University Press.

Cook, Haruko Minegishi. 1987. Social Meanings of the Japanese Sentence-Final Particle No. *Papers in Pragmatics*, 1(2): 123–68.

Cook-Gumperz, Jenny. 1986. *The Social Construction of Literacy*. Cambridge University Press.

Corder, S. Pit. 1973. *Introducing Applied Linguistics*. Harmondsworth: Penguin.

Coulthard, Malcom. 1977. *An Introduction to Discourse Analysis*. London: Longman.

Couper-Kuhlen, Elizabeth and Margret Selting (eds.) 1996. *Prosody in Conversation: Interactional Studies*. Cambridge University Press.

Crago, Martha Borgmann. 1988. Cultural Context in Communicative Interaction of Inuit Children. Unpublished Ph.D. dissertation, McGill University, Montreal.

Craig, Colette Grinevald. 1979. Jacaltec: Field Work in Guatemala. In T. Shopen (ed.), *Languages and Their Speakers* (pp. 3–57). Cambridge, MA: Winthrop.

Croft, William. 1990. *Typology and Universals*. Cambridge University Press.

Cruttenden, Alan. 1986. *Intonation*. Cambridge University Press.

Crystal, David. 1987. *The Cambridge Encyclopedia of Language*. Cambridge University Press.

Crystal, David and Derek Davy. 1969. *Investigating English Style*. Bloomington: Indiana University Press.

D'Andrade, Roy and Claudia Strauss (eds.). 1992. *Human Motives and Cultural Models*. Cambridge University Press.

Daniloff, R. and R. Hammarberg. 1973. On Defining Coarticulation. *Journal of Phonetics*, 1: 239–48.

Darnell, Regna. 1990. *Edward Sapir: Linguist, Anthropologist, Humanist*. Berkeley: University of California Press.

Darwin, Charles. 1965. *The Expression of the Emotions in Man and Animals*. University of Chicago Press.

De Martino, Ernesto. 1961. *La Terra del Rimorso*. Milan: Il Saggiatore.

De Mauro, Tullio. 1976. *Storia linguistica dell'Italia unita*, vol. 1. Bari: Laterza.

De Mulder, Walter. 1993. Intentionality and Meaning: A Reaction to Leilich's "Intentionality, Speech Acts and Communicative Action". *Pragmatics*, 3(2): 171–80.

DeLancey, Scott. 1981. An Interpretation of Split Ergativity and Related Patterns. *Language*, 57(3): 626–57.

Demuth, Katherine A. 1983. *Aspects of Sesotho Language Acquisition*. Unpublished Ph.D., Indiana University.

Dennett, Daniel. 1987. *The Intentional Stance*. Cambridge, MA: MIT Press.

Dilthey, Wilhelm. 1988. *Introduction to the Human Sciences*, trans. Betanzos, Ramon J. Detroit: Wayne State University Press.

Dixon, R. M. W. 1972. *The Dyirbal Language of North Queensland*. Cambridge University Press.

  1979. Ergativity. *Language, 55*, 59–138.

  1980. *The Languages of Australia*. Cambridge University Press.

  1988. *A Grammar of Boumaa Fijian*. University of Chicago Press.

  1994. *Ergativity*. Cambridge University Press.

Doke, Clement M. 1935. *Bantu Linguistic Terminology*. New York: Longmans, Green & Co.

Dolgin, Janet L., David S. Kemnitzer and David M. Schneider. 1977. *Symbolic Anthropology: A Reader in the Study of Symbols and Meanings*. New York: Columbia University Press.

Dorian, Nancy C. 1982. Defining the Speech Community to Include Its Working Margins. In S. Romaine (ed.), *Sociolinguistic Variation in Speech Communities* (pp. 25–33). London: Arnold.

  1993. A Response to Ladefoged's Other View of Endangered Languages. *Language, 69*(3): 575–9.

355

References

Dougherty, Janet W. D. 1985. *Directions in Cognitive Anthropology.* Urbana: University of Illinois Press.

Dowty, David. 1982. Grammatical Relations and Montague Grammar. In P. Jacobson and G. K. Pullum (eds.), *The Nature of Syntactic Representation* (pp. 79–130). Dordrecht: D. Reidel.

Drew, Paul and John Heritage (eds.). 1992. *Talk at Work.* Cambridge University Press.

Dreyfus, Hubert L. 1991. *Being-in-the-World: A Commentary on Heidegger's "Being and Time," Division I.* Cambridge, MA: MIT Press.

Du Bois, Jack. 1986. Self-Evidence and Ritual Speech. In W. Chafe and J. Nichols (eds.), *Evidentiality: The Linguistic Coding of Epistemology* (pp. 313–36). Norwood, NJ: Ablex.

Du Bois, John. 1987. The Discourse Basis of Ergativity. *Language,* 63: 805–55

    1993. Meaning without intention: Lessons from divination. In J. Hill and J. Irvine (eds.), *Responsibility and Evidence in Oral Discourse* (pp. 48–71). Cambridge University Press.

Dummett, Michael. 1973. *Frege: Philosophy of Language.* London: Duckworth.

Duranti, Alessandro. 1981. *The Samoan Fono: A Sociolinguistic Study.* Pacific Linguistics Monographs, Series B, vol. 80. Canberra: Australian National University, Department of Linguistics.

    1984a. Lauga and Talanoaga: Two Speech Genres in a Samoan Political Event. In D. L. Brenneis and F. R. Myers (eds.), *Dangerous Words: Language and Politics in the Pacific* (pp. 217–37). New York University Press.

    1984b. The Social Meaning of Subject Pronouns in Italian Conversation. *Text,* 4(4): 277–311.

    1985. Sociocultural Dimensions of Discourse. In T. A. V. Dijk (ed.), *Handbook of Discourse Analysis,* vol. 1: *Disciplines of Discourse* (pp. 193–230). New York: Academic Press.

    1988a. The Ethnography of Speaking: Toward a Linguistics of the Praxis. In F. Newmeyer (ed.), *Linguistics: The Cambridge Survey,* vol. 4: *Language: The Socio-Cultural Context* (pp. 210–28). Cambridge University Press.

    1988b. Intentions, Language and Social Action in a Samoan Context. *Journal of Pragmatics,* 12: 13–33.

    1990. Code Switching and Conflict Management in Samoan Multiparty Interaction. *Pacific Studies,* 14(1): 1–30.

    1991. Four Properties of Speech-in-Interaction and the Notion of Translocutionary Act. In J. Verschueren (ed.), *Pragmatics at Issue: Selected Papers of the 1987 International Pragmatics Conference, Antwerp, August 17–22, 1987* (pp. 133–50). Amsterdam: Benjamins.

    1992. Language and Bodies in Social Space: Samoan Ceremonial Greetings. *American Anthropologist,* 94: 657–91.

    1993a. Intentionality and Truth: An Ethnographic Critique. *Cultural Anthropology,* 8: 214–45.

    1993b. Intentions, Self, and Responsibility: An Essay in Samoan Ethnopragmatics. In

J. H. Hill and J. T. Irvine (eds.), *Responsibility and Evidence in Oral Discourse* (pp. 24–47). Cambridge University Press.

1994a. *From Grammar to Politics: Linguistic Anthropology in a Western Samoan Village*. Berkeley and Los Angeles: University of California Press.

1994b. Uguali ma non troppo. Identità collettive parzialmente coincidenti. *Rassegna di Psicologia*, 11: 41–60.

1996. Mediated Encounters with Pacific Cultures: Three Samoan Dinners. In P. Reill and D. Miller (eds.), *Visions of Empire: Voyages, Botany, and the Representation of Nature* (pp. 326–34). Cambridge University Press.

1997. Polyphonic Discourse: Overlapping in Samoan Ceremonial Greetings. *Text*.

Duranti, Alessandro and Donald Brenneis. 1986. The Audience as Co-Author. Special issue of *Text* (6–3): 239–347.

Duranti, Alessandro and Ernest Byarushengo. 1977. On the Notion of "Direct Object." In E. Byarushengo, A. Duranti and L. Hyman (eds.), *Haya Grammatical Structure* (pp. 54–71). Los Angeles: University of Southern California, Department of Linguistics.

Duranti, Alessandro and Elinor Ochs. 1986. Literacy Instruction in a Samoan Village. In B. B. Schieffelin and P. Gilmore (eds.), *Acquisition of Literacy: Ethnographic Perspectives* (pp. 213–32). Norwood, NJ: Ablex.

1990. Genitive Constructions and Agency in Samoan Discourse. *Studies in Language*, 14(1): 1–23.

Durie, Mark. 1987. Grammatical Relations in Acehnese. *Studies in Language*, 11(2): 365–99.

Durie, Mark. 1988. Preferred Argument Structure in an Active Language. *Lingua*, 74: 1–25.

Eckert, Penelope and Sally McConnell-Ginet. 1992. Communities of Practice: Where Language, Gender, and Power All Live. In K. Hall, M. Bucholtz and B. Moonwomon (eds.), *Locating Power. Proceedings of the Second Berkeley Women and Language Conference* (vol. 1, pp. 89–99). Berkeley: Berkeley Women and Language Group.

Eco, Umberto. 1976. *A Theory of Semiotics*. Bloomington: Indiana University Press.

Edwards, Jane A. and Martin D Lampert (eds.). 1993. *Talking Data: Transcription and Coding in Discourse Research*. Hillsdale, NJ: Lawrence Erlbaum.

Eibl-Eibesfeldt, Irenäus. 1968. Zur Ethologie des menschlichen Grussverhaltens: Beobachtungen an Balinese, Papus und Samoanern, nebst vergleichenden Bemerkungen. *Zeitschrift für Tierpsychologie*, 25: 727–44.

1970. *Ethology: The Biology of Behavior*. New York: Holt, Rinehart, & Winston.

1974. Similarities and Differences Between Cultures in Expressive Movements. In S. Weitz (ed.), *Nonverbal Communication* (pp. 20–33). New York: Oxford University Press.

Ekman, Paul (ed.). 1982. *Emotion in the Human Face*. 2nd edn. Cambridge University Press.

Ekman, Paul and Wallace V. Friesen. 1969. The Repertoire of Nonverbal Behavior: Categories, Origins, Usage, and Coding. *Semiotica*, 1: 49–98.

References

Ervin-Tripp, Susan. 1972. On Sociolinguistic Rules: Alternation and Co-occurrence. In J. J. Gumperz and D. Hymes (eds.), *Directions in Sociolinguistics: The Ethnography of Communication* (pp. 213–50). New York: Holt.

1973. The Structure of Communicative Choice. In A. S. Dil (ed.), *Language Acquisition and Communicative Choice: Essays by Susan Ervin-Tripp* (pp. 302–73). Stanford University Press.

Ervin-Tripp, Susan M. and Claudia Mitchell-Kernan. 1977. *Child Discourse*. New York: Academic Press.

Eschbach, Achim. 1990. Karl Bühler: Sematologist. In K. Bühler (ed.), *Theory of Language* (pp. xiii–xliii). Amsterdam/Philadelphia: John Benjamins.

Fabian, Johannes. 1983. *Time and the Other: How Anthropology Makes Its Object*. New York: Columbia University Press.

Farnell, Brenda. 1995. *Do You See What I Mean?: Plains Indian Sign Talk and the Embodiment of Action*. Austin: University of Texas Press.

Feld, Steven. 1982. *Sound and Sentiment: Birds, Weeping, Poetics, and Song in Kaluli Expression*. Philadelphia: University of Pennsylvania Press.

Ferguson, Charles. 1982. Simplified Registers and Linguistic Theory. In L. Obler and L. Menn (eds.), *Exceptional Language and Linguistics*. New York: Academic Press.

Fillmore, Charles J. 1966. Deictic Categories in the Semantics of Come. *Foundations of Language*, 2: 219–27.

1968. The Case for Case. In E. Bach and E. T. Harms (eds.), *Universals of Linguistic Theory* (pp. 1–88). New York: Holt.

1977a. The Case for Case Reopened. In P. Cole and J. M. Sadock (ed.), *Syntax and Semantics, Vol. 8: Grammatical Relations* (pp. 59–81). New York: Academic Press.

1977b. Topics in Lexical Semantics. In R. Cole (ed.), *Current Issues in Linguistic Theory* (pp. 76–138). Bloomington: University of Indiana Press.

1996. The Pragmatics of Constructions. In D. I. Slobin, J. Gerhardt, A. Kyratzis and J. Guo (eds.), *Social Interaction, Social Context, and Language: Essays in Honor of Susan Ervin-Tripp* (pp. 53–69). Mahwah, NJ: Lawrence Erlbaum.

Fillmore, Charles J., Paul Kay and Mary Catherine O'Connor. 1988. Regularity and Idiomaticity in Grammatical Constructions: The Case of Let Alone. *Language*, 64: 501–38.

Finegan, Edward. 1980. *Attitudes Toward English Usage: The History of A War of Words*. New York: Teachers College Press.

Finegan, Edward and Niko Besnier. 1990. *Language: Its Structure and Use*. New York: Harcourt.

Firth, Raymond. 1965. *Primitive Polynesian Economy*. New York: Norton.

1972. Verbal and Bodily Rituals of Greeting and Parting. In J. S. La Fontaine (ed.), *The Interpretation of Ritual: Essays in Honour of A. I. Richards* (pp. 1–38). London: Tavistock.

Ford, Cecilia. 1993. *Grammar in Interaction: Adverbial Clauses in American English Conversations*. Cambridge University Press.

Foucault, Michel. 1973. *The Order of Things: An Archaeology of Human Sciences*. New York: Vintage Books.

1979. *Discipline and Punish: The Birth of the Prison*. New York: Random House.

1980a. *Power/Knowledge: Selected Interviews & Other Writings 1972–1977*, ed. and trans. Colin Gordon. New York: Pantheon.

1980b. Questions on Geography. In C. Gordon (ed.), *Power/Knowledge: Selected Interviews & Other Writings 1972–1977* (pp. 63–77). New York: Pantheon.

1988. *Technologies of the Self: A Seminar with Michel Foucault*. ed. L. H. Martin, H. Gutman, and P. H. Hutton. Amherst: University of Massachusetts Press.

Fowler, C. 1985. Current Perspectives on Language and Speech Production: A Critical Overview. In R. Daniloff (ed.), *Speech Science* (pp. 193–278). San Diego: College-Hill Press.

Fowley, William and Robert Van Valin. 1984. *Functional Syntax and Universal Grammar*. Cambridge University Press.

Fox, Richard (ed.). 1991. *Recapturing Anthropology: Working in the Present*. Santa Fe, Mexico: School of American Research Press.

Frake, Charles O. 1964. A Structural Description of Subanum "Religious Behavior." In W. Goodenough (ed.), *Explorations in Cultural Anthropology* (pp. 111–29). New York: McGraw-Hill.

1969. The Ethnographic Study of Cognitive Systems. In S. A. Tyler (ed.), *Cognitive Anthropology* (pp. 28–41). New York: Holt, Rinehart, & Winston.

1975. How to Enter a Yakan House. In M. Sanchez and B. G. Blount (eds.), *Sociocultural Dimensions of Language Use* (pp. 25–40). New York: Academic Press.

Frege, Gottlob. [1892] 1952. On Sense and Reference. In P. Geach and M. Black (eds.), *Translations from the Philosophical Writings of Gottlob Frege* (pp. 56–78). Oxford: Blackwell.

Friedrich, Paul. 1986. *The Language Parallax: Linguistic Relativism and Poetic Indeterminacy*. Austin: University of Texas Press.

Gadamer, Hans-Georg. 1976. *Philosophical Hermeneutics*, trans. David E. Linge. Berkeley: University of California Press.

1986. *Truth and Method*, trans. Joel Weinsheimer and Donald G. Marshall. 2nd edn. New York: Continuum.

Gal, Susan. 1989. Between Speech and Silence: The Problematics of Research on Language and Gender. *Papers in Pragmatics*, 3(1): 1–38.

1991. Between Speech and Silence: The Problematics of Research on Language and Gender. In M. di Leonardo (ed.), *Gender at the Crossroads of Knowledge: Feminist Anthropology in the Postmodern Era* (pp. 175–203). Berkeley: University of California Press.

Garfinkel, Harold. 1967. *Studies in Ethnomethodology*. Englewood Cliffs, NJ: Prentice-Hall.

1972. Remarks on Ethnomethodology. In J. J. Gumperz and D. Hymes (eds.), *Directions in Sociolinguistics: The Ethnography of Communication* (pp. 301–24). New York: Holt, Rinehart, & Winston.

359

References

Garrett, Andrew. 1990. The Origin of NP Split Ergativity. *Language,* 66(2): 261–96.

Garvey, Catherine. 1984. *Children's Talk.* Cambridge, MA: Harvard University Press.

Garvin, Paul L. and S. H. Riesenberg. 1952. Respect Behavior in Ponape. An Ethnolinguistic Study. *American Anthropologist,* 54: 201–20.

Geertz, Clifford. 1973. *The Interpretation of Cultures.* New York: Basic Books.

1983. *Local Knowledge: Further Essays in Interpretive Anthropology.* New York: Basic Books.

1988. *Works and Lives: The Anthropologist as Author.* Stanford University Press.

Giddens, Anthony. 1979. *Central Problems in Social Theory: Action, Structure and Contradiction in Social Analysis.* Berkeley: University of California Press.

1984. *The Constitution of Society: Outline of the Theory of Structuration.* Berkeley: University of California Press.

Givón, Talmy. 1976. Topic, Pronoun, and Grammatical Agreement. In C. N. Li (ed.), *Subject and Topic* (pp. 149–88). New York: Academic Press.

(ed.). 1979. *Syntax and Semantics,* vol. 12: *Discourse and Syntax.* New York: Academic Press.

Gleason, H. A. Jr. 1972. Genetic Relationship Among Languages. In A. R. Keiler (ed.), *A Reader in Historical and Comparative Linguistics* (pp. 3–15). New York: Holt.

Gluckman, Max. 1965. *The Ideas in Barotse Jurisprudence.* New Haven: Yale University Press.

1972. *The Allocation of Responsibility.* Manchester University Press.

Godard, Daniele. 1977. Same Setting, Different Norms: Phone Call Beginnings in France and the United States. *Language in Society,* 6: 209–19.

Goffman, Erving. 1961. *Asylums: Essays on the Social Situation of Mental Patients and Other Inmates.* Garden City, NY: Anchor Books, Doubleday.

1963. *Behavior in Public Places: Notes on the Social Organization of Gathering.* New York: Free Press.

1964. The Neglected Situation. In John J. Gumperz and Dell Hymes, (eds.), The Ethnography of Communication. *American Anthropologist,* 66, (6), part II: 133–36.

1972. *Relations in Public.* Harmondsworth: Penguin.

1974. *Frame Analysis: An Essay on the Organization of Experience.* New York: Harper and Row.

1976. Replies and Responses. *Language in Society,* 5: 257–313.

1979. Footing. *Semiotica,* 25: 1–29.

1981. *Forms of Talk.* Philadelphia: University of Pennsylvania Press.

Gold, Raymond. 1969. Roles in Sociological Field Observations. In G. J. McCall and J. L. Simmons (eds.), *Issues in Participant Observation.* Reading, MA: Addison-Wesley.

Goodenough, Ward H. 1956. Componential Analysis and the Study of Meaning. *Language,* 32: 195–216.

1964. Cultural Anthropology and Linguistics. In D. Hymes (ed.), *Language in Culture and Society: a Reader in Linguistics and Anthropology* (pp. 36–9). New York: Harper & Row.

Goodwin, Charles. 1979. The Interactive Construction of a Sentence in Natural Con-

versation. In G. Psathas (ed.), *Everyday Language: Studies in Ethnomethodology* (pp. 97–121). New York: Irvington Publishers.

1981. *Conversational Organization: Interaction Between Speakers and Hearers*. New York: Academic Press.

1984. Notes on Story Structure and the Organization of Participation. In M. Atkinson and J. Heritage (eds.), *Structures of Social Action* (pp. 225–46). Cambridge University Press.

1987. Forgetfulness as an Interactive Resource. *Social Psychology Quarterly*, 50 (2): 115–30.

1993. Recording Human Interaction in Natural Settings. *Pragmatics*, 3 (2): 181–209.

1994. Professional Vision. *American Anthropologist*, 96(3): 606–33.

1996. Transparent Vision. In E. Ochs, E. Schegloff and S. A. Thompson (eds.), *Interaction and Grammar* (pp. 370–404). Cambridge University Press.

Goodwin, Charles and Alessandro Duranti. 1992. Rethinking Context: An Introduction. In A. Duranti and C. Goodwin (eds.), *Rethinking Context: Language as an Inter-active Phenomenon* (pp. 1–42). Cambridge University Press.

Goodwin, Charles and Marjorie Harness Goodwin. 1992a. Assessments and the Con-struction of Context. In A. Duranti and C. Goodwin (eds.), *Rethinking Context: Language as an Interactive Phenomenon* (pp. 147–89). Cambridge University Press.

1992b. Context, Activity and Participation. In P. Auer and A. d. Luzio (eds.), *The Contextualization of Language* (vol. 22, pp. 77–99). Amsterdam: Benjamins.

1996. Seeing as a Situated Activity: Formulating Planes. In Y. Engestrom and D. Middleton (eds.), *Cognition and Communication at Work* (pp. 61–95). Cambridge University Press.

Goodwin, Charles and John Heritage. 1990. Conversation Analysis. *Annual Reviews of Anthropology*, 19: 283–307.

Goodwin, Marjorie Harness. 1990. *He-Said-She-Said: Talk as Social Organization among Black Children*. Bloomington: Indiana University Press.

In press. By-Play: Negotiating Evaluation in Story-telling. In G. R. Guy, J. Baugh, D. Schiffrin and C. Feagin (eds.), *Towards a Social Science of Language: Papers in Honor of William Labov* (pp. 77–102). Philadelphia: John Benjamins.

Goody, Esther. 1972. "Greeting," "begging," and the Presentation of Respect. In J. S. La Fontaine (ed.), *The Interpretation of Ritual* (pp. 39–71). London: Tavistock.

Gordon, David and George Lakoff. 1975. Conversational Postulates. In P. Cole and J. Morgan (eds.), *Syntax and Semantics*, vol. 3: *Speech Acts* (pp. 83–106). New York: Academic Press.

Gossen, Gary H. 1974. *Chamulas in the World of the Sun: Time and Space in a Maya Oral Tradition*. Cambridge, MA: Harvard University Press.

Gouffé, C. 1966. Noms d'objets "ronds" en haussa. *Comptes rendus du Groupe Linguistique d'Etudes Chamito-Sémitiques*, 10: 104–13.

Graf, Fritz. 1992. Gestures and Conventions: The Gestures of Roman Actors and Orators. In J. Bremmer and H. Roodenburg (eds.), *A Cultural History of Gesture* (pp. 36–58). Ithaca, NY: Cornell University Press.

References

Graham, Laura. 1993. A Public Sphere in Amazonia? The Depersonalized Collaborative Construction of Discourse in Xavante. *American Ethnologist*, 20: 717–41.

1995. *Performing Dreams: Discourses of Immortality Among the Xavante of Central Brazil*. Austin: University of Texas Press.

Greenberg, Joseph H. (ed.). 1963. *Universals of Language*. 2nd edn. Cambridge, MA: MIT Press.

Greenberg, Joseph H., Charles A. Ferguson and Edith A. Moravcsik (eds.). 1978. *Universals of Human Language*, 4 vol. Stanford University Press.

Grice, H. P. 1971. Meaning. In J. F. Rosenberg and C. Travis (eds.), *Readings in the Philosophy of Language* (pp. 436–44). Englewood Cliffs, NJ: Prentice-Hall.

1975. Logic and Conversation. In P. Cole and N. L. Morgan (eds.), *Syntax and Semantics*, vol. 3: *Speech Acts* (pp. 41–58). New York: Academic Press.

Grimshaw, Allen (ed.). 1990. *Conflict Talk*. Cambridge University Press.

Grimshaw, Jane. 1990. *Argument Structure*. Cambridge, MA: MIT Press.

Gruber, Jeffrey S. 1965. Studies in Lexical Relations. Unpublished Ph.D. dissertation. Reproduced by the Indiana University Linguistic Club, Bloomington, MIT.

Gumperz, John J. 1964. Linguistic and Social Interaction in Two Communities. *American Anthropologist*, 66(6): 137–53.

1968. Types of Linguistic Communities. In J. A. Fishman (ed.), *Readings in the Sociology of Language* (pp. 460–72). The Hague: Mouton.

1972. Introduction. In J. J. Gumperz and D. Hymes (eds.), *Directions in Sociolinguistics: The Ethnography of Communication* (pp. 1–25). New York: Holt, Rinehart, & Winston.

1982a. *Discourse Strategies*. Cambridge University Press.

1982b. *Language and Social Identity*. Cambridge University Press.

1992. Contextualization and Understanding. In A. Duranti and C. Goodwin (eds.), *Rethinking Context: Language as an Interactive Phenomenon* (pp. 229–52). Cambridge University Press.

1996. The Linguistic and Cultural Relativity of Conversational Inference. In J. J. Gumperz and S. C. Levinson (eds.), *Rethinking Linguistic Relativity* (pp. 374–407). Cambridge University Press.

Gumperz, John J. and Dell Hymes (eds.). 1964. The Ethnography of Communication. *American Anthropologist*, 66, (6), part II.

1972. *Directions in Sociolinguistics: The Ethnography of Communication*. New York: Holt, Rinehart, & Winston.

Gumperz, John J. and Stephen Levinson. 1991. Rethinking Linguistic Relativity. *Current Anthropology*, 32: 613–23.

(eds.). 1996. *Rethinking Linguistic Relativity*. Cambridge University Press.

Haegeman, Liliane. 1994. *Introduction to Government and Binding Theory*. 2nd edn. Oxford: Blackwell.

Haiman, John. 1980. The Iconicity of Grammar. *Language*, 56: 515–40.

(ed.). 1985a. *Iconicity in Syntax*. Amsterdam: Benjamins.

1985b. *Natural Syntax: Iconicity and Erosion*. Cambridge University Press.

Hale, Kenneth. 1970. The Passive and Ergative in Language Change: The Australian Case. In S. Wurm and D. Laycock (eds.), *Pacific Linguistic Studies in Honour of Arthur Capell* (vol. 13, pp. 757–81). Canberra: Pacific Linguistics, Series C.

Hale, Ken, Michael Krauss, Lucille J. Watahomigie, et al. 1992. Endangered Languages. *Language*, 68(1): 1–62.

Hall, Edward T. 1959. *The Silent Language*. New York: Doubleday.
　1966. *The Hidden Dimension*. New York: Doubleday.

Hall, Kira and Mary Bucholtz (eds.). 1995. *Gender Articulated: Language and the Socially Constructed Self*. New York: Routledge.

Halliday, M. A. K. 1976. Anti-languages. *American Anthropologist*, 78(3): 570–84.

Hanks, William F. 1990. *Referential Practice: Language and Lived Space Among the Maya*. University of Chicago Press.
　1996. *Language and Communicative Practices*. Boulder, CO: Westview.

Haraway, Donna J. 1991. *Simians, Cyborgs, and Women: The Reinvention of Nature*. New York: Routledge.

Harding, Sandra. 1986. *The Science Question in Feminism*. Ithaca: Cornell University Press.

Harris, Marvin. 1976. History and Significance of the Emic/Etic Distinction. *Annual Review of Anthropology*, 5: 329–50.

Harvey, Penelope. 1991. Drunken Speech and the Construction of Meaning: Bilingual Competence in the Southern Peruvian Andes. *Language in Society*, 20: 1–36.
　1992. Bilingualism in the Peruvian Andes. In D. Cameron and et al. (eds.), *Researching Language: Issues of Power and Method* (pp. 65–89). London: Routledge.

Hatch, Elvin. 1973. *Theories of Man and Culture*. New York: Columbia University Press.

Haugen, Einar. 1980. How Should a Dialect be Written? In J. Göschel, P. Ivic' and K. Kehr (eds.), *Zeitschrift für Dialektologie und Linguistik* (vol. 26, pp. 273–82). Wiesbaden: Steiner.

Haviland, John B. 1979. Guugu Yimidhirr. In R. M. W. Dixon and B. J. Blake (eds.), *Handbook of Australian Languages* (pp. 27–180). Canberra: Australian National University Press.
　1986. "Con Buenos Chiles": Talk, Targets and Teasing in Zinacantan. *Text*, 6(3) (Special Issue on the Audience edited by A. Duranti and D. Brenneis): 249–82.
　1989. "Sure, Sure": Evidence and Affect. *Text*, 9(1): 27–68.
　1991. "That Was the Last Time I Seen Them, and No More": Voices Through Time in Australian Aboriginal Autobiography. *American Ethnologist*, 18(2): 331–61.
　1996. Projections, Transpositions, and Relativity. In J. J. Gumperz and S. C. Levinson (eds.), *Rethinking Linguistic Relativity* (pp. 271–323). Cambridge University Press.

Hawkins, John A. 1979. On Implicational and Distributional Universals of Word Order. *Language*, 55: 618–48.

Hays, Terence E. 1994. Sound Symbolism, Onomatopoeia, and New Guinea Frog Names. *Journal of Linguistic Anthropology*, 4(2): 153–74.

Heath, Christian. 1982. The Display of Recipiency: an Instance of Sequential Relationship Between Speech and Body Movement. *Semiotica*, 42.

References

1984. Talk and Recipiency: Sequential Organization in Speech and Body Movement. In M. Atkinson and J. Heritage (eds.), *Structures of Social Action* (pp. 247–66). Cambridge University Press.

Heath, Shirley Brice. 1983. *Ways with Words: Language, Life and Work in Communities and Classrooms*. Cambridge University Press.

Hegel, George W. F. 1967. *The Phenomenology of Mind*, trans. George Lichtheim. New York: Harper & Row.

Heidegger, Martin. 1962. *Being and Time*, trans. John Macquarrie and Edward Robinson. New York: Harper & Row.

1971. The Way to Language, *On the Way to Language* (pp. 111–36). New York: Harper & Row.

1977. Letter on Humanism. In D. F. Krell (ed.), *Martin Heidegger: Basic Writings* (pp. 193–242). New York: Harper & Row.

1985. *History of the Concept of Time. Prolegomena*, trans. Theodore Kisiel. Bloomington: Indiana University Press.

1988. *The Basic Problems of Phenomenology*. Rev. edn., trans., introduction and lexicon by Albert Hofstadter. Bloomington: Indiana University Press.

1992. *The Concept of Time*, trans. William McNeill. Oxford: Blackwell.

Heine, Bernd, Ulrike Claudi and Friederike Hünnemeyer. 1991. *Grammaticalization: A Conceptual Framework*. University of Chicago Press.

Heller, Monica S. 1982. Negotiation of Language Choice in Montreal. In J. J. Gumperz (ed.), *Language and Social Identity* (pp. 108–18). Cambridge University Press.

1995. Language Choice, Social Institutions, and Symbolic Domination. *Language in Society*, 24(3): 373–405.

Heritage, John. 1984. *Garfinkel and Ethnomethodology*. Cambridge: Polity Press.

1990/91. Intention, Meaning and Strategy: Observations on Constraints on Interaction Analysis. *Research on Language and Social Interaction*, 24: 311–32.

Heritage, John and David Greatbatch. 1991. On the Institutional Character of Institutional Talk: The Case of News Interviews. In D. Boden and D. H. Zimmerman (eds.), *Talk and Social Structure* (pp. 93–137). Berkeley: University of California Press.

Hill, Archibald. 1964. A Note on Primitive Languages. In D. Hymes (ed.), *Language in Culture and Society: A Reader in Linguistics and Anthropology* (pp. 86–9). New York: Harper & Row.

Hill, Jane. 1988a. Language, Culture, and Worldview. In F. J. Newmeyer (ed.), *Linguistics: The Cambridge Survey*, vol. 4: *Language: The Socio-Cultural Context*. Cambridge University Press.

1988b. Language, Genuine or Spurious? In P. Krosrkity (ed.), *The Ethnography of Communication: The Legacy of Sapir. Essays in Honor of Harry Hoijer 1984* (pp. 9–54). Los Angeles: UCLA Department of Anthropology.

Hill, Jane H. and Kenneth C. Hill. 1978. Honorific Usage in Modern Nahuatl of the Malinche Volcano Area. *Language*, 54 1: 123–55.

1986. *Speaking Mexicano: Dynamics of a Syncretic Language in Central Mexico*. Tucson: University of Arizona Press.

364

Hill, Jane H. and Judith T. Irvine (eds.). 1993. *Responsibility and Evidence in Oral Discourse*. Cambridge University Press.

Hill, Jane H. and Bruce Mannheim. 1992. Language and World View. *Annual Review of Anthropology*, 21: 381–406.

Hinde, Robert A. (ed.). 1972. *Non-Verbal Communication*. Cambridge University Press.

Hinton, Leanne, Johanna Nichols and John J. Ohala (eds.). 1994. *Sound Symbolism*. Cambridge University Press.

Hjelmslev, Louis. 1961. *Prolegomena to a Theory of Language. Revised Translation*, trans. Francis Whitfield. Madison: University of Wisconsin Press.

Hoijer, Harry. 1953. The Relation of Language to Culture. In A. L. Kroeber (ed.), *Anthropology Today* (pp. 554–73). University of Chicago Press.

   1961. Anthropological Linguistics. In C. Mohrmann, A. Sommerfelt and J. Whatmough (eds.), *Trends in European and American Linguistics 1930–1960* (pp. 110–25). Utrecht and Antwerp: Spectrum Publishers.

Hollan, Douglas. 1992. Cross-cultural Differences in the Self. *Journal of Anthropological Research*, 48(4): 283–300.

Holland, Dorothy and Naomi Quinn (eds.). 1987. *Cultural Models in Language and Thought*. Cambridge University Press.

Holm, John. 1988. *Pidgins and Creoles*, vol. 1: *Theory and Structure*. Cambridge University Press.

   1989. *Pidgins and Creoles*. vol. 2. *Reference Survey*. Cambridge University Press.

Hopper, Paul and Sandra A. Thompson. 1980. Transitivity in Grammar and Discourse. *Language*, 56: 251–99.

Hopper, Paul J. and Elizabeth Closs Traugott. 1993. *Grammaticalization*. Cambridge University Press.

Howe, James and Joel Sherzer. 1986. Friend Hairyfish and Friend Rattlesnake, or Keeping Anthropologists in Their Place. *Man*, 21: 680–96.

Hoy, David C. 1986. Must We Say What We Mean? The Grammatological Critique of Hermeneutics. In B. R. Wachterhauser (ed.), *Hermeneutics and Modern Philosophy* (pp. 397–415). Albany: SUNY Press.

Hudson, R. A. 1980. *Sociolinguistics*. Cambridge University Press.

Husserl, Edmund. 1931. *Ideas: General Introduction to Pure Phenomenology*. New York: Collier.

   1970. *Logical Investigations*, trans J. N. Findlay. New Jersey: Humanities Press.

Hutchins, Edwin. 1995. *Cognition in the Wild*. Cambridge, MA: MIT Press.

Hyman, Larry M. 1975. *Phonology: Theory and Analysis*. New York: Holt, Rinehart, & Winston.

Hymes, Dell. 1963. Objectives and Concepts of Linguistic Anthropology. In D. G. Mandelbaum, G. W. Lasker and E. M. Albert (eds.), *The Teaching of Anthropology* (pp. 275–302): American Anthropological Association. Memoir 94.

   1964a. General Introduction. In D. Hymes (ed.), *Language in Culture and Society: A Reader in Linguistics and Anthropology* (pp. xxi–xxxii). New York: Harper & Row.

   1964b. Introduction: Toward Ethnographies of Communication. In J. J. Gumperz and

D. Hymes (eds.), *The Ethnography of Communication* (pp. 1–34). Washington, DC: American Anthropologist (Special Issue).

(ed.). 1964c. *Language in Culture and Society*. New York: Harper & Row.

(ed.). 1971. *Pidginization and Creolization of Languages*. Cambridge University Press.

1972a. Models of the Interaction of Language and Social Life. In J. J. Gumperz and D. Hymes (eds.), *Directions in Sociolinguistics: The Ethnography of Communication* (pp. 35–71). New York: Holt, Rinehart, & Winston.

1972b. On Communicative Competence. In J. B. Pride and J. Holmes (eds.), *Sociolinguistics* (pp. 269–85). Harmondsworth: Penguin.

1974a. *Foundations in Sociolinguistics: An Ethnographic Approach*. Philadelphia: University of Pennsylvania Press.

1974b. Ways of Speaking. In R. Bauman and J. Sherzer (eds.), *Explorations in the Ethnography of Speaking* (pp. 433–51). Cambridge University Press.

1981. *"In Vain I Tried to Tell You": Essays in Native American Ethnopoetics*. Philadelphia: University of Pennsylvania Press.

Irvine, Judith. 1974. Strategies of Status Manipulation in Wolof Greeting. In R. Bauman and J. Sherzer (eds.), *Explorations in the Ethnography of Speaking* (pp. 167–91). Cambridge University Press.

1979. Formality and Informality in Communicative Events. *American Anthropologist*, 81: 773–90.

1989. When Talk Isn't Cheap: Language and Political Economy. *American Ethnologist*, 16(2): 248–67.

1995. The Family Romance of Colonial Linguistics: Gender and Family in Nineteenth-Century Representations of African Languages. *Pragmatics*, 5(2): 139–53.

Irvine, Judith and Susan Gal. In press. Language Ideology and Linguistic Differentiation. In P. Kroskrity (ed.), *Language Ideologies*. Santa Fe, NM: School of American Research Press.

Jackendoff, Ray. 1972. *Semantic Interpretation in Generative Grammar*. Cambridge, MA: MIT Press.

1987. The Status of Thematic Relations in Linguistic Theory. *Linguistic Inquiry*, 18: 369–411.

1990. *Semantic Structures*. Cambridge, MA: MIT Press.

Jackson, Bruce. 1987. *Fieldwork*. Urbana and Chicago: University of Illinois Press.

Jackson, Jean. 1974. Language Identity of the Colombian Vaupés Indians. In R. Bauman and J. Sherzer (eds.), *Explorations in the Ethnography of Speaking* (pp. 50–64). Cambridge University Press.

Jacquemet, Marco. 1994. T-offences and Metapragmatic Attacks: Strategies of Interactional Dominance. *Discourse and Society*, 5(3): 297–319.

Jakobson, Roman. 1932. Zur Struktur des russischen Verbums, *Charisteria Gvilelmo Mathesio ... oblata* (pp. 74–83). Prague: Cercle Linguistique.

1936. Beitrag zur allgemeinen Kasuslehre, Gesamtbedeutungen der russischen Kasus. *Travaux de Cercle Linguistique de Prague*, 6: 240–88.

1956. Two Aspects of Language and Two Types of Aphasic Disturbances. In R. Jakobson and M. Halle (eds.), *Fundamentals of Language* (pp. 53–82). The Hague: Mouton.

1960. Closing Statement: Linguistics and Poetics. In T. Sebeok (ed.), *Style in Language* (pp. 398–429). Cambridge, MA: MIT Press.

1968. Poetry of Grammar and Grammar of Poetry. *Lingua*, 21: 597–609.

1970. Shifters, Verbal Categories, and the Russian Verb, *Selected Writings*, vol. 2: *Word and Language* (pp. 130–47). The Hague: Mouton.

Jakobson, Roman, Gunnar Fante and Morris Halle. 1963. *Preliminaries to Speech Analysis*. Cambridge, MA: MIT Press.

Jakobson, Roman and Morris Halle. 1956. *Fundamentals of Language*. The Hague: Mouton.

James, Deborah and Sandra Clarke. 1993. Women, Men, and Interruptions: A Critical Review. In D. Tannen (ed.), *Gender and Conversational Interaction* (pp. 231–80). New York: Oxford University Press.

Jefferson, Gail. 1978. Sequential Aspects of Storytelling in Conversation. In J. Schenkein (ed.), *Studies in the Organization of Conversational Interaction* (pp. 219–48). New York: Academic Press.

Jelinek, Eloise. 1993. Ergative "Splits" and Argument Type. In J. Bobaljik and C. Phillips (eds.), *MIT Working Papers in Linguistics*, vol 18: *Papers on Case and Agreement, I* (pp. 15–42). Cambridge, MA: MIT Department of Linguistics.

Jespersen, Otto. 1923. *Language: Its Nature, Development, and Origin*. New York: George Allen & Unwin.

Johnson, Donna M. 1994. Who is We?: Constructing Communities in US-Mexico Border Discourse. *Discourse and Society*, 5(2): 207–31.

Johnson, Mark. 1987. *The Body in the Mind: The Bodily Basis of Meaning, Imagination, and Reason*. University of Chicago Press.

Jordan, Brigitte. 1993. *Birth in Four Cultures: A Crosscultural Investigation of Childbirth in Yucatan, Holland, Sweden, and the United States*. Prospect Heights, IL: Waveland Press.

Jourdan, C. 1991. Pidgins and Creoles: The Blurring of Categories. *Annual Review of Anthropology*, 20: 187–209.

Jupp, T. C., Celia Roberts and Jenny Cook-Gumperz. 1982. Language and the Disadvantage: The Hidden Process. In J. J. Gumperz (ed.), *Language and Social Identity* (pp. 232–56). Cambridge University Press.

Kant, Immanuel. 1798. *Anthropologie in pragmatischer Hindsicht*. Königsberg: Friederich Nicolovius.

Katz, Jerrold J. 1964. Analycity and Contradiction in Natural Language. In J. A. Fodor and J. J. Katz (eds.), *The Structure of Languages* (pp. 519–43). Englewood Cliffs, NJ: Prentice-Hall.

Kay, Paul and Chad K. McDaniel. 1978. The Linguistic Significance of the Meanings of Basic Color Terms. *Language*, 54(3): 610–46.

Keane, Webb. 1994. The Value of Words and the Meaning of Things in Eastern Indonesian Exchange. *Man* N.S., 29: 605–29.

References

Keating, Elizabeth. 1993. Correction/Repair as a Resource for Co-Construction of Group Competence. *Pragmatics*, 3(4): 411–23.

1996. Constructing Hierarchy: Women and Honorific Speech in Pohnpei, Micronesia. *International Journal of the Sociology of Language.*

1997. Honorific Possession: Power and Language in Pohpei, Micronesia. *Language in Society.*

In press. *Power Sharing: Language, Rank, Gender and Social Space in Pohnpei, Micronesia.* Oxford University Press.

Keenan, Edward L. 1972. On Semantically Based Grammar. *Linguistic Inquiry,* 3(4): 413–61.

1976. The Logical Diversity of Natural Languages. In S. R. Harnard, H. D. Steklis and J. Lancaster (eds.), *Origins and Evolution of Language and Speech* (pp. 73–91). New York: The New York Academy of Sciences.

Keenan, Edward and Bernard Comrie. 1977. Noun Phrase Accessibility Hierarchy and Universal Grammar. *Linguistic Inquiry,* 8: 63–99.

Keenan, Elinor Ochs. 1974. Conversation and Oratory in Vaninankaratra Madagascar. Unpublished Ph.D dissertation, University of Pennsylvania.

1975. A Sliding Sense of Obligatoriness: The Polystructure of Malagasy Oratory. In M. Bloch (ed.), *Political Language and Oratory in Traditional Society* (pp. 93–112). London: Academic Press.

1976. The Universality of Conversational Postulates. *Language in Society,* 5: 67–80.

Keesing, Roger. 1972. Paradigms Lost: The New Anthropology and the New Linguistics. *Southwest Journal of Anthropology,* 28: 299–332.

1974. Theories of Culture. *Annual Review of Anthropology,* 3: 73–97.

Keiler, Allan R. (ed.) 1972. *A Reader in Historical and Practical Linguistics.* New York: Holt.

Kendon, Adam. 1967. Some Functions of Gaze-Direction in Social Interaction. *Acta Psychologica,* 26: 22–63.

1973. The Role of Visible Behavior in the Organization of Social Interaction. In M. Von Cranach and I. Vine (eds.), *Social Communication and Movement: Studies of Interaction and Expression in Man and Chimpanzee* (pp. 29–74). New York: Academic Press.

1977. *Studies in the Behavior of Social Interaction.* Lisse: The Peter De Ridder Press.

1980. Gesture and Speech: Two Aspects of the Process of Utterance. In M. R. Key (ed.), *Nonverbal Communication and Language* (pp. 207–77). The Hague: Mouton.

1990. *Conducting Interaction: Patterns of Behavior in Focused Encounters.* Cambridge University Press.

1992. The Negotiation of Context in Face-to-Face Interaction. In A. Duranti and C. Goodwin (eds.), *Rethinking Context: Language as an Interactive Phenomenon* (pp. 323–34). Cambridge University Press.

1993. Human Gesture. In K. R. Gibson and T. Ingold (eds.), *Tools, Language and Cognition in Human Evolution* (pp. 43–62). Cambridge University Press.

Kendon, Adam and Andrew Ferber. 1973. A Description of Some Human Greetings. In

R. P. Michael and J. H. Crook (eds.), *Comparative Ecology and Behaviour of Primates* (pp. 591–668). London and New York: Academic Press.

Kendon, Adam, Richard M. Harris and Mary Ritchie Key. 1975. *Organization of Behavior in Face-to-Face Interaction*. The Hague: Mouton.

Kirch, Patrick Vinton. 1984. *The Evolution of Polynesian Chiefdoms*. Cambridge University Press.

Kochman, Thomas. 1972. Toward an Ethnography of Black American Speech Behavior. In T. Kochman (ed.), *Rappin' and Stylin' Out: Communication in Urban Black America* (pp. 241–64). Chicago: University of Illinois Press.

1981. *Black and White: Styles in Conflict*. University of Chicago Press.

Koerner, E. F. Konrad. 1992. The Sapir-Whorf Hypothesis: A Preliminary History and a Bibliographical Essay. *Journal of Linguistic Anthropology*, 2(2): 173–98.

Kondo, Dorinne. 1986. Dissolution and Reconstitution of Self: Implications for Anthropological Epistemology. *Cultural Anthropology*, 1: 74–88.

1990. *Crafting Selves*. University of Chicago Press.

Kripke, Saul A. 1982. *Wittgenstein: On Rules and Private Language*. Cambridge, MA: Harvard University Press.

Kroeber, Alfred L. [1923] 1963. *Anthropology: Culture Patterns and Processes*. New York: Harbinger Books.

Kroskrity, Paul V. 1993. *Language, History, and Identity: Ethnolinguistic Studies of the Arizona Tewa*. Tucson: University of Arizona Press.

Kuipers, Joel C. 1990. *Power in Performance: The Creation of Textual Authority in Weyewa Ritual Speech*. Philadelphia: University of Pennsylvania Press.

Kulick, Don. 1992. *Language Shift and Cultural Reproduction: Socialization, Self, and Syncretism in a Papua New Guinean Village*. Cambridge University Press.

Kuno, S. 1973. *The Structure of the Japanese Language*. Cambridge, MA: Harvard University Press.

Labov, William. 1966. *The Social Stratification of English in New York City*. Arlington: Center for Applied Linguistics.

1970. *The Study of Nonstandard English*. Champaign, IL: National Council of Teachers.

1972a. *Language in the Inner City: Studies in the Black English Vernacular*. Philadelphia: University of Pennsylvania Press.

1972b. The Logic of Nonstandard English, *Language in the Inner City: Studies in the Black English Vernacular* (pp. 201–40). Philadelphia: University of Pennsylvania Press.

1972c. *Sociolinguistic Patterns*. Philadelphia: University of Pennsylvania Press.

1984. Field Methods of the Project on Linguistic Change and Variation. In J. Baugh and J. Sherzer (eds.), *Language in Use: Readings in Sociolinguistics* (pp. 28–53). Englewood Cliffs, NJ: Prentice-Hall.

Ladefoged, Peter. 1975. *A Course in Phonetics*. New York: Harcourt Brace Jovanovich.

1992. Another View of Endangered Languages. *Language*, 68(4): 809–11.

Lakoff, G. 1972. Hedges: A Study in Meaning Criteria and the Logic of Fuzzy Concepts.

Papers from the Eighth Regional Meeting of the Chicago Linguistics Society, pp. 271–91.

1987. *Women, Fire, and Dangerous Things: What Categories Reveal About the Mind*. University of Chicago Press.

Lakoff, George and Mark Johnson. 1980. *Metaphors We Live By*. University of Chicago Press.

Lane, Harlan L. 1984. *When the Mind Hears: A History of the Deaf*. New York: Random House.

Langness, L.L. 1987. *The Study of Culture*. Rev. edn. Novato, California: Chandler & Sharp.

Lave, Jean. 1988. *Cognition in Practice*. Cambridge University Press.

1990. The Culture of Acquisition and the Practice of Understanding. In J. W. Stigler, R. A. Shweder, and G. Herdt (eds.), *Cultural Psychology: Essays on Comparative Human Development* (pp. 309–27). Cambridge University Press.

Lave, Jean and Etienne Wenger. 1991. *Situated Learning: Legitimate Peripheral Participation*. Cambridge University Press.

Lawrence, Denise and Setha Low. 1990. The Built Environment and Spatial Form. *Annual Review of Anthropology*, 19: 453–505.

Leach, Edmund. 1970. *Lévi-Strauss*. London: Fontana/Collins.

1972. The Influence of Cultural Context on Non-Verbal Communication in Man. In R. Hinde (ed.), *Non-Verbal Communication* (pp. 315–47). Cambridge University Press.

Lehmann, Winfred P. 1973. *Historical Linguistics. An Introduction*. 2nd edn. New York: Holt.

Lehrer, Adrienne. 1974. *Semantic Fields and Lexical Structure*. Amsterdam: North-Holland.

Leichter, Hope Jensen. 1984. Families as Environments for Literacy. In H. Goelman and A. Oberg (eds.), *Awakening to Literacy* (pp. 38–50). London: Heinemann.

Leilich, Joachim. 1993. Intentionality, Speech Acts and Communicative Action: A Defense of J. Habermas' and K. O. Apel's Criticism. *Pragmatics*, 3(2): 155–70.

Leont'ev, A. N. 1979. The Problem of Activity in Psychology. In J. V. Wertsch (ed.), *The Concept of Activity in Soviet Psychology* (pp. 37–71). Armonk, NY: M. E. Sharpe.

1981. *Problems of the Development of the Mind*. Moscow: Progress Publishers.

Lepore, Ernest and R. Van Gulick (eds.). 1991. *John Searle and His Critics*. Oxford: Blackwell.

Lévi-Strauss, Claude. 1955/1977. *Tristes Tropiques*, trans. John and Doreen Weightman. New York: Pocket Books.

1963a. *Structural Anthropology*. New York: Basic Books.

1963b. *Totemism*. Boston: Beacon Press.

1965. Le triangle culinaire. *L'Arc*, 26: 19–29.

1966. *The Savage Mind*. University of Chicago Press.

1978. *Myth and Meaning*. New York: Schocken Books.

Levinson, Stephen C. 1983. *Pragmatics*. Cambridge University Press.

1987. Pragmatics and the Grammar of Anaphora: A Partial Pragmatic Reduction of Binding and Control Phenomena. *Journal of Linguistics*, 23: 379–434.

1988. Putting Linguistics on a Proper Footing: Explorations in Goffman's Concepts of Participation. In P. D. and A. Wootton (ed.), *Erving Goffman: Exploring the Interaction Order* (pp. 161–227). Boston: Northeastern University Press.

Lewin, Bruno. 1971. Der interpersonale Bezug im Koreanische. In P. W. Pestman (ed.), *Acta Orientalia Neerlandica. Proceedings of the Congress of the Dutch Oriental Society Held in Leiden on the Occasion of its 50th Anniversary, 8th–9th May 1970* (pp. 196–205). Leiden: E. J. Brill.

Li, Charles N. (ed.). 1975. *Word Order and Word Order Change*. Austin: University of Texas Press.

(ed.). 1976. *Subject and Topic*. New York: Academic Press.

(ed.). 1977. *Mechanisms of Syntactic Change*. Austin: University of Texas Press.

Liberman, Alvin. 1970. The Grammars of Speech and Language. *Cognitive Psychology*, 1: 301–323.

Lieberman, Philip. 1975. *On the Origins of Language: An Introduction to the Evolution of Human Speech*. New York: Macmillan.

Lieberman, Philip and Sheila E. Blumstein. 1988. *Speech Physiology, Speech Perception, and Acoustic Phonetics*. Cambridge University Press.

Lindstrom, Lamont. 1992. Context Contests: Debatable Truth Statements on Tanna (Vanuatu). In A. Duranti and C. Goodwin (eds.), *Rethinking Context: Language as an Interactive Phenomenon* (pp. 101–24). Cambridge University Press.

Lounsbury, Floyd. 1956. Semantic Analysis of the Pawnee Kinship Usage. *Language*, 32: 158–94.

1969. The Structural Analysis of Kinship Semantics. In S. A. Tyler (ed.), *Cognitive Anthropology* (pp. 193–212). New York: Holt, Rinehart, and Winston.

Lowie, Robert H. 1940. Native Languages as Ethnographic Tools. *American Anthropologist*, 42(1): 81–9.

Lucy, John A. 1992a. *Grammatical Categories and Cognition: A Case Study of the Linguistic Relativity Hypothesis*. Cambridge University Press.

1992b. *Language Diversity and Cognitive Development: A Reformulation of the Linguistic Relativity Hypothesis*. Cambridge University Press.

(ed.) 1993. *Reflexive Language: Reported Speech and Metapragmatics*. New York: Cambridge University Press.

Lucy, John A. and Richard A. Shweder, 1979. *Whorf and His Critics*. Linguistic and Nonlinguistic Influences on Color Memory. *American Anthropologist*, 81: 581–615.

Luhmann, Niklas. 1981. *Gesellschafsstruktur und Semantik*, vol. 2. Frankfurt am Main: Suhrkamp Verlag.

Lyons, John. 1969. *Introduction to Theoretical Linguistics*. Cambridge University Press.

1977. *Semantics*. Cambridge University Press.

Macaulay, Ronald K. S. 1991a. "Coz it izny spelt when they say it": Displaying Dialect in Writing. *American Speech*, 66: 280–9.

371

References

1991b. *Locating Dialect in Discourse: The Language of Honest Men and Bonnie Lasses in Ayr*. Oxford University Press.

Maffi, Luisa. 1991. A Bibliography of Color Categorization Research, 1970–1990. In B. Berlin and P. Kay (eds.), *Basic Color Terms*, (paperback edn.) (pp. 173–89). Berkeley and Los Angeles: University of California Press.

Malinowski, Bronislaw. 1920. Classificatory Particles in the Language of Kiriwina. *Bulletin of the School of Oriental and African Studies*, 1: 33–78.

1922. *Argonauts of the Western Pacific*. New York: Dutton.

1923. The Problem of Meaning in Primitive Languages. In C. K. Ogden and I. A. Richards (eds.), *The Meaning of Meaning* (pp. 296–336). New York: Harcourt, Brace, & World, Inc.

[1935] 1978. *Coral Gardens and Their Magic*. 2 vols. London: Allan & Urwin.

Malotki, Ekkehart. 1983. *Hopi Time: A Linguistic Analysis of the Temporal Concepts in the Hopi Language*. Berlin: Mouton.

Maltz, Daniel N. and Ruth A. Borker. 1982. A Cultural Approach to Male-Female Miscommunication. In J. J. Gumperz (ed.), *Communication, Language and Social Identity* (pp. 196–216). Cambridge University Press.

Mandelbaum, Jenny. 1987. Recipient-driven Storytelling in Conversation. Unpublished Ph.D. dissertation, The University of Texas at Austin.

1993. Assigning Responsibility in Conversational Storytelling: The Interactional Construction of Reality. *Text*, 13(2): 247–66.

Mani, Lata. 1990. Multiple Mediations: Feminist Scholarship in the Age of Multinational Reception. *Feminist Review*, 35: 24–41.

Manicas, Peter T. 1987. *A History and Philosophy of the Social Sciences*. Oxford: Blackwell.

Mannheim, Bruce. 1991. *The Language of the Inka since the European Invasion*. Austin: University of Texas Press.

1992. A Semiotics of Andean Dreams. In B. Tedlock (ed.), *Dreaming: Anthropological and Psychological Interpretations* (pp. 132–53). Santa Fe, NM: School of American Research Press.

Martin, Laura. 1986. Eskimo Words for Snow: A Case Study in the Genesis and Decay of an Anthropological Example. *American Anthropologist*, 88: 418–23.

Martin, Samuel E. 1964. Speech Levels in Japan and Korea. In D. Hymes (ed.), *Language in Culture and Society: A Reader in Linguistics and Anthropology* (pp. 407–15). New York: Harper & Row.

Marx, Karl. 1845/1978. Theses on Feuerbach. In R. C. Tucker (ed.), *The Marx-Engels Reader*. 2nd edn. New York: Norton.

Marx, Karl. 1906. *Capital: A Critique of Political Economy*. New York: Random House.

Mauss, Marcel. 1935. Les techniques du corps. *Journal de psychologie normale et pathologique*, 39: 271–93.

1938. La notion de personne, celle de "moi". *Journal of the Royal Anthropological Institute*, 68 [English translation in Mauss 1985].

1979. *Sociology and Psychology: Essays*. London: Routledge & Kegan Paul.

1985. A Category of the Human Mind: The Notion of Person; The Notion of Self. In M. Carrithers, S. Collins and S. Lukes (eds.), *The Category of Person: Anthropology, Philosophy, History* (pp. 1–25). Cambridge University Press.

McConnell-Ginet, Sally. 1988. Language and Gender. In F. J. Newmeyer (ed.), *Linguistics: The Cambridge Survey*, vol. 4: *Language: The Socio-cultural Context* (pp. 75–99). Cambridge University Press.

McElhinny, Bonnie S. 1995. Challenging Hegemonic Masculinities: Female and Male Police Officers Handling Domestic Violence. In K. Hall and M. Bucholtz (eds.), *Gender Articulated: Language and the Socially Constructed Self* (pp. 217–43). New York: Routledge.

McTear, Michael. 1985. *Children's Conversation*. Oxford: Basil Blackwell.

Mead, Margaret. 1939. Native Languages as Field-work Tools. *American Anthropologist*, 41(2): 189–205.

1959. Apprenticeship Under Boas. In W. Goldschmidt (ed.), *The Anthropology of Franz Boas: Essays on the Centennial of his Birth. Memoir No. 89 of the American Anthropological Association* (vol. 61, pp. 29–45). San Francisco: American Anthropological Association and Chandler.

Mehan, Hugh. 1979. *Learning Lessons*. Cambridge, MA: Harvard University Press.

Merlan, Francesca. 1985. Split Intransitivity: Functional Oppositions in Intransitive Inflection. In J. Nichols and A. Woodbury (eds.), *Grammar Inside and Outside the Clause: Some Approaches to Theory from the Field* (pp. 324–62). Cambridge University Press.

Merleau-Ponty, Maurice. 1962. *Phenomenology of Perception*, trans. Colin Smith. London: Routledge.

Merritt, Marilyn. 1982. Distributing and Directing Attention in Primary Classrooms. In L. C. Wilkinson (ed.), *Communicating in the Classroom* (pp. 223–44). New York: Academic Press.

Mertz, Elizabeth and Richard J. Parmentier (eds.) 1985. *Semiotic Mediation: Sociocultural and Psychological Perspectives*. Orlando: Academic Press.

Milroy, James. 1980. *Language and Social Networks*. Oxford: Blackwell.

Milroy, James and Lesley Milroy. 1985. Linguistic Change, Social Network, and Speaker Innovation. *Journal of Linguistics*, 21: 339–84.

Milroy, Leslie. 1987. *Language and Social Networks*. 2nd edn. Oxford: Blackwell.

Milroy, Leslie and James Milroy. 1992. Social Network and Social Class: Toward an Integrated Sociolinguistic Model. *Language in Society*, 21: 1–26.

Milton, Kay. 1982. Meaning and Context: The Interpretation of Greetings in Kasigau. In D. Parkin (ed.), *Semantic Anthropology* (pp. 261–77). London: Academic Press.

Mitchell-Kernan, Claudia. 1972. Signifying and Marking: Two Afro-American Speech Acts. In J. J. Gumperz and D. Hymes (eds.), *Directions in Sociolinguistics: The Ethnography of Communication* (pp. 161–79). New York: Holt, Rinehart, & Winston.

Mithun, Marianne. 1986. On the Nature of Noun Incorporation. *Language*, 62: 32–7.

1991. Active/Agentive Case Marking and Its Motivation. *Language*, 67(3): 510–46.

References

Moerman, Michael. 1977. The Preference for Self-Correction in a Tai Conversational Corpus. *Language*, 53(4): 872–82.

1988. *Talking Culture: Ethnography and Conversation Analysis.* Philadelphia: University of Pennsylvania Press.

Monaghan, Leila. 1996. Signing, Oralism and Development of the New Zealand Deaf Community: An Ethnography and History of Language Ideologies. Unpublished Ph.D. Dissertation, University of California, Los Angeles.

1986. *Space, Text and Gender: An Anthropological Study of the Marakwet of Kenya.* Cambridge University Press.

Moore, Henrietta. 1994. *A Passion for Difference.* Bloomington: Indiana University Press.

Moravcsik, Edith. 1974. Object-Verb Agreement. *Working Papers in Language Universals. Stanford University*, 15: 25–140.

Morgan, Marcyliena. 1996. Conversational Signifying: Grammar and Indirectness Among African American Women. In E. Ochs, E. Schegloff and S. A. Thompson (eds.), *Interaction and Grammar* (pp. 405–34). Cambridge University Press.

(ed.). 1994. *Language and the Social Construction of Reality in Creole Situations.* Los Angeles: Center for Afro-American Studies, UCLA.

Morris, C. W. 1938. Foundations of the Theory of Signs. In O. Nuerath, R. Carnap and C. Morris (eds.), *International Encyclopedia of Unified Science* (pp. 77–138). University of Chicago Press.

Morrison, Toni. 1994. *The Nobel Lecture in Literature, 1993.* New York: Knopf.

Moshi, Lioba. 1993. Ideophones in KiVunjo-Chaga. *Journal of Linguistic Anthropology*, 3(2): 185–216.

Mühlhäusler, Peter. 1986. *Pidgin and Creole Linguistics.* Oxford: Blackwell.

Myers, Fred. 1986. *Pintupi Country Pintupi Self: Sentiment, Place, and Politics among Western Desert Aborigines.* Washington: Smithsonian Institution Press.

Nader, Laura. 1969 (ed.). *Law in Culture and Society.* Chicago: Aldine.

Narayan, Kirin. 1993. How Native is a "Native" Anthropologist? *American Anthropologist*, 95(3): 671–86.

Newman, Denis, Peg Griffin and Michael Cole. 1989. *The Construction Zone.* Cambridge University Press.

Nichols, Johanna and David A. Peterson. 1996. The Amerind Personal Pronouns. *Language*, 72(2): 336–71.

Nuckolls, Janis B. 1992. Sound Symbolic Involvement. *Journal of Linguistic Anthropology*, 2(1): 51–80.

1995. Quechua Texts of Perception. *Semiotica*, 145–69.

Nuyts, Jan. 1993. Intentions and Language Use. *Antwerp Papers in Linguistics*, no. 73.

1993. Intentions and the Functions of Language in Communication. *Protosoziologie*, 4: 15–31.

1994. The Intentional and the Socio-cultural in Language Use. *Pragmatics and Cognition*, 2(2): 237–68.

Ochs, Elinor. 1979. Transcription as Theory. In E. Ochs and B. B. Schieffelin (eds.), *Developmental Pragmatics* (pp. 43–72). New York: Academic Press.

374

1982. Talking to Children in Western Samoa. *Language in Society*, 11: 77–104.

1984. Clarification and Culture. In D. Shiffrin (ed.), *Georgetown University Round Table in Languages and Linguistics* (pp. 325–41). Washington, DC: Georgetown University Press.

1988. *Culture and Language Development: Language Acquisition and Language Socialization in a Samoan Village.* Cambridge University Press.

1992. Indexing Gender. In A. Duranti and C. Goodwin (eds.), *Rethinking Context.* Cambridge University Press.

1996. Linguistic Resources for Socializing Humanity. In J. J. Gumperz and S. C. Levinson (eds.), *Rethinking Linguistic Relativity* (pp. 406–37). Cambridge: Cambridge University Press.

1997. Narrative. In T. van Dijk (ed.), *Discourse as Structure and Process* (pp. 185–207). London: Sage.

Ochs, Elinor and Bambi B. Schieffelin. 1983. *Acquiring Conversational Competence.* Boston: Routledge & Kegan Paul.

1984. Language Acquisition and Socialization: Three Developmental Stories. In R. A. Shweder and R. A. LeVine (eds.), *Culture Theory: Essays on Mind, Self, and Emotion* (pp. 276–320). Cambridge University Press.

1995. The Impact of Language Socialization on Grammatical Development. In P. Fletcher and B. MacWhinney (eds.), *The Handbook of Child Language* (pp. 73–94). Oxford: Blackwell.

Ochs, Elinor, Ruth Smith and Carolyn Taylor. 1989. Dinner Narratives as Detective Stories. *Cultural Dynamics*, 2: 238–57.

Ochs, E. and C. Taylor. 1992. Mothers' Role in the Everday Reconstruction of "Father Knows Best." In K. Hall, M. Bucholtz and B. Moonwomon (eds.), *Locating Power: Proceedings of the 1992 Berkeley Women and Language Conference* (pp. 447–62). Berkeley: University of California, Berkeley.

Ochs, Elinor, Carolyn Taylor, Dina Rudolph and Ruth Smith. 1992. Story-telling as a Theory-building Activity. *Discourse Processes*, 15(1): 37–72.

Olmsted, D. L. 1950. Ethnolinguistics So Far. *Studies in Linguistics, Occasional Papers,* 2.

Ortner, Sherry B. 1979. *Sherpas Through Their Rituals.* Cambridge University Press.

1984. Theory in Anthropology Since the Sixties. *Comparative Studies in Society and History*, 26(1): 126–66.

Oswalt, Wendell H. 1986. *Life Cycles and Lifeways: An Introduction to Cultural Anthropology.* Palo Alto, CA: Mayfield.

Owusu, Maxwell. 1978. Ethnography of Africa: The Usefulness of the Useless. *American Anthropologist*, 80(2): 310–34.

Pace, David. 1983. *Claude Lévi-Strauss: The Bearer of Ashes.* London: Routledge & Kegan Paul.

Padden, Carol and Tom Humphries. 1988. *Deaf in America: Voices from a Culture.* Cambridge, MA: Harvard University Press.

Palmer, Gary B. and William R. Jankowiak. 1996. Performance and Imagination:

Toward an Anthropology of the Spectacular and the Mundane. *Cultural Anthropology*, 11(2): 225–58.

Pandolfi, Mariella. 1991. *Itinerari delle emozioni*. Milan: Franco Angeli.

Parmentier, Richard J. 1994. *Signs in Society: Studies in Semiotic Anthropology*. Bloomington: Indiana University Press.

Pawley, Andrew. 1974. Austronesian Languages, *Encyclopædia Britannica*, 13th edn. (pp. 484–93).

Peirce, Charles Sanders. 1940. Logic as Semiotic: The Theory of Signs. In J. Buchler (ed.), *Philosophical Writings of Peirce: Selected Writings*. London: Routledge & Kegan Paul.

Peters, Misja Shreuder, Milko van Gool and Ester Messing. 1992. A Bibliography on Space, Deixis, and Related Topics, with Index. *Cognitive Anthropology Research Group at the Max Plank Institute, Working Paper*, 15.

Philips, Susan. 1983. *The Invisible Culture: Communication in Classroom and Community on the Warm Springs Indian Reservation*. New York: Longman.

Philips, Susan, Susan Steele and Christina Tanz. 1987. *Language, Gender, and Sex in Comparative Perspective*. Cambridge University Press.

Philips, Susan U. 1972. Participant Structures and Communicative Competence: Warm Springs Children in Community and Classroom. In C. B. Cazden, V. P. John and D. Hymes (eds.), *Functions of Language in the Classroom* (pp. 370–94). New York: Columbia Teachers Press.

1992. The Routinization of Repair in Courtroom Discourse. In A. Duranti and C. Goodwin (eds.), *Rethinking Context: Language as an Interactive Phenomenon* (pp. 311–22). Cambridge University Press.

Pike, Kenneth L. 1954–56. *Language, in Relation to a Unified Theory of the Structure of Human Behavior*, parts I, II, III. Glendale, CA: Summer Institute of Linguistics.

1966. Etic and Emic Standpoints for the Description of Behavior. In A. G. Smith (ed.), *Communication and Culture: Readings in the Codes of Human Interaction* (pp. 152–63). New York: Holt, Rinehart, & Winston.

1971. *Language in Relation to a Unified Theory of the Structures of Human Behavior*. 2nd, rev. edn. The Hague: Mouton.

Pinker, Steven. 1994. *The Language Instinct: How the Mind Creates Language*. New York: William Morrow & Co.

Planck, Frans (ed.). 1979. *Ergativity: Towards a Theory of Grammatical Relations*. London: Academic Press.

Platt, J. T. and H. K. Platt. 1975. *The Social Significance of Speech: An Introduction to and Workbook in Sociolinguistics*. Amsterdam: North-Holland.

Platt, Martha. 1982. Social and Semantic Dimensions of Deictic Verbs and Particles in Samoan Child Language. Unpublished Ph.D. dissertation, University of Southern California.

Polhemus, Ted (ed.). 1978. *Social Aspects of the Human Body*. Harmondsworth: Penguin.

Pomerantz, Anita. 1978. Compliment Responses: Notes on the Co-operation of Multiple

Constraints. In J. Schenkein (ed.), *Studies in the Organization of Conversational Interaction* (pp. 79–112). New York: Academic Press.

1984. Agreeing and Disagreeing with Assessments: Some Features of Preferred/ Dispreferred Turn Shapes. In J. M. Atkinson and J. Heritage (eds.), *Structures of Social Action: Studies in Conversation Analysis* (pp. 57–101). Cambridge University Press.

Povinelli, Elizabeth A. 1995. Do Rocks Listen? The Cultural Politics of Apprehending Australian Aboriginal Labor. *American Anthropologist*, 97(3): 505–18.

Pullum, Geoffrey K. and William A. Ladusaw. 1986. *Phonetic Symbol Guide*. University of Chicago Press.

Putnam, Hilary. 1975. The Meaning of "Meaning," *Mind, Language and Reality. Philosophical Papers*, vol. 2 (pp. 215–71). Cambridge University Press.

Quirk, Randoph, Sidney Greenbaum, Geoffrey Leech and Jan Svartvik. 1985. *A Comprehensive Grammar of the English Language*. London: Longman.

Radford, Andrew. 1988. *Tranformational Grammar: A First Course*. Cambridge University Press.

Rappoport, Roy. 1974. Obvious Aspects of Ritual. *Cambridge Anthropology*, 2(1): 3–69.

Reddy, Michael. 1979. The Conduit Metaphor. In A. Ortony (ed.), *Metaphor and Thought*. Cambridge University Press.

Reill, Peter Hanns and David Philip Miller (eds.). 1996. *Visions of Empire: Voyages, Botany, and Representations of Nature*. Cambridge University Press.

Reisman, Karl. 1974. Contrapuntual Conversations in an Antiguan Village. In R. Bauman and J. Sherzer (eds.), *Explorations in the Ethnography of Speaking* (pp. 110–24). Cambridge University Press.

Resnick, Lauren B., John M. Levine and Stephanie D. Teasley (eds.). 1991. *Perspectives on Socially Shared Cognition*. Washington, DC: American Psychological Association.

Ricoeur, Paul. 1971. The Model of the Text: Meaningful Action Considered as Text. *Social Research*, 38: 529–62.

1981. *Hermeneutics and the Human Sciences*. Cambridge University Press.

Rogoff, Barbara. 1990. *Apprenticeship in Thinking*. New York: Oxford University Press.

Rogoff, Barbara and Jean Lave. 1984. *Everyday Cognition: Its Development in Social Context*. Cambridge, MA: Harvard University Press.

Romaine, Suzanne. 1982. What Is a Speech Community? In S. Romaine (ed.), *Sociolinguistic Variation in Speech Communities* (pp. 13–24). New York: Edward Arnold.

1984. On the Problem of Syntactic Variation and Pragmatic Meaning in Sociolinguistic Theory. *Folia Linguistica*, 18: 409–39.

1986. *Pidgin and Creole Languages*. London: Longman.

1994. Language Standardization and Linguistic Fragmentation in Tok Pisin. In M. Morgan (ed.), *Language in Creole Situations: The Social Construction of Identity* (pp. 19–41). Los Angeles: Center for Afro-American Studies.

Rosaldo, Michelle Z. 1980. *Knowledge and Passion: Ilongot Notions of Self and Social Life*. Cambridge University Press.

References

1982. The Things We Do With Words: Ilongot Speech Acts and Speech Act Theory in Philosophy. *Language in Society*, 11: 203–37.

Rosaldo, Renato. 1989. *Culture & Truth: The Remaking of Social Analysis*. Boston: Beacon Press.

Rosch, Eleanor. 1973. Natural Categories. *Cognitive Psychology* 7: 573–605.

1975. Universals and Cultural Specifics in Human Categorization. In R. Brislin, S. Bochner and W. Lonner (eds.), *Cross-Cultural Perspectives on Learning* (pp. 177–206). New York: Helstead Press.

1978. Principles of Categorization. In E. Rosch and B. Lloyd (eds.), *Cognition and Categorization* (pp. 27–48). Hillsdale, NJ: Lawrence Erlbaum.

Rosen, Lawrence. 1995a. Introduction: The Cultural Analysis of Others' Inner States. In L. Rosen (ed.), *Other Intentions: Cultural Contexts and the Attribution of Inner States* (pp. 1–11). Santa Fe, NM: School of American Research Press.

(ed.). 1995b. *Other Intentions*. Santa Fe, NM: School of American Research.

Rossi-Landi, Ferruccio. 1970. Linguistic Alienation Problems, *Linguaggi nella società e nella tecnica* (pp. 513–43). Milan: Edizioni di Comunità.

1973. *Il linguaggio come lavoro e come mercato*. Milan: Bompiani.

1983. *Language as Work and Trade: A Semiotic Homology for Linguistics and Economics*. South Hadley, MA: Bergin & Garvey.

Rumsey, Alan. 1990. Wording, Meaning, and Linguistic Ideology. *American Anthropologist*, 92(2): 346–61.

Rymes, Betsy. 1996. Naming as Social Practice: The Case of Little Creeper from Diamond Street. *Language in Society*, 25: 237–60.

Sacks, Harvey. 1972. On the Analyzability of Stories by Children. In J. J. Gumperz and D. Hymes (eds.), *Directions in Sociolinguistics: The Ethnography of Communication* (pp. 325–45). New York: Holt, Rinehart, & Winston.

1978. Some Technical Considerations of a Dirty Joke. In J. Schenkein (ed.), *Studies in the Organization of Conversational Interaction* (pp. 249–69). New York: Academic Press (edited by Gail Jefferson from four lectures delivered at the University of California, Irvine, Fall 1971).

1992a. *Lectures on Conversation*, vol. 1. Cambridge, MA: Blackwell.

1992b. *Lectures on Conversation*, vol. 2. Cambridge, MA: Blackwell.

Sacks, Harvey, Emanuel A. Schegloff and Gail Jefferson. 1974. A Simplest Systematics for the Organization of Turn-Taking for Conversation. *Language*, 50: 696–735.

1978. A Simplest Systematics for the Organization of Turn-Taking for Conversation. In J. Schenkein (ed.), *Studies in the Organization of Conversational Interaction* (pp. 7–57). New York: Academic Press.

Sacks, Oliver. 1989. *Seeing Voices: A Journey into the World of the Dead*. Berkeley and Los Angeles: University of California Press.

Sadock, Jerrold. 1980. Some Notes on Noun Incorporation. *Language*, 56: 300–19.

Sadock, Jerrold M. and Arnold M. Zwicky. 1985. Speech Act Distinctions in Syntax. In T. Shopen (ed.), *Language Typology and Syntactic Description*, vol. 1: *Clause Structure* (pp. 155–96). Cambridge University Press.

Sahlins, Marshall. 1976. *Culture and Practical Reason*. University of Chicago Press.

Said, Edward. 1978. *Orientalism*. London: Routledge & Kegan Paul.

1989. Representing the Colonized: Anthropology's Interlocutors. *Critical Inquiry*, 15: 205–25.

Salmond, Anne. 1975. Mana Makes the Man: A Look at Maori Oratory and Politics. In M. Bloch (ed.), *Political Language and Oratory in Traditional Society* (pp. 45–63). London: Academic Press.

Samarin, William J. 1967. Determining the Meanings of Ideophones. *Journal of West African Linguistics*, 4: 35–41.

1971. Survey of Bantu Ideophones. *African Language Studies*, 2: 130–68.

Sanjek, Roger (ed.). 1990a. *Fieldnotes: The Makings of Anthropology*. Ithaca: Cornell University Press.

1990b. The Secret Life of Fieldnotes. In R. Sanjek (ed.), *Fieldnotes: The Makings of Anthropology* (pp. 187–270). Ithaca: Cornell University Press.

1990c. A Vocabulary for Fieldnotes. In R. Sanjek (ed.), *Fieldnotes: The Makings of Anthropology* (pp. 92–121). Ithaca: Cornell University Press.

Sapir, Edward. 1921. *Language*. New York: Harcourt, Brace & World.

1924. Culture, Genuine and Spurious. *Journal of Sociology*, 29: 401–29.

1933. Language. *Encyclopaedia of the Social Sciences*, 155–69.

1949a. Cultural Anthropology and Psychiatry. In D. G. Mandelbaum (ed.), *Selected Writings of Edward Sapir in Language, Culture and Personality* (pp. 509–21). Berkeley and Los Angeles: University of California Press.

1949b. The Status of Linguistics as a Science. In D. G. Mandelbaum (ed.), *Selected Writings of Edward Sapir in Language, Culture and Personality* (pp. 160–6). Berkeley and Los Angeles: University of California Press.

1949c. The Unconscious Patterning of Behavior in Society. In D. G. Mandelbaum (ed.), *Selected Writings of Edward Sapir in Language, Culture and Society* (pp. 544–59). Berkeley: University of California Press.

1949d. The Psychological Reality of the Phoneme. In D. G. Mandelbaum (ed.), *Selected Writings of Edward Sapir in Language, Culture and Personality* (pp. 46–60). Berkeley and Los Angeles: University of California Press.

1993. *The Psychology of Culture: A Course of Lectures. Reconstructed and Edited by Judith T. Irvine*. Berlin: Mouton de Gruyter.

Sapir, J. David and J. Christopher Crocker (eds.). 1977. *The Social Uses of Metaphor*. Philadelphia: University of Pennsylvania Press.

Sarup, Madan. 1989. *An Introductory Guide to Poststructuralism and Postmodernism*. Athens, GA: University of Georgia Press.

Saussure, Ferdinand de. 1959. *Course in General Linguistics*, ed. Charles Bally and Albert Sechehaye, in collaboration with Albert Riedlinger, translated from the French by Wade Baskin. New York: Philosophical Library.

Saville-Troike, Muriel. 1989. *The Ethnography of Communication: An Introduction*. 2nd edn. Oxford: Blackwell.

References

Sawyer, R. Keith. 1996. The Semiotics of Improvisation: The Pragmatics of Musical and Verbal Performance. *Semiotica*, 108(3/4): 269–306.

Schegloff, Emanuel A. 1972a. Notes on a Conversational Practice: Formulating Place. In D. Sudnow (ed.), *Studies in Social Interaction* (pp. 75–119). New York: Free Press.

1972b. Sequencing in Conversational Openings. In J. J. Gumperz and D. Hymes (eds.), *Directions in Sociolinguistics: The Ethnography of Communciation* (pp. 346–80). New York: Holt, Rinehart, & Winston.

1979a. Identification and Recognition in Telephone Openings. In G. Psathas (ed.), *Everyday Language* (pp. 23–78). New York: Lawrence Erlbaum.

1979b. The Relevance of Repair for Syntax-for-Conversation. In T. Givón (ed.), *Syntax and Semantics 12: Discourse and Syntax* (pp. 261–88). New York: Academic Press.

1984. On Some Gestures' Relation to Talk. In J. M. Atkinson and J. Heritage (eds.), *Structures of Social Action* (pp. 266–96). Cambridge University Press.

1986. The Routine as Achievement. *Human Studies*, 9: 111–51.

1987. Between Macro and Micro: Contexts and Other Connections. In J. Alexander, R. M. B. Giesen and N. Smelser (eds.), *The Micro-Macro Link* (pp. 207–34). Berkeley: University of California Press.

1989. Harvey Sacks – Lectures 1964–1965. An Introduction/Memoir. *Human Studies*, 12 (3–4): 185–209.

1991. Reflections on Talk and Social Structure. In D. Bodem and D. H. Zimmerman (eds.), *Talk and Social Structure* (pp. 44–70). Berkeley and Los Angeles: University of California Press.

1992a. Introduction, in Harvey Sacks, *Lectures on Conversation,* vol. 1 (pp. ix–lxii). Cambridge, MA: Blackwell.

1992b. In Another Context. In A. Duranti and C. Goodwin (eds.), *Rethinking Context: Language as an Interactive Phenomenon* (pp. 191–227). Cambridge University Press.

Schegloff, Emanuel A., Gail Jefferson and Harvey Sacks. 1977. The Preference for Self-Correction in the Organization of Repair in Conversation. *Language*, 53: 361–82.

Schegloff, Emanuel A. and Harvey Sacks. 1973. Opening Up Closings. *Semiotica*, 8: 289–327.

1984. Opening Up Closings. In J. Baugh and J. Sherzer (eds.), *Language in Use: Readings in Sociolinguistics* (pp. 69–99). Englewood Cliffs, NJ: Prentice-Hall.

Schieffelin, Bambi B. 1979. Getting It Together: An Ethnographic Approach to the Study of the Development of Communicative Competence. In E. Ochs and B. B. Schieffelin (eds.), *Developmental Pragmatics* (pp. 73–110). New York: Academic Press.

1986. Teasing and Shaming in Kaluli Children's Interactions. In B. B. Schieffelin and E. Ochs (eds.), *Language Socialization across Cultures* (pp. 165–81). Cambridge University Press.

1990. *The Give and Take of Everyday Life: Language Socialization of Kaluli Children.* Cambridge University Press.

1994. Code-switching and Language Socialization: Some Probable Relationships. In J. Duchan, L. E. Hewitt and R. M. Sonnenmeier (eds.), *Pragmatics: From Theory to Therapy* (pp. 20–42). New York: Prentice Hall.

Schieffelin, Bambi B. and Rachelle Charlier Doucet. 1994. The "Real" Haitian Creole: Ideology, Metalinguistics, and Orthographic Choice. *American Ethnologist*, 21(1): 176–200.

Schieffelin, Bambi B. and P. Gilmore. 1986. *The Acquisition of Literacy*. Norwood, NJ: Ablex.

Schieffelin, Bambi B. and Elinor Ochs. 1986. *Language Socialization across Cultures*. Cambridge University Press.

Schieffelin, Bambi B., Kathryn Woolard and Paul Kroskrity (eds.). 1997. *Language Ideologies*. Oxford University Press.

Schieffelin, Edward L. 1976. *The Sorrow of the Lonely and the Burning of the Dancers*. New York: St. Martins Press.

Schiffrin, Deborah. 1994. *Approaches to Discourse*. Oxford: Blackwell.

Scholes, Robert J. and Brenda J. Willis. 1991. Linguists, Literacy, and the Intensionality of Marshall McLuhan's Western Man. In D. R. Olson and N. Torrance (eds.), *Literacy and Orality* (pp. 225–35). Cambridge University Press.

Schutz, Alfred. [1932]1967. *The Phenomenology of the Social World*, trans. G. Walsh and F. Lehnert. Evanston, IL: Northwestern University Press.

Scollon, Ronald and S. B. K. Scollon. 1981. *Narrative, Literacy, and Face in Interethnic Communication*. Norwood, NJ: Ablex.

Scribner, Sylvia and Michael Cole. 1981. *Psychology of Literacy*. Cambridge, MA: Harvard University Press.

Searle, John R. 1969. *Speech Acts: An Essay in the Philosophy of Language*. Cambridge University Press.

1975. Indirect Speech Acts. In P. Cole and J. L. Morgan (eds.), *Syntax and Semantics*, vol. 3 (pp. 59–82). New York: Academic Press.

1976. The Classification of Illocutionary Acts. *Language in Society*, 5(1): 1–23.

1983. *Intentionality: An Essay in the Philosophy of Mind*. Cambridge University Press.

1986. Meaning, Communication and Representation. In R. E. Grandy and R. Warner (eds.), *Philosophical Grounds of Rationality* (pp. 209–26). Oxford: Clarendon Press.

1990. Collective Intentionality and Action. In P. R. Cohen, J. Morgen and M. E. Rollsik (eds.), *Intention in Communication* (pp. 401–15). Cambridge, MA: MIT Press.

Searle, John R. and Daniel Vanderveken. 1985. *Foundations of Illocutionary Logic*. Cambridge University Press.

Severi, Carlo. 1989. Cristallizzazione e dispersione della conoscenza nella tradizione cuna. In G. R. Cardona (ed.), *La trasmissione del sapere: Aspetti linguistici e antropologici* (pp. 255–77). Rome: Bagatto.

Sherzer, Joel. 1973. Verbal and Non-Verbal Deixis: The Pointed Lip Gesture Among the San Blas Cuna. *Language in Society*, 2: 117–31.

1974. Namakke, Sunmakke, Kormakke: Three Types of Cuna Speech Event. In

R. Bauman and J. Sherzer (eds.), *Explorations in the Ethnography of Speaking* (pp. 263–82). Cambridge University Press.

1983. *Kuna Ways of Speaking: An Ethnographic Perspective*. Austin: University of Texas Press.

Sherzer, Joel and Regna Darnell. 1972. Outline Guide for the Ethnographic Study of Speech Use. In J. J. Gumperz and D. Hymes (eds.), *Directions in Sociolinguistics: The Ethnography of Communication* (pp. 548–54). New York: Holt, Rinehart, & Winston.

Shibatani, Masayoshi and Theodora Bynon (eds.). 1995. *Approaches to Language Typology*. Oxford: Clarendon Press.

Shore, Bradd. 1982. *Sala`ilua: A Samoan Mystery*. New York: Columbia University Press.

Shuy, Roger W., Walter A. Wolfram and William Riley. 1968. *Urban Language Study*. Washington, DC: Center for Applied Linguistics.

Silverstein, Michael. 1976a. Hierarchy of Features of Ergativity. In R. M. W. Dixon (ed.), *Grammatical Categories in Australian Languages* (pp. 112–71). Canberra: Australian Institute of Aboriginal Studies.

1976b. Shifters, Linguistic Categories, and Cultural Description. In K. H. Basso and H. A. Selby (eds.), *Meaning in Anthropology* (pp. 11–56). Albuquerque: University of New Mexico Press.

1977. Cultural Prerequisites to Grammatical Analysis. In M. Saville-Troike (ed.), *Linguistics and Anthropology: Georgetown University Round Table on Languages and Linguistics 1977* (pp. 139–51). Washington, DC: Georgetown University Press.

1979. Language Structure and Linguistic Ideology. In P. R. Clyne, W. F. Hanks and C. L. Hofbauer (eds.), *The Elements: A Parasession on Linguistic Units and Levels* (pp. 193–247). Chicago Linguistic Society.

1981. *The Limits of Awareness*. Austin: Southwest Educational Development Laboratory.

1985a. The Culture of Language in Chinookan Narrative Texts; or, On saying that . . . in Chinookan. In J. Nichols and A. Woodbury (eds.), *Grammar Inside and Outside the Clause* (pp. 132–71). Cambridge University Press.

1985b. The Functional Stratification of Language and Ontogenesis. In J. V. Wertsch (ed.), *Culture, Communication and Cognition: Vygotskian Perspectives* (pp. 205–35). Cambridge University Press.

1987. The Three Faces of "Function": Preliminaries to a Psychology of Language. In M. Hickmann (ed.), *Social and Functional Approaches to Language and Thought* (pp. 17–38). New York: Academic Press.

1992. The Indeterminacy of Contextualization: When is Enough Enough? In P. Auer and A. DiLuzio (eds.), *The Contextualization of Language*. Amsterdam: John Benjamins.

1993. Metapragmatic Discourse and Metapragmatic Function. In J. Lucy (ed.), *Reflexive Language* (pp. 33–58). New York: Cambridge University Press.

Slobin, Dan I. (ed.). 1967. *A Field Manual for Cross-Cultural Study of the Acquisition of*

Communicative Competence. Berkeley: Language Behavior Research Laboratory. University of California, Berkeley.

(ed.). 1985a. *The Crosslinguistic Study of Language Acquisition*, vol. 1. Hillsdale, NJ: Lawrence Erlbaum Associates.

1985b. The Crosslinguistic Evidence for the Language-making Capacity. In D. I. Slobin (ed.), *The Crosslinguistic Study of Language Acquisition*, vol. 2: *Theoretical Issues* (pp. 1157–256). Hillsdale, NJ: Lawrence Erlbaum Associates.

(ed.). 1992. *The Crosslinguistic Study of Language Acquisition*, vol. 3. Hillsdale, NJ: Lawrence Erlbaum Associates.

Soja, Edward W. 1989. *Postmodern Geographies: The Reassertion of Space in Critical Social Theory*. London and New York: Verso.

Sorensen, Arthur P., Jr. 1967. Multilingualism in the Northwest Amazon. *American Anthropologist*, 69: 670–84.

Spencer, Andrew. 1991. *Morphological Theory*. Oxford: Blackwell.

Sperber, Dan. 1985. Anthropology and Psychology. *Man*, 20: 73–89.

Spiro, Melford E. 1990. On the Strange and the Familiar in Recent Anthropological Thought. In J. W. Stigler, R. A. Shweder and G. Herdt (eds.), *Cultural Psychology: Essays on Comparative Human Development*. Cambridge University Press.

Spivak, Gayatri Chakravorty. 1985. Three Women's Texts and a Critique of Imperialism. *Critical Inquiry*, 12(1): 243–61.

Spradley, James P. 1980. *Participant Observation*. New York: Holt, Rinehart, & Winston.

Stocking, George W. Jr. (ed.). 1974. *The Shaping of American Anthropology, 1883–1911: A Franz Boas Reader*. New York: Basic Books.

Streeck, Jürgen. 1988. The Significance of Gesture: How it is Established. *International Pragmatics Association Papers in Pragmatics*, 2(1): 60–83.

1993. Gesture as Communication I: Its Coordination with Gaze and Speech. *Communication Monographs*, 60: 275–99.

1994. Gesture as Communication II: The Audience as Co-author. *Research on Language and Social Interaction*, 27: 239–267.

Streeck, Jürgen and Ulrike Hartge. 1992. Previews: Gestures at the Transition Place. In P. Auer and A. di Luzio (eds.), *Contextualization of Language* (pp. 135–58). Amsterdam: Benjamins.

Stubbs, Michael. 1983. *Discourse Analysis*. Oxford: Blackwell.

Suchman, Lucy A. 1987. *Plans and Situated Actions: The Problem of Human Machine Communication*. Cambridge University Press.

Swadesh, Morris. 1972. *The Origin and Diversification of Language*. ed. Joel Sherzer. London: Routledge & Kegan Paul.

Sweetser, Eve E. 1987. The Definition of *lie*. An Examination of the Folk Models Underlying a Semantic Prototype. In D. Holland and N. Quinn (eds.), *Cultural Models in Language and Thought* (pp. 43–66). Cambridge University Press.

Talmy, Leonard. 1985. Lexicalization Patterns: Semantic Structure in Lexical Forms. In T. Shopen (ed.), *Language Typology and Syntactic Description*, vol. 3: *Grammatical Categories and the Lexicon* (pp. 57–149). Cambridge University Press.

References

Tambaiah, Stanley J. 1968. The Magical Power of Words. *Man*, NS, 3: 175–208.

1973. Form and Meaning of Magical Acts: A Point of View. In R. Horton and R. Finnegan (eds.), *Modes of Thought: Essays on Thinking in Western and Non-Western Societies* (pp. 199–229). London: Faber & Faber.

1985. *Culture, Thought, and Social Action*. Cambridge, MA: Harvard University Press.

Tannen, Deborah. 1990. *You Just Don't Understand: Women and Men in Conversation*. New York: William Morrow & Co.

(ed.). 1993a. *Gender and Conversational Interaction*. New York: Oxford University Press.

1993b. The Relativity of Linguistic Strategies: Rethinking Power and Solidarity in Gender and Dominance. In D. Tannen (ed.), *Gender and Conversational Interaction* (pp. 165–88). New York: Oxford University Press.

Tarski, Alfred. 1956. *Logic, Semantics, Metamathematics*. Oxford: Clarendon Press.

Tedlock, Dennis. 1983. *The Spoken Word and the Work of Interpretation*. Philadelphia: University of Pennsylvania Press.

Testa, Renata. 1991. Negotiating Stories: Strategic Repair in Italian Multi-Party Talk. *Pragmatics*, 1(3): 345–70.

Tharp, R. and Robert Gallimore. 1988. *Rousing Minds to Life: Teaching, Learning, and Schooling in Social Context*. New York: Cambridge University Press.

Thomason, Sarah Grey and Terrence Kaufman. 1988. *Language Contact, Creolization, and Genetic Linguistics*. Berkeley: University of California Press.

Trier, Jost. 1934. Das sprachliche Feld. *Jahrbuch für Deutsche Wissenschaft*, 10.

Trubetzkoy, Nikolai. 1939. Gedanken zum Indogermanenproblem. *Acta Linguistica*, 1: 81–9.

Trudgill, Peter. 1974. *Sociolinguistics: An Introduction*. Harmondsworth: Penguin.

1978. *Sociolinguistic Patterns in British English*. London: Arnold.

Tyler, Stephen. 1978. *The Said and the Unsaid*. New York: Academic Press.

Tylor, Edward Burnett. 1871. *Primitive Culture*. London: John Murray.

1958. *The Origins of Culture. Part I of "Primitive Culture."* New York: Harper.

Urban, Gregg. 1988. Ritual Wailing in Amerindian Brazil. *American Anthropologist*, 90(2): 385–400.

1991. *A Discourse-Centered Approach to Culture: Native South American Myths and Rituals*. Austin: University of Texas Press.

Uyeno, T. 1971. A Study of Japanese Modality: A Performative Analysis of Sentence Particles. Unpublished Ph.D. dissertation, University of Michigan.

Vachek, Josef (ed.). 1964. *A Prague School Reader in Linguistics*. Bloomington: Indiana University Press.

1966. *The Linguistic School of Prague: An Introduction to Its Theory and Practice*. Bloomington: Indiana University Press.

Van Valin, Robert D. Jr. 1990. Semantic Parameters of Split Ergativity. *Language*, 66(2): 221–60.

Vološinov, Valentin Nikolaevic. 1973. *Marxism and the Philosophy of Language*, trans.

Ladislav Matejka and I. R. Titunik. New York: Seminar Press. (First Published 1929 and 1930).

von Humboldt, Wilhelm. [1836]1971. *Linguistic Variability and Intellectual Development*, trans. George C. Buck and Frithjof A. Raven. Philadelphia: University of Pennsylvania Press.

Vygotsky, L. S. 1978. *Mind in Society: The Development of Higher Psychological Processes*. Cambridge, MA: Harvard University Press.

Wallace, Anthony F.C. 1961. *Culture and Personality*. New York: Random House.

Walters, Keith. 1988. Dialectology. In F. J. Newmeyer (ed.), *Linguistics: The Cambridge Survey*, vol. 4: *Language: The Socio-Cultural Context* (pp. 119–39). Cambridge University Press.

Watson-Gegeo, Karen and Geoffrey White (eds.). 1990. *Disentangling: Conflict Discourse in Pacific Societies*. Stanford University Press.

Weinrich, Uriel. 1953. *Languages in Contact*. The Hague: Mouton.

Weinreich, Uriel, William Labov and Marvin I. Herzog. 1968. Empirical Foundations for a Theory of Language Change. In W. P. Lehmann and Y. Malkiel (eds.), *Directions in Historical Linguistics* (pp. 95–188). Austin: University of Texas Press.

Welmers, William E. 1973. *African Language Structures*. Berkeley: University of California Press.

Wertsch, James V. 1981. The Concept of Activity in Soviet Psychology: An Introduction. In J. V. Wertsch (ed.), *The Concept of Activity in Soviet Psychology* (pp. 3–36). Armonk, NY: M. E. Sharpe.

1985a. *Culture, Communication, and Cognition: Vygotskian Perspectives*. Cambridge University Press.

1985b. *Vygotsky and the Social Formation of Mind*. Cambridge, MA: Harvard University Press.

1991. *Voices of the Mind: A Sociocultural Approach to Mediated Action*. Cambridge, MA: Harvard University Press.

Whorf, Benjamin Lee. 1956a. An American Indian Model of the Universe. In J. B. Carroll (ed.), *Language, Thought, and Reality: Selected Writings of Benjamin Lee Whorf* (pp. 57–64). Cambridge, MA: MIT Press.

1956b. A Linguistic Consideration of Thinking in Primitive Communities. In J. B. Carroll (ed.), *Language, Thought, and Reality: Selected Writings of Benjamin Lee Whorf* (pp. 65–86). Cambridge, MA: MIT Press.

1956c. Linguistics as an Exact Science. In J. B. Carroll (ed.), *Language, Thought, and Reality: Selected Writings of Benjamin Lee Whorf* (pp. 220–32). Cambridge, MA: MIT Press.

1956d. The Relation of Habitual Thought and Behavior to Language. In J. B. Carroll (ed.), *Language, Thought, and Reality: Selected Writings of Benjamin Lee Whorf* (pp. 134–59). Cambridge, MA: MIT Press.

[1940]1956e. Science and Linguistics. In J. B. Carroll (ed.), *The Relation of Habitual Thought and Behavior to Language* (pp. 207–19). Cambridge, MA: MIT Press.

References

1956f. Grammatical Categories. In J. B. Carroll (ed.), *The Relation of Habitual Thought and Behavior to Language* (pp. 87–101). Cambridge, MA: MIT Press.

Wierzbicka, Anna. 1994. Semantic Universals and Primitive Thought: The Question of the Psychic Unity of Humankind. *Journal of Linguistic Anthropology*, 4(1): 23–49.

Willard, Dalls. 1972. The Paradox of Logical Psychologism: Husserl's Way Out. *American Philosophical Quarterly*, 9(1): 94–100.

Williamson, John B., David A. Karp, John R. Dalphin and Paul S. Gray (eds.). 1982. *The Research Craft: An Introduction to Social Research Methods*. Boston: Little Brown.

Witherspoon, Gary. 1977. *Language and Art in the Navajo Universe*. Ann Arbor: University of Michigan Press.

Wittgenstein, Ludwig. 1958. *Philosophical Investigations*, ed. G. E. M. Anscombe and R. Rhees, trans. G. E. M. Anscombe. 2nd edn. Oxford: Blackwell.

1960. *The Blue and Brown Books: Preliminary Studies for the "Philosophical Investigations."* New York: Harper & Row.

[1922] 1961. *Tractatus Logico-Philosophicus*. Translation by D. F. Pears and B. F. McGuinnes. London: Routledge & Kegan Paul.

1974. *Philosophical Grammar*, trans. Anthony Kenny, ed. Rush Rhees. Berkeley and Los Angeles: University of California Press.

Wolfson, Nessa. 1976. Speech Events and Natural Speech: Some Implications for Sociolinguistic Methodology. *Language in Society*, 5: 189–209.

Woodbury, Anthony C. 1984. Eskimo and Aleut Languages. In D. Damas (ed.), *Handbook of North American Indians*, vol. 5: *Arctic* (pp. 49–63). Washington, DC: Smithsonian Institution.

1985. Noun Phrase, Nominal Sentence, and Clause in Central Alaskan Yupik Eskimo. In J. Nichols and A. Woodbury (eds.), *Grammar Inside and Outside the Clause* (pp. 61–88). Cambridge University Press.

Woolard, Kathryn A. 1989. *Double Talk: Bilingualism and the Politics of Ethnicity in Catalonia*. Stanford University Press.

Woolard, Kathryn A. and Bambi B. Schieffelin. 1994. Language Ideology. *Annual Review of Anthropology*, 23: 55–82.

Worth, Sol and John Adair. 1972. *Through Navajo Eyes: An Exploration in Film Communication and Anthropology*. Bloomington Indiana University Press.

Yankah, Kwesi. 1995. *Speaking for the Chief: Okyeame and the Politics of Akan Royal Oratory*. Bloomington: Indiana University Press.

Zadeh, L. A. 1965. Fuzzy Sets. *Information and Control*, 8: 338–53.

1971. Quantitative Fuzzy Semantics. *Information Sciences*, 3: 159–76.

NAME INDEX

Abu-Lughod, Lila 95, 297n
Adair, John 117n
Agar, Michael H. 85n, 89
Agha, Asif 175, 306
Albó, Xavier 78
Allwood, Jens 220
Andersen, Elaine S. 70
Anderson, Benedict 81, 88, 305
Anderson, Stephen R. 125, 127, 321
Andersson, Lars-Gunnar 163n
Andrews, Avery 181n
Apel, Karl-Otto 319n
Appadurai, Arjun 95, 235
Argyle, Michael 123n
Armstrong, David F. 116, 168n
Aronoff, Mark 124
Asch, Patsy 123n
Asch, Timothy 123n
Atkinson, J. Maxwell 141n, 250, 260
Atran, Scott 29
Au, K. 295n
Austin, J. L. 15, 215, 218–36, 243, 278

Bach, Kent 225n
Baker, Gordon P. 238n
Bakhtin, Mikhail M. 75, 293
Bally, Charles 45
Barthes, Roland 168
Basso, Ellen B. 206, 277
Basso, Keith 5, 334
Bateson, Gregory 123n, 145, 254n
Baudillard, Jean 41n
Bauman, Richard 5, 10, 15, 16, 293
Bean, Susan S. 186n, 305n
Beatty, John 206
Benedict, Ruth 122
Benveniste, Emile 185, 305n
Berlin, Brent 65–6, 129–30, 205–6

Berliner, Paul F. 17
Besnier, Niko 119–20, 169, 268–9
Bhabha, Homi, K. 23
Biber, Douglas 70
Bilmes, Jack 260, 268n
Birdwhistell, Ray L. 145, 149
Bloch, Maurice 29, 30n, 275n, 292
Bloomfield, Leonard 79
Bloor, David 218n
Blumstein, Sheila E. 168
Boas, Franz 2n, 25, 27, 52–6, 122–3, 215n
Bogen, James 319n
Bolinger, Dwight 175
Borker, Ruth A. 238n
Bourdieu, Pierre 8, 9, 11, 16, 44–6, 48, 67, 163, 230
Boyer, Pascal 29, 30
Bremmer, Jan 145
Brenneis, Donald 16, 316, 338
Briggs, Charles L. 10, 15, 16, 105, 157, 293
Brown, Gillian xvi, 248
Brown, Penelope 209–11, 306
Brown, Roger 19
Bucholtz, Mary 19, 82
Bühler, Karl 219n, 282n, 284, 287, 329
Burke, Kenneth 288n
Burks, Arthur W. 17
Byarushengo, Ernest 128n
Bynon, Theodora xvi, 124, 132, 133n

Calame-Griaule, Genevieve 97
Cardona, Giorgio Raimondo 2n, 26, 125, 205
Carnap, Rudolf 162
Carroll, John B. 57, 58
Cassirer, Ernst 62–4, 67, 283
Caton, Steven C. 16
Chafe, Wallace 138, 192

Gonzales, Patrick 143–4
Goodenough, Ward H. 27, 29, 173
Goodwin, Charles 21, 124, 135, 142–3, 145–7, 151, 217, 246n, 255, 261n, 262, 266n, 269, 272–3, 299–300, 306, 318, 340
Goodwin, Marjorie H. 21, 141n, 142–3, 145, 151, 199, 266n, 294, 298, 306n, 307–10,
Goody, Esther 327
Gordon, David 226
Gossen, Gary H. 107–9
Gouffé, C. 206
Graf, Fritz 145n
Graham, Laura 277, 335
Greenbaum, Sidney 285
Greenberg, Joseph H. 133
Griaule, Marcel 97
Grice, H. P. 17n, 226, 228, 231–2
Griffin, Peg 10, 282n
Grimshaw, Allen 338
Grimshaw, Jane 181n
Gruber, Jeffrey S. 181n
Gumperz, John J. 13, 19–20, 33, 79, 81n, 107, 212, 285

Hacker, Peter M. S. 238n
Haegeman, Liliane 202n
Haiman, John 182n, 206–7
Hale, Kenneth 79n, 183
Hall, Edward T. 145
Hall, Kira 19, 82
Halle, Morris 34n
Halliday, M. A. K. 78, 133
Hammarberg, R. 167
Hanks, William F. 21, 37n, 209, 217, 277, 321–2
Haraway, Donna J. 98
Harding, Sandra 98
Harnish, Robert M. 225n
Harris, Marvin 173
Harris, Richard M. 145
Hartge, Ulrike 145
Harvey, Penelope 119–20
Hatch, Elvin 52n
Haugen, Einar 142
Haviland, John B. 102, 147–8, 159, 184–5
Hawkins, John A. 133
Hays, Terence E. 206
Heath, Shirley Brice 10, 198, 306n
Hegel, George W. F. 25, 86

Heidegger, Martin 11n, 21, 43, 44, 276, 319
Heine, Bernd 168n
Heller, Monica 18–9
Heritage, John 141n, 246n, 250, 255, 260, 316, 319
Herzog, Marvin I. 132
Hill, Archibald 215n
Hill, Jane 57, 59, 61, 77–9, 103, 111–12, 134, 157, 158, 270, 317
Hill, Kenneth C. 77–9, 103, 111–12, 134, 157, 158
Hinton, Leanne 205, 206
Hjelmslev, Louis 27
Hojer, Harry 3n, 336
Hollan, Douglas 228n, 235
Holland, Dorothy 39n
Holm, John 14n
Holquist, Michael 10
Hopper, Paul 193–5, 207
Howe, James 102
Hoy, David C. 319n
Hudson, R. A. xvi, 3, 79n, 280
Humphries, Tom 25, 333
Hünnemeyer, Friederike 168n
Hunt, George 53
Husserl, Edmund 208n, 318
Hutchins, Edwin 10, 31
Hyman, Larry M. 34, 168
Hymes, Dell 2, 4n, 10, 13, 14n, 15, 20, 52n, 74, 82, 265–7, 281, 288–90, 295,

Irvine, Judith 124, 131n, 136, 270, 292, 317, 327

Jackendoff, Ray 181n
Jackson, Bruce 85n, 340
Jackson, Jean 81
Jacoby, Sally 143–4
Jacquemet, Marco 203–4
Jakobson, Roman 15, 34–5, 37, 168, 207, 281, 284–8
James, Deborah 210n
Jankowiak, William R. 15, 16,
Jefferson, Gail 135, 141, 261, 315
Jelinek, Eloise 187
Jespersen, Otto 207
Johnson, Donna M. 298
Johnson, Mark 38, 64–5, 217
Jones, William 131
Jordan, Brigitte 344

389

SUBJECT INDEX